The Generative Lexicon

The Generative Lexicon

James Pustejovsky

The MIT Press
Cambridge, Massachusetts
London, England

© 1995 Massachusetts Institute of Technology

This book was set in Computer Modern by the author and printed and bound in the United States of America.

Library of Congress Cataloging-in-Publication Data

Pustejovsky, J. (James)
   The Generative Lexicon / James Pustejovsky.

      p.   cm.
   Based on the author's unpublished manuscript, "Towards a Generative Lexicon."
   Includes bibliographical references (p.) and indexes.
   ISBN 0-262-16158-3
   1. Semantics. 2. Generative grammar 3. Computational linguistics. I. Title
P325.P85 1995
401'.43–dc20
                                                            95–32875
                                                              CIP

Contents

Preface

This book is based on a larger unpublished manuscript, *Towards a Generative Lexicon*, written between 1988–1993. Many of the basic ideas for this manuscript are first explored in a general way in an article written in 1987 with Bob Ingria, entitled "Active Objects in Syntax and Semantics." Since the original publication of the article "Generative Lexicon" in the journal *Computational Linguistics* in 1991, what had started merely as a critique of theories of lexical sense enumeration has developed into a fairly specific proposal for how to perform lexical semantic analysis. Substantial new material has emerged from cooperative work with several colleagues. This includes the original work done with Bran Boguraev and discussion with Ted Briscoe and Ann Copestake in the context of their Acquilex research funded by Esprit in Europe. The work on unaccusativity stems from joint research with Federica Busa of Brandeis. Extensions and elaborations of the coercion analysis for aspectual predicates in French has been done in close collaboration with Pierrette Bouillon of ISSCO and the University of Paris.

Several chapters have been omitted for clarity of presentation and in some cases for clarity of the content. Hence, some topics that were expected to be included have been deleted entirely. For example, two important themes in generative lexical studies (the role played by Lexical Inheritance Theory and the theory of co-specification) are not examined in any depth in this monograph; both of these areas have become too large to make only passing reference to, and I felt the discussion possible in this monograph would do no justice to these issues. Regarding lexical inheritance, recent work in computational lexicography and semantics, much of it done in the context of the Acquilex project (and reported in Briscoe *et al.*, 1993) has pointed to new and exciting directions for how lexicons should be organized globally. The promise of realizing a *projective inheritance model*, as suggested in my 1991 article, awaits further investigation, although it is currently one of the topics of research at Brandeis in conjunction with Bran Boguraev at Apple.

The second major omission in this monograph is a comprehensive discussion of co-specification and processes of selection. This has proved to be a central concern in the applied computational research at Brandeis as well as the recent work on lexical acquisition and induction from corpora. In the present study, however, I have chosen to concentrate on the core mechanisms involved in semantic selection as they relate to syntactic expression. Because co-specification treats the subtle use and variation in selection below the level of conventional semantic and syntactic types, it is impossible to do it justice without extensive discussion. This can be found in Pustejovsky (forthcoming) and to a certain extent in Boguraev and Pustejovsky (1996).

Finally, I should point out that many questions relating to natural language semantics are not investigated in any great detail here. In particular, issues surrounding quantification and genericity are only touched on briefly, if at all. Furthermore, details of several of the mechanisms of composition are to be found not here but in other works, including Pustejovsky (1995b) and Pustejovsky and Johnston (forthcoming). My aim in the current work has been to outline what I feel is the necessary infrastructure for a truly generative, highly distributed, and lexically-based semantic theory for language.

James Pustejovsky
Brandeis University

Acknowledgments

The ideas contained in this work have been greatly influenced by conversations and interactions with numerous friends and colleagues. Those who have contributed to the specifics of this work include: Noam Chomsky, Bob Ingria, Bran Boguraev, Ted Briscoe, Federica Busa, Patrick Saint-Dizier, Nicholas Asher, Ray Jackendoff, Geoffrey Nunberg, Michael Johnston, Pierrette Bouillon, Scott Waterman, Sabine Bergler, Peter Anick, Paul Buitelaar, Evelyne Viegas, and David McDonald.

Early encouragement from Dave Waltz, Jane Grimshaw, Jim Higginbotham, Remko Scha, and Edwin Williams helped shape the direction of the work, and their influence is seen throughout the pages of this book. Critical interactions with many colleagues have been useful in sharpening my proposal and the specific analyses. In particular, George Miller, Jerry Hobbs, Manfred Bierwisch, Jürgen Kunze, Ewald Lang, Beth Levin, Barbara Grosz, Sergei Nirenburg, Aravind Joshi, Chuck Fillmore, Rick Alterman, Yorick Wilks, David Waltz, and Peter Cariani have provided various degrees of commentary and criticism, making, I believe, the resulting work much clearer than it might have been.

Large portions of the material reported on in this book have been presented in front of audiences from linguistics and computer science conferences and departments, including Brandeis, UMIST, MIT, University of Pennsylvania, Princeton, McGill, the University of Texas, Stuttgart, Humboldt University in Berlin, the CUNY Sentence Processing Conference in New York, IBM, SUNY Buffalo, Toronto, Toulouse, Cambridge University, University of Copenhagen, and Charles University in Prague. Many of the comments and questions from these interactions have found their way into the work presented here, and I would like to thank the participants of these talks for their critical and helpful remarks.

I would like to also thank the following for carefully reading the final manuscript: Bob Ingria, Federica Busa, Ann Copestake, Henk Verkuyl, Ted Briscoe, Nicholas Asher, Alex Lascarides, Anne-Marie Mineur, Michael Johnston, and Marc Verhagen.

I would like to give particular thanks to MIT Press, for their encouragement and editorial support of this project. To Harry Stanton, for his patience and faith, and to Amy Pierce, for her enormous help with guiding the book through the Press on time, and further expediting the publication. And finally, to Deborah Cantor-Adams, for her wonderful editorial help and support with the manuscript.

For moral support, there are really too many people to thank. I would like to thank my mother, Frances, for her constant energy and encouragement; Charlie and Helga Marqusee, for their wonderful creature comforts and Charlie's personal mail and delivery service; John Broglio, for lending me his apartment in Northampton to rewrite the manuscript; and to Brent Cochran, Peter Cariani, Bob Ingria, and Fede Busa, for their undeserved faith in me.

And finally and most significantly, to my family, Cathie, Zachary, and Sophia for always being there, and enduring the tedious hours and my testy moodiness.

This work was supported in part by grants from The Advanced Research Project Agency (MDA904-91-C-9328); the National Science Foundation (IRI-93-14955); Digital Equipment Corporation; and the National Institutes for Health.

I would like to dedicate this book to the memory of my father, George Harry Pustejovsky.

At this point, as it often happens in philosophy, we suddenly realize that the path of inquiry we hoped to open is already marked by the footprints of Aristotle.

Zeno Vendler
Linguistics in Philosophy

1 Introduction

This book deals with natural language semantics, and in particular the semantics of words, both alone and in combination, i.e. the problem of compositionality. Lexical semantics is the study of how and what the words of a language denote. Computational and theoretical linguists have largely treated the lexicon as a static set of word senses, tagged with features for syntactic, morphological, and semantic information. Under this view, different word senses have been generally associated with distinct lexical items. Nevertheless, formal theories of natural language semantics have done little to address two important issues:

- the creative use of words in novel contexts;
- an evaluation of lexical semantic models on the basis of compositionality.

In this study I examine the interaction of word meaning and compositionality as they relate to these concerns. I will argue that, by adequately accounting for the problem of creative word senses, we directly address the issue of compositionality. Our theory of lexical meaning will affect the general design of a semantic theory in several ways. If we view the goal of a semantic theory as being able to recursively assign meanings to expressions, accounting for phenomena such as synonymy, antonymy, polysemy, and metonymy, then compositionality depends ultimately on what the basic lexical categories of the language denote. The traditional view has been that words behave as either active functors or passive arguments. But we will see that if we change the way in which categories can denote, then the form of compositionality itself changes. Hence, if studied comprehensively, lexical semantics can be a means to reevaluate the very nature of semantic composition in language, in order to satisfy the goals of semantic theory.

First, I review some basic issues in lexical representation and present the current view on how to represent lexical ambiguity, both in theoretical and computational models. This view, incorporating "sense enumerative techniques," distinguishes word senses on the basis of finite feature distinctions. As I argue in chapter 3, however, such an approach, makes no distinction between what Weinreich (1964) calls *contrastive* and *complementary ambiguity*.[1] The former is basic homonymy, where a lexical item accidently carries several distinct and unrelated meanings, whereas the latter refers to logically related word senses of the same lexical item. I then turn to some further problems with the enumeration method for lexical description illustrated in chapter 3. It will be shown that the representations assumed by current theories are inadequate to account for the richness of natural language semantics.

As I show in chapters 2 and 3, most of the careful representation work has been done on verb classes (e.g., Levin, 1993). In fact, the semantic weight in both lexical and compositional terms usually falls on the verb. This has obvious consequences for how lexical ambiguity has been treated. In chapter 4, I discuss several devices which simplify our semantic description, but which fall outside the conception of enumerative lexical semantics. Looking at these devices closely, we notice that they point to a very different view of lexical semantics and how word meanings are combined.

Given the discussion in these chapters, the following conception of lexical semantic systems emerges. Under such a theory, a core set of word senses, typically with greater internal structure than is assumed in previous theories, is used to generate a larger set of word senses when individual lexical items are combined with others in phrases and clauses. I will refer to such an organization as a *generative lexicon*, and the operations which generate these "extended senses" as *generative devices*, including operations such as *type coercion* and *co-composition*. I discuss how this view supports an explanatory view of semantic modeling. I then examine the goals of linguistic theory in general and lexical semantics in particular. I argue that our framework of knowledge for lexical items must be guided by a concern for semanticality in addition to grammaticality. The model of semantic interpretation we construct should reflect the particular properties and difficulties of natural language, and not simply be an application of a ready-to-wear logical formalism to a new body of data. I will view natural languages as positioned on a hierarchy of semantic descriptions, characterized in terms of their underlying polymorphic generative power. I argue that natural languages fall within the *weakly polymorphic* languages, more expressive than *monomorphic*, but well below the power of unrestricted polymorphic languages. This particular characterization is rich enough to capture the behavior of logical polysemy as well as effects of co-compositionality.

Next, in chapter 5, I outline the type system for our semantics. A generative theory of the lexicon includes multiple levels of representation for the different types of lexical information needed. Among such levels are Argument Structure (for the representation of adicity information for functional elements), Event Structure (for the representation of information related to Aktionsarten and event type, in the sense of Vendler, 1967, and related work), Qualia Structure (for the representation of the defining attributes of an object, such as its constituent parts, purpose and function, mode of creation, etc.), and Inheritance Structure (for the representation of the relation between the lexical item and others in the lexicon). Chapter 6 presents in more detail the structure of qualia, and the role they play in distributing the functional behavior of words and phrases in composition.

Chapter 7 presents the application of the mechanisms outlined in chapters 5 and 6 to the polymorphic behavior of language. A variety of polymorphic types is studied and I consider what operations are needed to adequately account for the syntactic expressiveness of semantic types. In particular, I examine the role of coercion in the grammar as well as the need for other generative devices, such as selective binding and co-composition. There is no single form of polymorphism; rather, polysemy and type ambiguity are a result of several semantic phenomena in specific interaction.

Chapter 8 examines briefly what the consequences of qualia structure are for the semantics of nominals. Nouns can be formally characterizable in terms of three dimensions of analysis, involving argument structure, event type, and qualia structure. An analysis of nominal polysemy is presented, making use of the type system outlined in the previous chapters, and explaining in more detail the distinction between unified types and dot objects.

In the next two chapters, I outline some areas of grammar that can be greatly simplified if we apply to them principles of generative lexical analysis through the use of the generative devices and the type system presented in chapter 5. In particular, I treat argument selection as driven by semantic types, modulated by constraints on coercion rules, selective binding, and co-composition operations in the grammar. This approach will permit us to explain the polymorphic nature of verbs taking multiple syntactic types. In chapter 9, I discuss the role that qualia and event structure have in describing the way causal relations are lexicalized in language. Specifically, I look at the semantics of causative/inchoative verbs, aspectual predicates, experiencer predicates, and *modal causatives* such as *risk*.

Finally, I discuss how this view of lexical organization relates to current theories of metaphor and pragmatically-induced metonymy. I argue, on methodological grounds, for a strong distinction between commonsense knowledge and lexical structure, although the issue is clearly an empirical one. The types of creative polysemy examined in this work exhibit a regularity and systematicity across languages that is absent from patterns of pragmatic sense extension or modes of metaphor.

2 The Nature of Lexical Knowledge

Only a few years ago, it was conventional practice in both theoretical and computational linguistics textbooks to cover all that needed to be said regarding the lexicon in one quick chapter, before getting to the more interesting and substantive topics of syntactic form and semantic interpretation. Such an impoverished coverage today would scarcely reflect the vibrancy of the field of lexical research or the central role played by lexical knowledge in linguistic theory and processing models. It is now standardly assumed by most linguistic frameworks (both computational and theoretical) that much of the structural information of a sentence is best encoded from a lexicalized perspective.[1]

The most pressing problems for lexical semantics, I believe, are the following:

(a) Explaining the *polymorphic nature* of language;

(b) Characterizing the *semanticality* of natural language utterances;

(c) Capturing the *creative use of words* in novel contexts;

(d) Developing a richer, *co-compositional* semantic representation.

I believe we have reached an interesting turning point in research, where linguistic studies can be informed by computational tools for lexicology as well as an appreciation of the computational complexity of large lexical databases. Likewise, computational research can profit from an awareness of the grammatical and syntactic distinctions of lexical items; natural language processing (NLP) systems must account for these differences in their lexicons and grammars. The wedding of these disciplines is so important, in fact, that I believe it will soon be difficult to carry out serious computational research in the fields of linguistics and NLP without the help of electronic dictionaries and computational lexicographic resources (cf. Zampolli and Atkins, 1994, Boguraev and Briscoe, 1988). Positioned at the center of this synthesis is the study of word meaning, lexical semantics.

Before addressing these questions, I would like to discuss two assumptions that will figure prominently in my suggestions for a lexical semantics framework. The first is that, without an appreciation of the syntactic structure of a language, the study of lexical semantics is bound to fail. There is no way in which meaning can be completely divorced from the structure that carries it. This is an important methodological point, since grammatical distinctions are a useful metric in evaluating competing semantic theories.

The second point is that the meanings of words should somehow reflect the deeper conceptual structures in the cognitive system, and the domain it operates in. This is tantamount to stating that the semantics of natural language should be the image of nonlinguistic conceptual organizing principles, whatever their structure.

Computational lexical semantics should be guided by the following principles. First, a clear notion of semantic well-formedness will be necessary in order to characterize a theory of possible word meaning. This may entail abstracting the notion of lexical meaning away from other semantic influences. For instance, this might suggest that discourse and pragmatic factors should be handled differently or separately from the semantic contributions of lexical items in composition.[2] Although this is not a necessary assumption and may in fact be wrong, it will help narrow our focus on what is important for lexical semantic descriptions.

Secondly, lexical semantics must look for representations that are richer than thematic role descriptions (cf. Gruber, 1965, Fillmore, 1968). As argued in Levin and Rappaport (1986), named roles are useful at best for establishing fairly general mapping strategies to the syntactic structures in language. The distinctions possible with thematic roles are much too coarse-grained to provide a useful semantic interpretation of a sentence. What is needed, I will argue, is a principled method of lexical decomposition. This presupposes, if it is to work at all, (1) a rich, recursive theory of semantic composition, (2) the notion of semantic well-formedness mentioned above, and (3) an appeal to several levels of interpretation in the semantics (cf. Scha, 1983).

Thirdly, and related to the preceding point, lexical semantics must study all syntactic categories in order to characterize the semantics of natural language. That is, contrary to the recent trends in semantic representation, the lexicon must encode information for categories other than verbs. Recent work has done much to clarify the nature of verb classes and the syntactic constructions that each allows (cf. Levin 1985, 1993). Yet it is not clear whether we are any closer to understanding the underlying nature of verb meaning, why the classes develop as they do, and what consequences these distinctions have for the rest of the lexicon and grammar. The curious thing is that there has been little attention paid to the other lexical categories (but cf. Miller and Johnson-Laird,

1976, Miller and Fellbaum, 1991). That is, we have little insight into the semantic nature of adjectival predication, and even less into the semantics of nominals. Not until all major categories have been studied can we hope to arrive at a balanced understanding of the lexicon and the methods of composition.

Stepping back from the lexicon for a moment, let me say briefly what I think the position of lexical research should be within the larger semantic picture. Ever since the earliest attempts at real text understanding, a major problem has been that of controlling the inferences associated with the interpretation process. In other words, how deep or shallow is the understanding of a text? What is the unit of well-formedness when doing natural language understanding; the sentence, utterance, paragraph, or discourse? There is no easy answer to this question because, except for the sentence, these terms are not even formalizable in a way that most researchers would agree on.

It is my opinion that the representation of the context of an utterance should be viewed as involving many different *generative factors* that account for the way that language users create and manipulate the context under constraints, in order to be understood. Within such a theory, where many separate semantic levels (e.g., lexical semantics, compositional semantics, discourse structure, temporal structure) have independent interpretations, the global meaning of a "discourse" is a highly flexible and malleable structure that has no single interpretation. The individual sources of semantic knowledge compute local inferences with a high degree of certainty (cf. Hobbs *et al.*, 1988, and Charniak and Goldman, 1988). When integrated together, these inferences must be globally coherent, a state which is accomplished by processes of cooperation among separate semantic modules. The basic result of such a view is that semantic interpretation proceeds in a principled fashion, always aware of what the source of a particular inference is, and what the certainty of its value is. Such an approach allows the reasoning process to be both tractable and computationally efficient. The representation of lexical semantics, therefore, should be seen as just one of many levels in a richer characterization of contextual structure.[3]

Given what I have said, let us examine the questions presented above in more detail. First, let us turn to the issue of methodology. In this chapter, I shall review the most common methods used for semantic classification of lexical items, and characterize the richness of the problem of representing lexical semantic information.

It is the goal of any lexical semantic theory to adequately classify the lexical items of a language into classes predictive of their syntactic and semantic expression. Furthermore, such a theory should not merely map the meanings of lexical items per sentence, on an individual basis. Rather, it should capture the semantic relations between words in such a way which facilitates this mapping.

2.1 Semantic Classes and Categorial Alternation

Within the tradition of formal semantics, the most fundamental aspect of a word's meaning is perhaps its semantic type. On this view, categorial or type information determines not only how a word behaves syntactically, but also what the elements of the category refer to. For example, the verbs *love* and *hate* would be viewed as relations between individuals in the world, whereas the noun *woman* would pick out the set of all individuals in the world who are women. Logical operators such as *the* and *or* might be viewed as set-theoretic operations over sets of individuals in the world (cf. Montague, 1974, for example) or as procedural instructions (cf. Woods, 1975). Because type distinctions are generally so broad, lexical semantics further distinguishes selectional subsets of members of these categories. Conventionally, this is accomplished by applying standard distributional analysis on the basis of collocation and cooccurrence tests (cf. Chomsky, 1955, Harris, 1951). For example, the nouns *dog* and *book* partition into different selectional classes due to contexts involving *animacy*, while the nouns *book* and *literature* partition into different selectional classes due at least to a mass/count distinction (cf. Verkuyl, 1972, Pelletier and Schubert, 1989).

2.1.1 Verbal Alternations

A recently developed linguistic methodology for grouping the meanings of words into semantic classes is to study the syntactic patterns that words participate in (e.g., common grammatical alternations). For example, work begun in the MIT Lexicon Project and recently codified in Levin (1993), outlines a broad classification of verb argument alternations in English, in order to classify verbs into semantically unique classes. For example, the verbs *sink*, *roll*, and *break* all have both transitive and intransitive forms, where the lexical senses are related by the interpretive feature of causation. There are of course, numerous examples of intransitive verbs which have no zero-derived causative forms, e.g., *arrive, die, fall* (cf. Fillmore, 1968, Lakoff, 1970, Hale and Keyser, 1986, 1993, and Kunze, 1991):

(1) a. The boat <u>sank</u> in stormy weather.
     b. The plane <u>sank</u> the boat in stormy weather.

(2) a. The ball <u>rolled</u> down the hill.
     b. Bill <u>rolled</u> the ball down the hill.

(3) a. The bottle <u>broke</u> suddenly.
     b. Mary <u>broke</u> the bottle suddenly.

(4) a. The letter <u>arrived</u> on time.
     b. *The mailman <u>arrived</u> the letter on time.

(5) a. My terminal <u>died</u> last night.
     b. *The storm <u>died</u> my terminal last night.

(6) a. The block tower <u>fell</u>.
     b. *Zachary <u>fell</u> the block tower.
     c. Zachary <u>felled</u> the block tower.

While the sentences in (4b)–(6b) are ungrammatical, they are certainly understandable. The lexical semantics should specify what it is that these two classes share, such that they have grammatical intransitive forms, but equally important is the characterization of how they differ, such that the latter class permits no transitive form.

Other useful alternation patterns include the conative, as illustrated below in (7)–(10):[4]

(7) a. Mary <u>shot</u> the target.
     b. Mary <u>shot</u> at the target.

(8) a. Mary <u>scraped</u> the window.
     b. Mary <u>scraped</u> at the window.

(9) a. The cat <u>touched</u> my leg.
     b. *The cat <u>touched</u> at my leg.

(10) a. Mary <u>shot</u> the arrow (at the target).

      b. *Mary <u>shot</u> at the arrow.

The question is whether it is possible to identify the semantic discrimi-
nants leading to the distinct behavior of the transitive verbs above, while
still explaining why (9b)–(10b) are ungrammatical.[5] Perhaps even more
interesting is how the polysemy of those verbs taking multiple forms can
be represented lexically.

What the examples above clearly show is that participation in one
grammatical alternation does not sufficiently determine the semantic
class of the verb. In fact, even once a complete cataloguing of participation in alternation classes is achieved, we must ask ourselves just what
we have accomplished. Descriptively, we may have achieved a great deal,
in terms of how verbs behave according to semantically-labeled classes.
But we must realize that explaining the behavior of a verb's semantic
class can come only from acknowledging that the syntactic patterns in
an alternation are not independent of the information carried by the arguments characterized in the very patterns themselves. In other words,
the diversity of complement types that a verb or other category may
take is in large part also determined by the semantics of the complements themselves. One of the methodological points I will argue is that
alternation classifications do not constitute theory. Indeed, as Levin
(1993) herself points out, the theoretical mechanisms which give rise to
the descriptive distribution of syntactic behavior are not transparent in
the classes by themselves.

Still another kind of syntactic diagnostic that seems to have some
theoretical utility is polyadicity more narrowly construed. As Bresnan
(1982), Fillmore (1986), and Levin (1993) point out, there are not only
argument changing alternations such as those discussed above, but also
argument dropping alternations as well. The rule of "indefinite NP
deletion" is the term for the following alternation paradigm:

(11) a. The woman <u>ate</u> her meal quickly.

      b. The woman <u>ate</u> quickly.

(12) a. The dog <u>devoured</u> the cookie.

      b. *The dog <u>devoured</u>.

(13) a. John <u>drank</u> his beer feverishly.

b. John <u>drank</u> feverishly.

(14) a. John <u>gulped</u> his beer feverishly.
      b. *John <u>gulped</u> feverishly.

(15) a. Mary <u>hummed</u> a song while she walked.
      b. Mary <u>hummed</u> while she walked.

(16) a. Mary <u>performed</u> a song while she ate her dinner.
      b. *Mary <u>performed</u> while she ate her dinner.

In the examples here one might attribute the possibility of object-drop to an aspectual difference between the verbs being contrasted. That is, while *eat* denotes an activity of unbounded duration (at least lexically), *devour*, one might argue, denotes a transition. Although *devour* is generally considered a manner specification of the verb *eat*, it carries a completive implicature that is absent from *eat*. Similar remarks hold for the other two pairs above: while *drink* is an activity, *gulp* carries the implicature of completive aspect; and finally, while *hum* is an activity, *perform* has a completive aspect lexically.[6]

If this were a complete account of the above data, we might expect it to explain the patterns of deletion for the other cases of complement-dropping. This would seem difficult for many of the verbs entering into this alternation. For example, as Fillmore (1986) points out, there are cases where near synonyms seem to behave differently with respect to licensing of complement-drop (cf. (17) and (18)).

(17) a. Mary <u>tried</u> to start her car in the morning.
      b. Mary <u>tried</u> in the morning.

(18) a. Mary <u>attempted</u> to start her car in the morning.
      b. * Mary <u>attempted</u> in the morning.

As we can see, no one semantic parameter will be sufficient to explain all complement drop cases.[7]

In addition to transitive-intransitive polyadicity, there are well-documented ditransitive-transitive shifts such as those shown in (19)–(24) below (cf. Pustejovsky, 1992):

(19) a. John <u>gave</u> a book to Mary.

b. *John <u>gave</u> a book.

(20) a. John <u>gave</u> a lecture to the academy.
      b. John <u>gave</u> a lecture.

(21) a. John <u>mailed</u> a book to his brother.
      b. *John <u>mailed</u> a book.

(22) a. John <u>mailed</u> a letter to his brother.
      b. John <u>mailed</u> a letter.

(23) a. Bill <u>showed</u> a book to Mary.
      b. *Bill <u>showed</u> a book.

(24) a. Bill <u>showed</u> a movie to the audience.
      b. Bill <u>showed</u> a movie.

Thus, in certain cases, the otherwise obligatory expression of the goal argument is dropped and the verb becomes a simple transitive. What allows the alternation, I will argue in later chapters, is the interaction of the verbal semantics with semantic information from the complement itself.

Such grammatical alternations can be used throughout the grammar of a language to make semantic distinctions on the basis of syntactic behavior. Using category and selectional information as well as grammatical alternation data, words can be grouped into semantic classes following more or less predictable syntactic behaviors. Nevertheless, it is still necessary to explain why these and just these grammatical forms are part of a certain alternation class. This is addressed in chapter 9 below.

Finally, let us consider briefly one of the oldest semantic classifications for verbs, that of aspectual class or *Aktionsarten*. The essential idea behind this classification is that verbs and verb phrases differ in the kinds of eventualities in the world they denote. It is normally assumed that there are at least three aspectual types: *state, activity,* and *event,* where the last class is itself sometimes broken down into *accomplishment,* and *achievement* events.[8] For example, the verb *walk* in sentence (25) denotes an activity of unspecified duration. That is, the sentence itself does not convey information regarding the temporal extent of the activity, although deictically it is an event in the past which did terminate.[9]

(25) a. Mary <u>walked</u> yesterday.
      b. Mary <u>walked</u> to her house yesterday.

Such a sentence as (25a) is said to denote an *activity* (cf. Kenny, 1963, Vendler, 1967, Ryle, 1949, Mourelatos, 1978, Verkuyl, 1972, 1993, Dowty, 1979). Other examples of activity verbs are *sleep, run, work,* and *drink.* Sentence (25b) conveys the same information as (25a), with the additional constraint, however, that Mary terminated her activity of walking at her house. Although not making explicit reference to the temporal duration of the activity, (25b) does assert that the process has a logical culmination, whereby the activity is over when Mary is at home. This type of sentence is said to denote an *accomplishment* event.

Just as the verb *walk* seems to lexically default to an activity, there are verbs which seem to lexically denote accomplishments. For example, the verbs *build* and *destroy*, in their typical transitive use, denote accomplishment events because there is a logical culmination to the activity performed.

(26) a. Mary <u>built</u> a house.
      b. Mary <u>destroyed</u> the table.

In (26a) the existence of the house is the culmination of Mary's act, while in (26b), the nonexistence of something denotable as a table is the direct culmination or consequence of her act.

Creation-verbs are only the best example of accomplishments. *Performance*-verbs such as *play* permit both activity usage (27a) and accomplishment usage (27b), depending on the complement structure:[10]

(27) a. Mary <u>played</u> the piano (for hours).
      b. Mary <u>played</u> the sonata in 15 minutes.

As illustrated in (27b) above, one classic diagnostic for testing whether a verb or verb phrase denotes an accomplishment is modification by temporal adverbials such as *in an hour*, i.e., the so-called frame adverbials. Notice in (28) that both derived and lexical accomplishments license such modification, while activities (29) do not.

(28) a. Mary <u>walked</u> to the store in an hour.
      b. Mary <u>built</u> a house in a year.

(29)   a. *John <u>drank</u> in 20 minutes.
     b. *Mary <u>worked</u> in an hour.

The frame adverbial seems to require that the verb or verb phrase make reference to an explicit change of state, a precondition missing in (29a) and (29b).

   The last conventional aspectual classification is that of achievement. An achievement is an event that results in a change of state, just as an accomplishment does, but where the change is thought of as occurring instantaneously. For example, in sentences (30a), (30b), and (30c) the change is not a gradual one, but something that has a point-like quality to it. Hence, modification by *point adverbials* such as *at 3 pm* is suggestive that a sentence denotes an achievement (cf. Dowty, 1979).

(30)   a. John <u>died</u> at 3 pm.
     b. John <u>found</u> his wallet at 3 pm.
     c. Mary <u>arrived</u> at noon.

Of course, point adverbial modification is not restricted to achievements, as the examples with accomplishment verbs below show:

(31)   a. She <u>swam</u> the channel at 10:00 am.
     b. The pianist <u>performed</u> the sonata at noon.
     c. James <u>taught</u> his 3 hour seminar at 2:30 pm. d. He <u>delivered</u> his lecture at 4:00 pm.

Here the point-adverbial indicates the starting time of an event of some specific duration.

   What are apparently lexical properties of the verb can be affected by factors that could not possibly be lexical. For instance, consider the sentences in (32), where we see a shift in the meaning of *eat* from an activity as in (32a) to an accomplishment as in (32b). Similarly, the lexically specified accomplishment verb *build* mentioned above can appear with either a bare plural object or mass term, thereby assuming an activity reading (cf. (33a) and (33b)).

(32)   a. Mary <u>ate</u> cookies. (*activity*)
     b. Mary <u>ate</u> a cookie. (*accomplishment*)

(33)   a. Brown and Root Inc. <u>built</u> the runway in Tehran.

b. Brown and Root Inc. <u>builds</u> runways in Southwest Asia.

The presence of a bare plural object shifts the interpretation of a typically telic (or completive) event to an unbounded process (cf. Bach, 1986, Verkuyl, 1993, and Krifka, 1989 for details).

Another indication of an aspectual shift resulting from pluralization of the subject of achievement predicates comes from complementation patterns with aspectual predicates such as *begin* and *finish*. Normally, achievements are not grammatical as complements of these verbs, as illustrated in (34), but the same predicates with plural subjects suggests an aspectual distinction.

(34) a. *John began <u>finding</u> a flea on his dog.
      b. *The guest began to arrive.

(35) a. John began <u>finding</u> fleas on his dog.
      b. The guests began to <u>arrive</u>.

Finally, let us examine the behavior of *states*. Following Carlson (1977) and Kratzer (1989), we can distinguish two kinds of stative predicates *individual-level* and *stage-level*. Predicates such as *tall, intelligent,* and *overweight* might be thought of as properties that an individual retains, more or less, throughout its lifetime, and can be identified with the individual directly. These are *individual-level* predicates. Properties such as *hungry, sick,* and *clean* are usually identified with non-permanent states of individuals, and have been called *stage-level* predicates.[11] It is this class which typically appears in forms of the resultative construction as the culminating predicate, as shown in the sentences in (36).

(36) a. John drank himself <u>sick</u> with that cheap brandy.
      b. Watching the commercial on TV made John <u>hungry</u>.
      c. Bill wiped the counter <u>clean</u> before serving us our coffee.

None of these constructions typically permit individual-level predicates, as (37) clearly illustrates.

(37) a. *Bill ate himself <u>overweight</u> over the years.
      b. *John read himself <u>intelligent</u> with the *Great Books*.

One final characteristic for distinguishing activities from accomplishments, known as the "imperfective paradox" (cf. Bach, 1986, Dowty, 1979), involves the possible entailments from the progressive aspect. To illustrate the nature of this paradox, consider the sentences in (38).

(38) a. John is running. (Therefore, John has run.)
      b. John is building a house. (*Therefore, John has built a house.)

What this difference in entailment indicates is whether an action is homogeneous in nature or has a culmination of some sort. Sentence (38a) is an activity and entails the statement *John has run*. That is, John has already engaged in some running. Sentence (38b), on the other hand, does not allow the entailment *John has built a house* because building is not a homogeneous process, but rather culminates in a changed state, i.e., it is an accomplishment. Thus, if x *is* ϕ*ing* entails x *has* ϕ*ed*, then either the verb or the predicate is an activity. A theory of lexical semantics should be able to account for this behavior, and not just use it to classify propositions into aspectual types.

Summarizing, we have considered the following categorization of aspectual types for verbs, verb phrases, and sentences: ACTIVITIES: *walk, run, swim, drink*; ACCOMPLISHMENTS: *build, destroy, break*; ACHIEVEMENTS: *die, find, arrive*; and STATES: *sick, know, love, resemble, think, be*. Membership in an aspectual class determines much of the semantic behavior of a lexical item, but it should be noted that the aspectual properties of a sentence may change as the result of other factors, such as adverbial modification (both durative and frame), the structure of the NP in an argument position (e.g., definite vs. bare plural), or the presence of a prepositional phrase. Such non-lexical issues are problems in compositional semantics and are discussed in the context of "type-shifting" phenomena in Bach (1986), Link (1983), Krifka (1989), and Verkuyl (1993). In the discussion that follows, I will restructure the above classification slightly, by making reference to subevents and to an event focusing mechanism called *event headedness*.

2.1.2 Nominal Alternations

Nouns also have characteristic grammatical behaviors, depending on semantic category. For nouns as well, studying the behavior of grammatical alternations has certainly been the point of departure for the semantic classification of nominal types. Probably the most studied distinction for nominal semantics is that of *count* versus *mass*. This is a distinction which dates back to Aristotle, and more recently has played an integral role in the structuring of the semantic model for language (cf. Pelletier and Schubert, 1989, Link, 1983). How "stuff" is individuated will determine how we talk about it; hence, *sand*, although in fact composed of individual grains, is a mass noun and refers to undifferentiated stuff in our daily experience of it.[12] A *house*, on the other hand, is obviously perceivable as an individuated object and is classified as a count noun. As is well-documented, count nouns and mass nouns select for different quantifier types and allow very different patterns of predication.

(39) a. MASS NOUNS: much <u>sand</u>, more <u>water</u>;
     b. COUNT NOUNS: several <u>houses</u>, every <u>child</u>.

Not surprisingly, however, there are nouns that have both mass and count interpretations, and these will figure in our later investigations quite prominently. They include nouns such as *beer*, where we can talk about amounts of (40a) or quantities of (40b) the substance. Similarly, nouns such as *e-mail* refer either to the mass of correspondences I have or have sent, as in (41), or to the individual transaction or correspondence, seen in (42).

(40) a. Texans drink <u>a lot of beer</u>.
     b. Patsy relished <u>every beer she drank</u>.

(41) a. <u>More e-mail</u> is arriving every day.
     b. Is there <u>any e-mail</u> for me today?

(42) a. <u>The last e-mail I sent you</u> was yesterday.
     b. <u>Every e-mail</u> I send gets bounced.

A semantic distinction related to count and mass is that between individual and group nouns, and this is also differentiated by predicability. For example, group nouns satisfy semantic plurality requirements on selection, as shown in (43) below:

(43) a. The committee <u>met</u> for lunch.
     b. The crowd <u>dispersed</u> after the police introduced tear gas.

For purposes of anaphoric binding, group nouns do not parallel plural NPs completely, however.

So far, all the noun classes we have discussed have been *predicative* in a fairly direct way. That is, both *woman* and *water*, when used in full NPs, refer independently to something out in the world. *Relational* nouns, on the other hand, are dependent on another referent in terms of how they themselves denote. For example, *neighbor* and *brother* denote individuals standing in relation to at least one other individual in specific ways. The grammatical consequences of this semantic distinction have been long recognized, and give rise to the following interesting distinction;

(44) a. The men arrived yesterday.
      b. ?The neighbor arrived yesterday.
      c. The neighbors arrived yesterday.

(45) a. *The brother came home.
      b. The brothers came home together.

As Bierwisch (1983) and Eschenbach (1993) have pointed out, the two types of relational nouns can be distinguished with respect to pluralization behavior. Nouns such as *neighbor* and *sister* denote "horizontal relations," while *father* and *daughter* denote hierarchical relations. Within the latter class, the noun *daughter* is the dependent object in the relation, and behaves differently from *father*, which is the independent individual. Note that contextual salience will improve the acceptability of these NPs.

(46) a. *The daughter is in the house.
      b. ?The daughters are gathering upstairs.
      c. The fathers are meeting tomorrow.

Explicit mention of the independent variable in the relation, of course results in fully acceptable sentences:

(47) a. My daughter phoned me.
      b. John's brother is in town.
      c. My neighbor lent me a chainsaw.

The distinctions between count/mass, individual/group, and predicative/relational, are motivated by distinct grammatical behaviors as we as the underlying semantic distinctions perhaps giving rise to these differences. A more traditional method of nominal classification is based on taxonomies of the speaker's intuition or commonsense perspective of what the nouns denote in the world. For example, we might distinguish between "concrete referring" nouns, such as *woman, boy, horse* (all count nouns), as well as *grass, water,* and *gold* (mass nouns), and "abstract referring" nouns such as *time, place, age,* and *shape.* Such taxonomies of entity types are common in computational treatments of language phenomena, but are largely ignored or seen as irrelevant by the majority of theoretical linguists. The major exception to this is the semantic taxonomic tradition as carried out by Wierzbicka (1988) and Dixon (1991) and their colleagues. This tradition cannot be so quickly dismissed as is so often the case in theoretical circles. Many of the generalizations they hope to capture are legitimate goals for linguistic theory and cognitive science. More to the point, however, much of their work attempts to achieve these goals without always applying the proper tools of analysis.[13]

The structuring of such taxonomic information for nouns (and other categories as well) in computational linguistics and AI is not simply an exercise in domain modeling; it is necessary for driving the inferences that a language reasoning system must perform in order to understand a sentence. From primitives-based inferencing techniques such as Wilks (1975,1978) to commonsense metaphysics reasoning systems applied to language such as Hobbs *et al.* (1987), the taxonomic classification of objects in the world through language can be a serious enterprise and not merely metaphysical play.

These concerns have received renewed interest in computational approaches to language analysis both in computational linguistics and formal semantics, and point back to the work done on selection restriction from the 1960s and 1970s in the generative tradition. Where selectional features were seen as conditions on lexical insertion in previous theories, sortal specification is viewed in terms of type satisfaction within an interpreted model. I mention this trend because I believe there are important underlying motivations in both computational and theoretical linguistics communities for modeling the conceptual or epistemological ground assumptions for language research. Yet these motivations can differ dramatically and I hope to identify what the goals are for the diverse communities, and then outline what I think the common goals are for linguistic research in the different approaches.

2.1.3   Adjective Classes

Finally, let us turn briefly to the semantics of adjectives. By their very
nature, adjectives are generally taken to denote states. Some of the previous discussion on types of stativity, e.g., the individual-level vs. stage-
level distinction, will be a useful device for distinguishing adjectives as
well. This is related to but not identical with the oldest distinction applied to adjectives, that of accidental vs. necessary qualities (as used in
Aristotle and the scholastics). This distinction gives rise to the classification of properties such as *hungry*, *dirty*, and *broken* as accidental qualities as distinct from necessary qualities such as the properties *bipedal*
(of a species), *tall* (of an individual), and *hard* (of a substance). We
saw in the previous discussion that there are grammatical distinctions
to be made on the basis of this typological difference. One diagnostic
we did not consider concerns the progressive aspect, and the ability of
most stage-level predicates to enter into predicates with the progressive,
while individual-level predicates cannot, as illustrated below.

(48) a. The horse is being gentle with her rider.
      b. You're being so angry again!
      c. Stop being so impatient.

(49) a. *John is being tall today.
      b. *Aren't you being beautiful tonight!
      c. *Stop being so intelligent.

There are, of course, other ways to classify adjectives by virtue of
syntactically distinct behaviors, including the basic distinction between
predicative and attributive position, illustrated in (50)–(51).

(50) a. the alleged criminal
      b. *This criminal is alleged.

(51) a. the frightened boy
      b. The boy is frightened.

With respect to complementation patterns, there are structurally many
similarities between adjectives and verbs. For examples, just as there are

intransitive and transitive verbs, there are unary and binary predicative adjectives, which can be seen as intransitive and transitive forms. An adjective such as *old*, for example, takes no complement, as in (52a), while adjectives such as *envious* and *jealous* as in (52b) are inherently relational, and might be analyzed as transitive.

(52) a. Sophia is not <u>old</u>.
      b. John is <u>envious</u> of Mary's position.

Another structural distinction differentiates adjectives allowing movement-like behavior, such as *certain*, from non-alternating adjectives.

(53) a. Mary is <u>certain</u> to be the next President.
      b. It is <u>certain</u> that Mary will be the next President.

Perhaps the most celebrated example from this class involves the raising/control distinction seen with adjective pairs such as *easy* and *eager*.[14] Adjectives such as *eager*, *anxious*, and *unwilling* are subject-control predicates, and have no alternating construction, while *tough*-Movement adjectives such as *easy*, *tough*, and *difficult*, enter into the following alternation.

(54) a. It is <u>easy</u> to teach this class.
      b. This class is <u>easy</u> to teach.

(55) a. It is <u>dangerous</u> to drive on this road in the winter.
      b. This road is <u>dangerous</u> to drive on in the winter.

(56) a. It is <u>interesting</u> to imagine Bill President.
      b. Bill President is <u>interesting</u> to imagine.

These are particularly interesting from our perspective because of the underspecified meaning many of these adjectives assume in constructions such as (57) and (58) below:

(57) a. Jim has decided to give an <u>easy</u> exam.
      b. We're going to get a <u>difficult</u> exam for the final.

(58) a. Bill has to take a <u>dangerous</u> road to get here.
      b. John had an <u>interesting</u> suggestion.

Depending on the nominal, however, interpretation of the "ellipsed" infinitival may depend on local context, as the sentences in (59) illustrates.

(59) a. John is teaching an <u>easy</u> class this semester.
     b. Bill is taking an <u>easy</u> class this semester.

What is curious about these sentences is that the "understood predicate" in the NP *an easy class* is determined by the governing predicate in the VP; that is, in (59a) the class is *easy to teach* while in (59b) it is *easy to take*. This is not the case, however, with the NP *an easy/difficult exam*, where the ease or difficulty seems to refer in most cases to the taking of the exam.[15] This seems to depend on the semantics of the noun being modified. I will return to these examples in chapter 10, where local semantic context is able to bring out the appropriate reading compositionally, and the appropriate semantic distinctions are presented for differentiating between nouns such as *exam* and *class*.

Rather than first examining the grammatical behavior of adjectives, it might seem reasonable to look first at what concepts are expressible in a language adjectivally. This is the approach described in Dixon (1982), where he takes a field-descriptive perspective on the taxonomic classification of adjectives. Dixon distinguishes adjectives according to the general semantic field associated with the term. For example, he arrives at the following classes for adjectives from cross-linguistic study:

1. DIMENSION: big, little, large, small, long, short

2. PHYSICAL PROPERTY: hard, soft, heavy, light

3. COLOR: red, green, blue

4. HUMAN PROPENSITY: jealous, happy, kind, proud, cruel, gay

5. AGE: new, old, young

6. VALUE: good, bad, excellent, fine, delicious

7. SPEED: fast, quick, slow

8. DIFFICULTY: difficult, easy

9. SIMILARITY: alike, similar

10. QUALIFICATION: possible, probable, likely

Such classes can be very useful for descriptive purposes, but reveal little about the functional or relational properties of the predicate. For example, the adjectives *difficult* and *easy* are tough-movement predicates and behave the same with respect to this construction. In the class QUALIFICATION, however, the adjective *likely* allows raising while *possible* and *probably* do not. Similarly, the other semantic classes do not reflect a uniform syntactic behavior. What is needed, I believe, is a semantic classification that captures the intuitions listed by Dixon but based on the relational and logical behavior of the predicates and not on their folk-epistemology. I return to this discussion below in chapter 10.

2.2   Interlexical Relations

Besides grouping words into distinct semantic classes, lexical semantics is the study of how words are semantically related to one another. In this section, I will briefly examine five classes of lexical relations:

1. SYNONYMY

2. ANTONYMY

3. HYPONYMY AND LEXICAL INHERITANCE

4. MERONYMY

5. ENTAILMENT AND PRESUPPOSITION

Synonymy is generally taken to be a relation between words rather than concepts. One fairly standard definition states that two expressions are synonymous if substituting one for the other in all contexts does not change the truth value of the sentence where the substitution is made (cf. Lyons, 1977, Cruse, 1986).[16] A somewhat weaker definition makes reference to the substitution relative to a specific context. For example in the context of carpentry, *plank* and *board* might be considered synonyms, but not necessarily in other domains (cf. Miller *et al.*, 1990). It should be noted that if synonymy is defined by substitutability of expressions, then it is an intra-category relation, e.g., nouns for nouns, verbs for verbs, and so on.

Antonymy is a relation characterized in terms of semantic opposition, and, like synonymy is properly defined over pairs of lexical items rather than concepts. Examples of antonymy are *rise/fall, heavy/light, fast/slow*, *long/short* (cf. Cruse, 1986, Miller, 1991). It is interesting to observe that co-occurrence data illustrate that synonyms do not necessarily share the same antonyms. For example, *rise* and *ascend* as well as *fall* and *descend* are similar in meaning, yet neither *fall/ascend* nor *rise/descend* are antonym pairs. For further details see Miller *et al.* (1990).

By far the lexical relation most studied in the computational community is hyponymy, essentially the taxonomic relation defined in inheritance networks. For example, specifying *car* as a hyponym of *vehicle* is equivalent to saying that *vehicle* is a superconcept of the concept *car*, or that the set *car* is a subset of those individuals denoted by the set *vehicle*.

One of the most difficult lexical relations to define and treat formally is that of meronymy, the relation of parts to the whole. The relation is familiar from knowledge representation languages with predicates or slot-names such as `part-of` and `made-of` (cf. Brachman and Schmolze, 1985, Hobbs *et al.*, 1987). Similarly in the domain of planning, the issue of meronymy arises when defining the necessary or optional subparts of a plan or event (cf. Kautz, 1987, and Cohen *et al.*, 1990). For treatments of this relation in lexical semantics, see Miller *et al.* (1990) and Cruse (1986).

Another important respect in which words can be related is through entailment and presupposition. Although there is no complete agreement on how to define these relations, one fairly established distinction is the following. An expression A *semantically entails* an expression B if and only if every situation that makes A true, makes B true. On the other hand, A *semantically presupposes* B if and only if both (a) in all situations where A is true, B is true, and (b) in all situations where A is false, B is true (cf. Strawson, 1952, Keenan, 1972).[17]

To see how important these concepts are for determining lexical meanings, observe how (60a) entails the proposition denoted by sentence (60b).

(60)   a. John <u>killed</u> Bill.
       b. Bill <u>died</u>.
       c. Bill is <u>dead</u>.

That is, if there is a *killing* event, then there is also a *dying* event. Capturing such entailment relations was one of the motivations for lexical decomposition in linguistics in the 1960s, and still motivates much research (e.g., Jackendoff, 1983, Dowty, 1979).

That *kill* entails rather than presupposes an event associated with *dying*, becomes clear when examining the negation of (60a), where no dying event occurs. This is not the behavior of presupposition, however. Notice in (61)–(63) that the verb *manage* entails the complement event, but also carries a presupposition that the person *attempts* to do the action in the complement, whether it succeeds or not.

(61) a. Mary managed to finish the exam.
      b. Mary finished the exam.

(62) a. Mary didn't managed to finish the exam.
      b. Mary didn't finish the exam.

(63) Mary attempted to finish the exam.

Thus, the lexical semantics of a verb like *manage* must presuppose that the agent of the managing event also *attempts* to bring this event about (cf. Katz and Fodor, 1963, Karttunen, 1971, 1974, Seuren, 1985).

Similar presuppositions arise with the lexical semantics of verbs such as *sell* and *trade*, where possession or ownership is presupposed by the assertion of the relation.

(64) a. John is selling his piano.
      b. John owns a piano.

(65) a. Mary is trading her piano for a computer.
      b. Mary owns a piano.

For some lexical items, determining what the presuppositions are is not so straightforward. For example, the verb *forget* in (66a) and (66b) appears to presuppose the truth of the complement (hence, it is called a *factive* verb, cf. Kiparsky and Kiparsky, 1971).

(66) a. John forgot that he locked the door.
      b. John didn't forget that he locked the door.

That is, regardless of John's memory, there is a fact in the world that John locked the door. It would furthermore appear that this factivity is associated with the verb *forget*. Notice however, that in (67) there is no factive interpretation associated with the complement.

(67) John <u>forgot</u> to lock the door.

In fact, in some ways it appear to be counterfactive, in that the process of forgetting prevents the event from even occurring. We will return to issues of factivity in chapter 8.

3 The Logical Problem of Polysemy

In chapter 2, I reviewed the basic components of knowledge necessary for lexical description. In this chapter, I turn to the problem of lexical ambiguity. A proper treatment of the description of the semantics of lexical items in the language should permit us to adequately describe the behavior of ambiguity as well as the lexical selection process in the grammar. If done correctly, this should simplify both the grammatical and semantic description of the language. I explore two dimensions of the problem of lexical ambiguity and then discuss the simplest lexical model that is able to account for these phenomena.

3.1 Varieties of Sense Extension

It is certainly true that many words in a language have more than one meaning, a property usually called polysemy. But the ways in which words carry multiple meanings can vary. For example, Weinreich (1964) distinguishes two types of ambiguity, the first of which he calls *contrastive ambiguity*. This is seen where a lexical item accidently carries two distinct and unrelated meanings (i.e., homonymy). Examples of this are shown in (1)–(5) below.

(1) a. Mary walked along the <u>bank</u> of the river.
     b. HarborBank is the richest <u>bank</u> in the city.

(2) a. Drop me a <u>line</u> when you are in Boston.
     b. We built a fence along the property <u>line</u>.

(3) a. First we leave the gate, then we <u>taxi</u> down the runway.
     b. John saw the <u>taxi</u> down the street.

(4) a. The discussion <u>turned</u> on the feasibility of the scheme.
     b. The bull <u>turned</u> on the matador.

(5) a. The judge asked the defendant to approach the <u>bar</u>.
     b. The defendant was in the pub at the <u>bar</u>.

In the examples above, for whatever reason, the underlined items have more that one lexical sense. Whether these senses are historically related or accidents of orthographic and phonological blending, is largely irrelevant for purposes of lexicon construction and the synchronic study of meaning.

The other type of ambiguity Weinreich refers to, illustrated in (6)–(10) below, involves lexical senses which are manifestations of the same basic meaning of the word as it occurs in different contexts.

(6)   a. The <u>bank</u> raised its interest rates yesterday.
      b. The store is next to the newly constructed <u>bank</u>.

(7)   a. John crawled through <u>the window</u>.
      b. <u>The window</u> is closed.

(8)   a. Mary painted <u>the door</u>.
      b. Mary walked through <u>the door</u>.

(9)   a. The <u>farm</u> will fail unless we receive the subsidy promised.
      b. To <u>farm</u> this land would be both foolish and without reward.

(10) a. If the store is <u>open</u>, check the price of coffee.
      b. Zac tried to <u>open</u> his mouth for the dentist.

Following Weinreich's usage, I will refer to these sense distinctions as *complementary polysemies*. Somehow, our model of lexical meaning must be able to account for how the word for bank can refer to both an institution and a building, how the word for window can refer to both an aperture and a physical object, and how stative predicates can also refer to causative acts. In the examples above, there are two types of sense complementarity: (a) category preserving, and (b) category changing. I will define *logical polysemy* as a complementary ambiguity where there is no change in lexical category, and the multiple senses of the word have overlapping, dependent, or shared meanings. Hence, complementary polysemy is a slightly broader term than logical polysemy, since the former also describes how cross-categorial senses are related, for example with the use of *hammer* as both a noun and a verb.

In the next section I discuss the nature of contrastive ambiguity in more depth, and examine what factors in the grammar and what types of knowledge seem to be at play in the disambiguation process for this type of polysemy.

3.2   Contrastive Ambiguity

Making use of the distinction mentioned above, it quickly becomes clear that most work to date on ambiguity has dealt with contrastive ambiguity, the essentially arbitrary association of multiple senses with a single word; furthermore, if it has dealt with complementary polysemy at all, it has been cross-categorial ambiguity alone, usually treated as a subspecies of contrastive senses. In some sense this is not surprising, since given the current representational techniques and strategies for differentiating word senses, there would appear to be no reason to make a logical distinction between these types of ambiguity. This strategy, which I will call *sense enumeration lexicons (SELs)*, appears at first to adequately handle the sense differentiation for both ambiguity types.

Let us see what factors are at play in the disambiguation process for lexical items that have contrastive senses. Consider first, the ambiguities in sentence (11), presented in Waltz and Pollack (1987).

(11) John <u>shot</u> a few <u>bucks</u>.

In this sentence both the verb *shoot* and the noun *buck* are contrastively ambiguous, and this sentence asserts either that John was successful on a hunting trip or that he spent some money gambling. This example illustrates what could be called *pragmatically constrained disambiguation*, since comprehension of such an utterance is performed in a specific context of who John is and what activity he was involved in. Notice that lexical disambiguation does not occur independently for one lexical item, but rather, once the context or domain for one item has been chosen or identified, the ambiguity of the other items is also constrained. We will see that, while this is a property of contrastive ambiguity, it does not characterize sense narrowing in logical polysemy.

Consider next the sentence in (12) below, discussed in Hirst (1987, 1988).

(12) Nadia's <u>plane</u> taxied to the <u>terminal</u>.

Both the nouns *plane* and *terminal* are ambiguous.[1] Here *plane* has at least two senses, (1) as an aircraft and (2) as a tool used in carpentry. The noun *terminal* also has two senses, as (1) a computer terminal and (2) as a building at an airport, train station, or bus station. The

computational concern in the disambiguation of such lexical items is
the question of how to arrive at the appropriate word sense within a
given sentence, given particular strategies for contextual and pragmatic
priming.

Another example discussed in Hirst (1988) and similar examples discussed in Lascarides and Asher (1993) involve sentences such as (13)
below, and (14) mentioned in the previous section:

(13) Ross was escorted from the <u>bar</u> to the <u>dock</u>.

(14) a. The judge asked the defendant to approach the <u>bar</u>.
      b. The defendant was in the pub at the <u>bar</u>.

For a sentence such as (14a), although it is possible that a judge could
be at a drinking establishment and furthermore could refer to the individual as a defendant at this location, this is unlikely, given the normal
use of these terms. Hence, what is at play in these cases is an intuitive
notion of *priming* and *context setting* that is providing for the disambiguation of the lexical items in the sentence by virtue of the discourse
within which the sentence appears. From a theoretical perspective, the
major problems posed by contrastive ambiguity involve issues of discourse inferencing and the correct integration of contextual information
into processing.

Finally, there are some cases of contrastive ambiguity that do not
require context and pragmatic information for disambiguation, so much
as the disambiguation that comes by virtue of the predication relation in
the sentence. For example, in (15) below, the appropriate sense for the
noun *club* is arrived at by virtue of sortal knowledge of the NP appearing
in the inverted subject position (cf. Hirst, 1988).

(15) a. Nadia's favorite <u>club</u> is the five-iron.
      b. Nadia's favorite <u>club</u> is The Carlton.

Because of the way the appropriate sense is identified in this example, I
will refer to this as a case of *sortally constrained disambiguation.*

There are, of course, many finer distinctions to make in the nature of
contrastive ambiguity, as well as the in the strategies and information
sources that help disambiguate senses. My concern here, however, is to
compare this type of ambiguity with complementary polysemy, and to
explore what lexical representation is adequate for expressing such sense
distinctions.

3.3   Complementary Polysemy

Unlike the cases of ambiguity discussed in the previous section, complementary polysemy seems to entail a very different type of relation between senses. The sentences given in the first section above involving the nouns *door* and *window*, for example, are part of a larger set of alternations called *Figure-Ground Reversals*, which include a large class of nouns in the language, such as *fireplace, pipe, room, gate,* etc. The ambiguity in such nouns involves the two senses of 'aperture' and 'physical object' used to frame this aperture. This sense alternation is just one of many nominal alternations that can be described as logical polysemies, where the noun seems to have systematically related senses. These include:

(16)   Count/Mass alternations; *lamb*.
    a. The <u>lamb</u> is running in the field.
    b. John ate <u>lamb</u> for breakfast.

(17)   Container/Containee alternations; *bottle*.
    a. Mary broke the <u>bottle</u>.
    b. The baby finished the <u>bottle</u>.

(18)   Figure/Ground Reversals; *door, window*.
    a. The <u>window</u> is rotting.
    b. Mary crawled through the <u>window</u>.

(19)   Product/Producer alternation; *newspaper, Honda*.
    a. The <u>newspaper</u> fired its editor.
    b. John spilled coffee on the <u>newspaper</u>.

(20)   Plant/Food alternations; *fig, apple*.
    a. Mary ate a <u>fig</u> for lunch.
    b. Mary watered the <u>figs</u> in the garden.

(21)   Process/Result alternation; *examination, merger*.
    a. The company's <u>merger</u> with Honda will begin next fall.
    b. The <u>merger</u> will produce cars.

(22)   Place/People alternation; *city, New York*.
    a. John traveled to <u>New York</u>.
    b. <u>New York</u> kicked the mayor out of office.

Like the contextually determined disambiguation we encountered with the case of the noun *club* in the previous section, the correct sense within a logical polysemy is identified only by virtue of the context around it.

What distinguishes the senses in a logical polysemy from the contrastive cases we have discussed is the manner in which the senses are related. The biggest difference is that, while contextual priming and discourse setting helps disambiguate contrastive senses, it seems irrelevant to the issue of determining the sense of a logically polysemous noun. That is, while contrastive senses are contradictory in nature (that is, one sense is available only if every other sense is not available), complementary senses seem to have a much weaker shadowing effect. Both senses of a logically polysemous noun seem relevant for the interpretation of the noun in the context, but one sense seems 'focused' for purposes of a particular context. All of the pairs above seem to exhibit this logical relation between the senses of the noun.

Complementary polysemy is also seen in other categories as well. For example, adjectives such as *good* have multiple meanings, depending on what they are modifying.[2]

(23) a. a <u>good</u> car
      b. a <u>good</u> meal
      c. a <u>good</u> knife

In some sense, the adjective *good* is merely a positive evaluation of the nominal head it is modifying. Unlike the nominal polysemies above, however, there does not seem to be an alternation or focusing effect, but rather a functional dependency on the head being modified. Such adjective senses seem better classified as complementary polysemies rather than contrastive senses, although it is not clear what the exact relation is between these senses beyond a positive judgment. I return to this question in chapters 7 and 10 below.

Logical polysemy can also be seen as relating the multiple complement types that verbs select for, as in the sentences below.

(24) a. Mary <u>began</u> to read the novel.
      b. Mary <u>began</u> reading the novel.
      c. Mary <u>began</u> the novel.

Verbs such as *begin* are polysemous in that they must be able to select for a multiple number of syntactic and semantic contexts, such as Verb

Phrase, Gerundive Phrase, or Noun Phrase. To a large extent, the verb itself retains the same meaning, varying slightly depending on the type of complement it selects. Hence, this would appear to be a legitimate example of logical polysemy.

Other related senses which could possibly be viewed as polysemies take us further into the area of verbal alternations more broadly defined, such as the inchoative/causative alternation, seen below in (25) and (26).

(25) a. The bottle <u>broke</u>.
      b. John <u>broke</u> the bottle.

(26) a. The window <u>opened</u> suddenly.
      b. Mary <u>opened</u> the window suddenly.

These differ from the contrastive ambiguity cases presented in the previous section in several respects. Not only are the senses related in a well-defined way, but it is fairly uncontroversial that one sense (that in (25a) and (26a)) is actually entailed by the other sense. Thus, even such verbal alternations as these can be seen as logical polysemies as well.

These are but a few of the types of complementary polysemy that languages allow. The purpose of this discussion has been merely to introduce the distinctions in ambiguity types, and not to exhaustively study the nature of these polysemies themselves, something that is addressed in subsequent chapters. In the next section, I present the most elementary model for lexical semantics that would adequately describe the sense distinctions just discussed.

3.4   An Elementary Lexical Semantic Theory

Given the preliminary discussion of polysemy from the previous section, I present the simplest model of lexical design possible, and one which is widely assumed in both computational and theoretical linguistics. As I mentioned earlier, the form that a lexicon takes influences the overall design and structure of the grammar. The major part of semantic research until fairly recently has been on logical form and the mapping from a sentence-level syntactic representation to a logical representation language. Hence, it is not surprising that many assumptions regarding lexical meaning are based on models that are 10–20 years old.

Let us outline the problem in order to present the elementary model more clearly. Assuming that the core problem for natural language semantics is one of assigning the correct semantic interpretation to any string in the language, we would hope that the mapping between word forms and semantic forms can proceed in a well-defined and possibly deterministic process. The most direct way to account for the polysemies described in the previous section is to allow the lexicon to have multiple listings of words, each annotated with a separate meaning or lexical sense. This is certainly the simplest means of encoding sense variation in a lexical form, and furthermore has the smallest effect on the nature of the semantic operations in the grammar. Let us define such a dictionary as a *Sense Enumeration Lexicon (SEL)*, and characterize it directly as follows:

> A lexicon L is a *Sense Enumeration Lexicon* if and only if for every word w in L, having multiple senses $s_1, \ldots, s_n$ associated with that word, then the lexical entries expressing these senses are stored as $\{w_{s_1}, \ldots, w_{s_n}\}$.

Given this view of lexical sense organization, the fact that a word-form is ambiguous does not seem to compromise or complicate the compositional process of how words combine in the interpretation of a sentence.

For example, the two contrastive senses of the word *bank* as used above could be listed in a straightforward fashion as in (27) and (28) below, using a fairly standard lexical data structure of category type (CAT), and a basic specification of the genus term (GENUS), which locates the concept within the taxonomic structure of the dictionary.[3]

$$(27) \quad \begin{bmatrix} \textbf{bank}_1 \\ \text{CAT} = \textbf{count\_noun} \\ \text{GENUS} = \textbf{financial\_institution} \end{bmatrix}$$

$$(28) \quad \begin{bmatrix} \textbf{bank}_2 \\ \text{CAT} = \textbf{count\_noun} \\ \text{GENUS} = \textbf{shore} \end{bmatrix}$$

Assuming that selectional requirements for verbs are defined from the same set of features (or types) as the genus terms themselves, then disambiguation would appear to be merely the process of correctly matching the features of functor and arguments from the available set of lexical entries (cf. Hirst, 1987). For example, a verb such as *lend* might select, in one of its senses (for it will certainly have many senses in an SEL), for financial_institution as subject, shown below:

(29) The <u>bank</u> will <u>lend</u> the money to the customer.

$$(30) \quad \begin{bmatrix} \textbf{lend}_1 \\ \text{CAT} = \textbf{verb} \\ \text{SEM} = R_0(\theta_1, \theta_2, \theta_3) \\ \text{ARGSTR} = \begin{bmatrix} \text{ARG1} = \textbf{np} \ [\textbf{+financial\_institution}] \\ \text{ARG2} = \textbf{np} \ [\textbf{+money}] \\ \text{ARG3} = \textbf{np} \ [\textbf{+human}] \end{bmatrix} \end{bmatrix}$$

From the point of view of linguistic theory, this is a perfectly reasonable model for lexical design, since, as long as the structural and semantic requirements are satisfied, there is no reason to change or enrich the compositional mechanisms making use of this lexical knowledge.[4]

A similar approach applied to verbs would allow variation in complement selection to be represented as distinct senses, related through a sharing of the lexical sign itself. This is the strategy adopted in most current linguistic frameworks, in some fashion or other.[5] Informally, such an approach assumes each lexical item to be uniquely selective for a particular syntactic environment, as illustrated below for the verb *begin*. The semantics of each form, shown below simply as a relation $R_i(\theta_1, \theta_2)$, can be related to each other by a lexical redundancy rule or meaning postulate.

$$(31) \quad \begin{bmatrix} \textbf{begin}_1 \\ \text{CAT} = \textbf{verb} \\ \text{SEM} = R_1(\theta_1, \theta_2) \\ \text{ARGSTR} = \begin{bmatrix} \text{ARG1} = \textbf{np} \\ \text{ARG2} = \textbf{vp} \ [\textbf{+inf}] \end{bmatrix} \end{bmatrix}$$

$$(32) \quad \begin{bmatrix} \textbf{begin}_2 \\ \text{CAT} = \textbf{verb} \\ \text{SEM} = R_2(\theta_1, \theta_2) \\ \text{ARGSTR} = \begin{bmatrix} \text{ARG1} = \textbf{np} \\ \text{ARG2} = \textbf{vp} \ [\textbf{+prog}] \end{bmatrix} \end{bmatrix}$$

$$(33) \quad \begin{bmatrix} \textbf{begin}_3 \\ \text{CAT} = \textbf{verb} \\ \text{SEM} = R_3(\theta_1, \theta_2) \\ \text{ARGSTR} = \begin{bmatrix} \text{ARG1} = \textbf{np} \\ \text{ARG2} = \textbf{np} \end{bmatrix} \end{bmatrix}$$

Given this preliminary definition of sense enumeration lexicons, let us examine more carefully the way in which SELs are able to account for lexical selection and ambiguity in the two classes of ambiguity discussed in the previous section. We return to the sentence in (12), repeated below.

(34) Nadia's <u>plane</u> taxied to the <u>terminal</u>.

Assuming that the contrastive senses of *plane* and *terminal* can be distinguished by appropriate features or sorts (as illustrated in (35) and (36) for *plane*), then this example is similar to the disambiguation of the noun *club* given above.

$$(35) \quad \begin{bmatrix} \textbf{plane}_1 \\ \text{CAT} = \textbf{count\_noun} \\ \text{GENUS} = \textbf{aircraft} \end{bmatrix}$$

$$(36) \quad \begin{bmatrix} \textbf{plane}_2 \\ \text{CAT} = \textbf{count\_noun} \\ \text{GENUS} = \textbf{tool} \end{bmatrix}$$

That is, the contrastive senses of *plane* are *sortally constrained* or differentiated, hence discourse context is not really needed to select the appropriate sense. Assuming the sortal restrictions on the predicate *taxi* shown in (37) below, the subject is therefore disambiguated by strict type selection.

$$(37) \quad \begin{bmatrix} \textbf{taxi} \\ \text{CAT} = \textbf{verb} \\ \text{SEM} = P(\theta_1) \\ \text{ARGSTR} = \begin{bmatrix} \text{ARG1} = \textbf{np [+aircraft]} \end{bmatrix} \end{bmatrix}$$

As mentioned above, once one contrastive sense has been fixed in a sentence, pragmatically constrained disambiguation facilitates the narrowing of other contrastive senses in subsequent processing (cf. Small, Cottrell, and Tanenhaus, 1988). Assuming that the two senses for the noun *terminal* are $\textbf{terminal}_1$ (computer), and $\textbf{terminal}_2$ (a building for an aircraft), then selection of the appropriate sense is accomplished quite straightforwardly, given that the basic predication is fixed at this point in the processing.[6]

Let us turn to the representation of complementary polysemy. We saw above that variations in verb complementation have been encoded as enumerated lexical senses since the *Aspects*-Model (cf. Chomsky, 1965), and they appear to adequately describe syntactic distribution. I will attempt to analyze the cases of nominal polysemy discussed above in terms of SEL representations. These involved figure/ground reversals, container/containee alternations, and count/mass alternations, repeated below:

(38) a. The <u>lamb</u> is running in the field.
    b. John ate <u>lamb</u> for breakfast.

(39) a. Mary broke the <u>bottle</u>.
    b. The baby finished the <u>bottle</u>.

(40) a. The <u>window</u> is rotting.
    b. Mary crawled through the <u>window</u>.

Traditionally these have been treated as simple cases of sense enumeration, along the lines of contrastive ambiguity. Indeed, the representations below for the complementary senses of the noun *lamb* seem as well-motivated as the listings for *plane* given in (35) and (36).

$$(41) \quad \begin{bmatrix} \textbf{lamb}_1 \\ \text{CAT} = \textbf{count\_noun} \\ \text{GENUS} = \textbf{animal} \end{bmatrix}$$

$$(42) \quad \begin{bmatrix} \textbf{lamb}_2 \\ \text{CAT} = \textbf{mass\_noun} \\ \text{GENUS} = \textbf{meat} \end{bmatrix}$$

The fact that these two senses are logically related is not captured in the two representations above, but the senses are distinguished by type, which is usually the most important consideration for compositionality. One possible modification to the SEL framework we could make, which would differentiate contrastive from complementary senses for a lexical item, would be to store complementary senses in a single entry, distinguished by sense-identification number.

$$(43) \quad \begin{bmatrix} \textbf{lamb} \\ \text{SENSE}_1 = \begin{bmatrix} \text{CAT} = \textbf{mass\_noun} \\ \text{GENUS} = \textbf{meat} \end{bmatrix} \\ \text{SENSE}_2 = \begin{bmatrix} \text{CAT} = \textbf{count\_noun} \\ \text{GENUS} = \textbf{animal} \end{bmatrix} \end{bmatrix}$$

Thus, we could restate the definition of a sense enumeration lexicon to account for this distinction in how senses are stored:

(44) A lexicon L is a *Sense Enumeration Lexicon* if and only if for
     every word w in L, having multiple senses $s_1, \ldots, s_n$ associated
     with that word, then:

   (i) if $s_1, \ldots, s_n$ are <u>contrastive</u> senses, the lexical entries expressing
       these senses are stored as $w_{s_1}, \ldots, w_{s_n}$.

  (ii) if $s_1, \ldots, s_n$ are <u>complementary</u> senses, the lexical entry express-
       ing these senses is stored as $w_{\{s_1, \ldots, s_n\}}$.

   Every ambiguity is either represented by (i) or (ii) above.

This is in fact the approach taken by many researchers within both
theoretical and computational traditions. The advantage of this model
of lexical description is that the lexicon remains a separate and independent component or source of data, or a *plug-in* module from the
computational perspective. Hence, one can study properties of syntax
and semantic interpretation, knowing at least that the lexicon is a fixed
point of reference, interacting with other components of grammar in a
predictable and well-defined way. Nevertheless, in the next chapter, I
show how the sense enumerative lexicon model outlined above is inadequate for the purpose of linguistic theory. I will then outline what I think
are the necessary components for an adequate semantic description of
the language, as viewed from the lexicon.

4 Limitations of Sense Enumerative Lexicons

In this chapter I turn to some intrinsic problems with the enumeration method for lexical description described in the previous chapter. It will be shown that the representations allowed by sense enumeration lexicons are inadequate to account for the description of natural language semantics. It is important to note that a theory of lexical meaning will affect the general structure of our semantic theory in several ways. If we view the goal of a semantic theory as being able to recursively assign meanings to expressions, accounting for phenomena such as synonymy, antonymy, polysemy, metonymy, etc., then our view of compositionality will depend ultimately on what the basic lexical categories of the language denote. The standard assumption in current semantic theory requires that words behave as either active functors or passive arguments. As argued in Pustejovsky (1991a), however, if we change the way in which categories can denote, then the form of compositionality will itself change. Hence, our view of lexical semantics can actually force us to reevaluate the very nature of semantic composition in language.

I will show that there are three basic arguments showing the inadequacies of SELs for the semantic description of language.

(1) THE CREATIVE USE OF WORDS: Words assume new senses in novel contexts.

(2) THE PERMEABILITY OF WORD SENSES: Word senses are not atomic definitions but overlap and make reference to other senses of the word.

(3) THE EXPRESSION OF MULTIPLE SYNTACTIC FORMS: A single word sense can have multiple syntactic realization.

Each of these considerations points to the inability of sense enumerative models to adequately express the nature of lexical knowledge and polysemy. Taken together, it would seem that the frameworks incorporating SELs are poor models of natural language semantics.

I will argue that, although the conventional approach to lexicon design (i.e., sense enumeration) is sufficient for contrastive ambiguity, it is unable to address the real nature of polysemy. To adequately treat complementary polysemy, we must touch on every assumption we have regarding word meaning and compositionality. How this is accomplished without proliferating word senses is not a simple task and requires re-thinking the role played by typically non-functor elements in the phrase; that is, in order to maintain compositionality we must enrich the semantics of the expressions in composition. In the last section of this chapter, I outline a model of semantics built on this principle, called a *generative lexicon*.

4.1   The Goals of Lexical Semantic Theory

As mentioned above, I assume that the primary goal of a theory of lexical semantics, and with it a compositional semantics, is to both describe adequately the data and to be transparent regarding two points: the system must be learnable is an obvious way and the various phenomena of polymorphisms must be adequately addressed. I do not distinguish between the goals of theoretical linguistics and computational linguistics, but rather consider the use of computational tools and descriptions as an important part of the machinery for the analysis of linguistic theories. Furthermore, I believe the data set has necessarily expanded to include corpora, but we must be cautious with what inferences we draw from corpus data. In this respect, the criticism of Chomsky (1955, 1957) is just as relevant today as it was in the 1950s.

I will introduce a notion of *semanticality*, analogous to the view of grammaticality (cf. Chomsky, 1964), but ranging over semantic expressions rather than syntactic structures. Semanticality refers to the semantic well-formedness of expressions in a grammar. Within the standard assumptions of logical languages with truth-functional interpretations, an expression is either well-formed or not, and a sentence (i.e., an expression having a propositional type) is or is not a proposition. Hence, what would the definition of semanticality be if not simply a binary judgment on whether an expression is truth-functional or not?

Consider the way in which arguments are expressed in the language, and how this affects the acceptability of an utterance.

(1)   a. ?Mary kicked me with her foot.
      b. Mary kicked me with her left foot.

(2)   a. ?John buttered the toast with butter.
      b. John buttered the toast with an expensive butter from Wisconsin.

Although the (a)-sentences are not ungrammatical in any strict sense, they are semantically less acceptable than the b-sentences. As argued in chapter 9, the licensed expression of certain types of verbal arguments is predictable from the semantics of the expression and semantic operations in the grammar. The degree to which these conditions are met will intuitively define what is semantically well-formed or not, that is, its degree of semanticality. These include, for example, the conditions on closure of arguments in various positions (cf. chapter 9).

Other sentences such as (3b) and (3c) are semantically odd because of what we normally associate with the semantic possibilities of a noun such as *dictionary* and *rock*.

(3) a. Mary began the book.
     b. ?John began the dictionary.
     c. ??Mary began the rock.

These differ in semanticality in rather significant ways. The sentence in (3a) admits of two strong interpretations, that of doing what one normally does to a book as reader, *reading*, and that of doing what one normally does to a book as a writer, *writing*. There are, furthermore, any number of ways of beginning books. While (3b) has any number of interpretations regarding activities related to creating or constructing this object, it fails to readily allow an interpretation available to (3a), that of *reading* the dictionary. Of course, there are instances of individuals "beginning a dictionary," such as Malcolm X in prison, but in this case the dictionary is a form of narrative. That is, it is functioning in a different role, dictionary *qua* novel or narrative. There is no generally available interpretation for (3c) because of what we understand *begin* to require of its argument and our semantic knowledge or what rocks are and what you can do to them, with them, etc. This does not say that an interpretation is unavailable, however. The interpretive process in understanding is both stubborn and persistent, and as speaker/hearers of a community we accommodate to context and pragmatic effects in order to interpret otherwise semantically ill-formed expressions.

Another subtle example illustrating semanticality is the phenomenon illustrated in the pairs below, discussed in Grimshaw and Vikner (1993).

(4) a. ?The house was built.
     b. The house was built by accomplished builders.

(5)   a. ?The cookies were·baked.
      b. The cookies were baked in the oven.

The point of this discussion is that such distinctions in interpretation are real, systematic, and part of the language itself. Theses distinctions constitute a level of representation in the semantics, which operates according to its own set of constraints. By looking at levels of semantic representation, each with its own statement of semantic well-formedness, semanticality can become a metric reflecting the range of data and how semantic interpretation interacts with syntactic form.

It should be pointed out that what is *not* meant by semanticality is a correlation with the direct statistical frequency of occurrence of an expression in the corpus. Although the corpus can be used for data mining and a general notion of empirical verifiability for patterns and cooccurrences, it cannot be used as the only source of semanticality judgments, for example, as on the basis of probabilities. Work in this area that ignores the systematicity accompanying grammatical and semantic rule systems, therefore, is throwing away most of the data from which they hope to perform grammar induction.

4.2   The Creative Use of Words

The most convincing argument for the inadequacy of a theoretical model of description is to demonstrate that this model is unable to sufficiently account for the data being investigated. Another argument would be that the model accounts for the data, but in a *post hoc* fashion, without making any predictions as to whether a particular datum should be possible or not. I will show that SELs fail on both these descriptive criteria.

The first argument against the sense enumerative model concerns the creative use of words; that is, how words can take on an infinite number of meanings in novel contexts. This is not an argument from an "infinite polysemy" position (cf. Section 4.3 below) but from regular sense alternations that are as systematic as transformational regularities in the syntax.

Consider first the ambiguity of adjectives such as *good*, discussed in the previous chapter.

(6) a. Mary finally bought a good umbrella.
   b. After two weeks on the road, John was looking for a good meal.
   c. John is a good teacher.

Within an SEL, the only way to represent distinct senses for an adjective such as *good* would be by an explicit listing of senses in the received usage of the word: $good_1$, $good_2$, ... $good_n$. For the sentences in (10), this would correspond to the three fixed senses listed below.

good(1) to function well;

good(2) to perform some act well;

good(3) tasty.

The conditions which make an umbrella "good for something," however, are very different from those which make John a "good teacher". As Katz (1964) and Vendler (1967) point out, "goodness" is defined relative to a scale, and this scale may vary for each nominal the adjective applies to. One needn't search far to find natural applications of the adjective *good* that are not covered by the enumeration above; for example, *good weather*, *a good movie*, and *good children*. For each novel sense we encounter, the SEL approach must enter a new lexical item into the dictionary, creating one entry for each new sense. That is, the cardinality of the senses of *good* will equal (at least) the number of distinct types in the language to which the adjective applies.

As an alternative, one might simply keep the meaning of *good* vague enough to cover all the cases mentioned above. Then, world knowledge or pragmatic effects could further specify the manner in which something is good, by commonsense understanding of the phrase and the situation within which it is uttered. The problem with this strategy, however, is that the particular chunks of commonsense knowledge needed to interpret how *good* modifies in a specific phrase are actually part of the meaning of the noun being modified, and not simply part of world knowledge. If that is so, then deploying commonsense inference seems unnecessarily and heavy-handed. On the other hand, if such a move is not taken, then it remains for the theory to explain how these chunks of lexical knowledge are put to use in composition.[1]

Another example of the context-dependence of creative word use is illustrated very clearly with adjectives such as *fast* and *slow*, where the meaning of the predicate also varies depending on the head being modified. As mentioned above, an SEL model requires an enumeration of different senses for such words, to account for the ambiguity illustrated below (cf. Pustejovsky and Boguraev, 1993):[2]

(7) The island authorities sent out a <u>fast</u> little government <u>boat</u>, the Culpeper, to welcome us:
a boat driven quickly or *a boat that is inherently fast*

(8) a <u>fast typist</u>:
a person who performs the act of typing quickly

(9) Rackets is a <u>fast game</u>:
the motions involved in the game are rapid and swift

(10) a <u>fast book</u>:
one that can be read in a short time

(11) My friend is a <u>fast driver</u> and a constant worry to her cautious husband:
one who drives quickly

(12) You may decide that a man will be able to make the <u>fast</u>, difficult <u>decisions</u>:
a process which takes a short amount of time

As with the adjective *good*, the examples in (7)–(12) involve at least three distinct word senses for the word *fast*:

fast(1) to move quickly;

fast(2) to perform some act quickly;

fast(3) to do something that takes little time.

As argued in Pustejovsky and Boguraev (1993), for an actual lexicon, word senses would be further annotated with selectional restrictions: for instance, fast(1) should be predicated by the object belonging to a class of movable entities, and fast(3) should, ideally, know how to relate the action "that takes a little time"—reading, in the case of (10) above—to the object being modified. Upon closer analysis, each occurrence of *fast* predicates in a slightly different way. Again, any finite enumeration of word senses will not account for creative applications of this adjective in the language.

To illustrate this, consider the phrases *the fastest motorway* and *a fast garage* as used in (13) below.

(13) a. The Autobahn is the <u>fastest motorway</u> in Germany.

b. I need a <u>fast garage</u> for my car, since we leave on Saturday.

The adjective *fast* in sentence (13a) refers to a new sense, $fast_4$, i.e., the ability of vehicles on the motorway to sustain high speed. Should this be a separate lexical sense for *fast*? If it is not, then how is such an interpretation arrived at in the semantics? Notice that even this novel interpretation can be "blended" with other senses of the adjective in a sentence such as (14) below.

(14) The <u>fastest road</u> to school this time of day would be Lexington Street.

This incorporates the new sense, $fast_4$, with $fast_3$ given above; that is, the reference to *road* in (14) is implicitly a reference to a *route*, resulting from the goal PP within the NP; this subsequently allows a durative interpretation for the adjective, *fast*, meaning *quickly traversed*.

The other example given in (13b), *a fast garage* involves yet another sense, related to both $fast_2$ and $fast_3$, but the actual interval refers to the length of time needed for a repair by the garage, and not to the garage itself. This is similar to the sense in the phrase *fast typist*. With these novel uses of *fast*, we are clearly looking at new senses not covered by the enumeration given above.

The inability of an SEL to completely enumerate the senses for a particular lexical item is not limited to the above examples or constructions, by any means. For example, there are many ways to want, begin, or finish something:

(15) a. Mary <u>wants</u> another cigarette.

b. Bill <u>wants</u> a beer.

c. Mary <u>wants</u> a job.

(16) a. Harry <u>began</u> his class.

b. John <u>finished</u> his article.

c. We had better <u>postpone</u> our coffee until 11:00.

If the goal of semantic theory is to determine the well-formedness of an expression and then provide the interpretation of that expression, then we must somehow account for how we interpret the sentences in (15). Clearly, there is a contextual variability at play with a verb such as *want*, such that in (15a) it means "want to smoke," in (15b) it means "want to drink," and in (15c), it presumably assumes a general "want to have" interpretation. Of course, any of these interpretations are defeasible, but the only way within an SEL to capture each use of *want* is by explicit reference to the manner of the wanting relation.

(17)   a. **want**$_1$: *to want to smoke*;
       b. **want**$_2$: *to want to drink*;
       c. **want**$_3$: *to want to have*;

Similar remarks hold for the verbs in (16). Enumeration is unable to exhaustively list the senses that these verbs assume in new contexts. The difficulty here for semantics and computational lexicons is that word sense enumeration cannot characterize all the possible meanings of the lexical item in the lexicon. Somehow, lexical semantics must be able to account for the creative use of words in different contexts, without allowing for completely unrestricted interpretations.

If an SEL is to adequately explain sense extensions and the creative use of words, then there must also be in the grammar some system giving rise to the generation of new senses. Furthermore, this system must be sensitive enough to generate new senses that are *semantically appropriate* to a particular context; hence there is not a single generator. In fact, there must be as many sense generators as there are derivative senses for how an adjective applies to a noun; from our discussion above, this would mean that an infinite number of such generators would be necessary, given an open corpus of usage.

4.3   Permeability of Word Senses

While the first argument against sense enumerative models illustrated
the sense incompleteness problem, the second failing of SELs concerns
the problem of *fixed senses*. That is, the argument for a different organization of the lexicon is based on a claim that the boundaries between the
word senses in the analysis of *fast* above are too rigid. Even if we were
to assume that sense enumeration were adequate as a descriptive mechanism (a dubious assumption), it is not always obvious how to select the
correct word sense in any given context: consider the systematic ambiguity of verbs like *bake* (discussed by Atkins *et al.*, 1988), which require
discrimination with respect to *change-of-state* versus *creation* readings,
depending on the context (cf. the (a) versus (b) sentences respectively).

(18)   a. John <u>baked</u> the potatoes. (*change-of-state*)
        b. Mary <u>baked</u> a cake. (*creation*)

For purposes of the discussion here, the interesting fact is that the one
sense includes the other. The same holds for the other verbs in this sense
alternation class, such as *cook* and *fry*, shown below.

(19)   a. Mary <u>cooked</u> a meal.
        b. Mary <u>cooked</u> the carrots.

(20)   a. John <u>fried</u> an omelet.
        b. John <u>fried</u> an egg.

For both (19a) and (20a), the object comes into existence by virtue of
the process of cooking and frying, respectively, yet this is no different
than the activity responsible for the edible food resulting in (19b) and
(20b).

The problem here is that there is too much overlap in the "core" semantic components of the different readings; hence, it is not possible to
guarantee correct word sense selection on the basis of selectional restrictions alone. Another problem with this approach is that is lacks any
appropriate or natural level of abstraction. Herskovits (1987,1988), in
addressing the issue of lexical ambiguity of spatial prepositions, introduces the notion of an *ideal meaning* for a lexical item, which provides
the core semantics for the word. These undergo semantic deviations due

to convention or pragmatic factors, supplying additional or overriding information to the existing selectional restrictions of the preposition. Thus, from the core meaning of *in*, convention will elicit related but distinct senses for the preposition as used in the two expressions *the hole in the wall* and *the crack in the bowl*.

As these examples clearly demonstrate, partial overlaps of core and peripheral components of different word meanings make the traditional notion of word sense, as implemented in current dictionaries, inadequate; see Atkins (1991) for a critique of the flat, linear enumeration-based organization of dictionary entries. The only feasible approach would be to employ considerably more refined distinctions in the semantic content of the complement than is conventionally provided by the mechanism of selectional restrictions.[3]

Another problem for sense enumeration models of lexical knowledge is the inability to adequately express the logical relation between senses in cases of logical polysemy. For example, sense alternations involving nouns such as *window* and *door*, discussed in chapters 2 and 3, were analyzed as listings of sense pairs, such as that given for *window* below:

$$(21) \quad \begin{bmatrix} \textbf{window}_1 \\ \text{CAT} = \textbf{count\_noun} \\ \text{GENUS} = \textbf{aperture} \end{bmatrix}$$

$$(22) \quad \begin{bmatrix} \textbf{window}_2 \\ \text{CAT} = \textbf{count\_noun} \\ \text{GENUS} = \textbf{physical\_obj} \end{bmatrix}$$

The problem with this is that the logical relation that exists between the things in the world denoted by these expressions is not expressed, and these senses are embodied in the use of the word as in (23) below.

(23) John crawled through the broken window.

In chapters 7 and 8, we return to the question of how a single lexical item is able to denote two senses.

Another case of sense permeability involves adjectives which have complementary senses in well-defined contexts. These are cases of certain psychological predicates, discussed in Ostler and Atkins (1991, 1992), which have the ability to apparently change type. For example, adjectives like *sad* and *happy* are able to predicate of both individuals (24a) and (24b), as well as event denoting nouns (24c).

(24) a. The woman is sad$_1$.
    b. a sad$_1$ woman
    c. a sad$_2$ day / event / occasion

(25) a. The president is afraid$_1$.
    b. *the afraid$_1$ president
    c. *an afraid$_2$ day / event / occasion

(26) a. The man is frightened$_1$.
    b. a frightened$_1$ man
    c. *a frightened$_2$ day / event / occasion

We need to explain two things with such apparently polysemous adjectives. First, assuming these adjectives select for animate objects, what licenses the modification of a nonselected type such as a temporal interval?

$$(27) \quad \begin{bmatrix} \textbf{sad}_1 \\ \text{CAT} = \textbf{adjective} \\ \text{ARG1} = \textbf{animate\_ind} \end{bmatrix}$$

$$(28) \quad \begin{bmatrix} \textbf{sad}_2 \\ \text{CAT} = \textbf{adjective} \\ \text{ARG1} = \textbf{interval} \end{bmatrix}$$

Secondly, what constraints explain the inability of the adjectives in (25) and (26) to operate in a similar fashion? Within standard approaches to lexical semantics, these data would suggest two separate senses for each of these adjectives, one typed as predicating of animate objects, and the other predicating of intervals. Yet even with this solution, we must somehow explain that "a sad day" is still interpreted relative to a human judging the events of that interval as sad, and most naturally, in a causative relation. Briefly, as explored in Pustejovsky (1994), the distinction here seems to relate to the fact that the adjectives differ in their relational structure. That is, *sad*-adjectives do not take a prepositional object, except by adjunction, i.e., *sad about that*. The *frighten*-adjectives, being passive participles, are underlyingly relational, i.e., *frightened of snakes*, as are the *afraid*-adjectives, i.e., *afraid of swimming*. Apparently only the non-relational adjectives permit this shift in sense. Assuming that most of the interval or event denoting nominals carry a type of causative interpretation when modified by *sad*-adjectives—a sad occasion is one that causes one to be sad—then the polysemy is similar to the inchoative/causative pairs such as *break*.

Finally, another related type of adjectival polysemy involves modifiers such as *noisy*, which predicates of an individual or of a particular location.

(29)   a. a noisy$_1$ car
        b. the noisy$_1$ dog
        c. a noisy$_2$ room
        d. a noisy$_2$ cafeteria

Typical dictionary definitions will require at least two senses for the adjective *noisy*: (30) an object making noise; and (31) a location accompanied by noise.

$$(30) \quad \begin{bmatrix} \textbf{noisy}_1 \\ \text{CAT} = \textbf{adjective} \\ \text{ARG1} = \textbf{phys\_obj} \end{bmatrix}$$

$$(31) \quad \begin{bmatrix} \textbf{noisy}_2 \\ \text{CAT} = \textbf{adjective} \\ \text{ARG1} = \textbf{location} \end{bmatrix}$$

This representation, however, does not do justice to the meaning of this adjective. For these are not unrelated senses, since even with the location reading there is obviously a "noise-maker" present. Thus, we need some mechanism to strongly type an adjective like *noisy*, such that the first reading is somehow made available through a type of indirect modification. We return to this issue briefly below within the framework of a generative lexicon.[4]

4.4   Difference in Syntactic Forms

It is equally arbitrary to create separate word senses for a lexical item just because it can participate in distinct lexical realizations—and yet this has been the only approach open to computational lexicons which assume the ambiguity resolution framework outlined above. A striking example of this is provided by verbs such as *believe* and *forget*. The sentences in (32)–(36) show that the syntactic realization of the verb's complement determines how the proposition is interpreted semantically.

The *tensed-S* complement, for example, in (32) exhibits a property called "factivity" (cf. Kiparsky and Kiparsky, 1971), where the complement proposition is assumed to be a fact regardless of what modality the whole sentence carries. Sentence (35) contains a "concealed question" complement (cf. Baker, 1969, Grimshaw, 1979, Heim, 1979, and Dor, 1992), so called because the phrase can be paraphrased as a question. These different interpretation are usually encoded as separate senses of the verb, with distinct lexical entries.

(32) Madison Avenue is apt to <u>forget that</u> most folks aren't members of the leisure class. (*factive*)

(33) But like many others who have made the same choice, he <u>forgot to</u> factor one thing into his plans: Caliphobia. (*non-factive*)

(34) As for California being a state being run by liberal environmental loonies, let's not <u>forget where</u> Ronald Reagan came from. (*embedded question*)

(35) What about friends who <u>forget the password</u> or never got it? (*concealed question*)

(36) He leaves, <u>forgets his umbrella</u>, and comes back to get it. (*ellipsed non-factive*)

Under the standard SEL model, these would correspond to the separate senses below, where appropriate features have been introduced to distinguish the readings.

$$(37) \quad \begin{bmatrix} \textbf{forget}_1 \\ \text{CAT} = \textbf{verb} \\ \text{SEM} = R_2(\theta_1, \theta_2[-\text{FACTIVE}]) \\ \text{ARGSTR} = \begin{bmatrix} \text{ARG1} = \textbf{np} \\ \text{ARG2} = \textbf{vp} \ [+\textbf{inf}] \end{bmatrix} \end{bmatrix}$$

$$(38) \quad \begin{bmatrix} \textbf{forget}_2 \\ \text{CAT} = \textbf{verb} \\ \text{SEM} = R_2(\theta_1, \theta_2[+\text{FACTIVE}]) \\ \text{ARGSTR} = \begin{bmatrix} \text{ARG1} = \textbf{np} \\ \text{ARG2} = \textbf{s} \ [+\textbf{tns}] \end{bmatrix} \end{bmatrix}$$

$$(39) \quad \begin{bmatrix} \textbf{forget}_3 \\ \text{CAT} = \textbf{verb} \\ \text{SEM} = R_3(\theta_1, \theta_2) \\ \text{ARGSTR} = \begin{bmatrix} \text{ARG1} = \textbf{np} \\ \text{ARG2} = \textbf{np} \end{bmatrix} \end{bmatrix}$$

As discussed in Pustejovsky and Boguraev (1993), sensitivity to factivity would affect, for instance, the interpretation by a question-answering system: when asked *Did Mary lock the door?*, depending on whether the input was *Mary forgot that she locked the door* (factive), or *Mary forgot to lock the door* (non-factive), the answers should be *Yes* and *No* respectively. Such a distinction could be easily accounted for by simply positing separate word senses for each syntactic type, but this misses the obvious relatedness between the two instances of *forget*. It also misses not only the parallel between the question-like readings in (34) and (35), but also the similarity between the non-factive in (33) and the ellipsed non-factive in (36). Moreover, the general "core" sense of the verb *forget*, which deontically relates a mental attitude with a proposition or event, is lost between the separate senses of the verb. That is, the complement of *forget* is always factive in some respect, either directly, as in (32) with the tensed S complement, or with an infinitival VP.[5]

The proper approach, in our view, is to have one definition for *forget* which could, by suitable composition with the different complement types, generate all the allowable readings shown above (cf. chapter 7 below). Another example illustrating the property of multiple subcategorizations being associated with a common underlying meaning is the verb *remember*.

(40) John probably won't <u>remember</u> that he already fed the dog.
     (*factive*)

(41) The neighbor <u>remembered</u> to feed the dog.
     (*factive*)

(42) Mary can never <u>remember</u> where he leaves his car keys.
     (*embedded question*)

(43) Edith finally <u>remembered</u> her husband's name.
     (*concealed question*)

(44) John couldn't <u>remember</u> his lines for the play.
     (*concealed question*)

(45) Mary <u>remembered</u> the keys before she left.
     (*ellipsed factive*)

Other examples of multiple subcategorization involving concealed questions and concealed exclamations are given below (cf. Grimshaw, 1979 and Elliott, 1974).[6]

(46) a. John knows the plane's arrival time.
         (= what time the plane will arrive)
      b. Bill figured out the answer.
         (= what the answer is)

(47) a. John shocked me with his bad behavior.
         (= how bad his behavior is)
      b. You'd be surprised at the big cars he buys.
         (= how big the cars he buys are)

Although the underlined phrases syntactically appear as NPs, their semantics is the same as if the verbs had selected an overt question or exclamation. Similarly, the predicate *regret* takes S and NP complements, where both are interpreted factively, as in (48) below.

(48) a. Mary regretted that she had published the article in *Illustrated Semantics*.
      b. Mary regretted the article in *Illustrated Semantics*.
      c. John regretted publishing the photos in the magazine.
      d. John regretted the photos in the magazine.

For all of these cases, SELs would simply list the alternative structures along with their apparently distinct but related meanings. The fact that these senses are so related, however, suggests that this approach is missing the underlying generalization behind these syntactic forms.

Another interesting set of examples involves the range of subjects possible with causative and experiencer verbs.[7] Consider the sentences in (49) and (50).

(49) a. Driving a car in Boston frightens me.
      b. Driving frightens me.
      c. John's driving frightens me.
      d. Cars frighten me.
      e. Listening to this music upsets me.
      f. This music upsets me.

(50) a. John <u>killed</u> Mary.
     b. The gun <u>killed</u> Mary.
     c. The war <u>killed</u> Mary.
     d. John's pulling the trigger <u>killed</u> Mary.

As these examples illustrate, the syntactic argument to a verb is not always the same logical argument in the semantic relation. Although superficially similar to cases of general metonymy (cf. Lakoff and Johnson, 1982, Nunberg, 1978), there is an interesting systematicity to such shifts in meaning that we will try to characterize below as logical metonymy.

Finally, other verbal alternations involving reciprocal relations such as *meet* and *debate* are polysemous and allow reciprocal subject interpretation (cf. (51c) and (52c)); as the sentences in (54) show, however, the constraint on reciprocal interpretation for motion verbs must require that both subject and object be moving (cf. Levin, 1993, and Dowty, 1991).

(51) a. John <u>met</u> Mary.
     b. John <u>met</u> with Mary.
     c. John and Mary <u>met</u>.

(52) a. John <u>debated</u> Mary.
     b. John <u>debated</u> with Mary.
     c. John and Mary <u>debated</u>.

(53) a. A car <u>ran</u> into a truck.
     b. A car and a truck <u>ran</u> into each other.

(54) a. A car <u>ran</u> into a tree.
     b. *A car and a tree <u>ran</u> into each other.

These examples illustrate the inherent inability of SELs to capture the relatedness between senses in the above examples without the addition of more powerful mechanisms, such as meaning postulates. More generally, what emerges from these three independent arguments is the view that the sense enumerative model of lexical description is simply inadequate for describing the semantics of natural language utterances.

4.5   Semantic Expressiveness

In order to help characterize the expressive power of natural languages in terms of semantic expressiveness, it is natural to think in terms of semantic systems with increasing functional power. Furthermore, a natural way of capturing this might be in terms of the type system which the grammar refers to for its interpretation.

Let me begin the discussion on expressiveness by reviewing how this same issue was played out in the realm of syntactic frameworks in the 1950s. When principles of context-free and transformational grammars were first introduced, one of the motivations for the richness of these new systems was the apparent inadequacies of finite-state descriptions for the different natural language constructions that were being discovered (Chomsky, 1955, 1957). That is, wherever the structuralists did not appreciate that a particular construction was not sufficiently characterizable by finite-state description, the power of a more expressive grammar became necessary. When Chomsky and others argued that natural languages appeared to be not even context-free, but in fact appeared to require mechanisms moving out of the family of context-free languages, the motivation was clearly data-directed and seemed warranted by the most prevalent interpretations of what CFGs were.

An analogous situation holds in the semantics of natural language today. We have reached a point where we are discovering phenomena in language that are beyond the range of explanation, given the current makeup of our lexical semantic systems.

If we think of the view within SELs in terms of its generative capacity, we have what might be characterized as a *monomorphic language* (cf. Strachey, 1967). In a monomorphic language, lexical items are given a single meaning, that is, one type and denotation. Lexical ambiguity is handled by having a multiple listing of the word. The polysemy discussed in previous chapters with words such as *door* has forced monomorphic approaches to represent these senses as independent and separate lexical items. As we discovered, within monomorphic approaches to lexical meaning, the connection is captured at best by meaning postulates or lexical redundancy rules of some sort. Similar examples exist with an entire range of nominal types in natural languages, all of which seem to be logically polysemous; e.g., *fireplace, pipe, room*, etc. All of these have the meaning of both physical object and spatial enclosure (cf. Pustejovsky and Anick, 1988).

Something is clearly being missed in this approach; namely, the logical relationship that a door is an aperture defined by a physical object in a particular way. This particular definition leads us to a *complex typing* for this class of nominals, rather than as a simple set of individuals.

Summarizing our discussion of polysemy so far, it seems clear that the standard theory of lexical ambiguity can be characterized as a *monomorphic language (ML)* of types, with the following properties:

Monomorphic Languages A language where lexical items and complex phrases are provided a single type and denotation. In all these views, every word has a literal meaning. Lexical ambiguity is treated by multiple listing of words, both for contrastive ambiguity and logical polysemy. Treating the lexicon as an enumerative listing of word senses has been the predominate view, and adherents include Montague (1974), Levin (1985), and Levin and Rappaport (1988). Dowty (1979) has a more complex view of word senses which is still monomorphic, but the meaning postulates are more clearly defined than in Montague's model.

Although we will not discuss it here, the inverse of a restrictive theory such as that described above would be a theory denying the role of literal meaning entirely. Such a view is held by Searle (1979), for example. Viewed from the perspective we have adopted in this paper, such a theory might be termed an *unrestricted polymorphic language (UPL)* since the meaning is determined more by the context than any inherent properties of the language lexicon. Briefly, the properties of such a system are:

Unrestricted Polymorphic Languages No restriction on the type that a lexical item may assume. No operational distinction between subclasses of polymorphic transformations. Although not explicitly lexically based, the theory of Searle (1979) is polymorphic in a fairly unrestricted form. The contribution of "background knowledge" acts as the trigger to shift the meaning of an expression in different pragmatically determined contexts, and there is nothing inherent in the language that constrains the meaning of the words in context.

From our brief discussion above, I believe it is clear that what we want is a lexical semantic theory which accounts for the polysemy in natural language while not overgenerating to produce semantically ill-formed expressions. Furthermore, if our observations above are correct, then such a theory must be in part lexically determined and not entirely pragmatically defined. Such a theory would generate what I will term *weakly-polymorphic languages (WPLs)*. Several lines of research have pointed to capturing the flexibility of word meaning and semantic interpretation, from early observations made by Katz (1964), Wilks (1975), and Nunberg (1979) to the work reported in Klein and van Benthem (1987). The properties of such a system would be at least the following:

Weakly Polymorphic Languages   All lexical items are semantically active, and have a richer typed semantic representation than convention-ally assumed; semantic operations of lexically-determined type changing (e.g., type coercions) operate under well-defined constraints. Different subclasses of polymorphic operations are defined, each with independent properties and conditions on their application.

As with the increasing generative capabilities of families of grammars, the range of sense extensions for a lexicon (and with them the subsequent semantic expressions) increases as restrictions on generation are lifted. What natural language data seem to require is a semantic system falling outside of monomorphic languages (ML), but well below the language of unrestricted polymorphic languages (UPL), what we have called weakly-polymorphic languages (WPL):

$$ML \subseteq WPL \subseteq UPL$$

This is the view of semantics that I will present in the remainder of this book. I will describe the varieties of coercion types, and then outline an approach within generative lexicon theory, how best to constrain the ap-plication of coercion operations. The presentation of each phenomenon will be somewhat brief, in order to give a broader picture of how all cate-gories participate in generative processes giving rise to logical polysemy.

4.6   Generative Lexical Models

Given what I have said, I will outline what I think are the basic require-ments for a theory of computational semantics satisfying the require-ments outlined in the previous chapter. I will present a conservative approach to decomposition, where lexical items are minimally decomposed into structured forms (or templates) rather than sets of features. This will provide us with a generative framework for the *composition* of lexical meanings, thereby defining the well-formedness conditions for semantic expressions in a language.

We can distinguish between two distinct approaches to the study of word meaning: *primitive-based* theories and *relation-based* theories. Those advocating primitives assume that word meaning can be exhaustively defined in terms of a fixed set of primitive elements (e.g., Wilks, 1975a, Katz, 1972, Lakoff, 1971, Schank, 1975). Inferences are made through the primitives into which a word is decomposed. In contrast to this view, a relation-based theory of word meaning claims that there is no need for decomposition into primitives if words (and their concepts) are associated through a network of explicitly defined links (e.g., Quillian, 1968, Collins and Quillian, 1969, Fodor, 1975, Carnap, 1956, Brachman, 1979). This view relies on logical rules of inference to establish the connectedness between lexical meanings and propositions. In a sense, linguistic data are just another application of a general, more powerful set of reasoning devices needed for commonsense inference, naive physics, and micro-world modeling.

What I would like to do is to propose a new way of viewing decomposition, looking more at the generative or *compositional* aspects of lexical semantics, rather than decomposition into a specified *number* of primitives. Briefly, a generative lexicon can be characterized as a system involving at least four levels of semantic representations. These include the notion of *argument structure*, which specifies the number and type of arguments that a lexical item carries; an *event structure* of sufficient richness to characterize not only the basic event type of a lexical item, but also internal, subeventual structure; a *qualia structure*, representing the different modes of predication possible with a lexical item; and, a *lexical inheritance structure*, which identifies how a lexical structure is related to other structures in the dictionary, however it is constructed.

A set of generative devices connects these four levels, providing for the compositional interpretation of words in context. The most important of these devices for our discussion is a semantic transformation called *type coercion* which captures the semantic relatedness between syntactically distinct expressions. As an operation on types within a λ-calculus, type coercion can be seen as transforming a monomorphic language into one with polymorphic types (cf. Cardelli and Wegner, 1985, Klein and van Benthem, 1987). Argument, event, and qualia types must conform to the well-formedness conditions defined by the type system and the lexical inheritance structure when undergoing operations of semantic composition. Lexical items are strongly typed yet are provided with mechanisms for fitting to novel typed environments by means of type coercion over a richer notion of types.

If lexical items are to be thought of as carrying several parameters (or dimensions) of interpretation, then the question immediately arises as to how a particular interpretation is arrived at in a given context. This question is answered in part by the semantic operation of *type coercion*. Intuitively, the process works as follows. In the construction of a semantic interpretation for a phrase or sentence, a lexical item is able to coerce an argument to the appropriate type only if that word or phrase has available to it, an interpretation of the expected type. Assuming that objects are represented within a typed semantic formalism, we can define type coercion as follows:

> TYPE COERCION: a semantic operation that converts an argument to the type which is expected by a function, where it would otherwise result in a type error.

As I shall show in chapter 6, each lexical item has available to it a set of type shifting operators which are able to operate over the expression, changing its type and denotation, following specific semantic constraints.

In the next chapter, I turn to the general motivations of linguistic theory, and specifically, to the overriding principles motivating developments in lexical semantic research.

4.7   Strong vs. Weak Compositionality

Before looking at specific analyses of how ambiguity can be reduced, there are some important issues to address regarding compositionality in general.[8] We can view the principle of compositionality as being satisfied in at least two ways, which I will refer to as *weak* and *strong* compositionality. Briefly, the distinction can be articulated as follows. A basic Fregean concern with composition is not sufficient enough for a cognitive or computational model of natural language semantics. One must also be concerned with space (and possibly time) considerations within the system (i.e., for the algorithms therein). This means that two parameters are important for characterizing semantic devices:

(A) The degree of composition within an expression (i.e., how much unilateral or bilateral function application occurs within a phrase);

(B) How many explicitly defined senses are necessary to accomplish a unique interpretation of the phrase.

The first point I think is fairly clear. This refers to how functionally the elements in the phrase are treated, relative to the resulting interpretation. In most conventional approaches, only one element for each phrase is treated functionally. I have argued elsewhere that natural language exhibits a high degree of *cocomposition* that must be accounted for formally.

The second point refers to the linguistic and logical tradition of simply multiplying senses on demand for new contexts as needed to create new word senses. That is, as mentioned above, compositionality is achieved by enumeration of word senses. This gives rise to a system where the number of distinct lexical senses (i.e, lexical listings) needed in the lexicon rises proportional to the number of interpretations in the language. We will call this "weak compositionality." It may still be compositional, but it results in a system that captures generative expressiveness only by virtue of listing an infinite number of senses, an unfortunate state of affairs for a computational system.

A more adequate theoretical stance, I believe, is that where the number of lexical senses remains roughly constant relative to the space of possible interpretations in the language. On top of a simple type system are generative mechanisms, which through composition, produce the actual "senses in context" non-lexically up the tree, as it were. This is what I refer to as "strong compositionality." I believe this is a much more adequate model for cognitive concerns and computational tractability, while still preserving the principle of compositionality.[9] In what follows, I will explore the formal characteristics of some of these generative devices, as seen from the concerns of lexical semantics.

5 The Semantic Type System

5.1 Levels of Representation

In this chapter I detail the organization of lexical information within a generative lexicon. As should be clear from discussion in previous chapters, our goal is to provide a formal statement of language that is both expressive and flexible enough to capture the generative nature of lexical creativity and sense extension phenomena. To this end, I will characterize a generative lexicon as a computational system involving at least the following four levels of representations, mentioned briefly in chapter 4:

1. ARGUMENT STRUCTURE: Specification of number and type of logical arguments, and how they are realized syntactically.

2. EVENT STRUCTURE: Definition of the event type of a lexical item and a phrase. Sorts include STATE, PROCESS, and TRANSITION, and events may have subeventual structure.

3. QUALIA STRUCTURE: Modes of explanation, composed of FORMAL, CONSTITUTIVE, TELIC, and AGENTIVE roles.

4. LEXICAL INHERITANCE STRUCTURE: Identification of how a lexical structure is related to other structures in the type lattice, and its contribution to the global organization of a lexicon.

A set of generative devices connects these four levels, providing for the compositional interpretation of words in context. Included in these generative operations are the following semantic transformations, all involving well-formedness conditions on type combinations:

- TYPE COERCION: where a lexical item or phrase is coerced to a semantic interpretation by a governing item in the phrase, without change of its syntactic type.

- SELECTIVE BINDING: where a lexical item or phrase operates specifically on the substructure of a phrase, without changing the overall type in the composition.

- CO-COMPOSITION: where multiple elements within a phrase behave as functors, generating new non-lexicalized senses for the words in composition. This also includes cases of underspecified semantic forms becoming contextually enriched, such as *manner co-composition, feature transcription*, and *light verb specification*.

These three semantic transformations are important to our discussion of how to capture the semantic relatedness between syntactically distinct expressions.[1] Argument, event, and qualia types must conform to the well-formedness conditions defined by the type system and lexical inheritance structure when undergoing operations of semantic composition. Lexical items are strongly typed yet are provided with mechanisms for fitting to novel typed environments by means of type coercion over a richer notion of types, to be presented below in chapter 7.

By defining the functional behavior of lexical items at different levels of representation we hope to arrive at a characterization of the lexicon as an active and integral component in the composition of sentence meanings. Because of the more expressive mechanisms involved in composition, this approach will enable us to conflate different word senses into a single *meta-entry*, encoding regularities of word behavior dependent on context, and as a result, greatly reducing the size of the lexicon. Semantic underspecification for lexical items plays an important role in this restructuring of how composition operates. Following Pustejovsky and Anick (1988), I call such meta-entries *lexical conceptual paradigms (lcps)*. The theoretical claim here is that such a characterization constrains what a possible word meaning can be, through the mechanism of well-formed semantic expressions.

5.2   Argument Structure

Following the initial discussion above, I will assume that the semantics of a lexical item α can be defined as a structure, consisting of the following four components (cf. Pustejovsky, 1995a):

(1) $\alpha = \langle \mathcal{A}, \mathcal{E}, \mathcal{Q}, \mathcal{I} \rangle$

where $\mathcal{A}$ is the argument structure, $\mathcal{E}$ is the specification of the event type, $\mathcal{Q}$ provides the binding of these two parameters in the qualia structure, and $\mathcal{I}$ is an embedding transformation, placing α within a type lattice, determining what information is inheritable from the global lexical structure. Argument structure is by far the best understood of these areas, and is the logical starting point for our investigation into the semantics of words.

What originally began as the simple listing of the parameters or arguments associated with a predicate has developed into a sophisticated view of the way arguments are mapped onto syntactic expressions. For example, Chomsky's (1981) *Theta-Criterion* and Bresnan's (1982) *functional completeness* and *coherence* conditions require arguments to be expressed as syntactic constituents, and syntactic constituents to be bound to the argument structure. Chomsky's *Projection Principle* (Chomsky, 1981) further requires that such conditions are satisfied at all levels of linguistic representation. One of the most important recent contributions to the theory of grammar has been the view that argument structure itself is highly structured independent of the syntax. Williams' (1981) distinction between *external* and *internal* arguments and Grimshaw's proposal for a hierarchically structured representation (cf. Grimshaw, 1990) provide us with the basic syntax for one aspect of a word's meaning.[2]

The argument structure for a word can be seen as a minimal specification of its lexical semantics. By itself, it is certainly inadequate for capturing the semantic characterization of a lexical item, but it is a necessary component. Indeed, much research has been conducted on the assumption that argument structure is the strongest determinant or constraint on the acquisition of verb meaning in child language acquisition (cf. Gleitman, 1990, Fisher, Gleitman, and Gleitman (1991) and Pinker (1989) for discussion).

I will introduce a distinction between four types of arguments for lexical items, here illustrated for verbs;

1. TRUE ARGUMENTS: Syntactically realized parameters of the lexical item; e.g.,

    "John arrived late."

2. DEFAULT ARGUMENTS: Parameters which participate in the logical expressions in the qualia, but which are not necessarily expressed syntactically; e.g.,

    "John built the house out of bricks".

3. SHADOW ARGUMENTS: Parameters which are semantically incorporated into the lexical item. They can be expressed only by operations

of subtyping or discourse specification; e.g.,

"Mary buttered her toast with an expensive butter."

4. TRUE ADJUNCTS: Parameters which modify the logical expression, but are part of the situational interpretation, and are not tied to any particular lexical item's semantic representation. These include adjunct expressions of temporal or spatial modification; e.g.,

"Mary drove down to New York on Tuesday."

True arguments define those parameters which are necessarily expressed at syntax. This is the domain generally covered by the θ-criterion and other surface conditions on argument structure, as mentioned above. Verbal alternations between polysemous forms of a verb which result in the expression of true arguments should be distinguished from those alternations involving the expression of an optional phrase. The former include alternations such as the inchoative/causative alternation in (2), while the latter include cases such as the material/product alternation shown in the sentences in (3) (cf. Levin, 1993):

(2) a. The window broke.
     b. John broke the window.

(3) a. Mary carved the doll out of wood.
     b. Mary carved the wood into a doll.
     c. Mary carved a doll.
     d. ?Mary carved the wood.

Because the expression of the material is optional, its status as an argument is different from the created object. Such optional arguments in alternations such as the material/product pair I will call *default arguments*. They are necessary for the logical well-formedness of the sentence, but may be left unexpressed in the surface syntax. The conditions under which such arguments are ellipsed are discussed to some extent in chapter 9.

Intuitively, for an expression such as (4a) with true arguments A and B and a default argument C, the interpretation can be represented schematically in (4b).

(4) a. *A* verb *B* with *C*
     b. **verb'**(A,B,C)

If the default argument is unexpressed however, then existential closure on that argument gives the representation in (5).

(5) $\exists x[\textbf{verb'}(A,B,x)]$

Like default arguments, *shadow arguments* refer to semantic content that is not necessarily expressed in syntax, as with the incorporated semantic content in the verbs *butter* and *kick* in (6).

(6) a. Mary <u>buttered</u> her toast.
     b. Harry <u>kicked</u> the wall.

The "hidden argument" in (6a) is the material being spread on the toast, while in (6b) it is the leg which comes into contact with the wall. Unlike default arguments, however, which are optionally expressed due to conditions above the level of the sentence (i.e., discourse and contextual factors), shadow arguments are expressible only under specific conditions within the sentence itself; namely, when the expressed arguments stands in a subtyping relation to the shadow argument (cf. Wunderlich, 1987).[3] Observe the expressed shadow arguments in (7).

(7) a. Mary buttered her toast <u>with margarine</u> / *with butter.
     b. Harry kicked the wall <u>with his gammy leg</u> / *with his leg.
     c. Mary and John danced <u>a waltz</u> / *a dance.
     d. Harry elbowed me <u>with his arthritic elbow</u> / *with his elbow.

Because the conditions under which these arguments can be expressed are so specific, I will distinguish them in logical type from the larger class of default arguments.

The final class in our typology of argument types is defined more by complementarity than in terms of specific properties of the class; namely, *adjuncts*. I will have little to say about this type of argument here, except that they are associated with verb classes and not individual verbs. Hence, for example, the ability of the verb *sleep* to be modified by the temporal expression *on Tuesday* in (8a) is inherited by virtue of the verb's classification as an individuated event; similar remarks hold for the verb *see* and locative modifiers such as *in Boston* in (8b).

(8) a. John slept late <u>on Tuesday</u>.
     b. Mary saw Bill <u>in Boston</u>.

The above classification is a first attempt at refining the distinction
between argument and adjunct phrases. The theoretical consequences
of this move are potentially significant; namely, it is not just the lexical
properties of a single item which will determine the logical status of a
phrase as a certain argument type. Compositional operations may create
an argument or shadow an argument at a phrasal projection, by virtue of
compositionality in the phrase. In other cases, however, a true argument
is defaulted by virtue of a complement's semantics. For example, for the
verb *show*, the true argument expressing the GOAL argument in (9a), can
be *defaulted* by virtue of the semantics of the complement, as in (9b),
thereby becoming an optional argument.

(9) a. Mary showed her paintings <u>to John</u>.
     b. Mary showed a movie (<u>to John</u>).

That is, the phrase *show a movie* somehow demotes the otherwise true
GOAL argument to a default argument, giving it an optional status in
the syntax. I return to this topic in chapter 7.

Another consequence of this view of argument types is that default
arguments can be satisfied by full phrasal expression as a PP (cf. (10a)),
or as a phrase incorporated into a true argument, as in (10b):

(10) a. Mary built a house <u>with wood</u>.
      b. Mary built a <u>wooden</u> house.

In fact, when this occurs, the material is expressible as a shadow argument, as in (11) below.

(11) Mary built a <u>wooden</u> house <u>out of pine</u>.

In (10b) the default argument has effectively been saturated indirectly
as a modifier in the direct object, while in (11) further specification
by the phrase *out of pine* is licensed in the same manner as in shadow
arguments.[4]

From the discussion above, I will assume that the arguments for a
lexical item, ARG_1, ...,ARG_n, are represented in a list structure where
argument type is directly encoded in the argument structure, ARGSTR,

as shown in (12) below, where D-ARG is a default argument, and S-ARG is a shadow argument.

$$
(12) \quad
\begin{bmatrix}
\alpha \\
\text{ARGSTR} =
\begin{bmatrix}
\text{ARG}_1 & = & \ldots \\
\text{ARG}_2 & = & \ldots \\
\text{D-ARG}_1 & = & \ldots \\
\text{S-ARG}_1 & = & \ldots
\end{bmatrix} \\
\ldots
\end{bmatrix}
$$

For example, the lexical semantics for the verbs discussed above can now be partially represented with argument structure specifications, as illustrated in (13)–(15).

$$
(13) \quad
\begin{bmatrix}
\textbf{build} \\
\text{ARGSTR} =
\begin{bmatrix}
\text{ARG}_1 & = & \textbf{animate\_individual} \\
\text{ARG}_2 & = & \textbf{artifact} \\
\text{D-ARG}_1 & = & \textbf{material}
\end{bmatrix} \\
\ldots
\end{bmatrix}
$$

$$
(14) \quad
\begin{bmatrix}
\textbf{butter} \\
\text{ARGSTR} =
\begin{bmatrix}
\text{ARG}_1 & = & \textbf{human} \\
\text{ARG}_2 & = & \textbf{phys\_object} \\
\text{S-ARG}_1 & = & \textbf{butter}
\end{bmatrix} \\
\ldots
\end{bmatrix}
$$

$$
(15) \quad
\begin{bmatrix}
\textbf{kick} \\
\text{ARGSTR} =
\begin{bmatrix}
\text{ARG}_1 & = & \textbf{animate\_individual} \\
\text{ARG}_2 & = & \textbf{phys\_object} \\
\text{S-ARG}1 & = & \textbf{leg}
\end{bmatrix} \\
\ldots
\end{bmatrix}
$$

I have yet to discuss the formal conditions under which these arguments are licensed or expressed, but what should be clear from this discussion is the usefulness of the logical distinction in argument types, both descriptively in terms of coverage of construction types, and theoretically in terms of the formulation of principles of mapping from lexical semantic forms.

5.3   Extended Event Structure

It has become quite standard to acknowledge the role of events in verbal semantics. Conventionally, the event variable for a verb within an event-based semantics is listed as a single argument along with the logical parameter defined by a particular predicate or relation. For example, a lexical representation for the verb *build* merging aspects of both Davidson's (1967) and Parsons' (1990) analyses might be as follows:[5]

$$\lambda y \lambda x \lambda e[build(e, x, y) \wedge \theta_1(e, x) \wedge \theta_2(e, y)]$$

This assumes an atomic view on event structure, where internal aspects of the event referred to by the single variable are inaccessible. Moens and Steedman (1988) and Pustejovsky (1991b) argue that finer-grained distinctions are necessary for event descriptions in order to capture some of the phenomena associated with aspect and Aktionsarten. Assuming this is the case, we need a means for both representing the subeventual structure associated with lexical items while expressing the necessary relation between events and the arguments of the verb. In Pustejovsky (1995a), a mechanism called *Orthogonal Parameter Binding* is outlined, which allows us to bind into an expression from independent parameter lists, i.e., argument structure and event structure. Given a listing of arguments and an event structure represented as a listing of event variables,

[ARGSTR = ARG_1, ARG_2, ..., ARG_n]
[EVENTSTR = $EVENT_1$, $EVENT_2$, ..., $EVENT_n$]

we can view the semantics of the verb as being centrally defined by the qualia, but constrained by type information from the two parameter lists. The predicates in the qualia refer directly to the parameters:

[QUALIA = [... [Q_i = PRED($EVENT_j$,ARG_k)] ...]

I will return to the specifics of qualia structure in the next section. First, let us turn to the exact nature of the event argument list illustrated above, and what motivation exists for its structure.

Proceeding from our earlier discussion in chapter 2, I assume that events can be subclassified into at least three sorts: PROCESSES, STATES, and TRANSITIONS.[6] Furthermore, I assume a *subeventual* structure to these event sorts as well. This has the advantage of allowing principles of predicate-argument binding to refer to subevents in the semantic representation, a move which has significant theoretical consequences (cf. Grimshaw, 1990, and Pustejovsky, 1991b). As shown in Pustejovsky and Busa (1995), however, evidence from unaccusativity and the varied nature of causative constructions shows that this notion of event structure does not fully capture the underlying semantics of unaccusative constructions, with respect to how the subevents project to syntax.

Within an event semantics defined not only by sorts but also by the internal configurational properties of the event, we need to represent the relation between an event and its proper subevents. Extending the constructions introduced in van Benthem (1983) and Kamp (1979), we interpret an "extended event structure" as a tuple, $< E, \preceq, <, \circ, \sqsubseteq, * >$, where E is the set of events, $\preceq$ is a partial order of *part-of*, $<$ is a strict partial order, $\circ$ is overlap, $\sqsubseteq$ is inclusion, and $*$ designates the "head" of an event, to be defined below. An event structure with structured subevents such as that in Pustejovsky (1988, 1991), shown in (16) below,

(16)

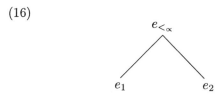

can be constructed in such a model as follows. Let us define an *event tree structure* in terms of the relation of "exhaustive ordered part of," $<_\alpha$:[7]

(17) a. $[_{e_3} \; e_1 \; <_\alpha \; e_2 \;] \; =_{def} \; <_\alpha (\{e_1, e_2\}, e_3)$
      b. $\forall e_1, e_2, e_3 [<_\alpha (\{e_1, e_2\}, e_3) \leftrightarrow e_1 \preceq e_3 \wedge e_2 \preceq e_3 \wedge e_1 < e_2 \wedge \forall e[e \preceq e_3 \rightarrow e = e_1 \vee e = e_2]]$

This definition states that the event e_3 is a complex event structure constituted of two subevents, e_1 and e_2, where e_1 and e_2 are temporally ordered such that the first precedes the second, each is a logical part of e_3, and there is no other event that is part of e_3. Verbs included in this description are causatives as well as inchoatives, as argued in chapter 9.

An event tree structure is not restricted to representing strictly sequential relations between subevents, but structures other orderings as well. For example, an event composed of two completely simultaneous subevents can be lexicalized with a relation we will call "exhaustive overlap part of," $\circ_\alpha$. It can be defined as follows (cf. Kamp, 1979, and Allen, 1984):

(18) a. $[_{e_3} \; e_1 \; \circ_\alpha \; e_2 \;] \; =_{def} \; \circ_\alpha(\{e_1, e_2\}, e_3)$

b. $\forall e_1, e_2, e_3 [\circ_\alpha(\{e_1, e_2\}, e_3) \leftrightarrow e_1 \preceq e_3 \wedge e_2 \preceq e_3 \wedge e_1 \sqsubseteq e_2 \wedge e_2 \sqsubseteq$
$e_1 \wedge \exists e[e \sqsubseteq e_1 \wedge e \sqsubseteq e_2 \wedge e = e_3] \wedge \forall e[e \preceq e_3 \rightarrow e = e_1 \vee e = e_2]]$

This event structure is denoted by verbs such as *accompany*, which involve two subevents occurring simultaneously. This can be illustrated in terms of an event structure tree as follows:

(19)

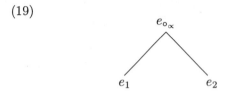

The interesting thing about such a verb is that, because it makes reference to an implicit event, it is aspectually underspecified, and assumes both telic and atelic interpretations, depending on the context.

(20)   a. John will accompany you to the store. (*telic*)
         b. Mary accompanied me while I was walking. (*atelic*)

In this sense, it is aspectually similar to the verb *go*, which also admits of multiple event interpretations.

Finally, the lexicalization of two basically simultaneous subevents, where one starts before the other, called "exhaustive ordered overlap," $< \circ_\alpha$, can be defined as follows, where *init* is a function over events, returning the initial part of that event, and *end* is a function returning the final part of the event:

(21)   a. $[_{e_3} e_1 < \circ_\alpha e_2] =_{def} < \circ_\alpha(\{e_1, e_2\}, e_3)$
         b. $\forall e_1, e_2, e_3 [< \circ_\alpha(\{e_1, e_2\}, e_3) \leftrightarrow e_1 \preceq e_3 \wedge e_2 \preceq e_3 \wedge e_1 \circ e_2 \wedge$
            $init(e_1) < init(e_2) \wedge end(e_1) = end(e_2) \wedge \forall e[e \preceq e_3 \rightarrow e =$
            $e_1 \vee e = e_2]]$

The relation $< \circ_\alpha$ above defines an event containing two subevents, e_1 and e_2, where e_1 starts before e_2. The event structure tree is shown below:

(22)

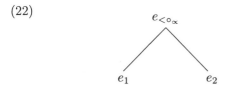

We shall see that because of this partial ordered relation, a type of causative relation exists between the subevents, but not in the same way as with the relation $<_\alpha$. Verbs such as *walk* will be analyzed as involving this subeventual structure, where two motion processes are structured in an overlapping relation; that is, the efficient motion of the legs bringing about the final motion of the body. I will argue that this relation is also present with control interpretations for aspectual predicates such as *begin*, with the associated entailments regarding causation.

Given what I have said so far, there are two facets of an event tree structure that need to be represented for a lexical structure: the specific events and their types; and the ordering restriction over these events. This is illustrated schematically in (23).

$$(23) \quad \begin{bmatrix} \alpha \\ \text{EVENTSTR} = \begin{bmatrix} \text{E}_1 = \dots \\ \text{E}_2 = \dots \\ \text{RESTR} = \dots \end{bmatrix} \\ \dots \end{bmatrix}$$

For example, the verb *build* is typically analyzed as involving a development process and a resulting state (cf. Dowty, 1979, Moens and Steedman, 1988, Pustejovsky, 1991b), ordered by the relation "exhaustive ordered part of," $<_\alpha$.

$$(24) \quad \begin{bmatrix} \textbf{build} \\ \text{EVENTSTR} = \begin{bmatrix} \text{E}_1 = \textbf{process} \\ \text{E}_2 = \textbf{state} \\ \text{RESTR} = <_\alpha \end{bmatrix} \\ \dots \end{bmatrix}$$

Unlike *build*, however, which constrains the types of its two subevents to PROCESS and STATE, the verb *accompany* permits either telic events, TRANSITIONS, or PROCESSES. The typing constraint, however, is similar to that for a coordinate structure in that they must be of like type:

$$(25) \quad \begin{bmatrix} \textbf{accompany} \\ \text{EVENTSTR} = \begin{bmatrix} \text{E}_1 = \tau_i \\ \text{E}_2 = \tau_i \\ \text{RESTR} = \circ_\alpha \end{bmatrix} \\ \dots \end{bmatrix}$$

Of course, there are many more possible relations between subevents than are actually realized in lexicalized forms in natural languages;[8] one of the principal goals of a semantic theory must be to constrain the model to reflect these restrictions.

The structural information discussed thus far for event structure, although necessary, is not sufficient to capture lexical distinctions that languages systematically make with respect to the relative prominence or importance of the subevents of a larger event. Talmy (1975,1976) and others have long noted that the event information conveyed by a verb can be much richer than the "sequence of events" structure encoded in the representations above. These grammatical observations, however, can be accounted for in terms of something I will call *event headedness* (cf. Pustejovsky, 1988). Event headedness provides a way of indicating a type of foregrounding and backgrounding of event arguments. An event structure provides a configuration where events are not only ordered by temporal precedence, but also by relative prominence. One instance of prominence for an event, e, is provided by the HEAD marker, annotated as e^*. The conventional role of a head in a syntactic representation is to indicate prominence and distinction. Rules of agreement, government, etc. militate in favor of marking structures in terms of heads of phrases. Within the interpretive domain of events, when viewed in a structural or configurational manner, the possibility of referring to heads becomes available. Informally, the head is defined as the most prominent subevent in the event structure of a predicate, which contributes to the "focus" of the interpretation. We can view $*$ as a relation between events, $*(e_i, e_j)$ ("e_i is a head of e_j"), where $e_i \preceq e_j$:

(26) $*(e_i, e_j) =_{def} [e_j \ldots e_i^* \ldots]$

Headedness is a property of all event sorts, but acts to distinguish the set of transitions, specifying what part of the matrix event is being focused by the lexical item in question. Adding the property of headedness to the event structure gives the following representation:

$$(27) \quad \begin{bmatrix} \alpha \\ \text{EVENTSTR} = \begin{bmatrix} E_1 = \ldots \\ E_2 = \ldots \\ \text{RESTR} = \ldots \\ \text{HEAD} = E_i \end{bmatrix} \\ \ldots \end{bmatrix}$$

Assuming that events have at most a binary event structure, and that there are three temporal ordering relations realized in language ($<_\alpha$, $\circ_\alpha$, and $< \circ_\alpha$) there are six possible head configurations with two events, given a single head; there are twelve possibilities, if unheaded and double-headed constructions are included. These are listed below along with an example of each type, where HEAD is indicated by an asterisk, and the event tree structure is given in a linear representation:

(28) a. $[_{e^\sigma}\ e_{1^*}\ <_\alpha\ e_2]$ — *build*
      b. $[_{e^\sigma}\ e_1\ <_\alpha\ e_{2^*}]$ — *arrive*
      c. $[_{e^\sigma}\ e_{1^*}\ <_\alpha\ e_{2^*}]$ — *give*
      d. $[_{e^\sigma}\ e_1\ <_\alpha\ e_2]$ — UNDERSPECIFIED
      e. $[_{e^\sigma}\ e_{1^*}\ \circ_\alpha\ e_2]$ — *buy*
      f. $[_{e^\sigma}\ e_1\ \circ_\alpha\ e_{2^*}]$ — *sell*
      g. $[_{e^\sigma}\ e_{1^*}\ \circ_\alpha\ e_{2^*}]$ — *marry*
      h. $[_{e^\sigma}\ e_1\ \circ_\alpha\ e_2]$ — UNDERSPECIFIED
      i. $[_{e^\sigma}\ e_{1^*}\ < \circ_\alpha\ e_2]$ — *walk*
      j. $[_{e^\sigma}\ e_1\ < \circ_\alpha\ e_{2^*}]$ — *walk home*
      k. $[_{e^\sigma}\ e_{1^*}\ < \circ_\alpha\ e_{2^*}]$ — *??*
      l. $[_{e^\sigma}\ e_1\ < \circ_\alpha\ e_2]$ — UNDERSPECIFIED

Intuitively, structure (28a) represents accomplishment verbs, where the initial event is headed, focusing the action bringing about a state; (28b) represents achievement verbs, for which the persistence of the final state is the focus of interpretation; (28c) illustrates events involving a relational predicate on each subevent, and characterizes unilateral transitions with three arguments, i.e., a subclass of ditransitive transfer verbs such as *give* and *take*. Predicate pairs such as *buy* and *sell* are characterized by (28e) and (28f) respectively, where there are two simultaneous events involved in the transaction, but only one is focused by the lexical item.

Finally, ordered overlap gives rise to the structure in (28i), where one event begins, and subsequently gives rise to another process which continues only while the first event continues to hold.

Notice that the structures in (28d), (28h), and (28l) are unheaded and hence ill-formed without further specification at surface structure (cf. chapter 9). The role of semantic underspecification will figure prominently in the analysis of verbal polysemy. In terms of event structure, polysemy occurs when a lexical expression is unspecified with respect to headedness, i.e., headless. Headless event structures admit of two possible interpretations. More generally, a predicate should be as many ways ambiguous as there are potential heads. This representation provides us with a mechanism for relating the logical senses of polymorphic verbs such as: *causative/unaccusative* predicates such as *break* and *sink*, associated with (28d); *argument inversion* predicates such as *rent*, associated with (28h); and *raising/control* predicates such as *begin* and *stop*, associated with (28l).[9]

There are several motivations for positing a head as part of an event structure, a matter that is discussed in Pustejovsky (1988) as well as in Pustejovsky and Busa (1995). When adjoined to predicates denoting transitions, prepositional and adverbial phrases not only can modify the entire event, but can also take scope over the individual subevents. In particular, heads seem to license certain types of modification. Observe that the durative adverbials in (29) modify the designated head of the event rather than the entire event structure.

(29)   a. John ran home <u>for an hour</u>.
       b. My terminal died <u>for two days</u>.
       c. Mary left town <u>for two weeks</u>.

The event tree structure is illustrated in (30) below, where, until the formal structure of qualia is presented in the next section, I refer informally to the expressions associated with each event in a tree structure.

(30)

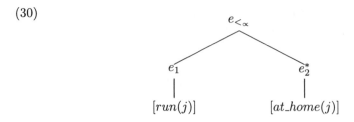

It is generally assumed that only processes and states license durative adverbials, yet modification by an adverbial in (29) is grammatical, even though the sentences denote telic events. Obviously, the available interpretation has the adverbial modifying the duration of the final state; in (29a) John spent an hour at home, in (29b) the terminal was dead for two days, and in (29c) Mary was out of town for a period of two weeks.

A similar phenomenon occurs with left-headed events (e.g., TRANSI-
TIONS), when modified by certain manner adverbs such as *carelessly* and
quietly; namely, modification is over the initial (headed) subevent.

(31) a. John built the house carelessly.
      b. Mary quietly drew a picture.

In (31a) *carelessly* modifies the act of building which brought the house
into existence; similar remarks hold for the sentence in (31b).[10] In the
event tree structure below, I assume a predicative approach to the relation between the object being drawn in the process e_1 and the resulting
picture in e_2, similar to Burge's (1972) treatment of mass terms. The
constitutive relation, CONST, defined below as an integral part of qualia
structure, gives the relationship between these two variables.

(32)

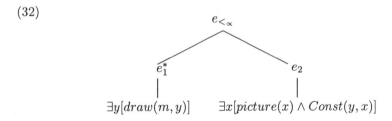

Evidence from event modification is only one of several arguments in favor of making reference to a focusing mechanism within an event structure (but cf. Pustejovsky (1988) for more discussion).

This complete our initial discussion of how lexical items make reference to events. In later chapters we will see how this view of event
structure is expressive enough to capture the polymorphic behavior of
verbal semantics while also being sufficiently constrained to not overgenerate semantic expressions.

5.4   Qualia Structure

In this section, I outline the structured representation which gives the
relational force of a lexical item, called the *qualia structure*. In some
sense, a generative lexicon analyzes all lexical items as relational to
a certain degree, but the manner in which this property is expressed
functionally will of course differ from category to category, as well as
between semantic classes. A more detailed discussion on the structure
of qualia is presented in chapter 6. Briefly, Qualia Structure specifies
four essential aspects of a word's meaning (or *qualia*):

- CONSTITUTIVE: the relation between an object and its constituent
  parts;
- FORMAL: that which distinguishes it within a larger domain;
- TELIC: its purpose and function;
- AGENTIVE: factors involved in its origin or "bringing it about".

This view of word meaning, inspired in part by Moravcsik's (1973) interpretation of Aristotle's modes of explanations (*aitiae*), emphasizes
aspects of a word's meaning that have been largely ignored by formal
treatments of lexical semantics. By looking at modes of *explanation* for
a word, we permit a much richer description of meaning than either a
simple decompositional view or a purely relational approach to word
meaning would allow. These qualia are in fact structures very much
like phrase structural descriptions for syntactic analysis, which admit
of something similar to transformational operations in order to capture
polymorphic behavior as well as sense creation phenomena. The latter
are the generative mechanisms covered in chapter 6.

There are two general points that should be made concerning qualia
roles:

(1) Every category expresses a qualia structure;

(2) Not all lexical items carry a value for each qualia role.

The first point is important for how a generative lexicon provides a
uniform semantic representation compositionally from all elements of
a phrase. This view of qualia structure is a natural extension of the
original applications where qualia for verbal representations were not

discussed. The second point allows us to view qualia as applicable or specifiable relative to particular semantic classes.

To begin our discussion, let us see how qualia structure encodes the meanings of nominals. We can think of qualia, in some sense, as that set of properties or events associated with a lexical item which best explain what that word means. For example, in order to understand what nouns such as *cookie* and *beer* mean, we recognize that they are a food-stuff and a beverage, respectively. While *cookie* is a term that describes a particular kind of object in the world, the noun *foodstuff* denotes by making functional reference to what we *do with* something, i.e., how we use it. In this case, the term is defined in part by the fact that food is something one eats, for a specific purpose, and so on. Similar remarks hold for the information related with the noun *beer*. The TELIC quale for the noun *food* encodes this functional aspect of meaning, represented informally as [TELIC= *eating*]. Likewise, the distinction between semantically related nouns such as *novel* and *dictionary* stems from what we do with these objects that is different. That is, although both objects are books in a general sense, how we use them differs: while one *reads* a novel, dictionaries are for *consulting*. Hence, the respective qualia values encoding this functional information for *novel* and *dictionary* are [TELIC= *reading*] and [TELIC= *consulting*]. This distinction, of course, is not the only way these concepts differ; the structure of the text in a novel is characteristically a narrative or story, while a dictionary is by definition a listing of words. This distinction is captured by the CONST (constitutive) role, expressing the internal structural differences. Finally, even with their overall similarity as expressed in identical FORMAL roles, novels and dictionary also differ in how they come into being (cf. Aristotle, *Metaphysics*), expressed in the AGENTIVE role. That is, while a novel is generally *written*, a dictionary is *compiled*.[11] As we shall see, however, the qualia are not simply a listing of interesting facts about an object or lexical item, but provide the jumping off point for operations of semantic reconstruction and type change, which in turn contribute to our overall goal of characterizing a natural language as polymorphic.

As in our previous discussion, I will employ a generic feature structure as the initial representation for the qualia structure. For a lexical item α, let us first characterize the roles as given in (33).

$$
(33) \quad
\begin{bmatrix}
\alpha \\
\cdots \\
\text{QUALIA} = \begin{bmatrix}
\text{CONST} = \ldots \\
\text{FORMAL} = \ldots \\
\text{TELIC} = \ldots \\
\text{AGENT} = \ldots
\end{bmatrix}
\end{bmatrix}
$$

The listing above tells us nothing about how a particular lexical item denotes, however. For example, although a novel's purpose is the activity of reading and it comes about by someone writing it, we do not want to claim that the common noun *novel* actually denotes such activities. Therefore, we cannot simply list the qualia values for an item, such as in (34), even though they are intuitively correct, without somehow binding them appropriately.

$$
(34) \quad
\begin{bmatrix}
\textbf{novel} \\
\cdots \\
\text{QUALIA} = \begin{bmatrix}
\text{CONST} = \textbf{narrative} \\
\text{FORMAL} = \textbf{book} \\
\text{TELIC} = \textbf{reading} \\
\text{AGENT} = \textbf{writing}
\end{bmatrix}
\end{bmatrix}
$$

Not only does this prove problematic from the view of predication, but it also ignores the data from previous chapters motivating a more polymorphic treatment of semantics. That is, the noun *novel* should predicate in some fairly conventional way (cf. chapter 7), but in particular contexts, it should permit of interpretations that are licensed both by local syntactic and semantic context as well as reconstruction from the semantics of the word, as with sentences such as *Mary enjoyed the novel.*

The solution to these concerns is to treat the qualia values as expressions with well-defined types and relational structures (cf. Pustejovsky, 1991, Copestake and Briscoe, 1992). For example, the arguments to the relation *read* are explicitly given in (35), indicating the proper binding of the predicating term:

$$
(35) \quad
\begin{bmatrix}
\textbf{novel} \\
\cdots \\
\text{QUALIA} = \begin{bmatrix}
\text{FORMAL} = \textbf{book(x)} \\
\text{TELIC} = \textbf{read(y,x)} \\
\cdots
\end{bmatrix}
\end{bmatrix}
$$

This is equivalent to the λ-expression below, as a partial denotation of the noun semantics for *novel*:

(36) $\lambda x[novel(x) \wedge \ldots \text{TELIC} = \lambda y[read(y,x)] \ldots]$

Given the representation in (35), it is now at least possible to see *where* contextual information comes from, in order to derive the "sense in context" effect, illustrated below with the verbs *begin* and *finish*. Determining *how* these readings are derived is the subject of chapter 7.

(37) a. Mary <u>began</u> a novel.
      b. John <u>finished</u> the cigarette.
      c. John <u>began</u> his second beer.

Qualia structure enables nouns, and consequently the NPs containing them, to encode information about particular properties and activities associated with the them. This in turn will provide the verb which governs the complement NP with the information required for "contextualizing the sense" of *begin* or *finish*. I return to this issue in later discussion in chapter 9.

Let me turn briefly now to the semantics of verbs and the role played by a qualia-based representation in the semantics. I defer a detailed discussion of verbal qualia until chapter 9. Continuing the discussion begun with the extended event structure in 5.3, I will distinguish broadly how modes of explanation map into a verb's event structure. Intuitively, a stative predicate corresponds to the FORMAL role in the qualia structure, e.g., that state of affairs which exists, without reference to how it came about. For example, the predicate *tall* might be represented as in (38), ignoring the details of argument structure for now:

$$
(38) \quad
\begin{bmatrix}
\textbf{tall} \\
\text{EVENTSTR} = \begin{bmatrix} \text{E}_1 = \textbf{e}_1\textbf{:state} \end{bmatrix} \\
\text{QUALIA} = \begin{bmatrix} \text{FORMAL} = \textbf{tall(e}_1\textbf{,x)} \\ \ldots \end{bmatrix}
\end{bmatrix}
$$

At first glance it might appear a gratuitous or superfluous move to simply shift the predicate *tall* into a particular named slot. What semantic motivation or generalization is captured by such a strategy? I argue in 10.1 that the distinction between stage-level and individual level predicates is actually not one of event-type, but rather is a qualia-based distinction, where stage-level predication involves reference to the bringing into being of the resulting state, i.e., the AGENTIVE quale.

Consider next the qualia structure associated with causative predicates (i.e., TRANSITIONS). These verbs are typically analyzed as involving an initial act or process followed by a resulting state. These two phases map directly into the AGENTIVE and FORMAL qualia roles, respectively. The transitive form of the verb *break* is illustrated in (39).

$$(39) \quad \begin{bmatrix} \textbf{break} & & \\ \text{EVENTSTR} & = & \begin{bmatrix} E_1 = e_1\text{:}\textbf{process} \\ E_2 = e_2\text{:}\textbf{state} \\ \text{RESTR} = <_\propto \end{bmatrix} \\ \text{QUALIA} & = & \begin{bmatrix} \text{FORMAL} = \textbf{broken}(e_2,y) \\ \text{AGENTIVE} = \textbf{break\_act}(e_1,x,y) \\ \cdots \end{bmatrix} \end{bmatrix}$$

Intuitively, this relates specific events and relational expressions to particular qualia roles. This corresponds roughly to the annotated event tree structures presented above, but where the expressions are now typed by named qualia.

Finally, predicates denoting a process are distinguished according to which mode of explanation the predicate is associated with. I will consider here only the distinction between AGENTIVE and FORMAL processes. As pointed out in Talmy (1975,1985), many languages distinguish active and passive classes of processes, where the former includes verbs of motion such as *run* and *move*, while the latter includes verbs such as *sleep* and *snore*. It should be pointed out that this distinction is not necessarily isomorphic to an unaccusative/unergative distinction in a language. The qualia structure for the active process class is illustrated below, with the verb *run*. For example, the verb *run* carries the qualia structure in (40) while the passive process verb *sleep* has the structure in (41).

$$(40) \quad \begin{bmatrix} \textbf{run} & & \\ \text{EVENTSTR} & = & \begin{bmatrix} E_1 = e_1\text{:}\textbf{process} \end{bmatrix} \\ \text{QUALIA} & = & \begin{bmatrix} \text{AGENTIVE} = \textbf{run\_act}(e_1,x) \\ \cdots \end{bmatrix} \end{bmatrix}$$

$$(41) \quad \begin{bmatrix} \textbf{sleep} & & \\ \text{EVENTSTR} & = & \begin{bmatrix} E_1 = e_1\text{:}\textbf{process} \end{bmatrix} \\ \text{QUALIA} & = & \begin{bmatrix} \text{FORMAL} = \textbf{sleep}(e_1,x) \\ \cdots \end{bmatrix} \end{bmatrix}$$

The relevance of this distinction in qualia binding is that processes are quantifiable in different ways, one of which is to specify explicitly the resulting state in the FORMAL role, by means of *co-composition*. This is possible only with active processes, and is illustrated with constructions such as *run to the store* and *run home* (cf. Hinrichs, 1985, Verkuyl and Zwarts, 1988, and Jackendoff, 1990). Quantification of passive processes generally does not allow the cognate construction, and is limited to modification by durative adverbials, as in *sleep for an hour, cough all night*. In later discussion, I will show how processes associated with more complex event structures, such as that proposed for the verb *walk* above, bind into both AGENTIVE and FORMAL qualia roles.

In this section, I have outlined informally how qualia structure contributes towards describing various aspects of noun and verb meaning. I have limited my discussion to these two categories in order to illustrate the basic descriptive power of this level of representation. In chapter 10 below and in Pustejovsky (1995b) I outline the appropriate extensions to qualia structure to encompass all categories.

5.5   The Interaction of Semantic Levels

In this section, I integrate the three levels of argument, event, and qualia structure, in order to construct a uniform language for lexical semantic representations. I will assume, for discussion, a system based on typed feature structures such as Carpenter's (1992) system, and following its application to lexical semantics described in Copestake *et al.* (1993). The type system has two parts; the type hierarchy itself, and the constraint system operating over the types. I will not discuss the details of the constraints within the typing language except as they relate to linguistic data and questions of generativity. I assume, furthermore, along with Sanfilippo (1993), that semantic class information may be inherited by subtyping specifications, providing constraints on the types of arguments.[12]

To illustrate how the three levels described in previous sections come together to provide an integrated representation, consider again the semantics of the verb *build*. We have already provided structures for each level of representation independently, and now we need to unify them in a coherent fashion. Recall that there are three arguments associated with the verb: two TRUE ARGUMENTS and one DEFAULT ARGUMENT. Furthermore, we analyzed the verb as a lexical accomplishment, containing two subevents, a process and a resulting state. These are bound to the qualia in the representation below.

$$(42) \quad \begin{bmatrix} \textbf{build} \\ \text{EVENTSTR} = \begin{bmatrix} \text{E}_1 = e_1\textbf{:process} \\ \text{E}_2 = e_2\textbf{:state} \\ \text{RESTR} = <_\propto \\ \text{HEAD} = e_1 \end{bmatrix} \\ \text{ARGSTR} = \begin{bmatrix} \text{ARG1} = \boxed{1}\begin{bmatrix} \textbf{animate\_ind} \\ \text{FORMAL} = \textbf{physobj} \end{bmatrix} \\ \text{ARG2} = \boxed{2}\begin{bmatrix} \textbf{artifact} \\ \text{CONST} = \boxed{3} \\ \text{FORMAL} = \textbf{physobj} \end{bmatrix} \\ \text{D-ARG1} = \boxed{3}\begin{bmatrix} \textbf{material} \\ \text{FORMAL} = \textbf{mass} \end{bmatrix} \end{bmatrix} \\ \text{QUALIA} = \begin{bmatrix} \textbf{create-lcp} \\ \text{FORMAL} = \textbf{exist}(e_2,\boxed{2}) \\ \text{AGENTIVE} = \textbf{build\_act}(e_1,\boxed{1},\boxed{3}) \end{bmatrix} \end{bmatrix}$$

The process is identified as that AGENTIVE act involving both the deep syntactic subject, ARG1, and the default argument, D-ARG1, which is related to the logical object by the CONSTITUTIVE relation of ARG-2. The FORMAL role expresses the resulting state of there being such an object ARG-2. Since this individual is defined as being made of the material of the default argument D-ARG1, and yet is logically distinct from it, as suggested in 5.3 above, there are two possibilities for existential closure on such an event structure, as illustrated in (43) and (44):

(43) a. John is building a house.
      b. $\exists z[build\_act(e_1, j, z) \wedge material(z) \ldots]$

(44) a. John built a house.
      b. $\exists z \exists y[build\_act(e_1, j, z) \wedge material(z) \wedge exist(e_2, y)$
         $\wedge house(y) \wedge e_1 < e_2]$

There are several consequences of this representation which we will not explore in this book. One result is that the binding problem in the imperfective (44) is overcome in a fairly natural way. That is, there is no assertion that a house exists in this atelic form of the event. Rather, this representation asserts no more than that the substance making up some (future) house has been acted upon.

The notion that concepts are associated with other concepts by some sort of explicit listing is, of course, not a very new or controversial notion. Indeed, much work in AI and computational approaches to word meaning has been concerned with providing "hooks" on word meanings, in order to facilitate inference. In some respects, qualia structure shares with these traditions the goal of capturing the meaning of a word as it relates to reasoning viewed in a much broader sense. But the principal motivation for qualia structure is not simply a listing of properties for a word. Rather, it can only be appreciated in the context of the generative mechanisms in the grammar which allow speakers to use the language creatively.

6 Qualia Structure

In this chapter I detail my assumptions about how lexical items encode semantic information in the qualia, and particularly, what the qualia structure conveys. In the previous chapter, I argued for associating functional semantic information with all categories, and how this move helps us towards achieving a more generative description of lexical sense derivation. The point of this chapter is to explore more fully the syntax of qualia structure and what its descriptive and explanatory role can be in a theory of word meaning and compositionality.[1]

6.1 Modes of Explanation

Aristotle's notion of modes of explanation (or *generative factors*), as pointed out by Moravcsik (1975), can be viewed as a system of constructive understanding and inference. These four factors drive our basic understanding of an object or a relation in the world. They furthermore contribute to (or, in fact, determine) our ability to name an object with a certain predication.[2]

Following our earlier discussion, assume that a lexical semantic structure is defined by the four interpretive levels, $<\mathcal{A}, \mathcal{E}, \mathcal{Q}, \mathcal{I}>$, and that furthermore there are four basic roles that constitute the qualia structure $\mathcal{Q}$ for a lexical item. Now let us elaborate on what these roles are and why they are a necessary component of the semantics. In 6.2 below, the qualia are given an informal interpretation, with possible values that each role may assume.[3]

1. CONSTITUTIVE: the relation between an object and its constituents, or proper parts.
   i. Material
   ii. Weight
   iii. Parts and component elements

2. FORMAL: That which distinguishes the object within a larger domain.
   i. Orientation
   ii. Magnitude
   iii. Shape
   iv. Dimensionality

v. Color

vi. Position

3. TELIC: Purpose and function of the object.

i. Purpose that an agent has in performing an act.

ii. Built-in function or aim which specifies certain activities.

4. AGENTIVE: Factors involved in the origin or "bringing about" of an object.

i. Creator

ii. Artifact

iii. Natural Kind

iv. Causal Chain

There are of course many ways of approaching the definition of a word, and qualia might seem at first to be a simple listing of case roles or named features associated with lexical items. This is not the case, however. What qualia structure tells us about a concept is the set of semantic constraints by which we understand a word when embedded within the language. The *mode* of explanation that characterizes a word as denoting a particular concept is potentially distinct from the manner in which that word is used in the language. That is, definition and word meaning need not have anything to do with grammaticalization or grammatical behavior. This is a fairly uninteresting claim about the relation between language and thought, and certainly unintuitive from a philosophical perspective. Yet, this is exactly what many models of semantics assume: namely, words have simple denotations, and the methods of composition are borrowed from general logical inference mechanisms.

The view within a generative lexicon is different. The qualia provide the structural template over which semantic transformations may apply to alter the denotation of a lexical item or phrase. These transformations are the generative devices such as type coercion, selective binding, and co-composition, which formally map the expression to a new meaning. These operations apply only by virtue of lexical governance relations; that is, their application is conditioned by the syntactic and semantic environment within which the phrase appears. For example, when we combine the qualia structure of an NP with that of a governing verb, we begin to see a richer notion of compositionality emerging, one which captures the creative use of words and the "sense in context" phenomena discussed in chapters 3 and 4.

A semantic representation is only useful if it facilitates a logical inference or interpretation. Furthermore, such information can be attributed to a specific lexical item only if it can be argued that the interpretive process is driven by language-specific representations or constraints rather than logical inference alone. Qualia are interesting in this respect, since they not only structure our knowledge of words, but also "suggest" interpretations of words in context. Consider, for example, how the NPs, both in subject and complement position contribute towards further specifying the interpretation of the verb *use* in the sentences in (1) and the NPs in (2) below.

(1) a. John used <u>the new knife</u> on the turkey.
    b. Mary has used <u>soft contact lenses</u> since college.
    c. This car uses <u>unleaded gasoline</u>.
    d. My wife uses <u>the subway</u> every day.

(2) a. the toners used in <u>copying machines</u>
    b. the yeast used <u>in beer</u>

In sentence (1a), our knowledge of knives as tools which can cut permits an economy of expression, whereby mention of the particular activity of cutting may be ellipsed. Similarly, in (1b), contact lenses are visual aids, and the use of them refers to the act of *wearing* them. The utility of a verb such as *use* is that it is semantically *light* (cf. Grimshaw and Rosen, 1990), what I will refer to as simply *underspecified*, with respect to the particular activity being performed. Sentence (1d), for example, is a near paraphrase of "My wife travels on the subway every day," an interpretation that is made possible by our knowledge of what the function of a subway is. Finally, the NPs in (2) show an interesting sense distinction, where the objects in (2a) are understood as standing in a functional part-of relation, while in (2b), the substance is interpreted as being part of the material used for the process of making beer.[4] The factors allowing us to determine which sense is appropriate for any of these cases are twofold: (1) the qualia structures for each phrase in the construction; and (2) a richer mode of composition, which is able to take advantage of this qualia information.

As further evidence of the way in which qualia structure elucidates an interpretation in context, consider the contextualized meanings for the verb *enjoy*, discussed in chapters 2 and 4 above, where the "ellipsed" predicate is supplied by information from the complement.

(3) a. Mary <u>enjoyed</u> the movie last night. (*watching*)
    b. John quite <u>enjoys</u> his morning coffee. (*drinking*)
    c. Bill <u>enjoyed</u> Steven King's last book. (*reading*)

Although there are certainly any number of ways of enjoying something, our understanding of these sentences is facilitated by default interpretations of properties and activities associated with objects. The qualia of an object can be seen as the initial points from which to construct interpretations that would otherwise be ill-formed. Hence, the TELIC roles for *movie, coffee,* and *book* somehow project the activities of *watching the movie, drinking his morning coffee,* and *reading Steven King's last book,* respectively, to the interpretation of the VP.

Notice that the contextualization of a sense for a verb need not come from the semantics of the complement, but can be influenced in obvious ways by the subject as well. For example, in (4a) there are two factors contributing to the interpretation of the ellipsed predicate; the qualia structures associated with the subject NP and the double object NPs. The complements are identified as names of airports, thereby allowing a default co-compositional interpretation of *landing, taking off,* and so on.

(4) a. Most commercial pilots <u>prefer</u> Kennedy to Logan.
    b. Most commercial pilots <u>prefer</u> New York to Boston.

Although this interpretation is also available for sentence (4a), it is more easily defeasible, since under this reading the complements must *inherit* the sortal typing of `airport` in the composition of the sentence, a process discussed in chapter 10.[5] Similar remarks hold for the semantic contribution made by the agentive nominals in (5) below, where the most likely interpretation is one that is not "suggested" by the VP semantics.

(5) a. Midwestern fish farmers are <u>preferring</u> catfish this year.
    b. Book sellers usually <u>prefer</u> cookbooks to textbooks around Christmas.

In other words, it is not the case that fish farmers are preferring to eat catfish and the book sellers are preferring to read the books, but rather, the farmers are raising the fish and the book sellers are selling the books. The TELIC roles from the agentive nominals in these examples seem to override any VP-internal interpretation available (cf. 10.2 for discussion).

Thus far, I have restricted my discussion to verbal and nominal semantics, yet the utility of qualia-based representations extends to the other categories as well. To demonstrate how, consider the phenomenon of adjectival submodification mentioned in chapters 2 and 4 above, and illustrated in (6) and (7).

(6) a. a <u>bright</u> bulb
     b. an <u>opaque</u> bulb

(7) a. a <u>fast</u> typist
     b. a <u>male</u> typist

The adjectives *bright* and *fast* in these examples are actually event predicates, modifying some aspect of the head noun. In fact, they each seem to make reference to a qualia-derived event associated with the noun. For a bulb, this is obviously reference to what function the bulb has, namely, its TELIC role, which would be *illumination*. For an agentive nominal such as *typist*, the TELIC makes direct reference to the process-denoting verb from which the nominal is derived. The adjectives *opaque* and *male*, on the other hand, make reference to the FORMAL role of the head. It appears as though adjectives are able to subselect on the basis of typing information contained within the qualia structure of the phrases they modify, although it is not yet obvious how this is accomplished. It is possible that the adjectives do not select for specific qualia in the head noun, but rather select a particular type, which is or is not available within the value of a quale role.

In the next section, I present a more detailed interpretation of the qualia structure as applied to nominal semantics. Issues relating to the grammatical consequences of this model will not be discussed until chapter 7.

6.2   The Qualia Structure of Nominals

In this section I explore in more detail the typing system necessary to characterize the semantics of NPs, and, in particular, the logically polysemous behavior of nominals such as *window* and *door*. The approach taken here is to introduce the analysis of a category in terms of the four levels of representation. In terms of nominals, this means viewing the semantic classification from the perspective of event structure, argument structure, and qualia structure. In this section I show how fine-grained distinctions are possible in the semantic behavior of nominal types based on the interaction of argument and qualia structures.

As mentioned earlier, I assume a system based on typed feature structures, as applied to lexical structures in Copestake *et al.* (1993). The type system includes the type hierarchy and the constraint system operating over the types. The hierarchy in 6.1, for example, illustrates how features are organized in a lattice structure, where nomrqs refers to the least upper bound type for the types entity, proposition, and event (cf. Copestake and Briscoe, 1992, Copestake, 1993, and Pustejovsky and Boguraev, 1993).

The details of the typing constraints will not be discussed here (but cf. Briscoe *et al.*, 1993); rather I will focus on the linguistic aspects of how a generative lexicon makes use of typed feature structures.

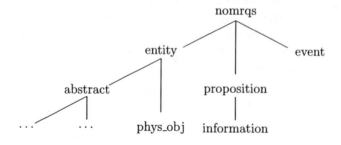

Figure 6.1
Fragment of a Type Hierarchy; cf. Copestake and Briscoe (1992), Pustejovsky and Boguraev (1993).

In chapters 3 and 4, I discussed the problem of logical polysemy and how nominals such as *window* and *door* in sentences (8) and (9) carry two distinct interpretations, each logically related to the other:

(8) a. John crawled through <u>the window</u>.
     b. Mary broke <u>the window</u>.

(9) a. Mary painted <u>the door</u>.
     b. Mary walked through <u>the door</u>.

Each noun has two word senses: a physical object denotation and an aperture denotation. Pustejovsky and Anick (1988) characterize the meaning of such "Double Figure-Ground" nominals as inherently relational, where both arguments are logically part of the meaning of the noun. In addition to the true arguments corresponding to the two senses, there is a default argument making reference to the plane within which the door or window is positioned.[6] There are many such classes of nominals, referring both to 2-dimensional objects such as *window* and *door*, as well as to 3-dimensional objects, such as *room*, *fireplace*, and *pipe*. They are interesting semantically, because they are logically ambiguous as well, referring to either the object or to the aperture, or to both. The ability of a lexical item to cluster multiple senses is what Pustejovsky and Anick (1988) referred to as a *Lexical Conceptual Paradigm (lcp)*. The intuition behind the notion of an lcp is that there is something inherent in the semantics of a noun such that it is able to project any of three separate senses of the noun in distinct syntactic and semantic environments. That is, the listing of the nouns in these separate environments is similar to a paradigmatic behavior. The notion of lcp is further extended in Pustejovsky and Boguraev (1993) in order to project syntactic behavior from the semantics of the noun characterized as an lcp.[7]

The lcp provides a means of characterizing a lexical item as a meta-entry. This turns out to be very useful for capturing the systematic ambiguities which are so pervasive in language. As discussed above, nouns such as *newspaper* appear in many semantically distinct contexts, able to function sometimes as an organization, a physical object, or the information contained in the articles within the newspaper.

(10) a. <u>The newspapers</u> attacked the President for raising taxes.

    b. Mary spilled coffee on <u>the newspaper</u>.
    c. John got angry at <u>the newspaper</u>.

What the notion of an lcp allows us to do is to treat these not as distinct senses, but as logical expressions of different aspects to the meta-entry for *newspaper*. Among the alternations that we can analyze in this way are those presented in chapter 4, namely nominal alternations exhibiting logical polysemy such as those repeated below.

(11) a. Count/Mass alternations; *lamb*.
      b. Container/Containee alternations; *bottle*.
      c. Figure/Ground Reversals; *door, window*.
      a. Product/Producer diathesis; *newspaper, Honda*.
      d. Plant/Food alternations; *fig, apple*.
      e. Process/Result diathesis; *examination, merger*.
      f. Place/People diathesis; *city, New York*.

Let us now examine an analysis of lcps within a type system such as that outlined here, to see how the appropriate structuring of types allows us to explain the polysemous behavior of the nominals in these classes. Imagine that we define G to be the *typing judgments* with respect to a grammar (cf. Gunter, 1992). A typing judgment consists of an assignment, g, an expression, α, and a type, τ. The judgment $g \vdash \alpha : \tau$ states that under assignment g, the expression α has type τ.[8] The rule of *application* can be stated using such typing judgments as follows, where the operator $\oplus$ indicates application:

(12)
$$\frac{\alpha : \sigma_1 \quad \oplus \quad \beta : \sigma_1 \rightarrow \sigma_2}{\beta(\alpha) : \sigma_2}$$

In addition to the application rule above, we will need conventional rules of *projection* and *abstraction*. For now, however, let us consider how to construct new types out of existing ones. Obviously, something like a recursive type constructor as shown in (13) is needed, here given as a rule:

(13)
$$\frac{\sigma_1 \quad \sigma_2}{\sigma_1 \rightarrow \sigma_2}$$

This would correspond to the rule of recursive types in Categorial Grammar, for example (cf. Lambek, 1958, Moortgat, 1988, van Benthem,

1991). In order to capture the behavior of the nouns above, however, a less conventional type construction is needed. Let us analyze the logical type relation between the polysemous senses of a lexical item such as *door* as a *dotted type*. The type constructor, *lcp*, creates this complex type for a term α which carries senses σ_1 and σ_2, giving the following rule:

(14) $$\frac{\alpha : \sigma_1 \quad \alpha : \sigma_2}{lcp(\alpha) : \sigma_1 \cdot \sigma_2}$$

This says effectively that two types are able to combine to become a complex type, treated here as a Cartesian type. The lcp itself is then represented by the *type cluster* consisting of the two base types and its dotted type, shown below:

(15) lcp $= \{\sigma_1 \cdot \sigma_2, \sigma_1, \sigma_2\}$

This is the paradigm of types associated with a lexical item by virtue of the type constructor *lcp*. Now imagine that σ_1 and σ_2 are the senses for a noun such as *door*, represented as the types phys_obj and aperture respectively. Then the lcp resulting from the type constructor *lcp* over these types would be the type cluster in (16).

(16) phys_obj.aperture_lcp $= \{$phys_obj.aperture, phys_obj, aperture$\}$

This is the lcp assigned to the lexical item *door*. All three types are available for expression by this noun, as we demonstrate in chapter 7.

Lexical conceptual paradigms illustrate very clearly that syntactic information is inheritable between lexical items. To illustrate this point, consider the class of process/result nominals such as *merger*, *joint venture*, *consolidation*, etc. These nominals are ambiguous between a process interpretation (the *act* of merging) versus the resulting entity or state (the merger which *results*). This is a property of the whole paradigm indicating that the alternation can be captured by an lcp.

The statement above suggests that there are actually three senses available to a lexical item associated with an lcp constructed from two base types. This is substantiated by data presented in chapter 8. For the example of *merger*, given above, this sense would essentially allow reference to the entire event of the merging, as well as either process and result reading, just as the tensed sentence equivalent of this NP does (cf. 8.3 for discussion). Consider the three senses for the noun *construction*.

(17) a. The house's <u>construction</u> was finished in two months.
      b. The <u>construction</u> was arduous and tedious.
      c. The <u>construction</u> is standing on the next street.

These three sentences make reference to the entire dotted type, the process, and the result of the process, respectively.

The type hierarchy in 6.2 below illustrates what the association is between types resulting from the constructor *lcp*.

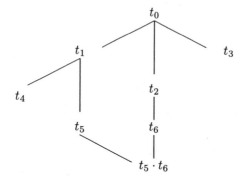

Figure 6.2
Type Hierarchy with Dotted Types

Unlike a feature unification operation, where two types σ_1 and σ_2 within a lattice can be characterized as having a unique greatest lower bound (glb), $\sigma_1 \sqcap \sigma_2$ (as used, for example, in Carpenter, 1992, and Copestake *et al.*, 1993), this is a different interpretation for how types are combined. The concept referred to by a lexical item corresponding to an lcp is not the *glb* of two types, but rather is the cluster of the two individual types along with the dotted type. Furthermore, this is not merely an operation of intersection on two types, but a much more structured and informative operation (cf. 8.3 below).

With this view of types, we can distinguish the senses of *newspaper* and *book* as in (18) below, and with this, explain the difference in logical polysemies available to these nouns (cf. 8.2).

(18)

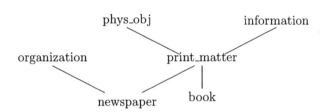

Given the discussion above, I now examine the specific properties of the qualia and how one can differentiate the semantic classes of nominals on the basis of argument type and qualia structure. I will assume that for two types α and β, seen as restrictions on the arguments x and y respectively, the complex or dotted type constructed from them is $\alpha \cdot \beta$. The argument associated with this type is notated $x.y$, and inherits the functional behavior of both types x and y.

6.2.1   The Interpretation of the FORMAL Quale

The most familiar equivalence class associated with nouns is its basic category description. The FORMAL quale distinguishes an object from a larger set. There are two possible structures associated with the FORMAL quale:

(19) a. *Simple Typing:* Value of FORMAL role is identical to sortal typing of the argument;

  b. *Complex (Dotted) Typing:* Value of FORMAL role defines the relation between the arguments of different types.

Concerning the first case, the typing of an argument for a nominal may exhaustively define the information contributed by the FORMAL quale. In fact, for nouns denoting simple types (and not dotted-types), the FORMAL is itself the typing restriction on the argument structure (i.e., the one referential argument). In such a case, the qualia structure has the following schematic form, minimally:[9]

$$(20) \quad \begin{bmatrix} \alpha \\ \text{ARGSTR} = \begin{bmatrix} \text{ARG1} = \mathbf{x}{:}\tau \end{bmatrix} \\ \text{QUALIA} = \begin{bmatrix} \text{FORMAL} = \mathbf{x} \end{bmatrix} \end{bmatrix}$$

By way of illustration, the nouns *man* and *woman* are sorts of human, distinguished by gender, a binary characterizing predicate. The distinction is inherent in the compositional make-up of the separation of these two sorts within the type human, and hence this feature is represented as a CONSTITUTIVE distinction, utilizing the predicate *male*, shown below.

$$(21) \quad \begin{bmatrix} \mathbf{man} \\ \text{ARGSTR} = \begin{bmatrix} \text{ARG1} = \mathbf{x}{:}\mathbf{human} \end{bmatrix} \\ \text{QUALIA} = \begin{bmatrix} \text{CONST} = \mathbf{male(x)} \\ \text{FORMAL} = \mathbf{x} \end{bmatrix} \end{bmatrix}$$

Now let us consider complex objects denoting dotted types. As I discussed in previous chapters, implicitly relational nouns such as *door*, *book*, *newspaper*, *window*, as well as process-result alternating nominals such as *destruction* and *examination* are classic cases of logical polysemy. The polysemy is encoded directly into the type of the object in the following manner. For a noun α denoting a complex (or dotted) type, e.g., $\tau_1 \cdot \tau_2$, the FORMAL quale defines how the arguments are related to each other. The type of the overall nominal is the complex type. The schematic form for the qualia structure for such nominals is given below:

$$(22) \quad \begin{bmatrix} \alpha \\ \text{ARGSTR} = \begin{bmatrix} \text{ARG1} = \mathbf{x}{:}\tau_1 \\ \text{ARG2} = \mathbf{y}{:}\tau_2 \end{bmatrix} \\ \\ \text{QUALIA} = \begin{bmatrix} \tau_1 \cdot \tau_2\_\text{lcp} \\ \text{FORMAL} = \mathbf{P(y,x)} \end{bmatrix} \end{bmatrix}$$

Conforming to the behavior of dotted types, in addition to the FORMAL defining the relation between arguments, there must be reference to the dotted argument $x.y$ in the qualia structure for this representation to be well-formed, e.g., $\texttt{R(e,w,x{\cdot}y)}$. A good example illustrating this point is the noun *book* and the related verb *read*. The activity of reading requires not just that the complement be information or propositional in nature, but that it is "readable"; that is, it must have some physical manifestation in order to be interpreted as symbolic. Furthermore, having only the property of physical manifestation is not sufficient for something to be readable; it must be something one can "read;" that is, it must be information.

An alternative interpretation of the dotted object is also possible.[10] One might build the relation between the types specified in the FORMAL role directly into the dot object itself. For example, the resulting type lattice would have the following structure:

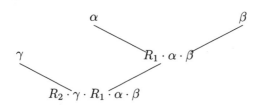

Figure 6.3
Dotted Type Hierarchy with Relations Built into the Dot Object

Judging between these alternatives seems difficult at this point, since the exact semantics of the resulting types is not yet well understood. In either case, the relations possible in the FORMAL quale which define exactly how the types are related must be constrained in a way that does not give rise to unattested complex types in language. We return to this question in 8.3.

6.2.2   The Interpretation of the AGENTIVE Quale

Knowledge of the "coming into being," in Aristotle's terms (*Physics II*), of an object is encoded in the AGENTIVE quale of the lexical item associated with it. The manner in which something is created is a mode of explanation that will distinguish natural kinds from artifacts. How something comes about is an important mode of explanation for distinguishing objects and events in the world.

If the lexical form is a noun, the AGENTIVE is represented as an event predicate, where the object being defined is typically bound to the second argument of the relation. For a simple typed nominal, the schematic qualia structure is as follows:

$$(23) \quad \begin{bmatrix} \alpha \\ \text{ARGSTR} = \begin{bmatrix} \text{ARG}1 = \mathbf{x}{:}\tau \end{bmatrix} \\ \text{QUALIA} = \begin{bmatrix} \text{FORMAL} = \mathbf{x} \\ \text{AGENTIVE} = \mathbf{R(e,y,x)} \end{bmatrix} \end{bmatrix}$$

The representation in (23) above corresponds to the semantics of artifacts. For example, viewed from the constraint of AGENTIVE, *qua* coming
into being, objects such as cookies, cakes, and bread are typically baked.
The process of baking, modulo such objects, is a creative activity, while
relative to objects such as potatoes, carrots, and other natural kinds, it
is simply a change of state predicate. As we discussed in previous chapters, to classify the verb *bake* as having both senses lexically specified is
to miss the semantic generalization the language is expressing; namely,
that certain objects come into being by virtue of an activity which can
otherwise simply change the internal state of an object. The sense is the
same, but manifests itself with overall effects differently, resulting in the
"sense in context" phenomenon.

The explanation of what brings something about is of course not restricted to nouns, and within nouns certainly not to artifacts and simple
typed objects. With the machinery of dotted types, we can provide a
unique value for the AGENTIVE quale of a lexical item. The methodological goal in GL is to associate individual qualia roles as unique values,
avoiding both conjunction and disjunction, except when motivated by
the semantics of particular lexical items. As discussed above, for a dot
object nominal, notice that the AGENTIVE may refer to the dotted argument directly (but cf. 8.3).[11]

$$(24) \quad \begin{bmatrix} \alpha \\ \text{ARGSTR} = \begin{bmatrix} \text{ARG}1 = \mathbf{x}{:}\tau_1 \\ \text{ARG}2 = \mathbf{y}{:}\tau_2 \end{bmatrix} \\ \text{QUALIA} = \begin{bmatrix} \tau_1 \cdot \tau_2\_\mathbf{lcp} \\ \text{FORMAL} = \mathbf{P(y,x)} \\ \text{AGENTIVE} = \mathbf{R(e,w,x.y)} \end{bmatrix} \end{bmatrix}$$

6.2.3   The Interpretation of the CONSTITUTIVE Quale

The CONSTITUTIVE (henceforth CONST) quale refers not only to the parts
or material of an object, but defines, for an object, what that object is
logically part of, if such a relation exists. The relation part_of allows
for both abstractions:

(25) a. $\lambda x \exists y [part\_of(y, x)]$
      b. $\lambda x \exists y [part\_of(x, y)]$

The function (25a) defines the more conventional part-of-relation, while
(25b) defines the relation between, for example, a hand and its body.
The example of the noun *hand* below shows how it encodes what it is
logically a part of:

$$
(26) \quad
\begin{bmatrix}
\textbf{hand} \\
\text{ARGSTR} = \begin{bmatrix} \text{ARG1} = \textbf{x:limb} \end{bmatrix} \\
\text{QUALIA} = \begin{bmatrix} \text{FORMAL} = \textbf{x} \\ \text{CONST} = \textbf{part\_of(x,y:body)} \end{bmatrix}
\end{bmatrix}
$$

That is, the relation in the CONST allows for reference to what something
is constituted of as well as what it constitutes, in part; i.e., a hand is
part of a body, and a body has a hand (cf. Vikner and Hansen's 1994
suggestion of this interpretation for the CONST role).

6.2.4 The Interpretation of the TELIC Quale

The TELIC quale defines what the purpose or function of a concept is,
if there is such a constraint associated with it.[12]   Rather than viewing the semantic functions associated with a lexical item (or concept)
in terms of traditional thematic role descriptions, I have argued that
lexical knowledge encodes the modes of explanation associated with a
word. For this reason, there is no simple one-to-one mapping between
θ-roles and qualia. For example, observe how the TELIC quale captures
aspects of several different θ-roles, but cannot be associated with any
one of them exhaustively.

Modes of Telic:

(i) *Direct Telic*: something which one acts on directly.

$$
\begin{bmatrix}
\alpha \\
\text{ARGSTR} = \begin{bmatrix} \text{ARG1} = \textbf{x:}\tau \end{bmatrix} \\
\text{QUALIA} = \begin{bmatrix} \text{FORMAL} = \textbf{x} \\ \text{TELIC} = \textbf{R(e,y,x)} \end{bmatrix}
\end{bmatrix}
$$

(ii) *Purpose Telic*: something which is used for facilitating a particular
      activity;

$$
\begin{bmatrix}
\alpha \\
\text{ARGSTR} = \begin{bmatrix} \text{ARG1} = \text{x:}\tau \end{bmatrix} \\
\text{QUALIA} = \begin{bmatrix} \text{FORMAL} = \text{x} \\ \text{TELIC} = \mathbf{R(e,x,y)} \end{bmatrix}
\end{bmatrix}
$$

Conforming to the first type above is the TELIC quale for a noun such as *beer*, where reference to the activity of drinking incorporates a variable for the noun as object of the predicate *drink*. The object's purpose is the activity given in the TELIC role.

$$
(27) \quad
\begin{bmatrix}
\textbf{beer} \\
\text{ARGSTR} = \begin{bmatrix} \text{ARG1} = \text{x:liquid} \end{bmatrix} \\
\text{QUALIA} = \begin{bmatrix} \text{FORMAL} = \text{x} \\ \text{TELIC} = \mathbf{drink(e,y,x)} \end{bmatrix}
\end{bmatrix}
$$

An example of the second type of TELIC use, that of purpose telic, is found with objects that are used in the performance of an activity, such as with tools, such as the noun *knife*.

$$
(28) \quad
\begin{bmatrix}
\textbf{knife} \\
\text{ARGSTR} = \begin{bmatrix} \text{ARG1} = \text{x:tool} \end{bmatrix} \\
\text{QUALIA} = \begin{bmatrix} \text{FORMAL} = \text{x} \\ \text{TELIC} = \mathbf{cut(e,x,y)} \end{bmatrix}
\end{bmatrix}
$$

It is, of course, just these sorts of relations between types of qualia that allow for some of the alternations seen in agents and instrumentals sharing causative structure.

(29) a. The hammer broke the glass.
      b. Mary broke the glass with the hammer.

(30) a. The knife cut the bread.
      b. John cut the bread with the knife.

Returning to the example of *book* from above, we can express the TELIC of a dotted type by direct reference to the dotted argument directly; read(P,w,x.y). With this representation of the TELIC for dotted types and the AGENTIVE of *book* given above, we can represent the complete qualia structure below:

$$(31) \quad \begin{bmatrix} \textbf{book} \\ \\ \text{ARGSTR} \; = \; \begin{bmatrix} \text{ARG1} \; = \; \textbf{x:information} \\ \text{ARG2} \; = \; \textbf{y:phys\_obj} \end{bmatrix} \\ \\ \text{QUALIA} \; = \; \begin{bmatrix} \textbf{information·phys\_obj\_lcp} \\ \text{FORMAL} \; = \; \textbf{hold(y,x)} \\ \text{TELIC} \; = \; \textbf{read(e,w,x.y)} \\ \text{AGENT} \; = \; \textbf{write(e',v,x.y)} \end{bmatrix} \end{bmatrix}$$

The predicates *read* and *write*, on this view, select for objects of just the dotted type specified by the restrictions, and no others. This point is taken up again in chapter 8 when the semantics of nominals is studied more closely.

6.2.5   Mapping from Qualia

In this section, I examine briefly what the consequences of qualia-based representations are for how arguments are mapped to syntax. Our strategy for projecting semantic arguments to syntax from underlying forms is very general, and would overgenerate unless constraints are operative in the grammar which block the expression of certain predicate-argument mappings. Given that event-headedness acts to foreground or "focus" a single quale of the verbal semantic representation, we will say that the abstracted quale that results from headedness must be saturated at s-structure. If one normally thinks of projection as specifying the appropriate grammatical functions to the arguments of a lexical item, such as (32):[13]

(32) $V(\underline{x}, y) \rightarrow$ x:SUBJ, y:OBJ

then it is clear what the task for a qualia-based representation is; namely to project from multiple semantic expressions to the appropriate grammatical functions in syntax. Whereas the PAS strategy accounts for how (32) is realized in syntax, projection in GL must make reference to qualia, thereby potentially complicating the lexicon to syntax mapping.

Within the approach taken here, the mapping illustrated in (32) is replaced with (33), which indicates the licensed projections from a particular quale, Q_i:[14]

(33) a. Q_i: $R(e_1, x, y) \longrightarrow$ x:SUBJ, y:OBJ
        b. Q_j: $P(e_2, y) \longrightarrow$ y:SUBJ

Given the presence of more than one qualia role, individual qualia compete for projection, and mechanisms such as headedness act as a filter to constrain the set of projectable qualia. The headed event, e^* projects the configuration (or template) associated with that event's predicate (i.e., its quale value). For example, from the qualia in (33), there are two possible mappings:

(34) a. Q_i: $R(e_1^*, x, y) \longrightarrow x$:SUBJ, y:OBJ
      b. Q_j: $P(e_2, y) \longrightarrow$ shadowed

(35) a. Q_i: $R(e_1, x, y) \longrightarrow$ shadowed
      b. Q_j: $P(e_2^*, y) \longrightarrow y$:SUBJ

To demonstrate this principle, consider the lexical representation for the verb *kill*.

(36)
$$
\begin{bmatrix}
\textbf{kill} \\[4pt]
\text{EVENTSTR} =
\begin{bmatrix}
\text{E}_1 = \textbf{e}_1\text{:process} \\
\text{E}_2 = \textbf{e}_2\text{:state} \\
\text{RESTR} = <_\alpha \\
\text{HEAD} = \textbf{e}_1
\end{bmatrix} \\[8pt]
\text{ARGSTR} =
\begin{bmatrix}
\text{ARG1} = \boxed{1}
\begin{bmatrix}
\textbf{ind} \\
\text{FORMAL} = \textbf{physobj}
\end{bmatrix} \\
\text{ARG2} = \boxed{2}
\begin{bmatrix}
\textbf{animate\_ind} \\
\text{FORMAL} = \textbf{physobj}
\end{bmatrix}
\end{bmatrix} \\[8pt]
\text{QUALIA} =
\begin{bmatrix}
\textbf{cause-lcp} \\
\text{FORMAL} = \textbf{dead}(\textbf{e}_2, \boxed{2}) \\
\text{AGENTIVE} = \textbf{kill\_act}(\textbf{e}_1, \boxed{1}, \boxed{2})
\end{bmatrix}
\end{bmatrix}
$$

Headedness will determine that the argument associated with the second subevent, e_2, cannot be expressed, since the qualia for the headed event expresses the template associated with that relation. This is illustrated in (37) below.

(37)

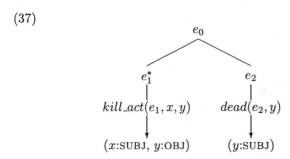

For an unergative verb such as *run*, the projection to subject follows
from the qualia structure, shown in (38).

$$(38) \quad \begin{bmatrix} \textbf{run} \\ \text{EVENTSTR} = \begin{bmatrix} \text{E}_1 = \textbf{e}_1\textbf{:process} \end{bmatrix} \\ \text{QUALIA} = \begin{bmatrix} \text{AGENTIVE} = \textbf{run\_act}(\textbf{e}_1,\textbf{x}) \\ \cdots \end{bmatrix} \end{bmatrix}$$

In addition to the mapping itself, the qualia of a lexical expression
must be "saturated" by the syntax. That is, the variables in the qualia
structure must be fully interpreted in the resulting syntactic structure
(Cf. Chomsky, 1981, 1986).

(39) QUALIA SATURATION: A qualia structure is saturated only if all
arguments in the qualia are *covered*.

(40) COVERING:
An argument x is covered only if:

(i) x is linked to a position in s-structure; or

(ii) x is logically dependent on a covered argument y; or

(iii) x is existentially closed by virtue of its type.

For the case of verbs such as *build*, discussed in chapter 9 where they
are referred to as *constitutive causatives*, an additional constraint is at
play. Because there is a default argument in the semantics of *build* (the
material z used by x to bring about y), the binding is different than for
a default causative relation. The qualia structure is repeated below in
(41) in an abbreviated form.

$$(41) \quad \begin{bmatrix} \textbf{build} \\ \cdots \\ \text{ARGSTR} = \begin{bmatrix} \text{ARG2} = \boxed{2} \begin{bmatrix} \textbf{artifact} \\ \text{CONST} = \boxed{3} \\ \text{FORMAL} = \textbf{physobj} \end{bmatrix} \\ \text{D-ARG1} = \boxed{3} \begin{bmatrix} \textbf{material} \\ \text{FORMAL} = \textbf{mass} \end{bmatrix} \end{bmatrix} \\ \text{QUALIA} = \begin{bmatrix} \textbf{create-lcp} \\ \text{FORMAL} = \textbf{exist}(\textbf{e}_2,\boxed{2}) \\ \text{AGENTIVE} = \textbf{build\_act}(\textbf{e}_1,\boxed{1},\boxed{3}) \end{bmatrix} \end{bmatrix}$$

With the initial event headed, we would expect the default argument, viz. the material to surface as the direct object, but this is not the case. Rather, the object which is constituted of this material is expressed as the object.

(42) a. Q_A: $R(e_1^*, x, f(y)) \longrightarrow x$:SUBJ, y:OBJ
      b. Q_F: $P(e_2, y) \longrightarrow$ shadowed

Formally, such a default argument can be viewed as a Skolem function of the argument it is dependent on, namely $f(y)$. Thus, given the calculus of relations in the qualia and the templates associated with them, the FORMAL argument in this case ends up bound to the object position in syntax.

It should be pointed out that the passive acts to head an event structure to a right-headed event. For a lexically left-headed event such as *kill*, this has the effect of shadowing the agent, and allowing expression of this argument only by adjunction. We return to this issue briefly in chapter 9 in the context of what licenses adjunction, but for further details of this proposal, see Pustejovsky (forthcoming).

As mentioned earlier, unergative and unaccusative verbs are distinguished by their qualia structures, but unergatives themselves are not a homogeneous class by any means. The lexical distinction between agent-like and non-agent-like processes was distinguished in chapter 5 in terms of the qualia being made reference to; namely, agent-like processes such as *run* are associated with the AGENTIVE quale while processes such as *sleep* are lexically associated with the FORMAL role. This is important for determining the manner in which adjuncts may co-compose with the verb to derive non-lexical senses, such as *run to the store* vs. *sleep a restful sleep*.

7 Generative Mechanisms in Semantics

In this chapter, we finally turn to the consequences of adopting a generative lexical approach to semantics, and the subsequent effect this has on the grammar in general. In the previous two chapters, we outlined the overall structure of the typing system incorporating the four levels of representation, as well as a more detailed examination of the semantics of qualia. Our goal in this chapter is to see what machinery is necessary in order to make use of the representations presented, i.e., event structure, qualia structure, and an argument structure with dotted types, so that the criteria of descriptive and explanatory adequacy can be satisfied for our semantic theory. What we hope to achieve is a model of meaning in language that captures the means by which words can assume a potentially infinite number of senses in context, while limiting the number of senses actually stored in the lexicon. The mechanism responsible for this polymorphic behavior of language is a set of generative devices connecting the different levels of lexical semantics, providing for the compositional interpretation of words in context. As mentioned in 5.1, included in these generative operations are the semantic transformations of *type coercion*, *selective binding*, and *co-composition*. Among co-compositional operations are transformations making use of semantically underspecified forms, such as manner co-composition, feature transcription, and light verb specification. All of these can be viewed as well-formedness conditions on type combinations in the grammar.

A major consequence of this approach is that the isomorphism between syntactic and semantic categories cannot be maintained for all levels of linguistic description, nor is it desirable. What this means is that a syntactic phrase cannot be interpreted outside of the syntactic and semantic context within which it appears. Rather, only by embedding the phrase can the appropriate denotation be determined. There are, however, canonical syntactic expressions for realizing semantic types, and these are presented in 7.4 below.

I first review the role played by type shifting in the literature, and how this tradition relates to the view of type coercion argued for in Pustejovsky (1991a, 1993) and elaborated here. Then, I outline the mechanisms of coercion and how we can make use of the richer semantic representations presented here to explain polysemy phenomena. The operations of selective binding and co-composition are discussed in 7.2 and 7.3. Finally, the study of how syntactic categories relate to semantic

types is taken up in section 7.4 , where the notion of lexical conceptual
paradigm is related to canonical syntactic forms.

7.1   Coercion and Type Shifting

Type shifting was first introduced as a way of allowing operators such
as negation and conjunction to change type according to what they
modified or took as arguments (cf. Geach, 1968, Strachey, 1967). Subsequent work in Rooth and Partee (1982), Partee and Rooth (1983),
Partee (1985), Klein and Sag (1985), and Chierchia (1984) developed
the mechanism to allow an NP, or any expression, in general, to change
its type (and hence its denotation) depending on the context. Briefly,
we can imagine an expression being assigned a default typing, where the
model defines what the well-defined and undefined type shiftings allowed
for that expression are. The types for an expression are related by what
Partee and Rooth (1985) call a *type ladder*. The utility of this proposal
is that it allows us to maintain a compositional semantics while also accounting for the different manifestations of an expression in a principled
way.

7.1.1   Parametric Polymorphism and Type Shifting

The example of conjunction studied in Partee and Rooth (1985) is perhaps the most obvious type shifting phenomenon in natural language,
and was independently classified as a *parametric polymorphism* in Strachey (1967). Leiß (1991) and Shieber (1992) treat conjunction operators
as operators taking *any* type as argument. For this reason, such lexical
items are said to be parametric polymorphic. For example, in English,
and is generally viewed as being able to conjoin almost any category at
any bar level, X^i. Although there are very few types of lexical items
which exhibit this behavior, it is helpful to see how this mechanism
works. The classic example illustrating type shifting within this operation is given in (1), where an individual, *John*, of type e is coordinated
with a quantified NP.

(1)   <u>John</u> and <u>every woman</u> arrived.

The NP *every woman* is of type <<e,t>,t>, and according to standard
typing restrictions on coordination within this approach, the conjuncts

must be of like type, which in this case they are not. Under this strategy, the sentence would be judged ill-formed even though it is fully grammatical. The solution to this difficulty is to *lift* the interpretation of *John* to that of a generalized quantifier, namely $\lambda P[P(j)]$, as shown in (2).

(2) a. [John]$_e$ and [every woman]$_{<<e,t>,t>}$:
  b. *every woman* $\in$ <<e,t>,t>: $\lambda P \forall x[woman(x) \rightarrow P(x)]$
  c. *John* $\in$ e type-shifts to <<e,t>t>: $\lambda P[P(j)]$

Type shifting has been useful for bringing together two distinct approaches to the semantics of interrogatives, as proposed recently by Groenendijk and Stokhof (1989). Other applications have also been proposed, and are explored in Partee (1985) and Dowty (1988).[1]

In Pustejovsky (1993) a particular application of type-shifting is discussed, illustrated in (3) below.

(3) John considers Mary *a fool*.

In (3), the type of the NP *a fool* is changed to that of a predicate, <e,t>. Thus, Mary (of type e) and the predicate can combine in the standard fashion. Following a suggestion in Partee (1985), we can represent the verb *consider* as selecting for an argument of a particular type, namely a predicative phrase.[2]

(4) a. John considers Mary *a fool*.
  b. *a fool*: $\lambda P \exists x[fool(x) \wedge P(x)]$, <<e,t>,t> $\Longrightarrow$ <e,t>
  c. *Mary*: $\in$ e

The type that *consider* selects for by default is <e,t>, as seen with the infinitival complement in (5), and it is exactly this type of complement selection which illustrates *type coercion*, to which I return below.[3]

(5) John considers [Mary]$_e$ [to be a fool]$_{<e,t>}$.

The attraction of type-shifting is that it will provide us with one of the tools needed for expressing the semantics-to-syntax mapping in the grammar; namely, it can capture the semantic relatedness between systematically ambiguous lexical items. For example, Klein and Sag (1985) show how the "raised" and "non-raised" forms with *believe* (cf. (6)), and *Equi* and non-*Equi* sentences with *prefer* (cf. (7)) can be accounted for (cf. also Gazdar, 1982). Their analysis in effect provides one solution to the polymorphic syntactic nature of these verbs.

(6) a. John believes <u>Mary to be honest</u>.
    b. John believes <u>that Mary is honest</u>.

(7) a. Mary prefers <u>to program in Commonlisp</u>.
    b. Mary prefers <u>for her students to program in Commonlisp</u>.

They suggest lexical entries for *believe* and *prefer* as shown in (8) and (9), where f_R and f_E are type-shifting operators for Raising and Equi, respectively.

(8) a. *believe* $\in$ <S,<NP,S>>
    b. $f_R(believe)$ $\in$ <VP,<NP,<NP,S>>>

(9) a. *prefer* $\in$ <S,<NP,S>>
    b. $f_E(prefer)$ $\in$ <VP,<NP,S>>

Lexically associated with each of these operators is a meaning postulate, ensuring the proper predication:[4]

(10) $\forall V \forall \mathcal{P}_1 \ldots \mathcal{P}_n \Box [f_R(\zeta)(V)(\mathcal{P}_1) \ldots (\mathcal{P}_n) \leftrightarrow \zeta(V(\mathcal{P}_1)) \ldots (\mathcal{P}_n)]$

(11) $\forall V \forall \mathcal{P}_1 \ldots \mathcal{P}_n \Box [f_E(\zeta)(V)(\mathcal{P}_1) \ldots (\mathcal{P}_n) \leftrightarrow \mathcal{P}_1 \{\lambda x [\zeta(V(x^*))(x^*)(\mathcal{P}_2)$
    $\ldots (\mathcal{P}_n)]\}]$

What these rules do is to ensure the appropriate predication of the lower predicate to the proper NP, the binding that is accomplished for example, by Binding Theory in Chomsky (1981, 1986). The operators in (8) and (9) permit the appropriate syntactic context to be licensed, but the resulting compositions require the meaning postulates in (10) and (11) for semantic well-formedness.[5] In other words, the type-shifting operator performs a destructive operation which the meaning postulate essentially acts to correct or undo.

A more conservative solution is suggested in Dowty (1985), where each particular grammatical usage of a verb is recorded in a separate lexical entry, what we characterized as sense enumeration in chapter 3 above. On this view, the relatedness between words is also captured via meaning postulates, and there is no single, "deep" type for a verb.[6]

These cases involving the verb *consider* illustrate that the type shifting of a phrase is often "licensed" by a particular lexical item. In this case, the governing verb *consider* licenses the shift in the second NP to be interpreted as a predicate. In just such cases, we can think of a verb *coercing* its argument to assume a certain type. In the next section, we will try to make this proposal more concrete in the hope of systematically accounting for why certain verbs allow the logical polysemy that they do.

As stated above, one of the most serious problems in lexical semantics is accounting for the systematic ambiguity of lexical items. It should be a general goal of semantic research to, whenever possible, reduce the amount of lexical ambiguity that the grammar requires. With this in mind, there are several constructions that have been treated as ambiguous verbs, but in fact lend themselves easily to a type shifting explanation. The first is a case discussed in McCawley (1979) and Dowty (1979) concerning the complement types of the verb *want*, as illustrated in (12):

(12) a. John wants <u>to have a car</u> until next week.
      b. John wants <u>a car</u> until next week.

As Dowty points out, the temporal adverbial *until next week* modifies a hidden or understood predicate in (12b), just as it modifies the overt predicate in (12a). To relate these word senses, Dowty suggests the null hypothesis, namely that the verb *want* is simply ambiguous, and has the following entries, related by meaning postulates.

(13) a. $want_1 \in$ <S,<NP,S>>
      b. $want_2 \in$ <VP,<NP,S>>
      c. $want_3 \in$ <NP,<NP,S>>

Similarly, Dowty (1985) argues in favor of the sense enumeration approach to these cases, partly because there are subtle differences in the verb meaning and the interpretation of the ellipsed predicate in each case, which must be accounted for somewhere, and presumably in the lexicon.[7] Consider for example, the context dependence of the ellipsed predicate in each example below.

(14) a. John wants <u>a beer</u>. (*to drink*)
      b. Mary wants <u>a book</u>. (*to read*)
      c. Harry wants <u>another cigarette</u>. (*to smoke*)

No general type shifting operator would give us the appropriately specific readings required for each of these examples. Dowty's solution is to have meaning postulates relate the major word senses for a verb such as *want*, and then allow pragmatic factors to supply the contextual information that embeds the verb sense in context. This is a reasonable approach given the limitations within conventional Montague Grammar, where information from the complement can in no way contribute to the overall composition of the phrase.

There is something missing in this solution, however, that is similar to the problems we encountered in previous chapters with the contextualization of senses for verbs such as *enjoy*, *begin*, and *finish*. Namely, the sense enumeration necessary to account for the behavior of these verbs is systematically associated with the complements as much as they are with constraints from the verb itself. The other problem with this solution is that the only way to establish the relation between verb senses is by meaning postulates. Although descriptively adequate, the meaning postulate solution for relating the different senses of *want*, for example, seems arbitrarily powerful and unconstrained.

Similar remarks hold for the verb type-shifting solution mentioned above. Namely, that although type shifting does allow various complement structures to be accepted by the same verb, what the operations are in fact doing is to create new subcategorization frames or semantic categories for each of the different complement types. There are two major problems with this approach. First, in most of the cases, it is not the meaning of the verb which is changing, but rather the selectional properties on the verb's complement. Once again, the association in meaning is done by a meaning postulate and not with any more restricted mechanism. The second problem is that it fails to capture the polysemous behavior of these complements when they appear in other syntactic environments. That is, the nature of these complements such as *a beer* and *a book* is such that they exhibit systematic polysemies that are independent of the verb *want*.

Given these remarks, we will adopt a different strategy in what follows. Consider again the full range of complementation for the verb *want*.

(15) a. Mary wants John to leave. (S [+INF])
      b. Mary wants to leave. (VP [+INF])
      c. Mary wants a beer. (NP)

Rather than type shifting the verb to accommodate each syntactic environment, let us assume that the type of the verb remains the same; that is, it is monomorphic with respect to semantic selection. What changes, however, is the syntactic type of the complement to the verb, which undergoes a type shifting operation by virtue of lexical governance from the verb. Such an operation I will call *type coercion*, because it is lexically governed type shifting. Following Cardelli and Wegner (1985) and Pustejovsky (1993), I will define coercion as follows:

(16) TYPE COERCION: a semantic operation that converts an argument to the type which is expected by a function, where it would otherwise result in a type error.

As mentioned above, Partee and Rooth (1982) suggest that all expressions in the language can be assigned a base type, while also being associated with a specific *type ladder*. Pustejovsky (1993) extends this proposal and suggests that each expression α may have available to it, a set of shifting operators, which we call Σ_α, which may operate over an expression, changing its type and denotation.

The rules of function application and composition may make reference to these operators directly, allowing us to treat the function as behaving polymorphically, while the argument is actually the shifting type. Hence, we can give an initial formulation of the rule of function application incorporating type coercion as follows:[8]

(17)   FUNCTION APPLICATION WITH COERCION (FAC): If α is of type c, and β is of type <a,b>, then,
  (i) if type c = a, then $\beta(\alpha)$ is of type b.
  (ii) if there is a $\sigma \in \Sigma_\alpha$ such that $\sigma(\alpha)$ results in an expression of type a, then $\beta(\sigma(\alpha))$ is of type b.
  (iii) otherwise a type error is produced.

To illustrate informally the effects of this rule, let us return to the ambiguity of *want* shown in (15) and (14) above. There are two things to explain: first, the different syntactic environments that are available as the complement types to the verb *want*; and secondly, the different interpretations that arise for the NP complement examples, which seems to require an enumeration of senses along with pragmatic enrichment for these cases. Rather than proposing different semantic types for the verb, i.e., separate and distinct lexical entries, let us propose that the verb's type remains constant, where the internal argument is uniformly typed as a `proposition`; if the syntactic form appearing in complement position matches this type, then the resulting structure is well-formed. If, however, the appropriate type is not present in complement position, it is *coerced* by the verb to match the type required by the typing restrictions on the verb. The tree in (18) below illustrates the relation between the "deep semantic type" and the syntactic realizations.

(18)

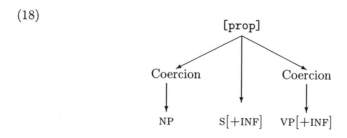

The mapping in (77) illustrates the ability of one semantic type to express itself in many syntactically distinct ways. From the perspective of syntactic categories, what this says is that a syntactic expression does not denote a single semantic type. Rather, it assumes a particular semantic type by virtue of context.[9]

What I am suggesting is that the syntactic forms associated with the argument of *want*, which appears to be a propositional type of some sort, are not uniquely realizable as these three syntactic forms for *want*, but are expressible by virtue of the semantic type itself. The methodology here is a fairly classic one in generative linguistics, arguing for the underlying properties of an expression on the basis of its distributional behavior. What we would expect, then is that something of like type would appear *mutatis mutandi* in different contexts with the same expressive abilities.

In the next section I formalize the operation of type coercion and show how it is an integral component to the grammar. It is but one part of the semantic system that allows us to capture the semantic creativity and sense extension phenomena discussed above. Only together with a richer representation system as embodied in the levels of argument, event, and qualia structure, can coercion appropriately apply to give rise to creative senses. In later sections, I also discuss two other generative devices required for adequately modeling the polymorphic behavior of language.

In sum, rather than assigning a new lexical entry to a verb every time a different syntactic environment for it is discovered or every time a new interpretation is need for a new context, we will "spread the semantic load" more evenly throughout the elements in composition. This is accomplished by the representations as well as the ability to make use of them through the generative operations discussed below.

7.1.2   Subtype Coercion

To demonstrate the formal properties of type coercion, it is useful to first examine what is perhaps the simplest case of coercion, one involving a very specific kind of semantic shifting, namely the case of *subtype coercion*. The formal properties accompanying types and subtypes are well known in the semantics and knowledge representation literature. Consider, for example, the sentences in (19) below, where both subject and object NPs are subtypes of the sortal specifications to the arguments of the verb.

(19)   a. <u>Mary</u> drives <u>a Honda</u> to work.
       b. <u>Tom</u> read <u>the Tractatus</u> on holiday.

Although this is a trivial point from the viewpoint of syntax, for a semantics with types, one must establish a relation between the type denoted by the NP in each of these argument positions and the type that is formally selected for by the verbs *drive* and *read*. The conventional relation given between these types is one of subtyping. Hence, within our typing system, we need to ensure that if a function selects for type τ_1 and the actually occurring form is τ_2, where τ_2 is a subtype of τ_1 ($\tau_2 \leq \tau_1$), it too should be accepted by the function as a legitimate argument. For example, assuming that the lexical representation for the noun *car* is given as in (20),

$$(20) \quad \begin{bmatrix} \textbf{car} \\ \text{ARGSTR} = \begin{bmatrix} \text{ARG1} = \textbf{x:vehicle} \end{bmatrix} \\ \text{QUALIA} = \begin{bmatrix} \text{FORMAL} = \textbf{x} \\ \text{TELIC} = \textbf{drive(e,y,x)} \\ \text{AGENTIVE} = \textbf{create(e,z,x)} \end{bmatrix} \end{bmatrix}$$

then by typing *Honda* as a subtype of car, we establish the following relation: Honda $\leq$ car $\leq$ vehicle. As with other lexical inheritance mechanisms, the more specific value for the AGENTIVE role in the structure below supersedes the more general value associated with an artifact in *car*, while still inheriting the values for the other qualia (cf. Beierle *et al.*, 1992 and Copestake *et al.*, 1993). Note that AGENTIVE and TELIC values are both inherited; the type specificity of the AGENTIVE for *Honda*, however, is locally defined.

(21)
$$
\begin{bmatrix}
\textbf{Honda} \\
\text{ARGSTR} = \begin{bmatrix} \text{ARG1} = \textbf{x:car} \end{bmatrix} \\
\text{QUALIA} = \begin{bmatrix} \text{FORMAL} = \textbf{x} \\ \text{TELIC} = \textbf{drive(e,y,x)} \\ \text{AGENTIVE} = \textbf{create(e,Honda-Co,x)} \end{bmatrix}
\end{bmatrix}
$$

Assuming that the internal type selected by the verb in sentence (19a) is `vehicle`, as illustrated below in the lexical representation for *drive*, then the selectional requirements can be satisfied just in case there exists the subtyping relation mentioned above, which acts to formally relate the type of the actual object to the lexically specified type.

(22)
$$
\begin{bmatrix}
\textbf{drive} \\
\text{EVENTSTR} = \begin{bmatrix} \text{E}_1 = \textbf{e}_1\textbf{:process} \\ \text{E}_2 = \textbf{e}_2\textbf{:process} \\ \text{RESTR} = <\text{o}_\alpha \end{bmatrix} \\
\text{ARGSTR} = \begin{bmatrix} \text{ARG1} = \textbf{x:human} \\ \text{ARG2} = \textbf{y:vehicle} \end{bmatrix} \\
\text{QUALIA} = \begin{bmatrix} \text{FORMAL} = \textbf{move(e}_2\textbf{,y)} \\ \text{AGENTIVE} = \textbf{drive\_act(e}_1\textbf{,x,y)} \end{bmatrix}
\end{bmatrix}
$$

Recall from chapter 6 that we defined a *typing judgment*, $g \vdash \alpha : \tau$, with respect to a grammar to be an assignment, g, an expression, α, and a type, τ, such that under assignment g, the expression α has type τ. We can define a *subtyping coercion* relation, Θ, for these judgments as follows (cf. Gunter, 1992):

(23)
$$
\frac{\alpha : \sigma_1, \quad \Theta[\sigma_1 \le \sigma_2] : \sigma_1 \to \sigma_2}{\Theta[\sigma_1 \le \sigma_2](\alpha) : \sigma_2}
$$

This says that, given an expression α of type σ_1, which is a subtype of σ_2, there is a coercion possible between σ_1 and σ_2, which changes the type of α in this composition, from σ_1 to σ_2 (cf. Beierle *et al.*, 1992). The typing relation between the subtype `Honda` and the type selected by the governing verb *drive* is respected by the coercion relation, Θ, as shown below:

(24) a. $\Theta[Honda \leq car] : Honda \rightarrow car$
      b. $\Theta[car \leq vehicle] : car \rightarrow vehicle$

Similarly, in (19b) above, The Tractatus $\leq$ book $\leq$ text defines a relation between the type selected by the verb *read* and the actual individual.

Having illustrated the general mechanism of type coercion with the subtyping relation, let us return to the complement coercion cases presented in the previous section. It will become clear that, although subtyping polymorphism and the complement coercions below are similar, in that they permit the variable functionality of a lexical item to be expressed in a single form, they are formally quite different. Subtype coercion follows the inferences available in a single type lattice, while true complement coercion requires reference to multiple types lattices, making use of information available through the qualia.

7.1.3   True Complement Coercion

Unlike parametric polymorphism, true type coercion involves the strict shifting of one type to another specified type, licensed by lexical governance. Furthermore, the shift is not arbitrary, but embeds the existing type into the resulting type by the proper coercion operation. Let us return to the paradigm mentioned in section 7.1:[10]

(25) a. Mary wants <u>a beer</u>.
      b. Mary wants <u>a cigarette</u>.

(26) a. Mary enjoyed <u>the movie</u>.
      b. Mary enjoyed <u>watching the movie</u>.

(27) a. John began <u>a book</u>.
      b. John began <u>reading a book</u>.
      c. John began <u>to read a book</u>.

In order to capture the semantic relatedness of these different verb forms (as well as the similarity of the complement denotations), we will need to invoke a coercion rule to ensure that the semantic type of the verb is satisfied in all these cases, regardless of syntactic form.[11]

The rule of function application with coercion (FAC) given in the previous section describes just how the semantic transformation comes about. For a lexical structure such as that associated with the verb *begin*, given below in a somewhat incomplete form (cf. 9.3 for details on aspectual coercion and control), the typing on the second argument is explicitly given as an event.

$$(28) \quad \begin{bmatrix} \textbf{begin} \\[2pt] \text{EVENTSTR} = \begin{bmatrix} E_1 = \textbf{transition} \\ E_2 = \textbf{transition} \\ \text{RESTR} = \;<\circ_\alpha \end{bmatrix} \\[2pt] \text{ARGSTR} = \begin{bmatrix} \text{ARG1} = \textbf{x:human} \\ \text{ARG2} = \textbf{e}_2 \end{bmatrix} \\[2pt] \text{QUALIA} = \begin{bmatrix} \text{FORMAL} = \textbf{P}(\textbf{e}_2,\textbf{x}) \\ \text{AGENTIVE} = \textbf{begin\_act}(\textbf{e}_1,\textbf{x},\textbf{e}_2) \end{bmatrix} \end{bmatrix}$$

This states that the complement to *begin* is actually an event of some sort (discussed in 9.3 and Pustejovsky and Bouillon, 1995). Regardless of the surface syntactic form of the complement, the semantic typing environment is the same, namely an event. Where that type is not directly satisfied, as in (27c) or (27b), a coercion applies to reconstruct the semantics of the complement. The coercion is, of course, successful only if the NP has available to it an *alias* of the appropriate type (Pustejovsky and Boguraev, 1993). An alias can be thought of as an alternative type that is available to a element, be it lexical or phrasal. For a sentence such as (27a), the event type is forced on the complement *a book*, and comes about by reconstructing an event reading from the qualia of the NP. Recall that the lexical structure for *book* is a dot object, making reference to two types, info and physobj.[12]

$$(29) \quad \begin{bmatrix} \textbf{book} \\[2pt] \text{ARGSTR} = \begin{bmatrix} \text{ARG1} = \textbf{x:info} \\ \text{ARG2} = \textbf{y:physobj} \end{bmatrix} \\[2pt] \text{QUALIA} = \begin{bmatrix} \textbf{info·physobj\_lcp} \\ \text{FORMAL} = \textbf{hold}(\textbf{y,x}) \\ \text{TELIC} = \textbf{read}(\textbf{e,w,x.y}) \\ \text{AGENT} = \textbf{write}(\textbf{e',v,x.y}) \end{bmatrix} \end{bmatrix}$$

Because the NP *a book* does not satisfy the type required by the predicate *begin*, the verb coerces the NP into an event denotation, one which is available from the NP's qualia structure through qualia projection (see below 7.4). There are two event readings associated with this NP, namely the values of the AGENTIVE and TELIC qualia roles. How an event is actually reconstructed to satisfy the typing environment is a result of the coercion operation itself. Consider the tree representation below, where semantic types are notated in brackets. According to the lexical structure in (28), the verb *begin* has two arguments, [human] and [event], and can be viewed as occupying a minimal syntactic projection for the verb, independent of any particular syntactic expression. That is, imagine for now the verb projecting semantic selectional information alone (cf. Chomsky, 1986).

(30)

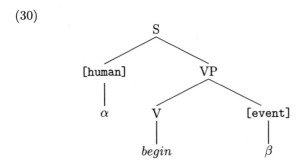

The statement of coercion on the complement from the governing verb *begin* can be seen as requiring it to recover an event-denoting expression, and then embed the NP semantics within this expression. This is illustrated schematically in (31) below.

(31)

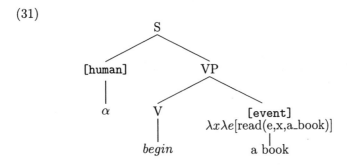

Ignoring issue of subject control and binding for now, what this demonstrates is that the semantic typing of an environment can be respected without changing the syntax of the expression. It should be pointed out

immediately that this does not operate without constraints, since the
expression being coerced itself projects the appropriate semantic type
required by the application rule.

To see more clearly how such coercion interpretations are formally
derived, consider the complement variations possible with the propositional attitude verb *believe*, given in (32).

(32) a. Mary believes that he left. (s [+TNS])
      b. Mary believes him to have left. (s [+INF])
      c. Mary believes the book. (NP)
      d. Mary believes John. (NP)

Assuming that the verb *believe* selects for a propositional type, **prop**,
as its complement, the tensed sentential complement in (32a) can be
viewed as direct satisfaction of this selected type. Similar remarks hold
for (32b), ignoring for this discussion, the exceptional case marking on
the complement subject *him* (cf. Chomsky, 1981).

Now notice the interpretation of the complement in (32c). Although
a definite NP such as *the book* is formally a generalized quantifier, with
type **<<e,t>,t**, the interpretation it assumes in this position is clearly
that of a proposition. We saw in (34) above that there are at least two
possible event interpretations associated with a noun such as *book* (and
subsequently with the NP containing it), but in fact there is neither an
event reading for (32c) nor is there a "reconstructed proposition" from
the qualia structure of the NP. How, then, does this reading come about?
Recall from our discussion in chapter 6 and the qualia structure in (34)
above that the semantics of *the book* is more complex than standardly
assumed for a nominal term phrase. Namely, the noun *book* is a complex
(or dot) object, and its type is **info·physobj**. Recall that this is the
result of the type constructor *lcp* repeated here applying to the two
types **info** and **physobj**:

$$(33) \quad \frac{\alpha : \texttt{info} \quad \alpha : \texttt{physobj}}{lcp(\alpha) : \texttt{info} \cdot \texttt{physobj}}$$

The dot object is the logical pairing of the senses denoted by the individual types in the complex type. That is, following the treatment taken for
relational nominals outlined in Pustejovsky (1989) and in Pustejovsky
(1994), we assume that nominals such as *book* are a sort of **container**,

which are further specified as a relation between a physical object and the textual information contained within it.

Along with the complex type, we need to define the operations over this object which effectively foreground a particular sense. The coercion operations projecting one type from the complex type are a special case of *type pumping* (or projection), and can be simply defined as Σ_1 and Σ_2 below. These two operations, together with the dot object itself will form the definition of the type cluster we called an lcp in the previous chapter.

(34) $\text{lcp} = \{\sigma_1 \cdot \sigma_2, \Sigma_1[\sigma_1 \cdot \sigma_2] : \sigma_1, \Sigma_2[\sigma_1 \cdot \sigma_2] : \sigma_2\}$

Hence, the lcp for *book* provides for the following aliases, licensing the polysemous behavior of the lexical item demonstrated previously. Assuming the operators Σ_1 and Σ_2 to be defined as above, then the full type cluster, first mentioned in 6.2, can be given as in (35c), with the appropriate derivation.

(35) a. $\Sigma_1[\text{info·physobj}]:\text{info}$
      b. $\Sigma_2[\text{info·physobj}]:\text{physobj}$
      c. $\text{info·physobj\_lcp} = \{\text{info·physobj}, \text{info}, \text{physobj}\}$

Intuitively, then, a book always denotes, in part, textual information. Because of the subtyping relations between these two types and the type proposition (prop):

> book $\leq$ text $\leq$ prop

the NP *the book* is able to "stand in" for a full propositional expression. This is illustrated in the tree structure below, once again showing semantic selection:

(36)

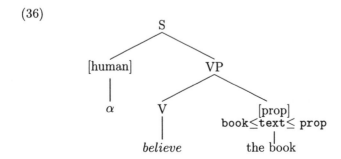

Given this discussion, we return to sentence (32c) and the coercion involving the NP, *the book*. The type derivation below shows both the application of the type pumping operator, Σ, and the subtyping relation, Θ. The lcp interpretation of *book*, and there exists a subtyping relation $\alpha \leq S'$.

$$(37) \quad \frac{\Sigma_1(\texttt{info} \cdot \texttt{physobj}) : \texttt{info} \quad , \quad \Theta[\texttt{info} \leq \texttt{prop}] : \texttt{info} \rightarrow \texttt{prop}}{\Theta[\texttt{info} \leq \texttt{prop}](\Sigma_1(\texttt{info} \cdot \texttt{physobj})) : \texttt{prop}}$$

The associated semantic interpretation is given below in (38).

(38) a. Mary believes the book.
     b. **believe(ˆ$\Theta(\Sigma_1$(the-book)))(Mary)** $\Rightarrow$
     c. **believe'(ˆΘ(the-book:info))(Mary)** $\Rightarrow$
     d. **believe'(ˆthe-book:prop)(Mary)**

What the composition in (38) illustrates is how the deep typing on the complement is satisfied by enriching the semantics of the object description as well as adding functionality to the manner in which phrases compose (cf. Pustejovsky, 1994).

Finally, consider how the typing requirement for a verb such as *sell*, selecting for a complement of type ind, is satisfied by the lcp of *book* (cf. (39)).

(39) Mary sold the book to John.

In sentence (39), the type physobj is available by application of the coercion operator Σ_2, and likewise, the type ind is available through subtyping with the coercion operator Θ: i.e., physobj $\leq$ ind.[13]

(40) a. Mary sold the book to John.
     b. **sell(John)($\Theta(\Sigma_2$(the-book)))(Mary)** $\Rightarrow$
     c. **sell(John)(Θ(the-book:physobj))(Mary)** $\Rightarrow$
     d. **sell(John)(the-book:ind)(Mary)**

Now let us return to the more difficult case of coercion involving the complement of *believe*, namely (32d) above, repeated below.

(41) Mary believes John. (NP)

Unlike the case of an NP such as *the book*, where the type required by selection was part of the underlying semantics of the expression, this is not the case in (41). What is similar, however, is the interpretation of the complement; namely, it refers to a proposition. Hence, under this view, there is coercion of an individual, *John*, to a propositional interpretation. In terms of typing, the shift simply involves taking the type of an NP like *John* (i.e., a generalized quantifier, `<<ind,prop>,prop>`) and coercing it to a proposition (`prop`).

(42) Type-shift: `<<ind,prop>,prop>` $\Rightarrow$ `prop`

By itself, of course, this is both uninteresting and unintuitive. It is one thing to simply provide the appropriate type shifting mechanisms to satisfy the type requirements of a complement, such as in (32c) and (32d). The task, however, is to explain why such a type is available as an interpretation to begin with. That is, why should *John* be able to metonymically project to a propositional denotation, and indeed, what would this mean? Intuitively, we understand this sentence to mean that, what John utters, typically or on this one occasion, is believed by Mary. Thus, there is an implicit relation between John and the proposition ϕ expressed by him, conveyed by some means of communication R, and it is this proposition which is being judged. The relation here is illustrated with an individual type, `ind`.

(43) *john* $\Rightarrow$ $\exists\phi\exists R[\phi \land [R(john,\phi)]]$

The proposition ϕ is not simply any proposition, but is construed as that which is communicated by John. Our knowledge of human agents as possible speakers or writers allows us to infer (semantically) that such a relation as R in (43) exists, and that it is sortally restricted to communicative acts. Further details, however, on what this relation is seems out of the domain of linguistic knowledge, and properly part of default reasoning and abduction (cf. Lascarides and Asher, 1993, Hobbs, 1987, and Hobbs *et al.*, 1988). Because the interpretation from the compositional semantics is conservative—by not completely specifying what the relation between the two types `prop` and `ind` is—I will refer to this particular application of type change as *minimal coercion*. That is, the typing environment is satisfied, but the semantics is not completely determined.[14] The associated semantic derivation is below.[15]

(44) a. Mary believes John.
     b. **believe**(ˆρ_2(**John**))(**Mary**) $\Rightarrow$
     c. **believe**(ˆ$\exists\phi\exists R[\phi \wedge [R(\textbf{John}, \phi)])])$(**Mary**) $\Rightarrow$
     d. **believe**(ˆ$\exists\phi\exists R[\phi \wedge [R(\textbf{John}, \phi)]])$(**Mary**)

As mentioned before, a complete interpretation is possible only with subsequent inferences operating to further specify what type of communicative relation R is defined as. This is not, however, lexical semantic information, but rather is supplied by other factors. For example, believing Daniel Schorr is probably to believe something that you heard him say *on radio*, while believing William Safire is most likely to believe something that he wrote. What this example illustrates is not only the natural limits of linguistic knowledge, but also how lexical semantics is able to license subsequent commonsense inferences, an issue we return to in chapter 10.

7.2   Co-composition

In this section we discuss those cases of verbal logical polysemy involving *co-composition* (Pustejovsky, 1991a). Briefly, co-composition describes a structure which allows, superficially, more than one function application. We begin by studying the polysemy of baking verbs to illustrate this point. In (45) below, the verb *bake* has two meanings, both a *change of state* sense and a *creation* sense (Atkins *et al.*, 1988).

(45) a. John <u>baked</u> the potato.
     b. John <u>baked</u> the cake.

Similarly, the verbs in (46)–(49) are ambiguous between a process reading and a transition reading, depending on the presence of a resultative adjectival. Normally, lexicons would have to enter both forms as separate lexical entries (cf. Levin and Rappaport, 1995).

(46) a. Mary <u>wiped</u> the table.
     b. Mary <u>wiped</u> the table dry.

(47) a. John <u>hammered</u> the metal.
     b. John <u>hammered</u> the metal flat.

(48) a. Mary <u>waxed</u> the car.

     b. Mary <u>waxed</u> the car clean.

(49) a. Mary <u>ate</u>.

     b. Mary <u>ate</u> herself sick.

In order to capture the logical polysemy in all these cases and obviate the need for multiple listings of words, Pustejovsky (1991a) proposed that the complements carry information which acts on the governing verb, essentially taking the verb as argument and shifting its event type. Here we will make this proposal more explicit and describe what mechanism makes such an operation available.

    Let us assume that the lexical structure for a verb such as *bake* is that given below.

$$(50)\quad \begin{bmatrix} \textbf{bake} \\ \text{EVENTSTR} = \begin{bmatrix} \text{E}_1 = \text{e}_1\text{:}\textbf{process} \\ \text{HEAD} = \text{e}_1 \end{bmatrix} \\ \text{ARGSTR} = \begin{bmatrix} \text{ARG1} = \boxed{1}\begin{bmatrix} \textbf{animate\_ind} \\ \text{FORMAL} = \textbf{physobj} \end{bmatrix} \\ \text{ARG2} = \boxed{2}\begin{bmatrix} \textbf{mass} \\ \text{FORMAL} = \textbf{physobj} \end{bmatrix} \end{bmatrix} \\ \text{QUALIA} = \begin{bmatrix} \textbf{state\_change\_lcp} \\ \text{AGENTIVE} = \textbf{bake\_act}(\text{e}_1, \boxed{1}, \boxed{2}) \end{bmatrix} \end{bmatrix}$$

I wish to claim that there is only one sense for *bake*, and that any other readings are derived through generative mechanisms in composition with its arguments. What needs to be explained, however, is why nouns such as *cake*, *bread* and *cookie* "shift" the meaning of the verb *bake*, while other nouns (such as *potato* and *garlic*) do not. Intuitively, we would like to capture the fact that the former objects are prototypically brought about by the activity they are in composition with, something that the qualia structure should be able to express. Assume that the qualia for *cake* makes reference to an AGENTIVE value of $\lambda y \lambda e \exists x[bake(e, y, x)]$.

$$(51)\quad \begin{bmatrix} \textbf{cake} \\ \text{ARGSTR} = \begin{bmatrix} \text{ARG1} = \text{x:}\textbf{food\_ind} \\ \text{D-ARG1} = \text{y:}\textbf{mass} \end{bmatrix} \\ \text{QUALIA} = \begin{bmatrix} \text{CONST} = \textbf{y} \\ \text{FORMAL} = \textbf{x} \\ \text{TELIC} = \textbf{eat}(\text{e}_2, \text{z}, \text{x}) \\ \text{AGENTIVE} = \textbf{bake\_act}(\text{e}_1, \text{w}, \text{y}) \end{bmatrix} \end{bmatrix}$$

Notice that the AGENTIVE makes reference to the very process within which it is embedded in this phrase, a relation which Pustejovsky (1991a) called *cospecification*.

The semantics for the VP *bake a cake* results from several operations. First, conventional function application binds the object into the argument structure of the verb *bake*. Secondly, a type of feature unification occurs, licensed by the identity of qualia values for AGENTIVE in the verb and its argument. That is, $Q_A(\texttt{bake}) = Q_A(\texttt{the cake})$.

The operation of co-composition results in a qualia structure for the VP that reflects aspects of both constituents. These include:

(A) The governing verb *bake* applies to its complement;

(B) The complement co-specifies the verb;

(C) The composition of qualia structures results in a derived sense of the verb, where the verbal and complement AGENTIVE roles match, and the complement FORMAL quale becomes the FORMAL role for the entire VP.

The derived sense results from an operation I will call *qualia unification*. The conditions under which this operation can apply are stated in (52) below (cf. also Keenan and Faltz, 1985):

(52) FUNCTION APPLICATION WITH QUALIA UNIFICATION: For two expressions, α, of type <a,b>, and β, of type a, with qualia structures QS_α and QS_β, respectively, then, if there is a quale value shared by α and β, $[_{QS_\alpha} \cdots [Q_i = \gamma]]$ and $[_{QS_\beta} \cdots [Q_i = \gamma]]$, then we can define the qualia unification of QS_α and QS_β, $QS_\alpha \sqcap QS_\beta$, as the unique greatest lower bound of these two qualia structures. Further, $\alpha(\beta)$ is of type b with $QS_{\alpha(\beta)} = QS_\alpha \sqcap QS_\beta$.[16]

Thus, we can derive both word senses of verbs like *bake* by putting some of the semantic weight on the NP. This view suggests that, in such cases, the verb itself is not polysemous. Rather, the creation sense of *bake* is contributed in part by the meaning of *a cake*, by virtue of it being an artifact. The verb appears polysemous because certain complements (i.e., those co-specifying the verb) add to the basic meaning by co-composition. The representation associated with this has the following structure:

(53)

$$
\begin{bmatrix}
\textbf{bake a cake} \\[4pt]
\text{EVENTSTR} = \begin{bmatrix} E_1 = \textbf{e}_1\textbf{:process} \\ E_2 = \textbf{e}_2\textbf{:state} \\ \text{RESTR} = <_\propto \\ \text{HEAD} = \textbf{e}_1 \end{bmatrix} \\[20pt]
\text{ARGSTR} = \begin{bmatrix}
\text{ARG1} \quad = \boxed{1}\begin{bmatrix} \textbf{animate\_ind} \\ \text{FORMAL} = \textbf{physobj} \end{bmatrix} \\[14pt]
\text{ARG2} \quad = \boxed{2}\begin{bmatrix} \textbf{artifact} \\ \text{CONST} = \boxed{3} \\ \text{FORMAL} = \textbf{physobj} \end{bmatrix} \\[14pt]
\text{D-ARG1} \quad = \boxed{3}\begin{bmatrix} \textbf{material} \\ \text{FORMAL} = \textbf{mass} \end{bmatrix}
\end{bmatrix} \\[36pt]
\text{QUALIA} = \begin{bmatrix} \textbf{create-lcp} \\ \text{FORMAL} = \textbf{exist}(\textbf{e}_2, \boxed{2}) \\ \text{AGENTIVE} = \textbf{bake\_act}(\textbf{e}_1, \boxed{1}, \boxed{3}) \end{bmatrix}
\end{bmatrix}
$$

The result of co-composition is a semantic representation at the VP level that is identical in structure to the lexical form for a creation verb such as *build*. What this claims is that the creation sense of *bake* embeds the change-of-state reading within it by systematic rules of composition.[17] The sense arises not by lexical enumeration, but *generatively* in the semantics itself.

As another brief example of how co-composition operates to give rise to "derived" senses, consider the lexical conflation examples first discussed in Talmy (1985), and characterized as *lexical subordination* in Levin and Rapoport (1988); namely, the systematic polysemy of the verb *float* and related verbs in the following construction:

(54) a. The bottle is floating in the river.
       b. The bottle floated under the bridge.

There is a systematic polysemy exhibited by these examples, where a process interpretation for the verb *float*, as in (54a), is shifted to a transitional reading in sentence (54b). A partial lexical representation for the verb is given in (55).

(55)

$$
\begin{bmatrix}
\textbf{float} \\[4pt]
\text{ARGSTR} = \begin{bmatrix} \text{ARG1} \quad = \boxed{1}\begin{bmatrix} \textbf{physobj} \end{bmatrix} \end{bmatrix} \\[10pt]
\text{EVENTSTR} = \begin{bmatrix} E_1 = \textbf{e}_1\textbf{:state} \end{bmatrix} \\[10pt]
\text{QUALIA} = \begin{bmatrix} \text{AGENTIVE} = \textbf{float}(\textbf{e}_1, \boxed{1}) \end{bmatrix}
\end{bmatrix}
$$

In (54b), both manner and motion aspects of meaning are conflated into a new sense of *float*. In Pustejovsky (1991a), it was suggested that directional PPs act as functions over the verb to give rise to a derivative verb sense through co-composition (cf. also Jackendoff, 1992a). More specifically, let us assume that the representation for the PP *into the cave* is that given below:

$$(56) \begin{bmatrix} \textbf{into the cave} \\ \text{ARGSTR} = \begin{bmatrix} \text{ARG1} &=& \boxed{1}\begin{bmatrix} \textbf{physobj} \end{bmatrix} \\ \text{ARG2} &=& \boxed{2}\begin{bmatrix} \textbf{the\_cave} \end{bmatrix} \end{bmatrix} \\ \text{EVENTSTR} = \begin{bmatrix} \text{E}_1 = e_1\text{:\textbf{process}} \\ \text{E}_2 = e_2\text{:\textbf{state}} \\ \text{RESTR} = <_\alpha \\ \text{HEAD} = e_2 \end{bmatrix} \\ \text{QUALIA} = \begin{bmatrix} \text{FORMAL} = \textbf{at}(e_2,\boxed{1},\boxed{2}) \\ \text{AGENTIVE} = \textbf{move}(e_1,\boxed{1}) \end{bmatrix} \end{bmatrix}$$

Notice that the PP carries the motion sense as part of its qualia structure, such that, when in composition with the verb *float*, the interpretation of the VP is roughly equivalent to the expression in (57), where the matrix predicate is temporally (and functionally) subordinated to the application of the PP.

(57) $\lambda x \lambda e_1 \exists e_2 [\circ(e_1, e_2) \wedge float(e_2, x)] \Rightarrow$ *while floating*

The result of the full composition is shown below in (58).

$$(58) \begin{bmatrix} \textbf{float into the cave} \\ \text{ARGSTR} = \begin{bmatrix} \text{ARG1} &=& \boxed{1}\begin{bmatrix} \textbf{physobj} \end{bmatrix} \\ \text{ARG2} &=& \boxed{2}\begin{bmatrix} \textbf{the\_cave} \end{bmatrix} \end{bmatrix} \\ \text{EVENTSTR} = \begin{bmatrix} \text{E}_1 = e_1\text{:\textbf{state}} \\ \text{E}_2 = e_2\text{:\textbf{process}} \\ \text{E}_3 = e_3\text{:\textbf{state}} \\ \text{RESTR} = <_\alpha (e_2, e_3) , \circ_\alpha(e_1, e_2) \\ \text{HEAD} = e_3 \end{bmatrix} \\ \text{QUALIA} = \begin{bmatrix} \text{FORMAL} = \textbf{at}(e_3,\boxed{1},\boxed{2}) \\ \text{AGENTIVE} = \textbf{move}(e_2,\boxed{1}), \textbf{float}(e_1,\boxed{1}) \end{bmatrix} \end{bmatrix}$$

What this analysis says is that the conflated sense for the verb *float* exists only phrasally and not lexically. Only co-compositional operations can contextualize the underlying sense to give rise to this interpretation.

In this section, I have illustrated but one way in which co-composition allows us to make use of semantic information in both functor and argument in a phrase, to result in the creation of senses that are not listed in the lexicon. Once a mechanism is in place which admits of making use of information from complements and other non-functor elements in a phrase, it is interesting to imagine how the notion of co-composition can be extended to handle other phenomena. Three applications are illustrative to this point; namely, *manner co-composition*, *feature transcription*, and *light verb specification*. I will present an analysis of one phenomenon related to the semantics of light verbs in chapter 10, and discuss several further applications of this mechanism involving the underspecification of semantic forms. The other phenomena mentioned here are discussed in Pustejovsky (forthcoming).[18]

7.3 Selective Binding

Now we return to the problem of adjectival polysemy presented earlier. In chapters 3 and 4, I discussed three types of polysemy with adjectival modification, repeated below:

(59) a. We will need a <u>fast</u> boat to get back in time.
      b. John is a <u>fast</u> typist.
      c. <u>Fast</u> drivers will be caught and ticketed.

(60) a. John put on a <u>long</u> album during dinner.
      b. I'd like a really <u>bright</u> bulb for my desk.
      c. Mary dumped the pasta into the <u>boiling</u> pot.

(61) a. The man is <u>sad</u>.
      b. John is a <u>sad</u> man
      c. That was truly a <u>sad</u> day (event, occasion).

These are interesting from our point of view because of the apparent noncompositional nature of the modification as well as the productivity of these constructions. Consider first the examples in (59). Recall that the standard view on selection within an SEL for these types of adjectives is to enumerate the senses. This requires that every finely-nuanced sense of *fast* must be typed specifically for the noun class or type it modifies. We observed, however, that the meaning of *fast* is determined largely by the semantics of the head it is in construction with. Following our discussion of qualia structure in 6.2, we can now give more substance to this observation.

In predicative position, adjectives such as *fast* are ambiguous as well, being able to modify both NPs (cf. (62)) as well as VPs (cf. (63) below).

(62) a. That was <u>fast</u>! You're back already?
      b. Your dog is <u>fast</u>.

(63) a. Emanuel Ax's hand moved so <u>fast</u> during the scherzo they were a blur.
      b. Mary was driving too <u>fast</u> to maintain control of the car.

Even in the individual predicative readings in (62), however, the interpretation of the modifier requires reference to an event. In (62a), the interpretation refers to the duration of the event of someone being gone, while in (62b), the property of being fast when moving is predicated of the dog. The two sentences in (63) are both standard event predicative interpretations.

There are two issues to be dealt with here: (a) adjectives such as *fast* are polysemous, being able to modify individuals or events; and (b) the interpretation of the adjective in context depends on the semantics of the head itself (cf. Bartsch, 1985).

Consider again the sentence in (59b) above. Treating the adjective *fast* as simply an intersective modifier would give us $\lambda x[typist'(x) \wedge fast'(x)]$. But how do we arrive at the interpretation of "John is a typist who is fast at typing?" Assume that the qualia structure for a deverbal agentive nominal such as *typist* is as follows:

(64)
$$
\begin{bmatrix}
\textbf{typist} \\
\text{ARGSTR} = \begin{bmatrix} \text{ARG1} = \textbf{x:human} \end{bmatrix} \\
\text{QUALIA} = \begin{bmatrix} \text{FORMAL} = \textbf{x} \\ \text{TELIC} = \textbf{type(e,x)} \end{bmatrix}
\end{bmatrix}
$$

If *fast* is an event predicate, then there is no standard mode of composition that would allow the desired interpretation for sentence (59b), namely, that in (65).

(65) $\lambda x[\dots Telic = \lambda e[type'(e,x) \wedge fast(e)]\dots]$

The adjective is able to make available a selective interpretation of an event expression contained in the qualia for the head noun.[19] What makes such an interpretation possible is a generative mechanism I will refer to as *selective binding*.

(66) SELECTIVE BINDING:

If α is of type $\langle a,a\rangle$, β is of type b, and the qualia structure of β, QS_β, has quale, q of type a, then $\alpha\beta$ is of type b, where

$$[\![\alpha\beta]\!] = \beta \cap \alpha(q_\beta).$$

The semantic device giving this interpretation can be seen as treating the adjective as a function and applying it to a particular quale within the N' that it is in composition with. This same interpretive mechanism will now allow us to account for the contextualized senses for evaluative adjectives such as *good*, discussed in chapters 2 and 3, and as used in (67) below.[20]

(67) a good knife: a knife that cuts well

Recall from chapter 6 that the qualia structure for *knife* is that given in (68).

$$(68) \quad \begin{bmatrix} \textbf{knife} \\ \text{ARGSTR} = \begin{bmatrix} \text{ARG1} = \textbf{x:tool} \end{bmatrix} \\ \text{QUALIA} = \begin{bmatrix} \text{FORMAL} = \textbf{x} \\ \text{TELIC} = \textbf{cut(e,x,y)} \end{bmatrix} \end{bmatrix}$$

Since *good* functions as an event predicate, it is able to selectively modify the event description in the TELIC quale of the noun, resulting in the interpretation given in (67).

Finally, consider the selective modification within the NP in sentence (69) below.

(69) a. John bought a long record.

b. a long record: a record whose playing time is long.

Assuming that the qualia structure for *record* is that given in (70) and that the adjective *long* has an interpretation as an event predicate, then the result is a selective interpretation over the TELIC event of "the record playing," as illustrated in (71).

$$(70) \quad \begin{bmatrix} \textbf{record} \\ \text{ARGSTR} = \begin{bmatrix} \text{ARG1} = \textbf{x:physobj} \\ \text{ARG1} = \textbf{y:info} \end{bmatrix} \\ \text{QUALIA} = \begin{bmatrix} \textbf{info·physobj\_lcp} \\ \text{FORMAL} = \textbf{R(x.y)} \\ \text{TELIC} = \textbf{play(e,x.y)} \end{bmatrix} \end{bmatrix}$$

(71) $\lambda x[\ldots Telic = \lambda e[play'(x)(e) \wedge long(e)]\ldots]$

Notice that, because the overall type of the NP does not change as a
result of the selective binding operation, sentences such as (69) are not
typing violations. That is, while the verb *buy* selects for an individual
for its internal argument, the adjective *long* selects for an event. Since
these types are both satisfied, but at different levels in the composition,
the sentence is well-formed.

What these adjectives demonstrate is not a violation or puzzle for
coercion and selection; rather, they serve to illustrate the subselective
binding properties of different classes of adjectives, as modifying different facets or qualia of the head, by virtue of their type. Modification by
an adjective such as *long, fast,* or *bright* , can be seen as event predication, selectively binding the appropriate quale of the head.[21] As we saw
above, the adjectives in these cases modify a distinguished event predicate (i.e., the TELIC quale) associated with the head, *read* for *book,* and
illuminate for *bulb.* Thus, *a long book* is interpreted as one taking a long
time to read, while *a bright bulb* is a bulb which shines brightly when
illuminated. These adjectives can be compared to modifiers such as *expensive* and *opaque* in the NPs in (72), both of which refer to the physical
object rather than an activity or state associated with the object.

(72)   a. an <u>expensive</u> book
       b. an <u>opaque</u> bulb

These adjectives can be seen as modifying the FORMAL role of the qualia
structure for these nouns.

There is another interesting phenomenon that might be explained by
qualia and selective binding mechanisms; namely, polysemous adjectives
such as *old* and *new* as used in *an old friend* and *a new neighbor,* with
the non-intersective interpretation. Representationally, the adjective selectively modifies in a way similar to *fast* and *long* in our analysis above.

(73)   a. an <u>old</u> friend: (a friend for a long time)
       b. $\lambda x \exists y[[Formal = friend(x,y) \wedge [Telic = \lambda e^S[\ friend\_state(e^S,x,y) \wedge long(e^S)\ ]]\ \ldots]$

The adjective *old* in this example is ambiguous between predication of
the individual and that of the friendship itself. The durative reading
faciliated by selective binding in (73a) does not seem to be available,

however, with non-relational nouns such as *movie* and *house*, as illustrated in (74):

(74) a. *an <u>old</u> movie: (one that I have had for a long time)
      b. *an <u>old</u> house: (one that I have had for a long time)

It is not clear whether this is a semantic or pragmatic distinction. While friendship is something that continues, and one can have any number of friendships, possession of a house is typically something that persists uniquely, in successive stages. Hence, the phrase in (74b) does not mean "a house that I've had for a long time," but rather assumes the sense of *previously lived in or owned.* Such an analysis, however, cannot explain why (74a) is not a possible interpretation for a noun such as *movie.*[22] In either case, it is the prepositional phrase *of mine* or the genitive which brings out the internal (i.e., selective) reading which is possible, namely, the sense of *former.*

In this section, I have tried to illustrate some further enrichments to the mechanisms of semantic composition, in order to capture the creative use of adjectives in adjective-noun constructions. The rule of selective binding is, in fact, an instance of a more general mechanism facilitating the selection of substructures through a path of features in the semantic description of a phrase. This is developed more fully in Pustejovsky and Johnston (forthcoming).

7.4   Semantic Selection

As stated in above chapter 4, the goal of lexical semantic theory is to provide the foundation on which projection to syntax can be accomplished. One of the avenues explored in this research is to determine to what extent syntactic behavior can be seen as following from semantic selection, and what is due to constraints on syntactic form. It is not our aim to completely reduce syntactic selection to underlying semantic types, a rather misguided goal in itself, since the semantic types would simply increase in specialization to reflect distinct syntactic patterning. Rather, the goal is to see how the grammar is affected by a specific approach to modeling lexical semantic knowledge. Although many of the problems in mapping semantic forms to syntax are left unanswered here, it is necessary to identify the scope of the changes that result from adopting a generative lexical approach to semantics.

There are two ways in which a generative lexicon as outlined above affects the mapping from lexical semantics to syntax:

(A) There is no one-to-one mapping from underlying semantic types to syntactic representations; rather, a syntactic phrase is only fully interpretable within the specific semantic context within which it is embedded;

(B) Because the representation of semantic information in the qualia structure, argument structure, and extended event structure is richer than what conventional models associate with a word, a more complex model of filtering and checking is necessary for restricting the output to actual syntactic form.

7.4.1   Canonical Syntactic Forms

Given the previous discussion of the mechanics and operation of coercion and other generative devices, what appears obvious is that the semantic type associated with an argument for a verb allows for a multiplicity of syntactic expressions; this forces us to address the issue of what role semantic selection is playing in general in the grammar. The view taken here is that the grammar associates a *canonical* syntactic form with a semantic type, but there are in fact many possible realizations for a type due to the different possibilities available from generative devices such as coercion and co-composition. Our methodology here, however, is to first look for semantic distinguishability between distinct sets of syntactic realizations. If no empirical evidence presents itself suggesting that two lexical items are truly distinguished in their semantic types, then the residual difference between these items is attributable to syntactic distinctions rather than semantic typing.

For an expression of a particular type, there is a unique syntactic realization, which is able to adequately express the semantics of the expression, and which can be seen as the most direct realization of the type, what I will call the *canonical syntactic form* (*csf*). The alternative syntactic forms which are available to an expression are licensed by virtue of principles of semantic "recoverability," such that the information conveyed by the expression whose canonical form is π is also able to be recovered by generative devices in another syntactic realization, π'. The proposal put forth here can be seen as an elaboration and extension of the ideas discussed in Chomsky (1986), where the notion of canonical syntactic realization is introduced.

In previous chapters, I discussed how semantic types can be expressed in the lexicalization process. The *lexical conceptual paradigm (lcp)* can be seen as the lexicalization of a number of distinct semantic types into one lexical form. The semantic type which results is a dot object, and the lcp itself is the type cluster of the individual types together with the dot object. The syntactic realizations for a semantic type are in part determined by virtue of the semantic type. Hence the form will exhibit the behavior of each type it is composed of in addition to the unique behavior of the dot object. The set of phrasal alternations associated with a semantic type is similar in nature to an lcp, in that they are determined by virtue of the semantic type. Unlike the lcp, however, which can be seen as taking a number of types and fusing them into a lexical item, the mapping from a single semantic type to syntactic forms is a one-to-many relation. What determines this mapping is the manner in which the generative devices are allowed to transform one semantic type into another, under a set of specified constraints.

Factors that are outside of the realm of the syntax-to-semantic mapping might restrict an otherwise legitimate set of mappings or syntactic possibilities. As we shall see in chapter 8, an lcp may not necessarily exist as a unique lexicalization, but may be distributed across several lexical entries. The lcp itself as a conceptual relation may exist, but logical polysemy in a single lexical item would not occur for that concept in this language. For example, while the noun *newspaper* is logically polysemous between the organization and the printed information-containing object, the noun *book* refers only to the latter, while the noun *author* makes reference to the "producer" of the book.

In what follows, I will discuss two examples of how the semantics of a lexical item is able to determine the resulting syntactic forms possible for complements to that item. The cases I wish to examine include selectional distinctions between the following two minimal pairs:

(75) a. the verbs *like* and *enjoy*;
　　 b. the interrogative selecting verbs *ask* and *wonder*.

What emerges from this discussion is that semantic selection can in fact be a good indicator of the syntactic behavior of a lexical item, but only when viewed together with the generative operations that connect the distinct syntactic forms for a particular semantic type.

Let us assume that, for any semantic type, τ, there is a unique *canonical syntactic form (csf)* that expresses this type as a syntactic object, X^i. Expressed as a function, *csf* can be viewed as that unique mapping from semantic types to syntactic forms, *csf*: $\tau \rightarrow X^i$, such that:

(76) For every type τ in the set of semantic types, there is a function, *canonical syntactic form (csf)*, such that $csf(\tau) = X^i$, except for
a. when $\tau = \top$, or
b. when $\tau = \bot$,
in which case *csf* is undefined.

A syntactic expression, Y^j, of type σ (where $csf(\sigma) = Y^j$), is substitutable for the *csf* of a type τ only if this type is fully recoverable from licensed semantic operations on σ.

For example, assume a verb is typed for selecting an argument of type τ, where $csf(\tau) = X^i$. The direct realization of this type as X^i is well-formed, assuming surface constraints are satisfied in the syntax; that is, $[V \ X^i \ ...]$ is a legitimate structure. Now consider the same verb appearing together with a syntactic phrase Y^j, of type σ_2; i.e., $[V \ Y^j \ ...]$. From what we have said above, this structure is well-formed only if τ is fully recoverable from σ_2. This is illustrated in (77) below.

(77)

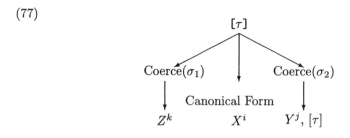

The resulting set of syntactic forms associated with a particular semantic type will be called a *phrasal paradigm*.[23] The operations ensuring recoverability on the semantic type in this case are exactly the generative devices introduced earlier in this chapter; namely, type coercion, selective binding, and co-composition. It should be pointed out that the overall enterprise of establishing a lexicon operating along the principles outlined in this work are to some extent independent of the success or failure of semantic selection determining syntactic behavior.

Let us turn now to specific examples illustrating this mechanism, beginning with the classic subcategorization differences between the verbs *enjoy* and *like*. Observe in (78) and (79) how these verbs differ in their complement selection behavior:

(78) a. Mary likes to watch movies.
     b. Mary likes watching movies.
     c. Mary likes movies.
     d. Mary likes (for) John to watch movies with her.
     e. Mary likes that John watches movies with her.
     f. Mary likes it that John watches movies with her.

(79) a. Mary enjoys watching movies.
     b. Mary enjoys movies.

The syntactic differences between these and other verbs are typically used as counterexamples to strong views of the semantic selection hypotheses (as held by Lakoff, 1971, Dixon, 1984, Wierzbicka, 1988, Chomsky, 1986). The discussion from the early literature on these differences were suggestive, but not conclusive of a real semantic type distinction. This was due, in part, to the lack of a sufficiently rich type system that was both linguistically motivated as well as formally characterized. Viewed within the current enterprise, however, there are diagnostics indicating that the semantics of these verbs are in fact distinguished by the type of complement each selects. Notice the distinction between these two verbs that emerges in the following discourse. Imagine that two roommates are discussing a chair in their apartment; speaker A utters sentence (80) to B, who in turn responds with sentence (81).

(80) I want to get rid of this chair.

(81) But I <u>like</u> that chair!

The statement made by B in (81) is difficult for A to question, since the questioner is not privy to the attitudes of the hearer, only to his or her actions. By uttering (81), B does not express any articulated attitude towards the object, although more explicit attitudes do exist. Consider now an alternate response to (80), that given in (82):

(82) But I <u>enjoy</u> that chair!

Sentence (82) expresses a very different relation with respect to the complement. In this case, the proposition is readily verifiable, since it says of an object, that the speaker stands in a relation of performing some activity with the object; as such, (82) can be doubted, questioned, or denied, since the judgment relies on the person's observable behaviors, entailed by the semantics of the selectional properties of the verb. Hence, (83) is a legitimate response for A to make for (82) but not for (81).

(83) But you never use it!

The distinction here is not just a pragmatic one, but is due to the underlyingly distinct types selected for by these verbs. Namely, the verb *enjoy* selects an event function, while *like* selects for an attitude towards any type, which I represent simply as the top most type available to interpretation, i.e., ⊤. This would include the semantic types `event`, `prop`, `property`, `ind`, and `factive`. These are shown with their respective canonical syntactic forms in (84).

(84)

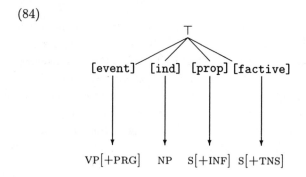

Because the verb *like* selects for ⊤, it has no unique *csf*. In fact, a unique *csf* exists only if there is a unique least upper bound in the type lattice.

Notice from the figure that there is still only one canonical syntactic form given for the proposition even though full sentential infinitival and PRO-form infinitivals are often considered in free variation, and constrained due to binding constraints. What this states is that PRO interpretation might be usefully associated with a coerced form of the complement. In (85), the two verbs are compared, where their syntactic behaviors are associated with distinct semantic typings:

(85)

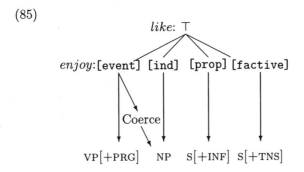

What this illustrates is how coercion, for example, operates under constraints to give the appearance of verbal polymorphism. The important thing to note from the previous discussion is that all and only those syntactic forms appear as complements to a verb for which there exists a legitimate path of coercion from their base semantic type.

Let us turn now to our second minimal pair illustrating the nature of the semantic selection relation, namely, the problem of interrogative complementation. In Chomsky (1986), continuing a discussion from Grimshaw (1979, 1981) and Pesetsky (1982), the idea of semantic selection is discussed in relation to interrogative complements and the problem of concealed questions. Observe the difference in selectional properties illustrated between (86) and (87)–(88) below.

(86) a. John asked me <u>what the temperature was</u>.
      b. John asked me <u>the temperature</u>.

(87) a. John wondered <u>what the temperature was</u>.
      b. *John wondered <u>the temperature</u>.

(88) a. John didn't care <u>what the temperature was</u>.
      b. *John didn't care <u>the temperature</u>.

The inability of the verbs *wonder* and *care* to take the NP form of the concealed question interpretation is attributed by Pesetsky (1982) to the absence of case assigned by these two verbs rather than to an underlying semantic distinction between the complements of *ask* versus *wonder* and *care*. The strategy employed in this work, however, is to assume that differences in syntactic expressibility should be first attributed to a semantic distinction in the verbs.[24]

The difference would appear to be that *ask* selects for a true interrogative (interpreted as a set of propositions), while *wonder* selects for an attitude towards a set of propositions. Even with this discussion, it might be argued that such a finely-articulated distinction between *ask* and *wonder* is not something that should be encoded in the semantics typing of the complements, since such a difference could not possibly be learned by the child in linguistic experience. Interestingly, such semantic distinctions seem to be more difficult for children to acquire, and the failure to make these subtle semantic differences is accompanied by a systematic misuse of the complement patterns associated with these verbs (cf. Pinker, 1984, 1989). If that is possible to maintain, then it is interesting to speculate that the semantic differences are motivated and furthermore obviate the case theory analysis for this example. The syntactic consequence of such a semantic split might be reflected in distinct tendencies towards transitivity, but that too would be as a result of the semantic typing.

What would the semantic types of these two verbs need to be, in order to give rise to both the appropriately fine-tuned interpretations mentioned above, as well as the syntactic forms possible for their complement position? Exactly that distinction made above; namely, *wonder* takes as its complement an attitude towards a question, while *ask* selects a question directly. Some useful work towards characterizing this distinction has already been made by Groenendijk and Stokhof (1989), who distinguish between *know* and *wonder* as *extensional* and *intensional* complement interrogatives, respectively.[25] Assume that semantic selection assigns the internal argument of *ask* the type `question`, which is a shorthand for the type `<s,t>`, where an interrogative is seen as a function from worlds to answers. Following the observations made in Groenendijk and Stokhof (1989) and others, let the type selected for by *wonder* be `<int,question>`, simply the intension of the type assigned to the complement of *ask*. This distinction turns out to have consequences for the syntactic complementation pattern for each verb, as we see below. The tree in (89) gives the two semantic types associated with the interrogative argument of the verbs *ask* and *wonder* along with their canonical and non-canonical syntactic forms.

(89)

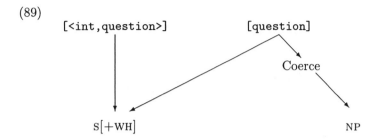

It is possible that the subtleties of such distinctions are not really appreciated or recognizable until larger segments (or units) of analysis in the language are investigated, such as the way these verbs are embedded in a particular discourse and context. This does not mean, however, that the information is not lexically encoded into distinct semantic types for the complements.

The NP complementation pattern for verbs like *ask* illustrates two aspect of the approach outlined here:

A. the ability of the verb to coerce its complement;

B. the ability of the complement to *metonymically reconstruct* the required coercing type from the semantic structure within the complement.

Without detailing the mechanisms behind these shifts in other classes, it is worth briefly looking at what the range of complementation patterns is for a small number of verbs, where the phrasal paradigm associated with each verb below is illustrative of a distinct semantic type

(90) LIKE-class: (*like, hate, prefer*)
    a. John would <u>hate</u> Bill to leave.
    b. John <u>hates</u> (it) that Bill left.
    c. John <u>hated</u> to lose the game.
    d. John <u>hated</u> losing the game.
    e. John <u>hated</u> that he lost the game.

(91) WAGER-class: (*wager, bet*)
    a. *John <u>wagered</u> Bill to have left.

b. John <u>wagered</u> that Bill left.

c. *John <u>wagered</u> to have left.

(92) MAINTAIN-class:

    a. *John <u>maintained</u> Bill to have left.

    b. John <u>maintained</u> (for a year) that Bill left.

    c. *John <u>maintained</u> to have left.

(93) TRY-class: (*try, attempt*)

    a. *John <u>tried</u> Bill to read the book.

    b. *John <u>tried</u> that Bill read the book.

    c. John <u>tried</u> to read the book.

    d. John <u>tried</u> the book.

(94) REMEMBER-class: (*remember, forget*)

    a. John <u>remembered</u> to lock the door.

    b. John <u>remembered</u> that he locked the door.

    c. John <u>remembered</u> locking the door.

    d. John <u>remembered</u> where he put the keys.

    e. John <u>remembered</u> his phone number.

(95) PERSUADE-class: (PERSUADE, CONVINCE)

    a. John <u>convinced</u> Mary to build a house.

    b. John <u>convinced</u> Mary that she should build a house.

    c. John <u>convinced</u> Mary that she had built a house.

From our previous discussion, it follows that the broader the selectional possibilities for a verb, the more general is the semantic type associated with the complement. We saw above that the verb *like* selects for the type $\top$, for which there is no specific *canonical syntactic form* (*csf*), but it is associated with the csfs for its immediate subtypes; hence, indirectly, it behaves as though it has several *csfs*, along with the derived syntactic expressions within the phrasal paradigm for each type. The verbs *forget* and *remember* select very generally for a factive interpretation of any type.

8 The Semantics of Nominals

8.1 Basic Issues

In this chapter, I give a general overview of how a generative lexical theory can contribute towards a classification of the different nominal types. In studying the semantics of nominals, we can distinguish four major areas of concern from the perspective of a lexical semantic theory:

(1) The distinction in complement-taking behavior between nouns and verbs;

(2) How nominalizations and event-denoting nominals are distinguished from their corresponding verbal representations and the events they denote: that is, what is the difference between an event represented as a sentence, and an event represented as an NP? And likewise, for facts and propositions, represented as sentences and NPs.

(3) The representation of logical polysemy in nominals, such as *window*, *record*, *book*, and how these implicitly relational nominals differ from relational nominals;

(4) How the semantics of nominals facilitates the richer compositional interpretation required for characterizing natural language semantics as polymorphic; that is, what allows for co-compositional interpretation in natural language?

The first two issues are of course related, and I will argue that they cannot be addressed independently of each other. Furthermore, a formal distinction in how nominals and verbs refer to event descriptions is necessary to show how the grammaticalization of events differs in these two syntactic domains. This is presented in 8.3 and 8.4. The third point was addressed in part in chapter 6, but many questions remain regarding the descriptive power and the exact nature of dot objects and how argument and event parameters interact in the qualia expressions. These issues are discussed below in 8.1 and 8.2, where I distinguish between *unified types* and *dotted types*. The former are a more formal interpretation of the orthogonal types of Pustejovsky and Boguraev (1993), incorporating the structures employed in Copestake (1992) and Copestake *et al.* (1993).

The last point above was touched on briefly in chapter 7, and will be the subject of later discussion. This concerns the exact manner in which coercion and co-composition rules makes use of qualia-based information.

The variation in the expression of complements between nouns and verbs has long been a major concern to linguists, and has motivated many of the shifts in the theory of grammar. We will not be able to address this issue until we have explored in somewhat more detail the semantics of nominals from a GL perspective.

As mentioned in chapter 6, for any category we can potentially distinguish three distinct dimensions along which the elements of that category can be analyzed semantically. With respect to nouns, the interpretation can vary according to the three dimensions below:

(A) ARGUMENT STRUCTURE: How many arguments the nominal takes; what they are typed as; whether they are simple, unified, or complex types.

(B) EVENT STRUCTURE: What events the nominal refers to, both explicitly and implicitly.

(C) QUALIA STRUCTURE: What the basic predicative force of the nominal is, and what relational information is associated with the nominal, both explicitly and implicitly.

The manner in which these three representational levels can help us classify the semantics and associated behavior of the different nominal types will become clear in the subsequent sections.

8.2   Nominals with Unified Types

For purposes of lexical representation, it is often necessary to allow a lexical item, making reference to a type in a lattice, to be able to inherit from multiple parents. For some conceptual structures and their associated lexicalizations, we will also need to employ a scheme allowing multiple inheritance. This has been explored in a generative lexicon to some extent in Pustejovsky and Boguraev (1993) and more generally in Copestake (1992) and Copestake et al. (1993). Previous attempts at structuring conceptual hierarchies (whether explicitly language related or not) have made heavy use of multiple inheritance, as systems have to grapple with accounting for the fact that, according to particular lexical-conceptual projections, biased by a variety of context factors, different aspects of objects become more or less prominent as context varies. Thus, as illustrated below, a "book" is_a "information," as well as a "physical_object; a "dictionary" is_a "physical_object," as well as "reference"; a "car" is_a both "vehicle" and an "artifact," and so forth. The conventional view on these sorts of inheritance relations is shown in the figure below.

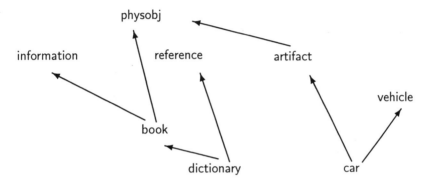

Figure 8.1
Conventional Representation of Inheritance Relations

Still, as descriptive as such relations may appear, models like these suffer from a very limited notion of lexical structure; one particular consequence of this is the ambiguity of class membership (or, in our terminology, 'hidden' lexical ambiguity). Thus, even though elaborate mechanisms have been proposed to control and limit the flow of information along the generalization/specialization links, there has been no theory to either (a) explain how to assign structure to lexical items, or (b) specify lexical relations between lexical items in terms of links between only certain aspects of their respective lexical structures. The approach presented here, with its several distinct levels of semantic description, and in particular the qualia structure, are relevant to just this issue.

On this view, a lexical item inherits information according to the qualia structure it carries. In this way, the different senses for words can be rooted into suitable, but orthogonal lattices. To illustrate this point, consider the two is_a relations below, and the differences in what relations the objects enter into.

	play is_a book	dictionary is_a book
read	ok	no
buy	ok	ok
consult	no	ok
begin	ok	no

Figure 8.2
Table of is-a relations

This table illustrates a serious problem with most current inheritance systems for lexical knowledge. Namely, although it might seem reasonable to think of both plays and dictionaries as "books," they behave very differently in terms of how they are selected by different relations. This suggests that a single lattice for inheritance is inadequate for capturing the different dimensions of meaning for lexical items.

In Pustejovsky and Boguraev (1993), a proposal is made in regards to the structure of Lexical Inheritance Theory, and the need for typed inheritance for lexical information. The proposal, although not fully formalized there, was to posit a separate lattice per role in the qualia structure. Briefly, inheritance through qualia amounts to the following relations for this example:

(1) a. book is_formal phys-object
     b. book is_telic information
     c. book is_agent information
     d. dictionary is_formal book
     e. dictionary is_telic reference
     f. dictionary is_agent compiled-material
     g. play is_agent literature
     h. play is_telic book

The different inheritance structures just mentioned can be illustrated by the diagram below.

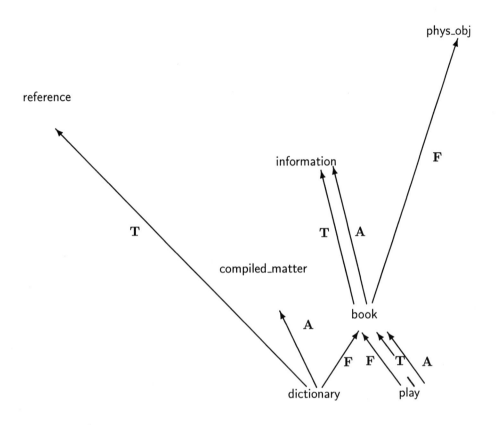

The qualia roles differentiate the lattice structures resulting in a *typed inheritance*, excluding the unwanted inferences listed above, and allowing only the desired ones.[1]

Let us now integrate this perspective into the typing system outlined in previous chapters. In Carpenter (1992), type unification is defined as the unique greatest lower bound, *glb*, for two types σ_1 and σ_2, i.e., $\sigma_1 \sqcap \sigma_2$. This will allow us to define those objects which are non-polysemous, yet do involve the logical conjunction of their types. For this reason, I will refer to these objects as *unified types*.

To illustrate the formal properties of nominals with unified types, consider the following examples. A type lattice provides the essential characteristics of a concept as a type in a hierarchy. Orthogonal inheritance arises not from the multiple assignment of essential typing of an object but from constraints on functional information about the object supplied by the qualia. The type hierarchy should be so constrained as to allow only orthogonal types to be unifiable (i.e., distinct qualia types); in other words, different qualia may unify to form a unified type, if the qualia unification is well-formed.

For example, given two orthogonal types σ and τ with qualia structures (2a) and (2b),

(2)   a. $\sigma = [_\sigma \ldots [Q_T = \alpha\,]]$
      b. $\tau = [_\tau \ldots [Q_A = \beta\,]]$

they may unify, $\sigma \sqcap \tau$, to form the unified type σ_τ, with the resulting qualia structure given in (3):

$$(3) \quad \begin{bmatrix} \sigma\_\tau \\ \text{QUALIA} = \begin{bmatrix} \text{TELIC} = \alpha \\ \text{AGENTIVE} = \beta \end{bmatrix} \end{bmatrix}$$

The creation of a concept (i.e., type) that refers both to a physical object and a proposition, however, is *not* a possible unified type, since the FORMAL qualia values for the two concepts are not unifiable. The ability to construct types that are otherwise outside of the set of unifiable types is something enabled by the construction of dot objects with the *lcp* type constructor, mentioned in 6.2, and discussed below.

Let us look at a few examples of unified types to illustrate what role the qualia are playing in supplying orthogonal dimensions of an object's denotation. Consider first the nominal *food*. As mentioned in chapter 6, the TELIC role specifies for a given concept its use or function; for *food* this value is the activity of *eating*. The construction of the type associated with food arises from a qualia-based constraint on the type physobj that it be edible.

$$(4) \quad \begin{bmatrix} \textbf{food} \\ \text{ARGSTR} = \begin{bmatrix} \text{ARG1} = \textbf{x:physobj} \end{bmatrix} \\ \text{QUALIA} = \begin{bmatrix} \text{FORMAL} = \textbf{x} \\ \text{TELIC} = \textbf{eat}(e^P,\textbf{y},\textbf{x}) \end{bmatrix} \end{bmatrix}$$

Similarly, the semantics for an artifactual object states minimally that it is something that was created, made, manufactured, or brought about by some human activity. The value of the AGENTIVE role for the type physobj indicates just this relation to the object, as shown in (5), where top is the top-level type in the lattice, as defined above in Section 7.4.1.

$$(5) \quad \begin{bmatrix} \textbf{artifact} \\ \text{ARGSTR} = \begin{bmatrix} \text{ARG1} = \textbf{x:top} \\ \text{D-ARG1} = \textbf{y:human} \end{bmatrix} \\ \text{QUALIA} = \begin{bmatrix} \text{FORMAL} = \textbf{x} \\ \text{TELIC} = \textbf{make}(\textbf{e}^T,\textbf{y},\textbf{x}) \end{bmatrix} \end{bmatrix}$$

This representation says nothing about the nature of the object except that it is human derived. That is, as an artifact, it could be a social construct, a verbal act, a physical object, and so on. Given the under-specified representation in (5) regarding what an artifact *is*, as opposed to how it came about, we can further restrict the type which partici-pates in the qualia relation, effectively *unifying* a subtype with the qualia structure for the concept `artifact`. For example, to represent artifacts that are physical objects, we would like a type which combines both the FORMAL value of a `physobj` and the AGENTIVE value of an `artifact`. Because we are treating the argument and the qualia relation both as types to be unified, it is possible to view the resulting lexical represen-tation as a *unified type*, effectively arriving at a type structure similar to Copestake's (1992) treatment of greatest lower bound types. The resulting qualia structure is shown in (6) below.

$$(6) \quad \begin{bmatrix} \textbf{phys\_artifact} \\ \text{ARGSTR} = \begin{bmatrix} \text{ARG1} = \textbf{x:physobj} \\ \text{D-ARG1} = \textbf{y:human} \end{bmatrix} \\ \text{QUALIA} = \begin{bmatrix} \text{FORMAL} = \textbf{x} \\ \text{AGENTIVE} = \textbf{make}(\textbf{e}^T,\textbf{y},\textbf{x}) \end{bmatrix} \end{bmatrix}$$

Another example of how the types instantiated as qualia structures can be unified to form new unified types is illustrated with the concepts of `tool` and artifactual `tool`. As discussed in chapter 6, a tool is simply defined as an object which has a TELIC value indicating a *purpose telic* rather than a *direct telic*. That is, the predicative argument is the first argument in the TELIC relation. Hence, for a word α, defining a TELIC value essentially classifies it as something that has a use;

$$(7) \quad \begin{bmatrix} \alpha \\ \text{ARGSTR} = \begin{bmatrix} \text{ARG1} = \textbf{x:top} \end{bmatrix} \\ \text{QUALIA} = \begin{bmatrix} \text{FORMAL} = \textbf{x} \\ \text{TELIC} = \textbf{R}(\textbf{e},\textbf{x},\textbf{y}) \end{bmatrix} \end{bmatrix}$$

Here again, this says simply that the object is usable in a certain capacity (i.e., TELIC), and says nothing about how it came about (i.e, AGENTIVE),

or what its basic type is, i.e., its FORMAL role. Hence, it could refer to
a naturally occurring object being used as a tool, or to a rhetorical
device used as a tool of persuasion. Restricting the nature of this object
to be both an `artifact` and a `tool`, however, creates a unified type,
`artifact_tool`, which is represented as in (8).

$$(8)\quad \begin{bmatrix} \alpha \\ \text{ARGSTR} = \begin{bmatrix} \text{ARG1} = \textbf{x:top} \\ \text{D-ARG1} = \textbf{y:human} \end{bmatrix} \\ \text{QUALIA} = \begin{bmatrix} \text{FORMAL} = \textbf{x} \\ \text{TELIC} = \textbf{R(e,x,y)} \\ \text{AGENTIVE} = \textbf{make(e}^T\textbf{,y,x)} \end{bmatrix} \end{bmatrix}$$

Nouns such as *knife*, discussed in 6.3 above, illustrate this operation
of type unification very clearly. Observe that the AGENTIVE value need
not be specified locally for *knife*, since lexical inheritance through the
FORMAL value will bind the AGENTIVE to the value inherited from the
type `artifact_tool`.

$$(9)\quad \begin{bmatrix} \textbf{knife} \\ \text{ARGSTR} = \begin{bmatrix} \text{ARG1} = \textbf{x:artifact\_tool} \\ \text{D-ARG1} = \textbf{y:physobj} \end{bmatrix} \\ \text{QUALIA} = \begin{bmatrix} \text{FORMAL} = \textbf{x} \\ \text{TELIC} = \textbf{cut(e,x,y)} \end{bmatrix} \end{bmatrix}$$

A look at the type lattice which results from such constructions illustrates the process of type unification, where unlabeled edges denote the
FORMAL quale.

(10)

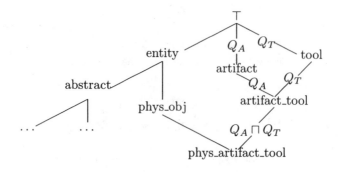

8.3   Nominals with Complex Types

Having discussed the properties of unified types, we turn now to the more complex structure associated with dot objects, first discussed in chapters 6 and 7. With the help of dotted types and qualia structure, we can analyze the inherently *relational* aspect of certain nominals without having to treat them as overtly relational in denotation. The dot object is a type which necessarily incorporates the meanings (i.e., types) of its simple types into the complex object. The examples I have used throughout this work have included nouns such as *book*, *door*, and *novel*. The manner in which such nouns are relational is expressed in the FORMAL quale, as outlined in 6.2. For the noun *book*, for example, a relation specifying a particular containment relation between an individual physical object and information is explicitly part of the make up of the noun's FORMAL role, as repeated below:

$$
(11) \quad
\begin{bmatrix}
\alpha \\
\text{ARGSTR} = \begin{bmatrix} \text{ARG1} = \mathbf{x}{:}\tau_1 \\ \text{ARG2} = \mathbf{y}{:}\tau_2 \end{bmatrix} \\
\text{QUALIA} = \begin{bmatrix} \tau_1 \cdot \tau_2\_\mathbf{lcp} \\ \text{FORMAL} = \mathbf{R(y,x)} \end{bmatrix}
\end{bmatrix}
$$

The predicative property of *book*, as discussed in chapter 6, is given by its type as a dot object. Hence, we can view the FORMAL quale here as the head or *predicative* qualia role in this structure, giving the equivalent representation in (12):

(12) $[\text{FORMAL} = x.y : R(x,y)]$

This is, in turn, translatable as the expression in (13) below:

(13) $\lambda x.y \exists R[book(x.y) \wedge \text{FORMAL} = R(x,y)\ldots]$

Notice that we have constructed a type $x.y$ in (13) above without concern for how it is related by subtyping in the lattice. Because of the qualia-based relation between the types in the FORMAL role of the object, there is no way of exhaustively defining the behavior or characteristics of the dot type in terms of the type lattice alone. We can, however, provide for a partial characterization of the type for purposes of type selection within the grammar. Namely, we need a mechanism for allowing an object $\alpha \cdot \beta$ to be selected in an environment less specific than either of its dot elements, α or β. I will call this particular coercion rule *Dot Object Subtyping*, $\Theta^{\cdot}$, and define it below.

(14)   DOT OBJECT SUBTYPING:

$$\frac{\gamma : \sigma_1 \cdot \sigma_2, \quad \Theta^{\cdot}[\sigma_1 \leq \tau, \sigma_2 \leq \tau] : \sigma_1 \cdot \sigma_2 \to \tau}{\Theta^{\cdot}[\sigma_1 \leq \tau, \sigma_2 \leq \tau](\gamma) : \tau}$$

This states that, given an expression γ of type $\sigma_1 \cdot \sigma_2$, which is a dot object, there is a subtyping relation possible between the dot object and a type τ, just in case τ is the least upper bound of both of the dot elements, σ_1 and σ_2; coercion furthermore allows the dot object to pass in an environment normally typed for τ.

To illustrate the utility of this operation, we need only recall the selectional properties of the verb *like*. By expressing a specific attitude towards a dot object such as a book, we do not commit ourselves to what specific aspect of the book causes me to like it. It might simply be its "bookness," independent of what information it contains (a dot element), what it looks like (another dot element), what I can do to it (a true coercion), and so on. In fact, the generic nature of the statement in (15a) suggests that it cannot be associated with any specific single process of reading or writing, since that would not entail a generic interpretation.

(15)   a. Mary likes the book.
       b. Mary liked the book.

(16)   a. ?Mary enjoys the book.
       b. Mary enjoyed the book.

This also explains why a generic interpretation for (16a) is only possible with an iterative telic event reading (i.e., every time Mary read that book, she enjoyed it). As argued in previous discussion, *enjoy* semantically selects for an event function and coerces its complement, if the appropriate type is not present.

The application of the dot object subtyping rule above to the type of *book* is illustrated in (18) below. Assume that book is a species of "printed material," associated with the type print_matter. Then, the lexical conceptual paradigm for this dot object is given in (17) below.

(17) print_matter_lcp = {physobj.info, physobj, info}

(18) a. Θ[physobj≤ T] :physobj→ T
      b. Θ[info≤ T] :info→ T
      c. Θ'[physobj≤ T,info≤ T] :physobj.info→ T

Hence, the type restriction for the complement position of *like* is satisfied by direct subtyping, as illustrated in (19).

(19)

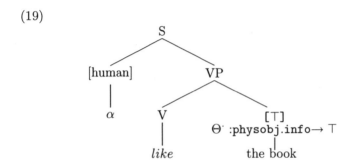

Now let us turn to how nominals denoting dot objects are different from relational nominals, such as *father* and *sister*. In chapter 6, I discussed simple and complex typed nominals, where the form of the qualia structure determined the general class of nominal a lexical item denotes. Hence, along the FORMAL dimension alone, we can distinguish between simple natural kind terms such as *rock* and *man*, as well as simple typed artifacts, such as *knife*, and complex typed nominals such as *book* and *record*. In spite of this difference in typing, however, all these noun classes are *predicative* nominals. The manner in which predicative nouns differ from nominals that are overtly relational in nature, such as *brother*, *sister*, and *neighbor*, must still be addressed. As discussed above in chapter 2, a relational noun denotes a set of individuals standing in relation to at least one other individual in a specific way.

(20) a. John's neighbor is visiting.
      b. Mary's brothers came home together.

In (20b), *Mary* stands in a particular relation to the head *brother*, which is given directly in the semantics of the noun's FORMAL role:

$$(21) \quad \begin{bmatrix} \textbf{brother} \\ \text{ARGSTR} = \begin{bmatrix} \text{ARG1} = \textbf{x:human} \\ \text{D-ARG1} = \textbf{y:human} \end{bmatrix} \\ \text{QUALIA} = \begin{bmatrix} \text{CONST} = \textbf{male(x)} \\ \text{FORMAL} = \textbf{brother\_of(x,y)} \end{bmatrix} \end{bmatrix}$$

The conditions under which the argument y is existentially closed or
bound to a constant are discussed in Eschenbach (1993) and elsewhere
(cf. Bierwisch,1983). The important point to notice about the representation above, however, is how the FORMAL quale differs from the forms
we have examined thus far.[2] That is, unlike a noun such as *cake* or *rock*,
with simple typing and a FORMAL value no different from the typing on
the argument, relational nouns have a "relational representation" in the
FORMAL quale. However, they must be distinguished from the complex
typed nominals such as *book*, which also carry a relational FORMAL value
(cf. (3)):

$$(22) \quad \begin{bmatrix} \alpha \\ \text{ARGSTR} = \begin{bmatrix} \text{ARG1} = \textbf{x:}\tau_1 \\ \text{ARG2} = \textbf{y:}\tau_2 \end{bmatrix} \\ \text{QUALIA} = \begin{bmatrix} \tau_1 \cdot \tau_2\textbf{\_lcp} \\ \text{FORMAL} = \textbf{P(y,x)} \end{bmatrix} \end{bmatrix}$$

The distinction between relational nominals and nouns such as *book* is
due to the latter being typed as dot objects. That is, although the
complex object denoted by *book* is partially defined by a relation in the
FORMAL quale, its actual type is quite distinct from a simple typed
relational nominal such as *brother*. The ability of such a noun to assume
one complex predicative interpretation, or one of two simple predicative
interpretations is what the lcp accomplishes (with the help of coercion
operators). I return to this point in chapters 9 and 10, when discussing
constraints on coercion.

It is perhaps worthwhile at this point to recall what the linguistic
motivation is for the existence of dot objects. There are, I believe, two
major reasons for admitting such objects into our semantics:

(i) SEMANTIC MOTIVATIONS: The knowledge we have of the concepts
    associated with doors, windows, books, computer programs, etc. is
    not characterizable as the conjunction of simple types (or properties)

in a conventional type hierarchy. The predicates and relations for the lexical item associated with such a concept are characteristic of that concept alone. For example, the concepts of "reading" and "writing" are not conceivable without the existence of the concept to which the activity is applied, i.e., the dot object of printed material.

(ii) LEXICAL MOTIVATIONS: The dot object captures a specific type of logical polysemy, one that is not necessarily associated with true complement coercion. There is strong cross-linguistic evidence suggesting that the way such concepts are lexicalized is systematic and predictable.

So far we have focussed our attention on what the dot object is not: it is not a unified type, created from the meet $\sqcap$ on types; nor is it a standard generalization (or join) on types, in the conventional sense of this operation (cf. Morrill, 1994). I have characterized it as a Cartesian type product of n types, with a particularly retricted interpretation. The product $\tau_1 \times \tau_2$, of types τ_1 and τ_2, each denoting sets, is the ordered pair $< t_1, t_2 >$, where $t_1 \in \tau_1$, $t_2 \in \tau_2$. But the pairing alone does not adequately determine the semantics of the dot object; rather, the relation, R, which structures the component types must be seen as part of the definition of the semantics for the lcp type constructor itself. That is, in order for the dot object $\tau_1 \cdot \tau_2$ to be well-formed, there must exist a relation R, that "structures" the elements of τ_1 and τ_2; i.e., $R(t_1, t_2)$. For nouns such as *book* and *record*, the relation R is a subtype of "containment," while for partially event-denoting nouns such as *lunch* and *sonata*, the relation is more complex (cf. 8.5 below).

For now, we might view the set of relations, $\{R_i\}$, as specialized type product operators, where the specific relation is built into the constructor itself:

(23) $\{R_i\} = \cdot_{R_1}, \cdot_{R_2}, \ldots, \cdot_{R_n}$

Then, for a dot object nominal such as *lunch*, which is polysemous between "event" and "food" interpretations (cf. 8.5), the appropriate dot object is that shown in (24).

(24) $\dfrac{lunch : \texttt{event}, \quad lunch : \texttt{food}}{lcp_{R_1}(lunch) : \texttt{event} \cdot \texttt{food}}$

The common noun *lunch* would then have the following interpretation:

(25) $\lambda x.y \exists R_1[lunch(x: \text{event}.y: \text{food}) \wedge \text{FORMAL}= R_1(x,y)\dots]$

With abstraction over tuples such as that in (25), we will need to generalize the semantics of determiners and quantifiers to apply polymorphically to any tuple type. This is discussed more fully in Pustejovsky (1995b), and in some respects, is similar to Morrill's (1994) treatment of parametric polymorphisms.

Given a mechanism for creating types such as dot objects, let us now turn to distinguishing different classes of polysemies for semantically related lexical items. Consider the nouns *book* and *newspaper*, which both refer to the type `print-matter`. This type has the lcp referred to above, repeated here:

(26) `print-matter_lcp = {physobj.info, physobj, info}`

As one would expect with this type, there is a logical polysemy for *newspaper* between the physical object that one purchases, and the information that one generally disbelieves or believes. Consider the sentences in (27), where `New York Times` is a subtype of `newspaper`.

(27) a. Eno the cat is sitting on <u>yesterday's New York Times</u>.
      b. <u>Yesterday's New York Times</u> really got me upset.

In addition to this complex of senses, represented by the dot object shown above, the noun *newspaper* refers logically also to the organization which publishes it, a sense which is unavailable to the noun *book*.

(28) a. <u>The newspaper</u> has just fired its sports editor.
      b. <u>The newspaper</u> is filing suit against the federal government for wire tapping.

(29) a. *<u>The book</u> has raised the price of paperbacks.
      b. *The author is suing <u>the book</u> for breach of contract.

While *newspaper* carries a sense corresponding to the organization which publishes the paper, the noun *book* is unable to denote the publisher of the book in these contexts. A concept such as that denoted by the noun *newspaper* is really a construction from types, one of which is itself a dot object.

(30) `newspaper_lcp = {print-matter.organization,`
    `print-matter, organization}`

As discussed in 8.6 below, whether a language actually *lexicalizes* the dot object represented above in (30) by a single lexical item or not, the concept exists potentially with this structure in the semantic representation for the language. We discuss split lexicalization below in 8.6.

From these considerations, the observation here is that dot objects are constructed in a pair-wise recursive fashion, as illustrated in (31) and (32) below. There may, in fact, turn out to be instances of dot objects that are constructed from three dot elements or more, but this is question open to further investigation.

(31) $$\frac{\alpha : \sigma_1 \quad \alpha : \sigma_2}{lcp_1(\alpha) : \sigma_1 \cdot \sigma_2}$$

(32) $$\frac{\beta : \sigma_3 \quad \beta : \sigma_1 \cdot \sigma_2}{lcp_2(\beta) : \sigma_3 \cdot (\sigma_1 \cdot \sigma_2)}$$

The lattice structure relating the type associated with `newspaper` to that for `print-matter` and `book` is shown in (33).

(33)

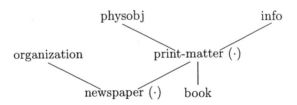

The way in which a noun such as *newspaper* denotes, however, is quite different from that of *book*, due to the type of lcp it belongs to. That is, the qualia structure for *newspaper* is a specialization of the lcp known as **product·producer**, where the AGENTIVE quale makes reference to the dot element denoting the producer, and the FORMAL quale refers to the product; the dot object itself does not appear in the qualia except to define the type itself:

(34)

$$
\begin{bmatrix}
\textbf{newspaper} \\[2pt]
\text{ARGSTR} = \begin{bmatrix} \text{ARG1} = \textbf{x:org} \\ \text{ARG2} = \textbf{y:info·physobj} \end{bmatrix} \\[10pt]
\text{QUALIA} = \begin{bmatrix} \textbf{org·info·physobj\_lcp} \\ \text{FORMAL} = \textbf{y} \\ \text{TELIC} = \textbf{read}(e_2,w,y) \\ \text{AGENT} = \textbf{publish}(e_1,x,y) \end{bmatrix}
\end{bmatrix}
$$

Hence, although *newspaper* is logically polysemous, it can not denote the complete dot object, as can *book*. Rather, one sense or the other is available for interpretation, but not both.[3]

Given this type of representational strategy, one might ask what the appropriate distinction is between nominals such as *book* and *novel*. Although *book* may refer to *novel* in many contexts, the latter is obviously more informative and less extensive in its selectional distribution. They are both dot objects, and in fact, *novel* is arguably a subtype of the dot object *book*. But this subtyping alone does not inform us of what distinguishes these concepts; namely, while a book is possibly an information holder of potentially any type of information, a novel is restricted to a specific structure and form of the information, e.g., a narrative. The relation between these nominals can therefore be characterized as the specialization of one dot element in the dot object. That is, for *book* denoting type `physobj·info`, the dot object associated with *novel* is `physobj·narrative`, where `narrative≤info`. This is illustrated in (35).

(35)

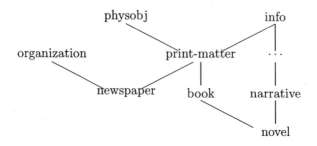

In this section, I have tried to better characterize the behavior and properties of the complex types known as dot objects. There are surely many questions that remain unanswered, but it is clear that the nature of the denotation relation for dot objects is distinct from the unified types presented in 8.2.

8.4   Propositions and Event Descriptions

In order to understand the position taken here with regard to event descriptions and nominalizations, it is necessary to digress briefly about our assumptions regarding the treatment of tense, and the distinction between propositions and events in semantics. I will make some very particular assumptions about the relation between events, propositions, and facts. An untensed utterance such as *Mary build a house* will denote a set of events, and becomes a proposition only by virtue of being "tensed" (cf. Verkuyl, 1993). A fact is a proposition generally judged to be known as true. An unsaturated proposition, typically denoting a propositional function, will be replaced by an *event function*, to be defined below. The way in which a sentence denotes events is distinct from the way NPs are event-denoting. To make this clearer, let us compare the reference to the event of Mary's arriving, expressed as first a sentence in (36a) and as an NP in (36b).

(36)   a. Mary arrived at 3 pm.
       b. Mary's arrival at 3 pm.

Although both (36a) and (36b) ostensibly may refer to the same event, they do not express the same content about this event, since (36a) is an assertion of an event having occurred while (36b) denotes an event without an assertion that it has occurred. In order to make this distinction clearer, we will distinguish the way in which events are quantified as NPs or sentences. In (36a), the event is tensed and thereby interpreted as a proposition. I will argue that only through tensing of an event-selecting predicate can the event in (36b) contribute propositional information;

(37) Mary's arrival was at 3 pm.

Our assumptions regarding the connection between propositions and events is essentially the following: both untensed sentences and NPs may denote event descriptions, but the manner with which they denote is quite different, distinguished by their types. A proposition is seen as the result of applying tense to an event description. To this end, I assume that tense acts as a generalized quantifier over event descriptions, and behaves in many respects similarly to $SPEC$ in an NP structure.

The proper name of an individual object is typically construed as denoting a type e directly. Let the simplest cases of event reference also be an individual, e^σ. Both are types that refer to individuated objects, either spatial (e) or spatio-temporal (e^σ). Consider the proper named event *The Vietnam War* or *Vietnam* as in (38) below.

(38) We will never forget <u>Vietnam</u>.

Just as the proper name Nixon is typed e, and yet is understood to refer to a particular individual, there is no reason for us to treat *Vietnam* any differently, in terms of presupposition or existential closure due to the name alone. Consider the following two sentences.

(39) a. I read a book about <u>Nixon</u>.
      b. I read a book about <u>The Vietnam War</u>.

Since books can be about anything, the preposition *about* obviously selects for a type that covers both e and e^σ. Let us call this type a "general individual," g, where $e \leq g$, $e^\sigma \leq g$. The way *about* predicates is illustrated in (40) below.

(40) $\lambda g \lambda x [about(x, g)](Vietnam_{e^\sigma})$

The type for a quantifier such as *every* or *a* is now represented as shown in (41), where g is the general individual type:

(41) $<<g,t>,<<g,<e^\sigma,t>>,<e^\sigma,t>>>>$

For example, the quantifier *a* will have the following denotation, where $\mathcal{F}$ is a variable of type $<g,<e^\sigma,t>>$.

(42) $[\![a]\!] = \lambda P \lambda \mathcal{F} \lambda e \exists x [P(x) \wedge \mathcal{F}(e, x)]$

The interpretation of NPs such as *a woman* or *a war* as generalized quantifiers is differentiated by a sortal specification on the lambda expression as well as the "predicate" variable, $\mathcal{F}$, as illustrated in (43) and (44) below, where $\mathcal{F}_e$ denotes a sortally specified $<e,<e^\sigma,t>>$-type variable for individuals, and $\mathcal{F}_{e^\sigma}$ is a sortally specified $<e^\sigma,<e^\sigma,t>>$-type variable for events.

(43) $\lambda\mathcal{F}_e\lambda e\exists x[woman(x) \wedge \mathcal{F}_e(e,x)]$

(44) $\lambda\mathcal{F}_{e^\sigma}\lambda e_2\exists e_1[war(e_1) \wedge \mathcal{F}_{e^\sigma}(e_2,e_1)]$

The variable notating a generalized quantifier will remain $\mathcal{P}$, with sortally specified variables for individual-denoting and event-denoting expressions of type $<<e,<e^\sigma,t>>,<e^\sigma,t>>>>$ and $<<e^\sigma,<e^\sigma,t>>,<e^\sigma,t>>>>$, given as $\mathcal{F}_e$ and $\mathcal{F}_{e^\sigma}$, respectively.

Let us analyze what the interpretation of a verb is on this view, and the resulting VP which it projects. The expression in (45a) is the standard lower type functional description of a predicate where the subject applies to it, i.e., $NP'(VP')$; (45b) expresses the higher type functional description, which applies to its subject, i.e., $VP'(NP')$, where $\mathcal{P}$ is the variable for the redefined generalized quantifier mentioned above.

(45) a. $[VP] = \lambda x\lambda e[VP(e,x)]$
       b. $[VP] = \lambda\mathcal{P}\mathcal{P}(\lambda x\lambda e[VP(e,x)])$

Now let us examine the role that tense plays in creating a propositional reading. In fact, the relation is more abstract than tense, since in some languages, aspect is primary and tense secondary. Given the tense/aspect system of a language, it is the presence of the tense/aspect marker that anchors the proposition. Since the examples in this section are in English, in which tense is the relevant marker, I will refer to "tense" through the rest of this discussion, but understand that this is meant for expository purposes only, and is not meant to be a substantive claim about how other languages utilize tense as opposed to aspect (cf. Comrie, 1976,1980).

Assume that tense is treated as a function over event descriptions, $\mathcal{E}$, which are of type $<e^\sigma,t>$, and is itself of type $<<e^\sigma,t>,t>$. The anchoring relation *anch* embeds an event within an interval structure, as explored in Verkuyl (1993) and Kamp and Reyle (1993) (cf. also Enç, 1983).

(46) $[Tns_\alpha] = \lambda\mathcal{E}\exists i\exists e[\alpha(i,n) \wedge anch(i,e) \wedge \mathcal{E}(e)]$

To illustrate how these changes bring out the distinction between event descriptions in NPs and those at the sentence level, let us look at the difference between the interpretations of the sentences in (47a) and (47b).

(47) a. A man <u>arrived</u> yesterday.
      b. A man's <u>arrival</u> occurred yesterday.

Let us assume that the denotations for the basic tenses in English are as given in (48), where n is the *now* operator as used in Kamp (1979) and Kamp and Reyle (1993).

(48) a. $[\![PAST]\!] = \lambda \mathcal{E} \exists i \exists e [i \leq n \wedge anch(i, e) \wedge \mathcal{E}(e)]$
      b. $[\![FUT]\!] = \lambda \mathcal{E} \exists i \exists e [n \leq i \wedge anch(i, e) \wedge \mathcal{E}(e)]$
      c. $[\![PRES]\!] = \lambda \mathcal{E} \exists i \exists e [n \subseteq i \wedge anch(i, e) \wedge \mathcal{E}(e)]$

Assume that the underlying lexical representation for the verb *arrive* is that given in (49), where: the event structure shows it to be a lexically specified telic right-headed event, i.e., an achievement; the argument structure specifies a single argument and a default argument of the location achieved.

$$(49) \begin{bmatrix} \textbf{arrive} \\ \text{ARGSTR} = \begin{bmatrix} \text{ARG}_1 = \textbf{x:ind} \\ \text{D-ARG}_1 = \textbf{y:location} \end{bmatrix} \\ \text{EVENTSTR} = \begin{bmatrix} \text{E}_1 = \textbf{e}_1\textbf{:process} \\ \text{E}_2 = \textbf{e}_2\textbf{:state} \\ \text{RESTR} = <_\propto \\ \text{HEAD} = \textbf{e}_2 \end{bmatrix} \\ \text{QUALIA} = \begin{bmatrix} \text{FORMAL} = \textbf{at(e}_2\textbf{,x,y)} \\ \text{AGENTIVE} = \textbf{arrive\_act(e}_1\textbf{,x)} \end{bmatrix} \end{bmatrix}$$

Because of event headedness, the right subevent is prominent, and the projection to syntax is mediated through those qualia making reference to that subevent, in this case the FORMAL role. Hence, this expression reduces to the lexical forms shown in (50) below, where $\exists y$:loc is a restricted quantification over locations.

(50) a. $\lambda x \lambda e \exists y$:$\text{loc}[arrive(e, x, y)]$
      b. $\lambda \mathcal{P} \mathcal{P}(\lambda x \lambda e \exists y$:$\text{loc}[arrive(e, x, y)])$

The semantic type of the unsaturated VP associated with the sentence in (47a) is an eventual function, $<e, \mathcal{E}>$, which is equivalent to the type <ind,<event,prop>> shown below.

(51)

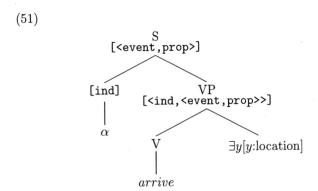

The denotation for the subject NP, *a man*, is the revised generalized quantifier expression, making reference to event descriptions:

(52) $\lambda \mathcal{F}_e \lambda e \exists x[man(x) \wedge \mathcal{F}_e(e, x)]$

Application of the VP to the subject NP results in the event description-denoting sentence denotation, shown in (53) below:

(53) a. $\lambda \mathcal{P} \mathcal{P}(\lambda x \lambda e \exists y: \texttt{loc}[arrive(e, x, y)])(\lambda \mathcal{F} \lambda e \exists x[man(x) \wedge \mathcal{F}(e, x)])$
      b. $\lambda \mathcal{F} \lambda e \exists x[man(x) \wedge \mathcal{F}(e, x)](\lambda x \lambda e \exists y: \texttt{loc}[arrive(e, x, y)])$
      c. $\lambda e \exists x[man(x) \wedge \lambda x \lambda e \exists y: \texttt{loc}[arrive(e, x, y)](e, x)]$
      d. $\lambda e \exists x[man(x) \wedge \exists y: \texttt{loc}[arrive(e, x, y)]]$

Then, given the interpretation of the past tense marker as (54), we arrive at the propositional structure in (55).

(54) $[\![ed]\!] = \lambda \mathcal{E} \exists x \exists e[i \leq n \wedge anch(i, e) \wedge \mathcal{E}(e)]$

(55) a. $\lambda \mathcal{E} \exists i \exists e[i \leq n \wedge anch(i, e) \wedge \mathcal{E}(e)](\lambda e \exists x[man(x) \wedge \exists y: \texttt{loc}[arrive$
      $(e, x, y)]])$
      b. $\exists i \exists e[i \leq n \wedge anch(i, e) \wedge \lambda e \exists x[man(x) \wedge \exists y: \texttt{loc}[arrive(e, x, y)]]$
      $(e)]$
      c. $\exists i \exists e[i \leq n \wedge anch(i, e) \wedge \exists x[man(x) \wedge \exists y: \texttt{loc}[arrive(e, x, y)]]]$

What this illustrates is the functional property of tense, and how it can be viewed as applying to event descriptions (i.e., the denotations of untensed sentences), in a way that is similar to the quantifier within an

NP. That is, both untensed sentences and common event nouns denote event descriptions. As mentioned earlier, *Tense* functions as the specifier of *S*, just as *Det* is the specifier of *NP*.

Now let us see how NPs refer to events in the simplest case. More complicated modes of reference will be considered below and in the next section. Consider a simple event denoting nominal such as *war*, as in the sentence in (56).

(56) A war occurred last year.

I will assume that an NP may denote an event in one of two ways; either it denotes an individual proper name event, such as *Thanksgiving* or *Mardi Gras*, of type e^σ; or it denotes a quantified expression of an event description, such as *every war*, which is of type $<<e^\sigma,t>,<e^\sigma,t>>$, as shown in (57) below.

(57) $[\![every\ war]\!] = \lambda \mathcal{F}_{e^\sigma} \lambda e_1 \exists e_2 [war(e_2) \wedge \mathcal{F}_{e^\sigma}(e_1, e_2)]$

The qualia structure for *war* is shown in (58), where I assume that the logical agent of the activity is the join of the two parties (cf. Link, 1983, Krifka, 1989).

$$
(58)\quad
\begin{bmatrix}
\textbf{war} \\
\text{ARGSTR} = \begin{bmatrix} \text{D-ARG}_1 = \textbf{x:ind} \\ \text{D-ARG}_2 = \textbf{y:ind} \end{bmatrix} \\
\text{EVENTSTR} = \begin{bmatrix} \text{E}_1 = \textbf{e}_1\textbf{:process} \\ \text{HEAD} = \textbf{e}_1 \end{bmatrix} \\
\text{QUALIA} = \begin{bmatrix} \text{AGENTIVE} = \textbf{war\_act}(\textbf{e}_1,\textbf{x}{\oplus}\textbf{y}) \end{bmatrix}
\end{bmatrix}
$$

The basic predicative force of the noun is to denote an event between two individuals, both of which are represented as default arguments, and are optionally expressed in the syntax. They must be logically represented, however, because of the interpretation necessary for NPs such as those in (59).[4]

(59) a. the war between the U.S. and Vietnam
      b. France's war with Russia
      c. the American war with Vietnam

There are, furthermore, other uses of nouns such as *war* where there is an extended sense of *attack* or *assault*, such as *the war on drugs* and *the war on poverty*.

A verb such as *occur*, selecting an event argument, is represented by
the following expression:

(60) $\lambda \mathcal{P}_{e^{\sigma}} \mathcal{P}_{e^{\sigma}} (\lambda e_2 \lambda e_1 [occur(e_1, e_2)])$

The semantic selection on the subject for this verb is similar to the
tree given in (61), where we have simplified the typing for the event
description selected by the verb.

(61)

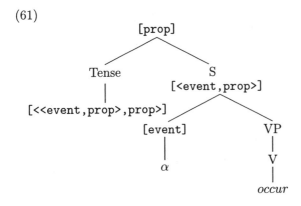

The event description in the subject position is only anchored by virtue
of tensing, which is itself only available by verbal predication. The result,
however, is the same as with a sentential event description, namely a
proposition.

(62) a. $\lambda \mathcal{E} \exists i \exists e_2 [i \leq n \wedge anch(i, e_2) \wedge \mathcal{E}(e_2)](\lambda e \exists e_1 [war(e_1) \wedge$
          $[occur(e, e_1)]])$
      b. $\exists i \exists e_2 [i \leq n \wedge anch(i, e) \wedge \lambda e_3 \exists e_1 [war(e_1) \wedge [occur(e_3, e_1)]](e_2)]$
      c. $\exists i \exists e_2 [i \leq n \wedge anch(i, e_2) \wedge \exists e_1 [war(e_1) \wedge [occur(e_2, e_1)]]]$

In the next section, we will return to the example in (47b) above, repeated below:

(63) A man's <u>arrival</u> occurred yesterday.

First, however, we will need to examine how complex events are constructed with the lcp type constructor into dot objects, the subject of
the next section.

Finally, let us revisit the semantics of true complement coercion involving event selection, in order to examine the role played by the mechanisms introduced here for tense binding into the complement. Recall from 7.4, that sentences such as (64) require coercion on the complement to reconstruct the type selected for by the verb, as well as to provide an appropriate interpretation of the complement.

(64) John enjoyed *War and Peace*.

The complement of *enjoy* is an event description, $<e,\mathcal{E}>$.

(65)

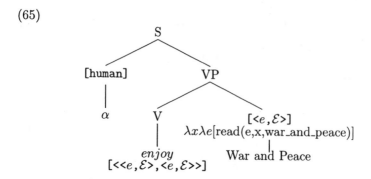

The formal derivation associated with this coercion is shown below.

(66) a. John enjoyed *War and Peace*.
      b. $\lambda e^{T}[\mathbf{enjoy'}(Q_{T}(\mathbf{WP}))(\mathbf{John})(e^{T})] \Rightarrow$
      c. $\lambda e^{T}[\mathbf{enjoy'}(\lambda x, e[read(\mathbf{WP})(x)(e)])(\mathbf{John})(e^{T})] \Rightarrow$
      d. $\mathbf{John}\{\lambda x, e^{T}[\mathbf{enjoy'}(\lambda x, e[read(\mathbf{WP})(x)(e)](x^{*}))(x^{*})(e^{T})]\} \Rightarrow$
      e. $\mathbf{John}\{\lambda x, e^{T}[\mathbf{enjoy'}(\lambda e[read(\mathbf{WP})(x^{*})(e)])(x^{*})(e^{T})]\} \Rightarrow$
      f. $\lambda e^{T}[\mathbf{enjoy'}(\exists e[read(\mathbf{WP})(\mathbf{John})(e)])(\mathbf{John})(e^{T})]$

In this section, I have briefly presented a view of how events and propositions are related through the treatment of tense as a function over event descriptions. Many questions have been left unanswered, such as the relation between events and propositions to facts, as well as further consequences to the analysis of tense as a generalized quantifier. I defer discussion of these issues to Pustejovsky (forthcoming).

8.5   Varieties of Nominalization

In Davidson (1967) and Parsons (1981), the connection between nominalizations and events was explored, and the motivation for adding an event variable to verbs as well as to nouns such as *burning* and *arrival* was supported by inference patterns that mirror the sentential structures associated with such nouns. For example, consider the pair of sentences in (67), where in (67a), two sentences are connected by a temporal connective, while in (67b) a nominalization is predicated in a way that results in a reading similar to (67a).

(67)   a. When wood burns, it requires oxygen.
       b. The burning of wood requires oxygen.

This pair illustrates how *ing*-nominalizations and sentences contribute similar information for purposes of inferences. Davidson's point was to elevate the event to a first-order object in the logic, such that quantification over such objects would be possible with event nominals such as the *ing*-phrase in (67b) above just as it is with sentences as in (67a). Higginbotham (1983, 1985), Verkuyl (1990, 1993) and Grimshaw (1990) extend this notion to the role that event quantification has on the syntax and examine a broad function of nominalization types with respect to event quantification.

One of the remaining difficult questions in event semantics is to formally characterize the linguistic devices which facilitate an interpretation of these sentences as making similar if not identical causal statements. To illustrate this point, consider the sentences in (68).

(68)   a. Charcoal <u>requires</u> oxygen to burn.
       b. The burning of charcoal <u>requires</u> oxygen.
       c. When charcoal burns, it <u>requires</u> oxygen.
       d. Every burning of charcoal <u>requires</u> oxygen.

There are several things to point out about these sentences. First, the quantified expression in (68d) is simply a more explicit wording of what is implicitly stated in (68b) and (68c). Secondly, the statement in (68a) brings out the functional dependency between the subject phrase *charcoal* and the rationale clause *to burn*; namely, that only together with the rationale clause does the subject satisfy the event selecting property of the verb *require*.

Let me illustrate this point with some further data. Observe how *require* is polymorphic in that it selects either for an event directly as subject (cf. (69a)), or allows a split construction with control of an infinitival VP (cf. (69b)).

(69) a. Making this dive <u>requires</u> having both wet and dry suits.
      b. The divers <u>require</u> both wet and dry suits to make this dive.
      c. For the divers to make this dive <u>requires</u> (having) both wet and dry suits.
      d. Making this dive <u>requires</u> the divers to have both wet and dry suits.

Notice how the near synonym *need*, however, does not allow both constructions.

(70) a. *Making this dive <u>needs</u> having both wet and dry suits.
      b. The divers <u>need</u> both wet and dry suits to make this dive.

(71) a. *Animals breathing <u>need</u> oxygen.
      b. Animals <u>need</u> oxygen to breath.
      c. *Every breathing of animals <u>needs</u> oxygen.

While the verb *need* is patterning more like a *want*-verb,[5] *require* seems to relate an event to another event. The verb in these generic propositions can be seen as making reference to a quantification over events or states of affairs, resulting in a meaning like the following, where $\circ$ is temporal overlap as discussed in chapter 5:

(72) $\forall e \forall x \forall l : \text{loc}[burn(e,x) \land at(e,x,l) \rightarrow \exists e'[\circ(e,e') \land at(e',y,l) \land oxygen(y)]$

I am not concerned in this section, however, with justifying the relevance of events—which we have discussed previously in any case—as much as establishing the way that linguistic items make reference to them. To fully understand the contribution made by nominals to causal inference, we must first explain the distinctions in event-denoting types.

We saw from Section 8.5 that simple event-denoting nominals such as *war* have a fairly direct representation in a qualia-based structure. What would the qualia structure and event-denoting properties for a nominal such as *burning* be, such that the readings in (68) could be correlated?

Notice that this is not answered by merely placing a Davidsonian-like event variable in both the nominal and verbal expressions, as in (73).

(73) $\forall e \forall x [burning(e, x) \land wood(x) \rightarrow \exists y[oxygen(y) \land require(x, y)]]$

Regardless of the overall expressiveness of this statement, this move simply ignores the polymorphic behavior of the verb *require* and what it is telling us about the underlying semantics of the sentences in (69) above. Namely, that even when an individual appears in subject position (as in (69b)), the underlying reference that is required by the verb is to an *event description*.

The representation of *ing*-nominals such as *burning* should make reference to the same event description as the verb, while still requiring the expression of the argument, as the ungrammatical forms in (74) suggest.[6]

(74) a. *The burning requires oxygen.
     b. *Burning requires oxygen.

The event description associated with *burning* is illustrated in (75). Notice that the AGENTIVE argument, x, is necessarily expressed, as indicated by the argument structure assignment.

(75) $\begin{bmatrix} \textbf{burning} \\ \text{ARGSTR} = \begin{bmatrix} \text{ARG}_1 = \textbf{x:physobj} \end{bmatrix} \\ \text{EVENTSTR} = \begin{bmatrix} \text{E}_1 = \textbf{e}_1\textbf{:process} \\ \text{HEAD} = \textbf{e}_1 \end{bmatrix} \\ \text{QUALIA} = \begin{bmatrix} \text{AGENTIVE} = \textbf{burn\_act(e}_1\textbf{,x)} \end{bmatrix} \end{bmatrix}$

The emphasis in the interpretation of the sentences above seems to be on the initial aspect of the event being referred to, an observation pointed out by Asher (1993). In fact, this appears to be a property of *ing*-nominals in general, at least for left-headed events, as we shall see below. Asher (1993) claims that this is due to the aspectualizing nature of the nominalization suffix *-ing*, resulting in an interpretation similar to the progressive form in the verbal system.

(76) a. The launching of the Space Shuttle occurred at 10:30 pm.
     b. The launching of the Space Shuttle was aborted.

Extending Asher's observation, we might compare the *ing*-nominalizer
to agentive nominals created by suffixation with the *-er* and *-or* suffixes,
such as *baker* and *advisor*. That is, for an event e_0 seen as a pair of
subevents, e_1 and e_2, related through a temporal relation, R, where
$R(e_1, e_2)$, then the *agentive* process nominal would be derived by a kind
of externalization, i.e., $R(\underline{e_1}, e_2)$. In fact, this is similar to the headedness
operation we encountered in chapter 5.

An alternative view might be that the *ing*-nominal denotes the complete event in a way identical to both simple events such as *party* and
war as well as polysemous event nominals such as *examination*, discussed
below. Indeed, one might argue that the verbs in both (76a) and (76b)
are coercing predicates, changing the event denoted by *the launching of
the Space Shuttle* to an aspectualized interpretation, forcing reference to
the preparatory phase of the launching event. The fact that you can
say (76b) at all might suggest that this NP already denotes a complete
event. Following this argument, the verb *abort* is the aspectualizer, not
the *ing*-suffix on the nominal form. The associated verbs, such as *cut
short*, *terminate*, as well as causatives such as *stop* and *quit* are also
aspectualizing predicates, and seem to perform similar operations over
events. Thus, the *ing*-nominal seems to denote the completed event as
much as the other nominalizers, and not simply the initial phase of the
event.

As plausible as this analysis seems, it does not appear to withstand
scrutiny from two observations:

A. Right-headed transitions (i.e., achievements) are much less acceptable as *ing*-nominals than are processes and left-headed transitions.

B. There is no interpretation of *ing*-nominals as the result of an event,
   as there is with *ion*-nominalizations, such as *destruction*.

Regarding the first point, given what we have said, one would expect
right-headed transitions (such as *arrive* and *die*) to be ill-formed as
ing-nominals, since the result of the nominalization is to effectively
head the process subevent of the event structure; i.e., $ing(R(e_1, e_2)) =
ing(R(e_1^*, e_2))$, where $*$ indicates headedness. Hence, we might expect
that an operation resulting in a double-headed event structure would
be less acceptable than the application of the suffix to event-denoting
relations which are already left-headed, or are unheaded. This seems

to be supported by the contrasting behavior of *arriving* and *arrival*, as illustrated in (77)–(79) below. For some reason, the *ing*-form is grammatical only when some reference is also made to the culminating state of the event, as in (77b).[7]

(77) a. *The arriving of John was greeted with mixed reactions.
      b. ?The arriving of John late was met with mixed reactions.

(78) a. The arrival of John was greeted with mixed reactions.
      b. The arrival of John late was met with mixed reactions.

(79) a. John's arrival was graceful.
      b. The arrival of the train is expected for 3:00 pm.

Regarding the second point made above, notice that *ing*-nominals are not actually polysemous between process and result readings, as are most *-ion* nominalizations such as *destruction*.

(80) a. *The destroying (of the city) was widespread.
      b. The destruction was widespread.

(81) a. *The constructing (of the house) has adequate stability.
      b. The construction has adequate stability.

The way in which the lexical structure reflects this single sense, making reference only to the initial event, is illustrated in the representation in (82) of the semantics for the *ing*-nominal form *constructing*.

$$
(82) \quad
\begin{bmatrix}
\textbf{constructing} \\
\text{EVENTSTR} =
\begin{bmatrix}
E_1 = e_1\text{:}\textbf{process} \\
\text{D-}E_1 = e_2\text{:}\textbf{state} \\
\text{RESTR} = <_\alpha \\
\text{HEAD} = e_1
\end{bmatrix} \\[2em]
\text{ARGSTR} =
\begin{bmatrix}
\text{ARG1} = \boxed{2}
\begin{bmatrix}
\textbf{artifact} \\
\text{CONST} = \boxed{3} \\
\text{D-ARG1} = \boxed{1}
\begin{bmatrix}
\textbf{animate\_ind} \\
\text{FORMAL} = \textbf{physobj}
\end{bmatrix} \\
\text{FORMAL} = \textbf{physobj}
\end{bmatrix} \\[2em]
\text{D-ARG2} = \boxed{3}
\begin{bmatrix}
\textbf{material} \\
\text{FORMAL} = \textbf{mass}
\end{bmatrix}
\end{bmatrix} \\[2em]
\text{QUALIA} =
\begin{bmatrix}
\text{FORMAL} = \textbf{exist}(e_2, \boxed{2}) \\
\text{AGENTIVE} = \textbf{construct\_act}(e_1, \boxed{1}, \boxed{3})
\end{bmatrix}
\end{bmatrix}
$$

In order to fully understand the inability of these nominals to carry the resulting event reading, we must look more closely at nominalizations which do exhibit this polysemy, such as *examination, destruction,* and *arrival.* Recall from chapter 6, that there are in fact three senses associated with these nominals, as demonstrated in (83).

(83) a. The house's <u>construction</u> was finished in two months.
      b. The <u>construction</u> was interrupted during the rains.
      c. The <u>construction</u> is standing on the next street.

I will argue that these process-result nominals are best treated as denoting dot objects, where both the dot elements are typed as events. This results in a class of **event·event** nominalizations, which are logically polysemous between process and result interpretations (cf. (17b) and (17c), respectively), but also admit of a third interpretation, that given by the dot object itself (cf. (17a)).

The nominalized form for the accomplishment verbs derived by this process will be logically polysemous in exactly the way that the aspectual system operates over their respective verbal forms. That is, (i) the *process* reading in the nominal is the *imperfective* construction for the verbal; (ii) the *result* reading in the nominal is the *perfect* construction for the verbal; and (iii) the dot object reading in the nominal is the *simple* construction for the verbal form. To illustrate this parallel, consider the three sentence pairs in (84)–(86) below. Sentence (84a) and (84b) demonstrate how the force of the simple past is captured by the dot object nominalization sense; the sentences in (85) show the past imperfective sense being covered by the process nominalization sense; and finally, sentence (86b) illustrates how the result nominalization sense covers the present perfect sense in (86a).

(84) a. John <u>constructed</u> the roof frame for the house yesterday.
      b. John's <u>construction</u> of the roof frame for the house was done yesterday.

(85) a. John <u>was constructing</u> the roof frame, when he fell from the ladder.
      b. John fell from the ladder during the <u>construction</u> of the roof frame.

(86) a. Now that John <u>has constructed</u> the roof frame, he can start
          shingling.
      b. With the <u>construction</u> of the roof frame complete, John can
          start shingling.

Now let us examine what type structure for these nominalizations
would allow these three interpretations. I will argue that the polysemy
exhibited by these nominalizations is formally the same as that seen
with the nominals *book*, *newspaper*, and so on. Namely, two types are
constructed to form a dot object with the *lcp* type constructor. In the
case of this class of event nominalizations, the types are both events, such
that the dot object is itself an event. For an event e_1 of type **process**
and another event e_2 of type **state**, the dot object is a complex type,
$e_1 \cdot e_2$, as shown below.

(87) process·result_lcp = {process·result, process, result}

To illustrate how this type is integrated into the representation of the
nominal's semantics, consider the noun *examination*.

(88)

$$
\begin{bmatrix}
\textbf{examination} \\[4pt]
\text{EVENTSTR} = \begin{bmatrix} E_1 = \textbf{process} \\ E_2 = \textbf{state} \\ \text{RESTR} = <_\alpha \end{bmatrix} \\[18pt]
\text{ARGSTR} = \begin{bmatrix} \text{ARG1} = \boxed{1}\begin{bmatrix}\textbf{animate\_ind} \\ \text{FORMAL} = \textbf{physobj}\end{bmatrix} \\[12pt] \text{ARG2} = \boxed{2}\begin{bmatrix}\textbf{physobj} \\ \text{FORMAL} = \textbf{entity}\end{bmatrix}\end{bmatrix} \\[24pt]
\text{QUALIA} = \begin{bmatrix}\text{FORMAL} = \textbf{examine\_result}(e_2, \boxed{2}) \\ \text{AGENTIVE} = \textbf{examine\_act}(e_1, \boxed{1}, \boxed{2})\end{bmatrix}
\end{bmatrix}
$$

In some sense, the only thing different about this dot object is the typing
on the dot elements. That is, whereas a book is a dot object composed
of **information** and **physobj**, related by the FORMAL relation of containment (cf. 6.4 and 8.2), an examination is a dot object composed of
process and **state**, related by the RESTR relation in the event structure
of precedence. It should be pointed out that the operation of headedness on the verbal representation is similar to the coercion operation
selecting a dot element within the dot object of a complex event. We
can, in fact, for purposes of discussion, assume that they are the same
operation applying over different expressions.

As another example, consider the representation for the nominalization *arrival* shown in (90), accounting for the polysemy exhibited in (89) below.

(89) a. The party will begin after John's <u>arrival</u>.
      b. John's <u>arrival</u> was flamboyant.

$$
(90) \quad
\begin{bmatrix}
\textbf{arrival} \\[4pt]
\text{ARGSTR} =
\begin{bmatrix}
\text{ARG}_1 = \textbf{x:ind} \\
\text{D-ARG}_1 = \textbf{y:location}
\end{bmatrix} \\[12pt]
\text{EVENTSTR} =
\begin{bmatrix}
\text{E}_1 = \textbf{e}_1\textbf{:process} \\
\text{E}_2 = \textbf{e}_2\textbf{:state} \\
\text{RESTR} = <_\alpha
\end{bmatrix} \\[16pt]
\text{QUALIA} =
\begin{bmatrix}
\textbf{process·state\_lcp} \\
\text{FORMAL} = \textbf{at}(\textbf{e}_2,\textbf{x},\textbf{y}) \\
\text{AGENTIVE} = \textbf{arrive\_act}(\textbf{e}_1,\textbf{x})
\end{bmatrix}
\end{bmatrix}
$$

Unlike with the *ing*-nominal *arriving*, the form above denotes a dot object, and carries the polysemy inherent with that typing. The type cluster associated with *arrival* is the same as that given above for the other process-result nominals, and a specific single dot element sense is arrived at by the headedness operation mentioned earlier in chapter 8.

For nominalizations such as *construction* and *development*, which are derived from verbs of creation, the result interpretation corresponds either to the individual which is created as a result of the initial process, or to the state itself. This is due to the fact that the FORMAL role of these verbs makes reference both to a state and to the object created. Verbs of destruction such as *destroy*, however, do not allow this sense, because the object is not predicated within the FORMAL role. This effect is demonstrated below with the verb *develop* and the nominalization *development*. The full lexical semantic structure for a verb like *develop* is given below in (91).

$$
(91) \quad
\begin{bmatrix}
\textbf{develop} \\[4pt]
\text{EVENTSTR} =
\begin{bmatrix}
\text{E}_1 = \textbf{process} \\
\text{E}_2 = \textbf{state} \\
\text{RESTR} = <_\alpha \\
\text{HEAD} = \textbf{e}_1
\end{bmatrix} \\[10pt]
\text{ARGSTR} =
\begin{bmatrix}
\text{ARG1} = \boxed{1}
\begin{bmatrix}
\textbf{animate\_ind} \\
\text{FORMAL} = \textbf{physobj}
\end{bmatrix} \\[8pt]
\text{ARG2} = \boxed{2}
\begin{bmatrix}
\textbf{artifact} \\
\text{CONST} = \boxed{3} \\
\text{FORMAL} = \textbf{physobj}
\end{bmatrix} \\[8pt]
\text{D-ARG1} = \boxed{3}
\begin{bmatrix}
\textbf{material} \\
\text{FORMAL} = \textbf{mass}
\end{bmatrix}
\end{bmatrix} \\[10pt]
\text{QUALIA} =
\begin{bmatrix}
\text{FORMAL} = \textbf{exist}(\text{e}_2, \boxed{2}) \\
\text{AGENTIVE} = \textbf{build\_act}(\text{e}_1, \boxed{1}, \boxed{3})
\end{bmatrix}
\end{bmatrix}
$$

The effect of the nominalizing suffix -*ment* is to create a dot object, process·state, where in this case, the FORMAL quale predicates of the individual as well as of the state.

Now consider some other typing possibilities available with the use of dot objects. Grimshaw (1990) and others have made much of the grammatical distinctions between *examination*, mentioned above, and nominals such as *exam*. What is it that gives rise to the differences between *exam* and *examination* in (92)–(94) below?

(92) a. The examination was long.
    b. *The examination was on the table.

(93) a. The exam was long.
    b. The exam was on the table.

(94) a. The examination of the students.
    b. * The exam of the students.

Grimshaw's analysis is partially correct, yet fails to observe that both these nouns are actually logically polysemous, in different ways, however. Notice that *exam* is polysemous in a manner similar to that of *book*. An exam contains an information object, such as that denoted by book, but specifically, of the type of question. This information object is part of the type of *exam*, along with the process of taking the exam. Thus, the exam is both *the set of questions* and the event of the *asking of the questions*. This is the polysemy in the nominal *exam*, represented in (95) below.

$$
(95) \quad
\begin{bmatrix}
\textbf{exam} \\
\text{ARGSTR} = \begin{bmatrix} \text{ARG1} = \textbf{x:question} \end{bmatrix} \\
\text{EVENTSTR} = \begin{bmatrix} \text{E}_1 = \textbf{e}_1\textbf{:process} \end{bmatrix} \\
\text{QUALIA} = \begin{bmatrix} \textbf{question·process\_lcp} \\ \text{FORMAL} = \textbf{ask(e}_1\textbf{,z,x)} \\ \text{AGENT} = \textbf{make(e}_2\textbf{,y,x)} \end{bmatrix}
\end{bmatrix}
$$

This representation expresses the polysemy that an exam can refer to the set of questions which compose the event of the examination, or the event itself. The questions, like any information objects, can also have physical manifestation, but need not (e.g., an oral exam). The logical polysemy, therefore, arises from the combination of the inherent polysemy possible in the type of information object of question, and the event of the examination itself.

In terms of qualia structure, the noun *exam* behaves like the event nominals *sonata* and *symphony*. Therefore, it is important to acknowledge that the major difference between *exam* and *examination* is that they are polysemous in very different ways. *Exam* is an event artifact while *examination* is purely an event with no physical object denotation. The dot object associated with *sonata* appears to make reference to both an event and an information type of music, as shown in (96).[8]

(96) a. Mary is in Harvard Square looking for <u>the Bach sonatas</u>.
      b. We won't get to the concert until after <u>the Bach sonata</u>.

The qualia structure for these event-objects (using Dowty's, 1979 terminology), such as *sonata* and *symphony* can be given as follows:

$$
(97) \quad
\begin{bmatrix}
\textbf{sonata} \\
\text{ARGSTR} = \begin{bmatrix} \text{ARG1} = \textbf{x:music} \end{bmatrix} \\
\text{EVENTSTR} = \begin{bmatrix} \text{E}_1 = \textbf{e}_1\textbf{:process} \end{bmatrix} \\
\text{QUALIA} = \begin{bmatrix} \textbf{music·process\_lcp} \\ \text{FORMAL} = \textbf{perform(e}_1\textbf{,w,x)} \\ \text{TELIC} = \textbf{listen(e',z,e}_1\textbf{)} \\ \text{AGENT} = \textbf{compose(e'',y,x)} \end{bmatrix}
\end{bmatrix}
$$

The first thing to notice is that the lexical item directly denotes an event, as well as an information type of music.[9] The FORMAL relation is that which specifically relates the types making up the dot object. That is, just as the two types in *book* are defined by a specific containment relation, the event and the music are related by the relation of *performing*.

Now consider other nominals which appear to be simple events, but are in fact dot objects making reference to a simple events. This is seen in nouns such as *lecture, class,* and *lunch.* These have the same type of logically polysemous behavior as that exhibited above with *exam* and *sonata.*

(98)   a. Hurry up, Zac, your lunch is getting cold!
       b. We can talk about it during lunch.

(99)   a. John is still writing tomorrow's lecture.
       b. John's lecture lasted over three hours.

(100) a. John is late for his 11:00 class.
       b. John is throwing a barbecue brisket party for his class.

Next consider the dot object created by an event type and a proposition. This is the representation for lexical items such as *belief* and *regret.*

$$
(101) \quad
\begin{bmatrix}
\textbf{belief} \\
\text{ARGSTR} \; = \; \begin{bmatrix} \text{ARG1} \; = \; \textbf{x:prop} \\ \text{D-ARG1} \; = \; \textbf{y:human} \end{bmatrix} \\
\text{EVENTSTR} \; = \; \begin{bmatrix} \text{E}_1 \; = \; \textbf{e}_1\textbf{:state} \end{bmatrix} \\
\text{QUALIA} \; = \; \begin{bmatrix} \textbf{state·prop\_lcp} \\ \text{FORMAL} \; = \; \textbf{x} \\ \text{FORMAL} \; = \; \textbf{believe(e}_1\textbf{,y,x)} \end{bmatrix}
\end{bmatrix}
$$

That is, the nominal denotes both the complement proposition and the state of having this attitude, as illustrated in (102), where the lcp type constructor has created the new type.

$$
(102) \quad \frac{\alpha : \textbf{state}, \quad \alpha : \textbf{prop}}{lcp(\alpha) : \textbf{state} \cdot \textbf{prop}}
$$

Notice that case assignment through the preposition *in* appears to be the only option available to a coerced NP complement with the nominalized form of the coercing verb, but not to all nominalizations.

(103) a. Mary believes that John is sick.
       b. Mary believes the story.
       c. Mary believes John.

(104) a. Mary's belief that John is sick.

   b. Mary's <u>belief</u> in the story.
   c. Mary's <u>belief</u> in John.

The important thing to realize with this analysis is that the nominal
belief is a dot object, and therefore denotes both the state of believing
something as well as the proposition of belief itself.

   Now let us turn briefly to the semantics of purported factive nominalizations. Asher (1993) claims that all the NPs in (105) below are factive.
The corresponding sentential structures are given in (106).

(105) a. The <u>collapse</u> of Carthage is a fact.
       b. John informed Sue of Mary's <u>departure</u>.
       c. The <u>collapse</u> of the stock market is a real possibility.

(106) a. That Carthage <u>has collapsed</u> is a fact.
       b. John informed Sue that Mary <u>has departed</u>.
       c. That the stock market <u>will collapse</u> is a real possibility.

Although it is true that these NPs carry factive readings, I would argue that the NPs themselves are not factive outside of these selectional
environments, but simply event descriptions admitting a single interpretation as result event nominals. The factive interpretation exhibited
above in (105) is due to the *coercive property* of factive predicates such
as *inform* and *be a fact* rather than the inherent semantics of the event
nominal itself. There are two types of data suggesting this is correct.
First, these event nominals appear in other contexts without factive interpretations, as demonstrated in (107). Secondly, factivity is an interpretation that many NPs assume when placed within a factive coercive
environment such as the complement of *inform* and as subject of *be a
possibility*, as illustrated in (108). That these NPs are not necessarily factive seems to correlate with the lack of tense/aspect anchoring,
behaving, in effect, as *irrealis* expressions.

(107) a. The <u>collapse</u> of the stock market was prevented by government
          intervention.
       b. The thief's <u>departure</u> was stopped by the police.

(108) a. Cathie informed me of your <u>blister</u>.
       b. A <u>thunderstorm</u> is a real possibility.
       c. John informed his parents of his <u>scholarship</u>.

The semantic selection structure below shows how *inform* is a factive predicate which coerces its complement to a factive interpretation.

(109)

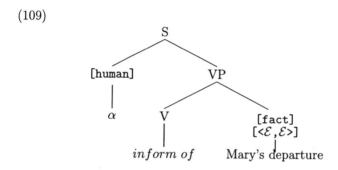

Following Asher's (1993) treatment of factives, the resulting interpretation for the NP shown above in (109) reveals that the factive reading is coerced onto the event description in a manner similar to true complement coercion discussed in 8.1.3. The factive sense in context for this NP is given in (110).

(110) $\exists i \exists e \exists f [i \leq n \land anch(i, e) \land fact(f) \land f = depart(e, mary)]$

The important point to realize, however, is that this is not a reading inherent in the NP's semantics, but one arising through coercion (cf. Asher, 1993 and Zucchi, 1993).[10]

In this section, I have tried to give a general perspective on how a generative lexicon captures the polysemy inherent in many nominalization processes, as well as the inability of other nominals to behave polysemously.

8.6   Lexicalization and LCPs

In this section, I explore what the consequences are generally for lexicalization theory given the notions of lcp and qualia structure in the semantics. The characterization of how meaning maps to lexical form is explored, as is the correspondence between lexicalized semantic expressions and expressions with similar structures, derived compositionally in the syntax.

From our discussion above, we can think of logical polysemy as resulting from a complex object, which is constructed from other objects with a type constructor, which we called *lcp*. The type cluster associated with a lexical paradigm (lcp) allows the realization of a number of senses, but is itself a functionally defined structure. Given such a system, the process of conceptual lexicalization is affected, such that two distinct situations may arise within a given language. For any possible lcp, lcp_i, constructed in the type system, the language may express this paradigm through the unique expression of a single lexical item, or it may *split* this lcp into distinct lexical forms. The former case is illustrated schematically in (111), where the type cluster $\{t_1, t_2, t_1 \cdot t_2\}$ is associated with the word w_i.

(111)

The second possibility is illustrated in (112), where the dot object does not actually result in a logical polysemy in the lexical system for the language.

(112)

This distinction allows us to capture a number of interesting lexicalization phenomena in language, particularly with cross-linguistic lexical comparisons (cf. Pustejovsky and Busa, forthcoming). For now, let us restrict our discussion to English. Compare the nouns *sale*, *purchase*, and *transaction*, and how they relate to the dot object.

The result of the *lcp* type constructor shown below represents the type of the nominalization *transaction*, independent of the financial aspect associated with selling and buying.

(113) $$\frac{\alpha : \texttt{give} \quad \alpha : \texttt{take}}{lcp(\alpha) : \texttt{give} \cdot \texttt{take}}$$

Notice that this nominal is unable to refer to the individual types, each representing a unilateral event of transfer, but only to the dot object itself. Thus, *transaction* appears to be a case of split lexicalization within the *lcp* of this type cluster, since it cannot make reference to the individual events. The other lexical items in this split lexicalization are the nominals *purchase* and *sale*, which do refer to the individual events, while still requiring reference to the entire type cluster. Because of this split, there is no logical polysemy associated with these nouns, in terms of the process-result ambiguity. This is not to say that these nouns cannot enter into logical polysemies. Just as the noun *exam* is not polysemous with respect to one type polysemy which *examination* is (i.e., process-result), it does exhibit the process-object polysemy, as discussed above. Interestingly, the noun *purchase* seems to be logically polysemous between the event and the object involved in the transaction, while the noun *sale* is not. Hence, the former behaves in some respects like the dot objects mentioned in the previous section, while *sale* seems to denote only the event.

(114) a. The government prohibits the <u>purchase</u> of illegal drugs.
       b. The <u>purchases</u> I made today are in the back of the truck.

(115) a. The <u>sale</u> of the house this month seems quite likely now.
       b. *The <u>sales</u> I made today are already distributed throughout Boston.

This may be related to the distinction we saw between the physical object sense associated with the result reading of creation-verb nominalizations such as *building*, *construction*, and *creation*, which is absent from the nominalizations for verbs of destruction. The lexical representation for *purchase* is given in (116) below.

$$
(116) \quad
\begin{bmatrix}
\textbf{purchase} \\
\text{ARGSTR} =
\begin{bmatrix}
\text{ARG1} = \textbf{x:human} \\
\text{ARG2} = \textbf{y:physobj} \\
\text{D-ARG1} = \textbf{z:human}
\end{bmatrix} \\
\text{EVENTSTR} =
\begin{bmatrix}
\text{E1} = \textbf{e}_1\textbf{:process} \\
\text{E2} = \textbf{e}_2\textbf{:state} \\
\text{RESTR} = <_\alpha \\
\text{HEAD} = \textbf{e}_1,\ \textbf{e}_2
\end{bmatrix} \\
\text{QUALIA} =
\begin{bmatrix}
\textbf{process·physobj\_lcp} \\
\text{CONST} = \textbf{part\_of(e}_1\textbf{·e}_2\textbf{,give·take)} \\
\text{FORMAL} = \textbf{have(e}_2\textbf{,x,y} \\
\text{TELIC} = \textbf{buy\_act(e}_1\textbf{,x,y,z)}
\end{bmatrix}
\end{bmatrix}
$$

In closing our discussion of lexicalization, it is interesting to compare how the semantic field around a particular lexical item is structured relative to other words in the same language. For example, while nouns such as *apple, lemon, grape* are polysemous between the product and the producer of the product senses as in (117), there are many words that have only one sense or the other, as in (118).[11]

(117) a. We have planted <u>apples</u> in the field behind the house.
       b. There are <u>apples</u> in that basket.

(118) a. The <u>pines</u> are growing tall.
       b. *We have collected <u>pines</u> for the wreath. (*pine cones*)

The tree and the fruit contained on this tree are both logical senses for the word *apple*, while *pine* is simply unable to refer to *pine cone*. It is the structure behind these concepts which gives rise to the polysemy. That is, an lcp relating product and producer for food items simply does not apply to pines, given our current dietary habits. If pine cones were to be edible or eaten, then the semantic conceptualization between the tree and the cone would change as well, possibly permitting the polysemy as a result. It is possible that factors relating to suppletion phenomena may also be at play with sense assignment in such cases.

8.6.1 Referential Transparency

To close this section, I would like to briefly explore the role that qualia structure might play in the modes of reference for an object. In the classification of nominal types, there are several standard distinctions made in the way that NPs refer. For example, the distinction between pronouns, proper names, and descriptions is important both for anaphoric binding phenomena as well as for the obvious interpretive differences in these types (cf. Chomsky, 1981). What qualia structure permits us to do, however, is to look at the relative transparency or opacity of how a noun refers, as expressed in the value of the noun's qualia structure. I will refer to this property as *referential transparency*, and define it as follows:

(119) The REFERENTIAL TRANSPARENCY of an NP is a characterization of the specificity of qualia values for that NP.

    (i) If an NP is only weakly constrained by the values of its qualia, then it is *referentially opaque*.

    (ii) If an NP is strongly constrained by the values of its qualia, then it is *referentially transparent*.

Determining whether the qualia for an item are weakly or strongly constrained depends, of course, on where the qualia predicates fall in the lattice structure of the global type hierarchy. This is, of course, not "reference" in the technical sense, but the term does captures the intuitive distinction between the informativeness of the nominal types. In reality, of course, there is a range of transparency and these are not absolute categories, except in the case of pronominal elements, which are semantically weak, in general. Pronouns such as *she*, *himself*, and *it* are referentially opaque NPs, in that there is no mode of explanation (i.e., quale) suggesting how this term denotes. The qualia structure for such pronominals are lexically devoid of specific relational information. Knowing what the reference of *he* is does not require my understanding of what the TELIC or AGENTIVE role of that individual is, for example.

At the other end of the spectrum are nouns such as *baker*, *lecturer*, and *bread*, which we understand only by virtue of knowing the way in which these objects satisfy the typing requirements established by the qualia that they carry. The knowledge we have of these objects is therefore more specific, and our use of the words referring to these concepts has distinct consequences. Namely, they are referentially transparent in that the modes of explanation for these words are specified more clearly to the hearer. This is illustrated most clearly when seen in composition with predicates, such as *begin* and *enjoy*, as in (120) below.

(120) a. The lecturer began at 3:00 pm.

b. Mary enjoyed <u>the cake</u>.

Although certainly a defeasible inference, the referential transparency
of the subject in (120a) suggests the activity that is begun, while a
similar transparency of the object in (120b) suggests the manner in
which the cake is enjoyed. Both pronouns and proper names, however,
are uninformative in this respect, as demonstrated by the sentences in
(121).

(121)   a. <u>Mary</u> began at 3:00 pm.
        b. Mary enjoyed <u>it</u>.

As we will see in chapter 10, the degree of transparency of an NP will
determine the default interpretation of how a phrase is semantically reconstructed within a coercive environment. This parameter will also
determine the way that individuals are described and referred to in discourse.

9 The Lexical Semantics of Causation

In this chapter, I explore how extended event structure and qualia structure interact in the semantics of verbs to account for the polysemy associated with certain verbal alternations. In particular, I will show how the theory of event headedness outlined in chapter 5 gives us a constrained mechanism for lexically underspecifying the semantics of verbs exhibiting polysemy in alternation classes involving causation. The representation responsible for the polymorphic behavior of these verbs is a fairly basic statement of event causation, called the *Default Causative Paradigm*. In section 9.1, I demonstrate how both causative and unaccusative forms for verbs such as *sink* and *break* share the same underlying semantic representation, but project to distinct syntactic environments because of event headedness on this default causative expression. Analogously, aspectual verbs such as *begin* and *start*, which have both raising and control readings are analyzed in section 9.2 as logically polysemous in a similar fashion. In many respects, these alternations are formally similar to the behavior of dot object nominals such as *door* and *book*, which was discussed in previous chapters. Section 9.3 briefly examines the event structures associated with non-lexical (synthetic) causatives for comparison to the lexicalization phenomena discussed in previous sections. In Section 9.4, I show how the semantic representation of experiencer predicates is based on an underlying causal relation, similar to those discussed in 9.1 and 9.2, which is responsible for the syntactic binding violations associated with these constructions. Finally, in 9.5, I explore a limited class of verbs I will call *modal causative*, such as *risk* and *gamble*, and their associated semantic and grammatical properties.

9.1 How Language Encodes Causation

Our language of causal relations is only as rich as the descriptive mechanisms we employ for encoding how objects and events interact in the world. Much of the groundwork towards such a descriptive formalism for causal reasoning has been elucidated in the AI and computational linguistics community. For example, Wilks (1978) develops a taxonomy of causal relations as motivated by the reasoning necessary for language understanding systems. Allen (1984), Eberle (1988), and Kowalski and Sergot (1986) each explore what possible temporal connections can exist

between propositions taken as individual events, in order to structure
an event-based logic for planning or reasoning. Kamp (1979) and van
Benthem (1983) are both serious explorations addressing the same issues
from the perspective of philosophical logic. Finally, Hobbs *et al.* (1987)
presents an extremely rich language exploring not only possible causal
connections, but also constraints on actually realized temporal binding
between events.

Most work from formal semantics has tended to take a more conservative approach to describing how events, as described in linguistic
expressions, are combined to facilitate causal inference. Recent work in
Discourse Representation Theory (DRT) (cf. Kamp and Reyle, 1993,
and Asher, 1993) has concentrated on event quantification in discourse,
which makes no use of internal subeventual structure. Hence, lexical
causation has not been explored in great detail in these frameworks
(cf. however, Kamp and Roßdeutscher, 1992). Parsons (1990) explicitly
mentions how certain verbs encode causation, but limits his inquiry to
a small class of causative predicates, without examining the issue more
generally throughout the language.

The approach taken in this work has been to build explicitly and
extensively from the work mentioned above, in order to examine whether
there is a general methodology for determining what information should
be encoded in the lexical item itself, and furthermore, why. In other
words, the goal is to study not only what causal relations are possible,
but which relations are justifiably represented in the semantics of natural
languages. In some sense, the entire structure of a generative lexicon is
organized around this strategy; namely, to provide an account for why
certain causal relations and explanatory modes are lexicalized in the
ways they are, as well as how they project to the particular syntactic
environments they govern.

One point that deserves mention is that there are identifiable and formally characterizable constraints on the representations which encode
causal relations. Given that we are concerned with the *lexicalization* of
causation, and not its general form, there are several conditions that
must be met within a lexical expression. Capturing the necessary and
sufficient conditions on causation in the physical world are, of course,
beyond the scope of this work, and, fortunately, irrelevant for much of
this investigation. Both Bach (1986) and Chomsky (1994), echoing remarks made by Reichenbach (1978), argue that the conceptualization

of the world through linguistic structures within a model of the semantics of natural language need not reflect the currently accepted view of reality for those concepts. For example, the constraints on how language lexicalizes causation will not reflect or embody principles from quantum mechanics. If anything, our causal conceptualizations seem to be remarkably Aristotelian in nature. Analytic traditions addressing the issue of causation, nevertheless, typically adopt a causal statement satisfying at least the following properties:

(1) a. conditionalness;
     b. one-sided dependence;
     c. invariability;
     d. uniqueness;
     e. productivity.

For example, statement (1) below is illustrative of this approach:

(2) If event e_1 happens, then and only then, event e_2 is always produced by it.

The statement in (2) makes no mention of the semantic participants in the events nor what their relation to each other must be in order to construe this expression as a coherent causal relation. Furthermore, while conditions (1a) and (1b) are encoded directly into the semantics of lexical items, invariability, uniqueness, and productivity seem to be represented indirectly at best.

From a naive metaphysics point of view, these properties can be restated as the following linguistic constraints. First, there must exist a precedence relation between the causing event and the resulting event. Given the three relations described in chapter 5, $<_\propto$, $< \circ_\propto$, and $\circ_\propto$, only the first two would play any role in the causal explanation of a lexical item. That is, the causing event (i.e., the AGENTIVE quale) can completely precede or precede and overlap the resulting event. Secondly, the events must cohere in some way, such that the lexical item is predicated of the same individual over at least two consecutive events. We will refer to this property as *argument coherence*.

(3)   ARGUMENT COHERENCE:

The relation expressed by the causing event and that expressed by the resulting event must make reference to at least one parameter in common. This reference can be direct or indirect:

a. DIRECT CAUSATION :

$$\left[\text{QUALIA} = \left[\begin{array}{l} \text{FORMAL} = \alpha\_\text{result}(e_2,y) \\ \text{AGENTIVE} = \alpha\_\text{act}(e_1,x,y) \end{array} \right] \right]$$

b. INDIRECT (CONSTITUTIVE) CAUSATION :

$$\left[\text{QUALIA} = \left[\begin{array}{l} \text{CONST} = \text{part\_of}(z,y) \\ \text{FORMAL} = \alpha\_\text{result}(e_2,y) \\ \text{AGENTIVE} = \alpha\_\text{act}(e_1,x,z) \end{array} \right] \right]$$

The lexicalization of direct reference causation is schematically shown in the event tree structure in (4), where argument coherence and precedence of the causing event to the resulting event are both present. This accounts for a variety of change of state verbs, such as *bake*, *kill*, *drop*, *move*, and so on, as well as verbs such as *die*, *arrive* and other right-headed events (see below). Constitutive causation, discussed briefly in chapter 5 in connection with the semantics of creation verbs such as *build*, is discussed more fully in Pustejovsky (forthcoming).[1]

(4)

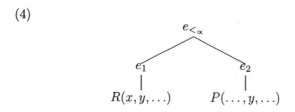

As argued in chapters 5 and 7 above, the qualia can be seen as structuring the relations which make reference to the sortally defined arguments and subevents for the lexical item.

(5) $\lambda y \lambda x \lambda e_1 \lambda e_2 \exists P \exists R \ [\alpha: \text{AGENTIVE}=[R(e_1, x, y)] \wedge$
      $\text{FORMAL}= [P(e_2, y)] \wedge e_1 <_\alpha e_2]$

This says that a predicate α is a relation between two subevents and two individuals such that some relation exists between x and y in the "bringing about" (the AGENTIVE role) of the resulting state of y (the

FORMAL role), where this state, $P(e_2, y)$ did not hold before. The event tree structure in (4) and the equivalent qualia structure in (5) are underspecified, however, in that there is no event head in the structure. The representation in (5), referred to as the *Default Causative Paradigm (DCP)* in Pustejovsky and Busa (1995), embodies the simplest type of causative relation that can be associated with a lexical item, and one that is realizable in a number of syntactic forms.[2]

Our aim here is to arrive at a semantic expression that is both informative regarding the connection between the arguments, but also predictive of the grammatical behavior of the verb with respect to syntactic realization. As mentioned in chapter 6, richer semantic representations such as that in (5) need to be effectively filtered or constrained from binding to syntactic expressions which are not admissible in the grammar. Furthermore, the semantic type should not only map to the syntactic possibilities accompanying a verb, but should also elucidate the connection between these various forms. A more explicit statement of the DCP is shown in (6), illustrating the specific temporal restriction between subevents, as well as their sortal restrictions.

$$
(6) \quad
\begin{bmatrix}
\alpha \\
\text{EVENTSTR} =
\begin{bmatrix}
\text{E}_1 = \mathbf{e_1{:}process} \\
\text{E}_2 = \mathbf{e_2{:}state} \\
\text{RESTR} = <_\alpha \\
\text{HEAD} =
\end{bmatrix} \\
\text{ARGSTR} =
\begin{bmatrix}
\text{ARG}1 = \boxed{1} \\
\text{ARG}2 = \boxed{2}
\end{bmatrix} \\
\text{QUALIA} =
\begin{bmatrix}
\textbf{default-causative-lcp} \\
\text{FORMAL} = \alpha\_\text{result}(e_2, \boxed{2}) \\
\text{AGENTIVE} = \alpha\_\text{act}(e_1, \boxed{1}, \boxed{2})
\end{bmatrix}
\end{bmatrix}
$$

As I will demonstrate, this paradigm accounts for most lexical forms of causation in natural language. Because of event headedness, there are (at least) three lexical semantic classes associated with this structure;

(7) a. LEFT-HEADED EVENTS : e.g., Direct causative accomplishments, such as *kill, murder*, etc.

   b. RIGHT-HEADED EVENTS : e.g., Direct causative achievements, such as *die, arrive*.

   c. HEADLESS EVENTS : e.g., causative/unaccusative verbs, such as *sink, break, burn*.

I argue in 9.2 and 9.3 that it is the semantic underspecification occasioned by a lexically headless event which gives rise to the polysemy exhibited by the predicates in the causative/unaccusative alternation and in the raising/control alternation.

9.2   Causation and Unaccusativity

Let us now see how the underspecification mentioned above gives rise to the verbal polysemy associated with unaccusativity. The purely syntactic characterization of split intransitivity in language fails to capture the semantic relatedness between the causative and unaccusative forms for the verbs in any systematic way. In fact, these analyses can be seen as employing sense enumerative lexicons (as described in chapters 3 and 4), with all the shortcomings of that approach. The work of Van Valin (1990), Zaenen (1993), and others has illustrated the problem in failing to link "unaccusativity" to the lexical semantics of the elements in the sentence more intimately (cf. also Abraham, 1986); yet Levin and Rappaport (1989, 1995) have explained the syntactic behavior of these verbs in terms of fixed-form, lexically determined verb classes. Pustejovsky and Busa (1995) argue that a description of the behavior of unaccusatives in terms of fixed classes does not capture the relatedness between the constructions involved in the diathesis alternation or in the unaccusative/unergative alternation of the same predicate. As a result, the sense enumerative lexical approach is not able to explain how unaccusativity can also arise non-lexically, through composition with other elements in the sentence. Within the framework presented here, however, where the number of senses remains fairly constant with respect to the possible space of interpretations, a set of generative devices allows us to determine semantic selection of complements by the rules of composition. These rules operate over underspecified lexical representations, such that the behavior of a predicate can be predicted from the configurational properties of different parameters in the semantic representation.

First we examine briefly the behavior of unaccusatives in Italian, where the data suggest that the causative/inchoative alternation can be analyzed as a systematic form of *logical polysemy*. We will see that the alternation shown below in (8) with the Italian verb *affondare (sink)* requires neither a multiple listing of the entries (as in Levin and Rappaport, 1992, 1995, nor lexical rules as in Copestake, 1993), and Sanfilippo, 1993).

(8) a. I nemici hanno affondato la nave.
        "The enemy sank the boat."
     b. La nave è affondata.
        "The boat sank."

The characteristic behavior of verbs such as *affondare* is that, when occurring as intransitives, they assume the auxiliary selectional properties of unaccusatives such as *arrivare* (arrive), and are distinguished from unergative verbs such as *camminare* (walk). Chierchia (1989) suggests that the lexical representation for unaccusatives is in fact an underlying causative.[3] Pustejovsky and Busa (1995) extend this notion by combining it with the concept of underspecified event structures and argue that those unaccusatives which also have causative counterparts are logically polysemous because of the headless nature of the event structure representation of the predicate, e.g., as with *affondare* in (12). As I will demonstrate, whether the verb surfaces as an unaccusative or a transitive causative will be determined by which subevent in the semantic representation is headed. For *affondare*, the unheaded event tree structure is shown in the tree below.

(9)

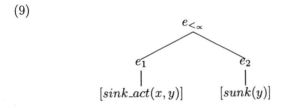

Compare this structure to a lexically right-headed predicates such as *arrivare* (*arrive*) and *morire* (*die*), which have only unaccusative realizations, as demonstrated in the sentences in (10) and (11).

(10) a. Il pacchetto è arrivato.
         "The package arrived."
      b. *Il postino ha arrivato il pacchetto.

"The mailman arrived the package."

  c. *Il postino ha fatto arrivare il pacchetto.

     "The mailman has made arrive the package."

(11) a. Gianni è morto.

      "Gianni died."

    b. *La pallottola ha morto Gianni."

     *"The bullet died Gianni."

Recall from chapter 8, that the semantics for the English verb *arrive* includes a specification that the resulting state in the transition, e_2, is the head. This is true of the Italian verb *arrivare* as well. In fact, all lexical unaccusative verbs will be analyzed as right-headed binary event structures, meeting the following constraints on event structure:

$$(12) \quad \begin{bmatrix} \alpha \\ \text{EVENTSTR} = \begin{bmatrix} E_1 = e_1\text{:process} \\ E_2 = e_2\text{:state} \\ \text{RESTR} = <_\alpha \\ \text{HEAD} = e_2 \end{bmatrix} \\ \dots \end{bmatrix}$$

For *arrivare* in particular, the lexical structure is given in (13) (cf. chapters 6 and 7) .[4]

$$(13) \quad \begin{bmatrix} \textbf{arrivare} \\ \text{ARGSTR} = \begin{bmatrix} \text{ARG}_1 = \textbf{x:ind} \\ \text{D-ARG}_1 = \textbf{y:location} \end{bmatrix} \\ \text{EVENTSTR} = \begin{bmatrix} E_1 = e_1\text{:process} \\ E_2 = e_2\text{:state} \\ \text{RESTR} = <_\alpha \\ \text{HEAD} = e_2 \end{bmatrix} \\ \text{QUALIA} = \begin{bmatrix} \text{FORMAL} = \textbf{at}(e_2,\textbf{x},\textbf{y}) \\ \text{AGENTIVE} = \textbf{arrive\_act}(e_1,\textbf{x}) \end{bmatrix} \end{bmatrix}$$

The status of the location argument, y, as a default argument, obviates its obligatory expression in the syntax, while still allowing such constructions as that in (14).

(14)   Il pacchetto è arrivato a casa.

       "The package arrived home."

According to the mapping principles outlined in chapter 6, the realization of such a lexical structure is dictated by the effect that headedness has on argument expression. In particular, recall that only arguments associated with the headed event are obligatorily expressed at surface structure. The headless events, along with their arguments, are *shadowed*, resulting in an interpretation with quantificational closure over these arguments (cf. below in 6.2.5). This is repeated in (15) and (16) below.

(15) Q_i: $R(e_1^*, x, y) \longrightarrow$ x:SUBJ, y:OBJ
$\quad\;\;$ Q_j: $P(e_2, y) \longrightarrow$ shadowed

(16) Q_i: $R(e_1, x, y) \longrightarrow$ shadowed
$\quad\;\;$ Q_j: $P(e_2^*, y) \longrightarrow$ y:SUBJ

For a lexically-determined unaccusative such as *arrivare*, the mapping is unambiguous, and there is but one syntactic realization possible, namely expression of the "deep object" argument as the subject in an intransitive structure. This is illustrated in the tree below.

(17)

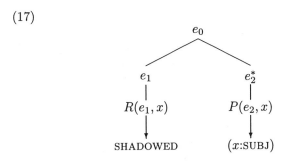

What is important to note is that, although a direct causative construction is not possible with *morire* (die) and *arrivare* (arrive), reference to the initial subevent in the event structure above is still possible with certain adjunct phrases, as shown in (18a)–(18d).

(18) a. Gianni è morto per una polmonite.
$\qquad$ "John died from pneumonia."
$\quad\;$ b. Il tetto è crollato per il peso della neve.
$\qquad$ "The roof collapsed from the weight of the snow."
$\quad\;$ c. Maria è arrossita per l'imbarazzo.
$\qquad$ "Mary blushed out of embarrassment."

d. Gianni è annegato per il maltempo.
"John drowned from bad weather."

The PP *per una polmonite* in (18a) is not a true adjunct, but is in
fact adding specificity to the relation in the event associated with the
AGENTIVE quale for the verb. Schematically, this is represented by the
mapping given in (19): below.

(19)

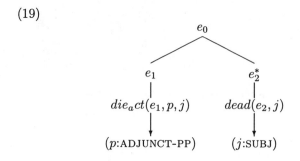

As suggested above, whereas lexical unaccusatives such as *arrivare* are
right-headed underlyingly, the polysemy possible with *affondare* (sink)
is due to an underspecified event structure. The lexical form for the verb
affondare is given in (20) below.

(20)
$$
\begin{bmatrix}
\textbf{affondare} \\
\text{EVENTSTR} = \begin{bmatrix} E_1 = \textbf{process} \\ E_2 = \textbf{state} \\ \text{RESTR} = <_\propto \end{bmatrix} \\
\text{ARGSTR} = \begin{bmatrix} \text{ARG1} = \boxed{1}\begin{bmatrix} \textbf{physobj} \\ \text{FORMAL} = \textbf{entity} \end{bmatrix} \\ \text{ARG2} = \boxed{2}\begin{bmatrix} \textbf{physobj} \\ \text{FORMAL} = \textbf{entity} \end{bmatrix} \end{bmatrix} \\
\text{QUALIA} = \begin{bmatrix} \textbf{default-causative-lcp} \\ \text{FORMAL} = \textbf{sink\_result}(e_2, \boxed{2}) \\ \text{AGENTIVE} = \textbf{sink\_act}(e_1, \boxed{1}, \boxed{2}) \end{bmatrix}
\end{bmatrix}
$$

By its headless nature, the lexical entry for *affondare* makes available two
grammatical constructions, the unaccusative in (12b) and the causative
in (12a). The realization as an unaccusative gives rise to a right-headed
event structure, by foregrounding the resulting state of the boat, and
consequently shadowing the arguments and the subevents in the agentive. Realization as a causative gives rise to a left-headed event structure,

by foregrounding the AGENTIVE predicate and projecting all arguments therein. In other words, given an unheaded event structure α we can express α via any one of its roles, namely either through the AGENTIVE, or through the FORMAL role. As discussed in chapter 5, this strategy for projecting semantic arguments from underlying forms is needed in order to filter the expression of "unheaded" arguments. In other words, given the presence of more than one qualia role, individual qualia "compete" for projection, and the mechanism of headedness acts as a filter to constrain the set of projectable arguments. The quale for the headed event, e^*, projects the configuration (or template) associated with that quale. In chapter 5, I described how the qualia of a lexical expression must be "saturated" by the syntax. This condition is repeated below in (21), along with the definition of *covering*.[5]

(21)   QUALIA SATURATION :
       A qualia structure is saturated only if all arguments in the qualia are covered.

(22)   COVERING:
       An argument α is covered only if:
   (i) it is linked to a position in s-structure; or
   (ii) it is logically dependent on a covered argument β; or
   (iii) it is closeable by virtue of its type.

The realization of an unaccusative takes place by heading the culminating event and by abstracting the only argument in the relation associated with the headed quale, namely the "deep object," *la nave*. This is shown below in (23):

(23)

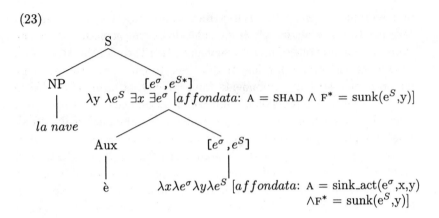

Projection of the left-headed event gives rise to a causative transitive construction, as illustrated in the tree in (24) below.

(24)

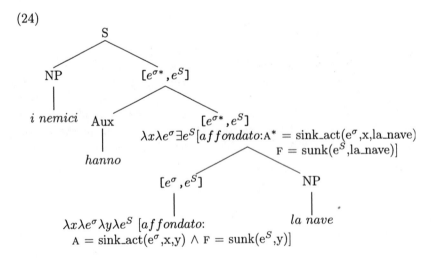

What these two structures illustrate is how event headedness acts to constrain the form of the semantic representation and its syntactic realization. The strategy within this analysis is to allow for gross potential overgeneration of syntactic mappings from semantic expressions, and constrain the output (or restrict the licensing) of generated forms. This is essentially the strategy employed by Chomsky (1986), where, without constraints, the statement on how an expression is formed would appear much too general to actually match the data. Constraints or parameters on the applicability of the strategy, however, restrict the expressiveness of the rules.

The analysis thus far has illustrated how both causative and unaccusative forms of this verb class can usefully be derived from an underlying causative representation. Following the discussion in Pustejovsky and Busa (1995), let us briefly examine the conditions under which defaulted and non-headed arguments are realized as adjuncts rather than as direct arguments. Chierchia (1989) and Roeper (1987,1993) have discussed the conditions under which the agent (under normal thematic interpretations) is accessible for control of rationale clauses (e.g., (25)).

(25) a. Giovanni ha affondato la nave per incassare l'assicurazione.
          "John sank the boat to collect insurance."
      b. * La nave è affondata per incassare l'assicurazione.
          "The boat sank to collect insurance."

Chierchia (1989) argues that the unaccusative form of *affondare* is a zero reflexivization form of the transitive counterpart, where the underlying causative semantics is preserved, but the causing event is interpreted statively. It will become clear from independent considerations, that this analysis falls under the Default Causative Paradigm presented above, and accounts for a range of acceptable adjuncts to these verbs.

From our previous discussion on headedness in chapter 5, given a left-headed predicate, one should in fact expect adjuncts to modify the head:

(26) a. Il nemico ha affondato la nave dall'aereo.
          "The enemy sank the boat from the plane."
      b. La nave è stata affondata dall'aereo.
          "The boat was sunk from the plane."
      c. * La nave è affondata dall'aereo.
          "The boat sank from the plane."

In (26a), *dall'aereo* modifies an event and not the agent, since it denotes the locatum of the event that brought about a sinking. The passive in (26b), as expected, licenses the same adjunct since the agent in the initial subevent is also accessible. However, in (26c) the same adjunct is ungrammatical. On the basis of the examples below, it appears that it is not accessibility to the agent that crucially determines the licensing of the adjunct for unaccusatives, but rather accessibility to an event.

(27) a. La nave è affondata per l'esplosione.
         "The boat sank from the explosion."
      b. ?La nave è affondata per la bomba.
         "The boat sank from the bomb."
      c. *La nave è affondata per l'aereo.
         "The boat sank from the plane."

There are two things to point out concerning these data. First, (27a) contrasts with (26c) in that the *per*-PP is able to make reference to the initial event itself, while the *dal*-PP makes reference to the agent of the event itself.

In some sense, this is analogous to the rule of passivization. Grimshaw (1990) discusses the fact that in the passive the agent has the status of a special kind of adjunct, namely an a-adjunct which is systematically headed by the preposition *by*. With regard to event structure, headedness has the effect of shadowing the non-headed event, which can only be accessed by a special kind of adjunct, and in the case of unaccusatives, one that can construe a coherent causal chain by selecting the proper subevent. This seems to be exactly what the preposition *per* is doing in the examples above. The different degrees of grammaticality of examples (27a-c) show that it is not a question of binary acceptability, but rather, that there is a range of grammaticality judgments explained by the degree to which the adjunction satisfies (i.e., "is coherent with respect to") the default causative paradigm. In order to capture this degree of "semanticality," as argued in chapter 4, we need to appeal to the richer descriptive notions of type coercion and nominal qualia structures. This is explored in more detail in Pustejovsky and Busa (1995, forthcoming).[6]

If unaccusativity is characterized as a property of an expression satisfying the DCP with a right-headed event, then one might expect there to be non-lexical unaccusatives, as long as these conditions are satisfied. In fact, this appears to explain the behavior of *correre* (run) when appearing in a dative goal context, as in (28b).

(28) a. Gianni ha corso.
          "John has run."
      b. "Gianni è corso a casa.
          "John ran home."

While *correre* behaves like an unergative in (28a), it is clear that (28b) is an unaccusative form for the same verb. The verb need not be entered into multiple semantic classes, however, since (28b) is a non-lexical unaccusative, derived by co-composition with the PP-phrase *a casa* (cf. Pustejovsky and Busa, 1995). By allowing a verb's membership in a particular semantic class to emerge from the composition of the sentence it appears in, we obviate the need to enumerate separate senses for the distinct semantic classes associated with that verb. This ability is as significant as the operation of coercion towards providing an explanation for why these verbs are polysemous in the way that they are.

One final example will illustrate the usefulness of the notion of derived unaccusativity. This involves the meaning shift associated with creation verbs such as *build*, as in (29a).

(29) a. Tension is building.
      b. Mary's presence is building tension among the other faculty.

It would appear as though *build* has shifted from its normal status as a *constitutive causative* verb, which has no unaccusative form.

(30) a. *The house built/is building quickly.
      b. The construction crew built the house quickly.

As shown in Pustejovsky and Busa (1995), by selecting an abstract noun as object, the *mode* of causation for the verb changes from a constitutive to a direct causative, allowing this use of *build* to satisfy the DCP. That is, while typically the direct object of a constitutive causative makes reference to a default argument as the value of its CONST quale (e.g., material as part of the artifact that is built), the qualia structure for an abstract noun such as *tension* does not distinguish the contents of the CONST and FORMAL qualia (cf. Pustejovsky, 1995b); consequently, the possibility of a constitutive causative interpretation disappears as well. The relevant structure for the derived sense of *build* as used in the VP *build tension* is shown in (31).

$$(31) \begin{bmatrix} \textbf{[build tension]} \\ \text{ARGSTR} = \begin{bmatrix} \text{ARG1} = \boxed{1} \begin{bmatrix} \textbf{animate\_ind} \\ \text{FORMAL} = \textbf{physobj} \end{bmatrix} \\ \text{ARG2} = \boxed{2} \begin{bmatrix} \textbf{tension} \\ \text{FORMAL} = \textbf{abstract} \end{bmatrix} \end{bmatrix} \\ \text{QUALIA} = \begin{bmatrix} \textbf{create-lcp} \\ \text{FORMAL} = \textbf{exist}(e_2, \boxed{2}) \\ \text{AGENTIVE} = \textbf{build\_act}(e_1, \boxed{1}, \boxed{2}) \end{bmatrix} \end{bmatrix}$$

Ignoring for now the specifics of the co-composition, the resulting qualia structure for the above VP mirrors that of the lexical structure for a direct causative, repeated below in (32):

$$(32) \begin{bmatrix} \alpha \\ \text{QUALIA} = \begin{bmatrix} \text{FORMAL} = \alpha\_\text{result}(e_2, y) \\ \text{AGENTIVE} = \alpha\_\text{act}(e_1, x, y) \end{bmatrix} \end{bmatrix}$$

This, in turn, appears to license the unaccusative form for the verb *build* that we see in sentence (29a). These issues are explored in more detail in Pustejovsky and Busa (forthcoming).

In this section, I have outlined a general strategy for representing both causatives and unaccusatives as related to an underlying causal relation. As we saw, this supports the view put forth in Chierchia (1989), where unaccusativity is analyzed as a causative. Furthermore, by making use of underspecified representations in the event structure, the model allows us to capture the polysemy inherent in this class of polymorphic verbs.

9.3 Aspectual Causatives and Coercion

In chapter 7, it was argued that much of the polysemous behavior of verbs which take multiple subcategorizations could be explained in terms of deep semantic selection and type coercion. For aspectual verbs such as *begin* and *finish*, shown in (33) and (34) below, it was suggested that the verb selects for the semantic type of `event function`. If the appropriate type is absent from the local environment (i.e., if the complement is not an event function), then coercion applies, making use of semantic information associated with the complement, in order to reconstruct the proper type. For the two examples given below, the default predicates associated with the TELIC roles of the complements are *reading* and *drinking* respectively, although within the right context, any number of interpretations is possible.

(33) a. John began to read the book. (VP[+INF])
      b. John began reading the book. (VP[+PRG])
      c. John began the book. (NP)

(34) a. Mary finished drinking her beer. (VP[+PRG])
      b. Mary finished her beer. (NP)

Whatever the specific value of the embedded "predicate" in these examples, the coercion analysis requires there to be an event function associated with the complement of the verb. In Pustejovsky and Bouillon (1995), this analysis is extended to cover the behavior of French aspectual predicates, and is refined in two respects: (a) constraints on the applicability of coercion, motivated by data in Pustejovsky and Anick (1988) and Godard and Jayez (1993), are presented in order to restrict the overgeneration of semantic expressions; and (b) the nature of the selectional properties of aspectual predicates is given a more formal treatment, while explaining the polysemy between the control and raising senses of these predicates.

As discussed in chapter 7, a semantic type projects to a *canonical syntactic form* (*csf*) along with the forms allowable from licensed coercion operations. Together, these forms constitute what we called a *phrasal paradigm*, and the type surfaces as one of three possible forms for *begin*, and one of two forms for *finish*, depending on which coercion rules are applicable. There is, however, only one semantic type being selected for, and the clustering of the particular syntactic forms appearing as surface complement types in (33) and (34) are systematically projected by virtue of this semantic type. That is, a verb such as *begin*, selecting for an event, will paradigmatically allow for the expression of the grammatical forms shown above, assuming surface syntactic constraints are satisfied. For this reason, the structuring of this kind of linguistic knowledge, where this event type has its syntactic expression as any one of the surface types in (33) or (34) was called a *phrasal paradigm* in chapter 7. In line with the discussion from chapter 7, the NP *the book* in (33c) is coerced to the appropriate type required by its governing verb, in this case an event. What makes coercion possible in this case is the availability of the selected type, given as part of the NP's *qualia structure*, indicating, for example, that the TELIC role for *book* is the event function of reading, while the AGENTIVE role is an event function of writing. The result of applying this coercion operator to an NP is effectively to create an *extension* of the NP meaning, called a *metonymic reconstruction*. In the case of the NP *the book*, for example, the coercion operators provide two event function interpretations: namely, *reading the book* and *writing the book*. These interpretations are generated by virtue of the type of the selected complement and the availability of such types in the qualia structure of the complement itself.

There are several interesting things to note about the above application of coercion. First, such "reconstructive operations" on the semantics of the complement are by no means universally applicable, even with aspectual predicates. The constraints necessary to limit coercion operations, however, can be stated in a principled manner, and demonstrate not the overgeneration of coercive operations, but rather that such semantic operations are finely-tuned to the type structures of the elements in composition. This is discussed in more detail in Pustejovsky and Bouillon (1995).

The second observation concerns the ability of many aspectual verbs to appear in raising constructions as well as the control structures already mentioned above in (33) and (34). Consider, for example, the sentences in (35) and (36).

(35) a. The war began to reach into Bosnia.
      b. It began to rain.
      c. The party began early.
      d. *The book began.

(36) a. *The war finished reaching into Bosnia.
      b. *It finished raining.

Notice that a raising construction is possible with referential NPs as in (35a), pleonastic NPs (35b), and event-denoting nominals (35c). Interestingly, what might appear to be an instance of coercion in the subject position of (35d) is not well-formed. As shown in Pustejovsky and Bouillon (1995), however, this is not a possible metonymic reconstruction to the type selected by *begin*. Observe, furthermore, that some aspectual predicates such as *finish* allow only the control structure, and are ungrammatical with raising constructions.

This is relevant to our current discussion of how causation is lexically encoded in language for the following reason; namely, it is no accident that both raising and control constructions exist for the same aspectual predicate, given that causative and unaccusative forms exist for the same predicate, as with *sink*. That is, we can view the relation between these two constructions as one involving causation in much the same way as the default causative paradigm. It has long been noted, of course, that pairs such as that in (37) are related by a causative interpretation of some sort (cf. Perlmutter, 1967, Levin, 1993).

(37) a. The movie began.
      b. Mary began the movie.

The construction in (37a) is essentially an unaccusative form, while that in (37b) can be easily interpreted as its causative counterpart.

This solution, however, need not be restricted to the event-nominal cases in (37) above, but can be extended to include the distinction between raising and control senses of the same verb. That is, *begin* exhibits a logical polysemy between control and raising senses, where the unaccusative form is associated with the raising construction and the control structure is associated with the causative form. The lexical semantics for verbs that exhibit control and raising behavior is a causative representation.

The alternation displayed above is licensed by the headless nature of the event structure representation of the predicate *begin*. Whether it surfaces as a raising verb or a transitive control verb will be determined by which subevent is headed. If the initial event is headed, a control structure results. If, however, the final event is headed, a raising construction results.

In Pustejovsky and Bouillon (1995), it is argued that much of the confusion associated with the coercion data arise from this ambiguity. Although these senses are distinct, they are logically related types, where only the control sense allows coercion. The idea of analyzing aspectual verbs as essentially ambiguous is not new, but was already proposed by Perlmutter (1970) for English, and Lamiroy (1987) for French. The traditional method for distinguishing between control and raising verbs involves a battery of diagnostics testing for selection, agentivity and controllability (cf. Dowty, 1979 and Zaenen, 1993). Perhaps the best indicator of a raising predicate is that it imposes no selectional restrictions on its subject, as illustrated with the verb *seem* in (38).

(38) a. The lake seems to have frozen.

b. A riot seems to have happened yesterday.

c. This fact seems to have escaped Mary's attention.

The subject in each sentence in (38) is restricted by the embedded predicate in the VP selected for by the verb *seem*. A control predicate, on the other hand, imposes clear and obvious restrictions on the subject NP (cf. (39));

(39) a. Mary tried to leave the party.

     b. *A riot tried to happen yesterday.

There are also syntactic constraints imposed by control predicates that are absent in raising constructions:[7]

(40) a. There seems to be a riot going on now.

     b. *There attempted to be a riot.

Perlmutter (1970) uses *force*-complement constructions as another clear indication of a control verb. Compare (41a) with (41b).

(41) a. Mary forced John to begin writing his thesis.

     b. *Mary forced it to begin raining yesterday.

The sentence in (41a) illustrates that the matrix object stands in a control relation to the embedded VP. Observe, however, that the ungrammatical sentence in (41b) illustrates that a "raised" NP cannot satisfy the selectional constraints imposed by *force*.

(42) a. I am forcing you to begin reading the book by Proust.

     b. *I am forcing it to begin to rain.

The well-formedness of object complement coercion with aspectual predicates such as *begin* is conditioned by the event sort of the qualia associated with the NP itself. Thus, only NPs having associated transition events will allow coercion and control. This is not to say, however, that *begin* selects only for transition events. There are, of course, perfectly grammatical examples of process or state complements, as shown in (43) below:

(43) a. The acid is beginning to corrode the marble.

     b. It is beginning to rain.

c. The snow began to fall at midnight.
d. The war is beginning to reach into Bosnia.
e. John is beginning to bleed.
f. John is beginning to be annoyed by the noise.
g. John is beginning to be ill.

The above examples illustrate the use of *begin* as a raising verb. The two senses of the verb *begin* conform to the observation that Perlmutter originally made, namely, that *begin* functions as both a *raising* and a *control* verb.[8] As a Raising verb, the event sort specified as the complement to *begin* may be any sort. As a control verb, it appears that the complement must be a TRANSITION.[9]

Finally, as pointed out in Jacobson (1990), VP-ellipsis can be used as a diagnostic for determining whether a complement is part of a raising or control construction in English; namely, only control complements enter into this construction. Notice that in (44), the only fully grammatical sentence involves an overt control interpretation of *begin*, that in (44b).

(44)   a. *John began to bleed and Mary began, too.
       b. John began to read the book, and Mary began, too.

These considerations together suggest that there are in fact two constructions associated with *begin*, namely control and raising.

To see how these senses are related, let us present the lexical semantics for *begin*, illustrated in (45) below.

$$
(45) \quad
\begin{bmatrix}
\textbf{begin} \\
\text{EVENTSTR} =
\begin{bmatrix}
E_1 = e_1\textbf{:process} \\
E_2 = e_2\textbf{:event} \\
\text{RESTR} = \ < \circ_\alpha
\end{bmatrix} \\
\text{ARGSTR} =
\begin{bmatrix}
\text{ARG1} = \textbf{x:human} \\
\text{ARG2} = \textbf{ef}_1 = \texttt{<x,<e}_2\texttt{,t>>:event-function}
\end{bmatrix} \\
\text{QUALIA} =
\begin{bmatrix}
\text{FORMAL} = \textbf{P(e}_2\textbf{,x)} \\
\text{AGENTIVE} = \textbf{begin\_act(e}_1\textbf{,x,ef}_1\textbf{)}
\end{bmatrix}
\end{bmatrix}
$$

What emerges from this representation are two typing assignments for *begin*, corresponding to the two senses:

(46)   a. *begin* as a Control verb: $<<e,\mathcal{E}>,<e,\mathcal{E}>>$
       b. *begin* as a Raising verb: $<e^\sigma,\mathcal{E}>$

Given that event-headedness acts to foreground or 'focus' a single quale of the verbal semantic representation, the effect of heading the final event from the lexical structure in (45), i.e., the FORMAL role, corresponds to the raising interpretation; what is asserted is simply the initiation of an event, without explicit reference to causal preconditions of the event.

Consider now the semantics of the control interpretation of *begin*, and how it interacts with coercion on the complement.

(47) Mary began a book.

Assume the qualia structure for *book* to be as given in (48).

(48)
$$\begin{bmatrix} \textbf{book} \\ \text{ARGSTR} = \begin{bmatrix} \text{ARG1} = \textbf{x:info} \\ \text{ARG2} = \textbf{y:physobj} \end{bmatrix} \\ \text{QUALIA} = \begin{bmatrix} \textbf{info·physobj\_lcp} \\ \text{FORMAL} = \textbf{hold(y,x)} \\ \text{TELIC} = \textbf{read}(e^T,\textbf{w,x}) \\ \text{AGENT} = \textbf{write}(e^T,\textbf{v,x}) \end{bmatrix} \end{bmatrix}$$

By heading the initial event in the lexical representation associated with *begin*, we arrive at a shadowing of the culminating event, while the control relation is expressed as subject and event function complement.

(49)

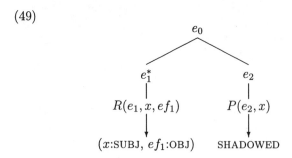

$$e_0$$

$$e_1^* \qquad\qquad e_2$$

$$R(e_1, x, ef_1) \qquad P(e_2, x)$$

$$(x\text{:SUBJ}, \ ef_1\text{:OBJ}) \qquad \text{SHADOWED}$$

Following the discussion in chapter 7, the qualia can also be seen as type pumping operations, giving rise to new types for coercive environments. Thus for example, the type available to an expression α with quale Q_i of type τ, can be seen as allowing the following type inference:

(50)
$$\frac{\alpha : \sigma \ \oplus \ Q_i[\sigma, \tau] : \sigma \to \tau}{Q_i[\sigma, \tau](\alpha) : \tau}$$

This says that, given an expression α of type σ, there is a coercion possible between σ and τ, which changes the type of α in this composition from σ to τ. We will illustrate the application of this coercion operation below, as used in the *begin* example above in (47). Because of the qualia structure of the complement inherited from that of its head *book*, the typing requirements specified by the governing verb *begin* are satisfied just in case the type of the NP is coerced to an event function.

As illustrated below in (51), coercion applies to the complement NP, where reconstruction with either the TELIC or AGENTIVE qualia will result in the appropriate type selected by the verb. We illustrate the derivation within the VP where the TELIC role has been selected.

(51)
$$\frac{begin : (e \to \mathcal{E}) \to (e \to \mathcal{E}) \quad \oplus \quad \dfrac{a\ book{:}e \quad \oplus \quad Q_T[e,(e \to \mathcal{E})]{:}e \to (e \to \mathcal{E})}{Q_T[e,(e \to \mathcal{E})](e){:}(e \to \mathcal{E})}}{begin\ the\ book : e \to \mathcal{E}}$$

This corresponds to the selection tree structure shown below.

(52)

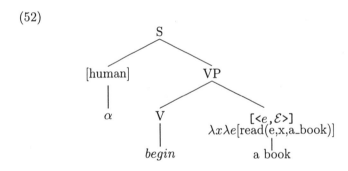

This states that the TELIC role of *the book*, $\lambda x \lambda e^T[read(e^T, x, a\text{-}book)]$, is available as an alias for shifting the type of the NP. This metonymically reconstructed type, $\langle e, \mathcal{E}\rangle$, is identical to that selected by the verb *begin* in complement position. After the coercion operation, the derivation proceeds as if a full predicate were present in the syntax.[10]

The result of heading the final event in *begin* gives rise to either direct event selection, as in (53a) below, or a raising construction, as in (53b).

(53) a. The party began at midnight.
      b. Snow began to fall.

In (53a), the typing of the predicate is satisfied directly by the event description in subject position (ignoring some technical details). For the construction in (53b), I assume that raising is accomplished by function composition (FC), in the manner of Jacobson (1990). In particular, the raising verb *begin*, of type $<e^\sigma, \mathcal{E}>$, imposes the type e^σ on its complement. Assuming the VP *to fall*, for example, in (53b), is $<e, \mathcal{E}>$, then $FC(\texttt{begin,to fall})$ returns the expression $\lambda \mathcal{P}[begin(fall(\mathcal{P}))]$.

Finally, let me turn briefly to the semantics of the verb *finish* and how the semantic type selected by this verb corresponds to a different canonical form as well as the associated phrasal paradigm. There are two things to note about *finish*. Notice first that *finish* differs from *begin* in that it is not logically polysemous, having only a control sense. That is, the raising examples in (54) are ungrammatical.

(54) a. *It has finished raining.
      b. *The sun has finished shining in my eyes.
      c. *The acid finished corroding the marble.

This would suggest that *finish* is not lexically underspecified with respect to headedness, as is *begin*, but is already specified with a head. It is this lexical specification that gives rise to the control reading only.[11]

Consider now the sentences in (55), which appear to be raising constructions, contradicting the claim made above about *finish* being lexically specified as a control verb.

(55) a. The leaves have finished falling.
      b. The paint has finished drying.

These data would suggest that a raising construction is possible with *finish* with some nominals. But the sentences in (55) are best analyzed as *pseudo-control* cases, and they are restricted to a certain well-defined class of nominals. In general, these verbs do not pass the standard raising tests, but nouns such as *paint* and *leaves* are exceptions because they carry qualia information indicating a kind of "autonomy of behavior" relative to certain predicates. Hence, *paint*, for example, is construed as a pseudo-agent in the control relation because of this property; i.e., it can dry on its own.

It is interesting to observe that another type of intransitive construction is possible with *finish*; namely, if the event nominal in subject position has an agentive component (cf. (56b) and (56c)), then a control interpretation is possible in what would otherwise appear to be an intransitive (i.e., raising) construction. Pustejovsky and Bouillon (1995) refer to these as *intransitive control* constructions.

(56) a. ??The party finishes at midnight.
      b. Class will finish at 2:00 pm.
      c. The talk will finish by noon.

(57) a. *The rain will finish by noon.
      b. The rain will stop by noon.

While *classes* and *talks* have an apparent agentivity and controllable component to them, *parties* are less controllable, resulting in the less acceptable (56a). Since *rain* is completely uncontrollable, it is ungrammatical in an intransitive control construction with the verb *finish* (cf. (57a)). The verb *stop*, however, allows a raising interpretation and permits the intransitive raising construction in (57b). This verb is interesting because it has both control and raising senses, yet does not allow complement coercion at all. Observe that *stop* appears in the sentences in (58) with a non-control construction, assuming the sense of "prevent:"

(58) a. John stopped Mary from smoking in his house.
      b. Mary stopped the man from hitting her.
      c. John stopped the bomb from exploding.

In fact, there is a kind of coercion possible in complement position with *stop*, essentially reconstructing an ellipsed predicate, as in (59).

(59) a. John stopped the car. (*from moving*)
      b. The referee stopped the clock. (*from moving*)
      c. Mary stopped the record. (*from playing/moving*)

What these data suggest is that the complement type of *stop* is not an event function, as with *begin*, but rather simply an event, where the type of the verb is $<e^\sigma, <e, \mathcal{E}>>$. That is, these verbs are not strict obligatory control verbs, such as *try* and *begin*, but impose "available controller" binding, as with verbs such as *want* (cf. Chomsky, 1981, Dowty, 1985, and Farkas, 1988). It is worth noting that, with the complement of *stop* specified as e^σ, it is clear that coercion is not possible since this is not among the type aliases for the NP complements (cf. Pustejovsky and Bouillon, 1995 for discussion).[12]

9.4 Experiencer Predicates

Given the general statement of causation presented above, it is interesting to speculate on what role verbal qualia might play in other lexical causatives. For example, as has been long noted and as was mentioned in chapter 2, the verb *kill* allows for a broad range of possible subject types, as long as the causal relation between the argument in subject position and the resulting state is coherent in some way.

(60) a. John <u>killed</u> Mary.
       b. The gun <u>killed</u> Mary.
       c. The storm <u>killed</u> Mary.
       d. The war <u>killed</u> Mary.
       e. John's shooting Mary <u>killed</u> her.

In Pustejovsky (1991a), it was suggested that *kill* selects for an event and coerces its subject to this type, in a manner similar to the interpretations of *enjoy* and *begin*. This is essentially correct, but the details are more complicated, and in fact, more interesting.

Assume that the lexical representation for the verb *kill* is as given in (61), where the initial subevent is headed.

$$
(61) \quad
\begin{bmatrix}
\textbf{kill} \\[4pt]
\text{EVENTSTR} =
\begin{bmatrix}
\text{E}_1 = e_1\text{:}\textbf{process} \\
\text{E}_2 = e_2\text{:}\textbf{state} \\
\text{RESTR} = <_\propto \\
\text{HEAD} = e_1
\end{bmatrix} \\[20pt]
\text{ARGSTR} =
\begin{bmatrix}
\text{ARG1} = \boxed{1}\,[\,\textbf{top}\,] \\
\text{ARG2} = \boxed{2}
\begin{bmatrix}
\textbf{animate\_ind} \\
\text{FORMAL} = \textbf{physobj}
\end{bmatrix}
\end{bmatrix} \\[20pt]
\text{QUALIA} =
\begin{bmatrix}
\textbf{dc\_lcp} \\
\text{FORMAL} = \textbf{dead}(e_2, \boxed{2}) \\
\text{AGENTIVE} = \textbf{kill\_act}(e_1, \boxed{1}, \boxed{2})
\end{bmatrix}
\end{bmatrix}
$$

In sentence (60a) above, the process John engaged in such that Mary died is left completely unspecified. In (60d), on the other hand, the particular action is completely specified by the event description in subject position. This example illustrates how qualia unification can fully specify what is left underspecified with an animate argument in (60a). The cases of (60b-d), on the other hand, are causally coherent because of coercion and qualia-based selection. That is, in (60b), the NP *the gun* must participate in the relation within the AGENTIVE quale in some significant way, just as in (60c), *the storm* is a coherent cause only if Mary stands in a relation to this event, such that the storm could effect such a change of state, e.g., she was in the middle of the storm, etc. Hence, even sentences with an event nominal as subject (as in (60c) and (60d) must respect argument coherence in order for the causal relation to be satisfied (cf. Croft, 1986 for discussion of this idea).

The above discussion is important because the semantics of DCP verbs such as *kill* and *break* is suggestive of the underlying causative nature of experiencer predicates, such as those shown below in (62).

(62) a. Books <u>bore</u> me.
  b. The movie <u>frightened</u> Mary.
  c. The newspaper <u>angered</u> John.
  d. Listening to Mary <u>irritates</u> Alice.

We can view these sentences as involving a metonymic reconstruction of the subject to an event, and in particular, to an experiencing event between the surface object and the surface subject. That is, in (62), it is *(my reading) books* which bores me, *(Mary's watching) the movie* which frightened her, *(my seeing) John's face* which scared me, and *(Alice's) listening to Mary* which irritates her.[13]

We can, of course, experience objects in any number of ways. That is, one need not read books in order to be bored by them. One can be bored by looking at them, shopping for them, writing them, or thinking about them. This is not in any way inconsistent with the GL approach. The qualia determine two types of information in the context of coercion:

i. Type and sort information which the qualia must satisfy;

ii. Specific qualia values which are the explanatory modes in understanding a word.

For words such as *film* and *book*, the TELIC quale role value of *watch* and *read* respectively are not optional in any sense, but are part of the semantics of the words. When an NP enters into a coercive environment, such as here with experiencer verbs, the qualia values act only to determine the default assignment for how the type environment is reconstructed. Thus, it seems that linguistic evidence supports an underlying semantic type of an event as the subject, which would directly explain what the connection between the subject and object of the experiencing relation is. The underlying semantics of psychological predicates is a causative structure where the surface subject is the logical object of an experiencing event. On this view, the lexical representation for the verb *anger* has something like the following form, where $Exp(x,y)$ is a sortally restricted relation of experiencing (e.g., hearing, seeing, watching, etc.), and $<$ is a strict partial order of temporal precedence:

(63) $\Box \forall x \forall y \forall e [anger(e, y, x)] \rightarrow \exists e_1 \exists e_2 \exists Exp[Exp(e_1, x, y) \wedge \neg angry(e_1, x) \wedge angry(e_2, x) \wedge \neg e_2 < e_1]$

This states that a verb such as *anger* involves someone who directly experiences something, and as a result becomes angry. What is interesting about examples such as (62a) and (62b) is that the semantics of the NP in surface subject position contributes information to the interpretation of what kind of experiencing event is involved. That is, the qualia structure projected by the NP *books* contributes the particular manner in which I became bored in (62a), namely the NP's TELIC role of *reading*. Similarly, our knowledge of movies as something that we watch and experience in a particular manner is encoded in the TELIC role of *movie* in sentence (62b). The event projected from the noun *movie*, viz., *watch*, in turn satisifies the selectional requirements of the verb *frighten* on its subject. The complete semantic form assigned to this verb is not the default causative paradigm discussed in section 9.2 (i.e., dcp-lcp), but rather is a causative act which predicates a certain state of the person performing the act, hence, the experience. Thus, unlike the direct causative we encountered in the lcp expression of argument coherence (cf. Section 9.1 above), an experiencer verb exhibits *experienced causation*, as shown in (65).

(64)   DIRECT CAUSATION:

$$\left[\text{QUALIA} = \left[\begin{array}{l} \text{FORMAL} = \alpha\_\text{result}(e_2, y) \\ \text{AGENTIVE} = \alpha\_\text{act}(e_1, x, y) \end{array} \right] \right]$$

(65)   EXPERIENCED CAUSATION:

$$\left[\text{QUALIA} = \left[\begin{array}{l} \text{FORMAL} = \alpha\_\text{result}(e_2, x) \\ \text{AGENTIVE} = \alpha\_\text{act}(e_1, x, \dots) \end{array} \right] \right]$$

Experiencer predicates do obey argument coherence, but by controlling or being in control of the causing action. As a specific example of this representation, consider the semantics for the verb *anger*.

(66)

$$
\begin{bmatrix}
\textbf{anger} \\
\text{EVENTSTR} = \begin{bmatrix} E_1 = e_1\text{:}\textbf{process} \\ E_2 = e_2\text{:}\textbf{state} \\ \text{RESTR} = < \circ_\alpha \\ \text{HEAD} = e_1 \end{bmatrix} \\
\text{ARGSTR} = \begin{bmatrix} \text{ARG1} = \boxed{1}\begin{bmatrix} < \boxed{2}, <e_1,t>> \end{bmatrix} \\ \text{ARG2} = \boxed{2}\begin{bmatrix} \textbf{animate\_ind} \\ \text{FORMAL} = \textbf{physobj} \end{bmatrix} \end{bmatrix} \\
\text{QUALIA} = \begin{bmatrix} \textbf{experiencer\_lcp} \\ \text{FORMAL} = \textbf{angry}(e_2, \boxed{2}) \\ \text{AGENTIVE} = \textbf{exp\_act}(e_1, \boxed{2}) \end{bmatrix}
\end{bmatrix}
$$

Notice that the temporal restriction is different from default causatives, and involves a precede and overlap relation between the experiencing process and the resulting experienced state.

That is, if doing something angers me, then I need not complete the activity before I become angry. The major difference between DCP verbs and experiencer verbs, however, is the necessary control relation that exists between the coerced predicate in the subject position and the individual who appears in object position. That is, just as the coercing control verbs *enjoy* and *begin* were analyzed as selecting for event functions in the complement position, experiencer predicates select for an event function in subject position. For NPs such as *the newspaper* and *the movie*, the qualia structure is able to drive a metonymic reconstruction to the type coerced by the predicate, an event function. The event structure associated with the sentence in (62c), for example, is illustrated below in (67), where a specific process has been specified, by virtue of the TELIC role from the qualia structure of *the newspaper*.

(67)

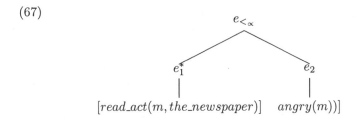

$$e_{<\alpha}$$

$$e_1^* \qquad\qquad e_2$$

$$[read\_act(m, the\_newspaper)] \qquad angry(m))]$$

Notice that the mapping to syntactic form from the headed event, e_1, is different from that associated with the DCP causatives, such as *kill*.

(68)

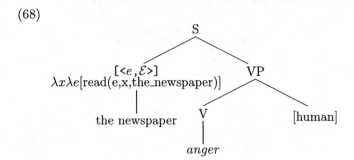

It is important to note that the conditions on how the qualia of the subject NP are made available through type coercion will vary from verb to verb, even within the experiencers. For example, one sees what appears to be a controlled versus non-controlled perception distinction emerging with the sentences in (69a) and (69b) respectively.

(69)   a. The sign <u>startled</u> Mary.
       b. The sign <u>angered</u> Mary.

That is, the verb *startle* seems to select for direct perceptual experiences such as given by direct visual and auditory stimuli, e..g, *seeing* and *hearing*. In sentence (69a), the default interpretation of the experiencing relation between Mary and the sign refers to her simply seeing it. The verb *anger*, on the other hand, requires of the subject that the experiencing event is controlled and intentional; hence, the predicates associated with the reconstructed event functions for the subject of *anger* will reflect this distinction. In (69b), for example, Mary must at least *read* the sign to be angered by it. Although it is certainly true that the mere presence of the sign in this location could make Mary angry, that is not a possible interpretation for (69b).[14]

There is a non-trivial issue of the aspectual properties of experiencer predicates that I have not addressed here. This is the fact that the resulting aspectual class of an experiencer predicate in context is determined by the *reconstructed event type* from the subject position. Consider the following sentences:

(70)   a. The flash of lightning frightened John.
      b. The electrical storm frightened John.

(71)   a. The sudden ring of the telephone frightened John.
      b. The ringing telephone frightened John.

That is, the point-like property of the event in the subject of (70a) is inherited by the overall experiencing event denoted by the sentence. Likewise, the bounded process event in the subject of (70b) influences the aspectual interpretation of the whole sentence as well. Similar remarks hold for the distinction in (71). This is related to the analysis of how complements influence the aspectual properties of their governing verbs, as presented in Verkuyl (1993). Although this phenomenon must be accounted for in the aspectual characterization of the experiencer verbs, I will defer discussion of this issue to Pustejovsky (forthcoming).

To conclude this section, let us discuss briefly what the consequence of this analysis of experiencers is for the well-known phenomenon of binding violations associated with this class of verbs. Following Chomsky (1981), the normal constraints on anaphoric binding will refer to properties of *precedence*, *c-command*, and *binding domain*. As discussed in Belletti and Rizzi (1985), Pesetsky (1987), and Grimshaw (1990), *frighten* and other experiencer verbs violate these constraints by allowing anaphoric binding into a subject which itself c-commands the antecedent, as shown in (72).[15]

(72)   a. The pictures of each other frighten the teachers.
      b. *Each other's students frighten the teachers.
      c. The picture of himself frightened John.

(73)   *The students of each other fear the teachers.

The psych-predicates patterning like *fear* behave predictably with respect to binding, while the *frighten*-class data are not accounted for without specific stipulations on the conditions for anaphoric reference.[16]

Recall from our previous discussion that experiencer verbs select for an event function in subject position, and are coercive on this position. This explained why control is possible into subject position from the object, as seen in (74).

(74)   a. PRO_i Seeing Mary so happy pleased $John_i$.

  b. PRO$_i$ Driving his car in Boston frightens John$_i$.

Assuming this analysis is correct, then we would actually expect the
kind of apparent c-command violations shown above in (72) to surface,
given the actual underlying structure of the causative relation between
the surface object and the event this individual engages in.

  To clarify this point, consider again the sentence in (72c). The event
tree structure illustrating this proposition is shown in (75) below, where I
have simplified some of the quantificational structure of the proposition.

(75)

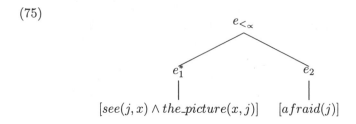

$$e_{<\alpha}$$

$$e_1^* \qquad\qquad e_2$$

$$[see(j,x) \wedge the\_picture(x,j)] \qquad [afraid(j)]$$

As becomes clear from the above structure, the ability to bind into the
subject of an experiencer predicate is not due to specific statements on
the ordering of θ-roles or the licensing of inverse predication, but follows simply from the *event function* interpretation of the subject. This,
furthermore, is the same reason control is possible into this position.

  It should be pointed out that binding into subject position is not
unilaterally acceptable, as the sentences in (76) illustrate.

(76)   a. *Himself$_i$ frightened John.
       b. *Each other$_i$ upset the teachers.

(77)   ?Each other$_i$'s students upset the teachers.

Given the coercion possible into the subject position of verbs such as
frighten and *upset*, one might expect the sentences in (76) to be acceptable. But notice that no coherent reconstruction from the reflexive
is possible directly. That is, coercion applies to the subject NP, but
because they are referentially opaque, there is nothing in the qualia
structure of these anaphors to reconstruct to the type required by the
governing verb.

9.5 Modal Causatives

In this section, I discuss briefly how lexical items encode modally subordinated causal relations or modally subordinated effects of an action. This is seen in the semantics of verbs such as *risk*, and I show how a semantic representation encoding this modal dimension affects the possible syntactic realization of the arguments to this verb.[17]

Most lexical causatives encode the certainty of the causal relation as an inherent part of their semantics. That is, if *x killed y*, or *x broke y*, then some event brought about the resulting state; in order to add the force of uncertainty, the verb must be modally subordinated by the syntax, as shown in (78).

(78) a. John <u>may kill</u> the tree by watering it so much.
      b. Mary <u>may break</u> the glass if she puts it in the dishwasher.

Some verbs, however, appear to encode the uncertainty of the resulting state which follows an action directly into the semantics of the lexical item itself. An example of such a lexical item is the verb *risk*, which lexically encodes the modality of the causal relation expressed syntactically above in (79).

(79) a. John <u>risks</u> killing the tree by watering it so much.
      b. Mary <u>risks</u> breaking the glass by putting it in the dishwasher.

This verb, studied in Fillmore and Atkins (1990) along with its nominal form, is interesting because of its strange complement-taking behavior. Namely, there is an unusual complementarity to the expression of the internal argument that leads Fillmore and Atkins to analyze this verb as motivation for constructions within a construction grammar (cf. Fillmore, 1987 and Goldberg, 1994).

(80) a. Mary <u>risked</u> death to save her son.
      b. Mary <u>risked</u> her life to save her son.

(81) a. Mary <u>risked</u> illness.
      b. Mary <u>risked</u> her health.

(82) a. John <u>risked</u> bankruptcy doing that.

    b. John <u>risked</u> his own solvency doing that.

What is interesting about these examples is that the direct object in each (a) sentence stands in complementary distribution to those in the (b) sentences, yet they are semantically near paraphrases of each other. Whatever the thematic or case structure of the verb is, it is clear that the presence of one argument acts to completely shadow the expression of the other.

    In their investigation of this word, Fillmore and Atkins (1990) argue that the semantic roles associated with the verb *risk* must include the following named relations:

(83) a. HARM: a potential unwelcome development or result;
       b. VICTIM: the individual who will potentially be harmed;
       c. DEED: the act which brings about the risky situation;
       d. GOAL: that which is achieved by the act;
       e. POSSESSION: something valued by the victim.

According to their analysis, there is no obvious compositional solution to the selection and assignment of the appropriate case roles as exhibited in the above data, and this is seen as evidence in support of a construction grammar solution. From our perspective, however, the complementary expression of the HARM and POSSESSION roles in the sentences above is indicative of a deeper relation between the roles and the nominalizations that express them. Namely, the HARM role always indicates the *privation* of a possible POSSESSION role, but in complementary semantic distribution.[18]

    This minor observation—that one argument of *risk* is the privative of another—points to an interesting fact about the complement types for this verb. That is, there are actually three basic syntactic patterns for the verb *risk* (for these arguments), as shown below in (84):

(84) a. Mary risked <u>death</u> to save John.
       b. Mary risked <u>her life</u> to save John.
       c. Mary risked <u>losing her life</u> to save John.

Given that these NPs—which according to Fillmore and Atkins' analysis, each assume a different case role—stand in complementary distribution to each other, then it is plausible to consider them as different expressions of the same underlying role, namely a *privative stative event*. Assume that the noun *death* is the privative of *life*, and *illness* is the privative of *health*, and so on. The phrasal expression of this role, *losing one's life*, is also privative, and it must be explained why the syntactic variability of the same semantic type is expressible in three different forms.

I believe that the complement taking behavior of *risk* follows from the following assumptions:

a. The direct object argument is typed a PRIVATIVE STATE.

b. There is no distinction between HARM and POSSESSION roles.

c. The verb may coerce its complement, giving rise to variable (nominally dependent) interpretations of the semantic type. Essentially, PRIVATIVE is acting as a function over NP denotations.

d. The semantics of lexical items makes reference to privative/nonprivative pairs. Qualia structure provides the semantic mechanism for reconstructing a privative interpretation for a lexical item.

How do these assumptions relate to the three grammatical forms available for this unique semantic type? We can think of PRIVATIVE as functioning as a coercion operator over a semantic expression, where, for example, given the nominal *health*, a metonymic reconstruction of this stative nominal is returned, which satisfies the privative typing environment of *risk*, without changing the meaning of the NP itself.

(85)   Metonymic Reconstruction by Coercion :
        a. PRIVATIVE(*health*)   =   *losing one's health*
        b. PRIVATIVE(*life*)   =   *losing one's life*
        c. PRIVATIVE(*solvency*)   =   *losing one's solvency*

In (85a), the privative typing requirement is directly satisfied by a number of lexical items, i.e., *sickness*, *illness*, which are both lexically privative, or by the actual gerundive phrase given. Similarly, the lexical privative for (85b) is *death*, and for (85c) is *bankruptcy*.

The modal nature of the resulting state brought about by the action performed in a sentence with *risk* is encoded as part of the lexical semantics of the verb. That is, a modal causative statement must be allowed in the semantics of lexical items. We can express the conditional nature of this resulting state in the qualia structure of the verb *risk* directly. The qualia structure for *risk* can be given as follows:

(86) $\lambda e_2 \lambda x \lambda e_1$ [*risk*: FORMAL=$[P(e_2, x) \vee \neg P(e_2, x)]$
     $\wedge$ AGENTIVE=$[R(e_1, x)]]$

This states that an individual x, by performing the activity e_1, will end up either in the state $P(e_2, x)$, or $\neg P(e_2, x)$. More specifically, this denotes the possibility that the activity in $R(e_1, x)$ results either in the continuation of the relevant state holding of x, $P(e_2, x)$, or its negation, $\neg P(e_2, x)$. The disjunction in the FORMAL role is the uncertainty of how the action will effect the subject.[19] This furthermore explains why there are three expressions corresponding to the type of PRIVATIVE STATE. Namely, the type can be satisfied by selecting $\neg P(e_2, x)$ from the FORMAL quale, and either finds a lexicalized form for this privative expression, such as *illness*, or it is forced to grammaticalize the privative of the positive form, *health*, giving rise to *losing one's health*. Finally, the non-privative, $P(e_2, x)$, can be selected, and interpreted, because of coercive reconstruction, as the privative in this context.[20]

In order to account for the modal nature of the causal relation expressed in the verb *risk*, it was sufficient to allow a disjunctive statement in the qualia structure, something I have avoided thus far, for obvious reasons. If we can maintain the interpretation of disjunctive expressions within qualia as interpreted relative to their modal force, then the nature of the semantic system will be extremely constrained. It is not clear, however, what other types of modal causatives exist in natural language, and whether they will be so easily treated by a disjunctive analysis.

9.6   Conclusion

In this chapter, I have tried to illustrate how a generative lexical approach to semantics is able to structure the space of possible lexicalizations for causal relations in language. Many topics, therefore, have been ignored, among them the semantics of resultative constructions, morphologically derived causatives, as well as the relation to syntactic causatives.

What we have seen is a number of possible lexical forms for the expression of causation. In particular, we examined three basic structures satisfying the condition on argument coherence, summarized below.

(87) DIRECT CAUSATION:

$$\left[\text{QUALIA} = \left[\begin{array}{l} \text{FORMAL} = \alpha\text{\_result}(e_2,y) \\ \text{AGENTIVE} = \alpha\text{\_act}(e_1,x,y) \end{array} \right] \right]$$

(88) EXPERIENCED CAUSATION:

$$\left[\text{QUALIA} = \left[\begin{array}{l} \text{FORMAL} = \alpha\text{\_result}(e_2,x) \\ \text{AGENTIVE} = \alpha\text{\_act}(e_1,x,\ldots) \end{array} \right] \right]$$

(89) INDIRECT (CONSTITUTIVE) CAUSATION:

$$\left[\text{QUALIA} = \left[\begin{array}{l} \text{CONST} = \textbf{part\_of}(z,y) \\ \text{FORMAL} = \alpha\text{\_result}(e_2,y) \\ \text{AGENTIVE} = \alpha\text{\_act}(e_1,x,z) \end{array} \right] \right]$$

In closing this discussion, it might be useful to compare briefly how lexically-encoded causation, with its condition on coherence, compares to causative constructions involving the verbs *make*, and *have*, and the Italian causative, *fare*.

As many have observed, the distinction between *make* and causative *have* in English involves the controllability of the event. But a notion of co-agency is also at play, brought about by agreement or contractual obligations. For example, while (90a) is clearly odd under normal interpretations, the same statement with *have* is acceptable, and furthermore refers to an agreed-upon event, which the subject is in control of, but mediated by the co-agency.

(90) a. ?We made the painters paint the house.
　　 b. We made the painters repaint the house.
　　 c. *We made the house painted.

(91) a. We had the painter paint the house.
　　 b. We had the painter repaint the house.
　　 c. We had the house painted.

Interestingly, (90b) is grammatical because of this same notion of (breach of) contractual agreement, somehow allowing the force of *make* to be licensed. Both forms are grammatical with *have*. Such subtle distinctions are not generally possible in English with lexical causatives, but do exist as derivational distinctions in causative types in some languages, e.g., Hindi, (cf. Saksena, 1980).[21]

How does this relate to the lexicalization of causative relations? Consider the structural alternatives to the transitive causative *kill* in Italian, illustrated in (92a)–(92d) below.

(92) a. Il fumo ha fatto morire Gianni di cancro.
          "His smoking caused John to die of cancer."
      b. Il suo comportamento ha fatto morire Maria di crepacuore.
          "His behavior caused Mary to die of heartbreak."
      c. Il divorzio ha fatto morire Maria di crepacuore.
          "The divorce caused Mary to die of heartbreak."
      d. Gianni ha fatto morire Maria.
          "John caused Mary to die."

When a verb encodes causation, it must obey the condition on argument coherence, as discussed above. Within the interpretation of a syntactic causative, however, there is no argument coherence at all. That is, while *kill* exhibits argument coherence on the affected object, *fare* in (92) does not. Rather, it exhibits *event coherence* on the event denoted by the dying, and not the affected object itself. Hence, there are many possible interpretations for these causatives, some due to qualia unification, others left underspecified by the semantics. The event tree structure in (93) illustrates how the semantics for a verb such as *fare* cannot necessarily bind into the arguments of the affected event, as is the case with a lexical causative.

(93)

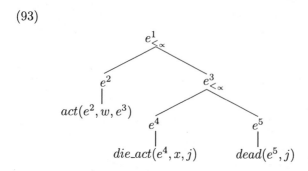

The interpretation of causative constructions is, of course, much too large an issue to do justice to here, and this discussion has been merely suggestive of how syntactic causatives necessarily differ from lexicalized causal relations.

10 Consequences of a Generative Lexicon

10.1 Co-composition and Verbal Semantics

The representations assumed from previous discussion for causative verbs such as *open*, shown in (1) below, are motivated in large part to allow headedness from an underspecified event representation to project to either a causative or unaccusative construction, as outlined in chapter 9.

(1)

$$
\begin{bmatrix}
\textbf{open} \\
\text{EVENTSTR} = \begin{bmatrix} E_1 = e_1\text{:process} \\ E_2 = e_2\text{:state} \\ \text{RESTR} = <_\alpha \end{bmatrix} \\
\text{ARGSTR} = \begin{bmatrix} \text{ARG1} = \boxed{1} \\ \text{ARG2} = \boxed{2} \begin{bmatrix} \textbf{physobj} \\ \text{FORMAL} = \textbf{entity} \end{bmatrix} \end{bmatrix} \\
\text{QUALIA} = \begin{bmatrix} \textbf{dc-lcp} \\ \text{FORMAL} = \textbf{open\_result}(e_2, \boxed{2}) \\ \text{AGENTIVE} = \textbf{open\_act}(e_1, \boxed{1}, \boxed{2}) \end{bmatrix}
\end{bmatrix}
$$

Such a representation provides us with a great deal more structure, in terms of granularity of the semantic description for the lexical item, while also connecting directly with the syntactic expressiveness of the semantic types. But notice that the structural semantic description for the predicate in this case is quite different from the cases discussed previously, such as *sink, kill,* and the other verb classes. Namely, the lexical representation for the predicate being defined, *open,* itself makes reference to a predicate with the same name in the FORMAL role. The qualia do actually distinguish the verb *open* from the stative adjective in this representation, by referring to the **open_result** predicate rather than any particular lexicalized form for it in the language. Nevertheless, what is distinctly different about verbs such as *open, close, break, repair,* and *fix,* is the functional dependence that the verb has on the argument denotation for arriving at the appropriate interpretation of the verb in context. To better understand this connection, consider the following sentences:

(2) a. Mary <u>opened</u> the letter from her mother.
  b. The rangers have <u>opened</u> the trail for the summer.
  c. John <u>opened</u> the door for the guests.

(3) a. Mary <u>broke</u> the teapot this morning.
     b. Federica's television <u>broke</u> during the Oscars.
     c. Mary <u>broke</u> the stick in two.

What each sentence in (2) asserts about its complement is that the function or purpose associated with the object of the predicate is available for use. That is, the object's TELIC role is shared, in a modally subordinated form, as the value of the FORMAL role for the main predicate *open*. For a noun such as *letter*, the TELIC is specified as the event function $\lambda z \lambda e \exists x.y[read(e, z, x.y)]$; this expression is embedded into a modal context within the FORMAL role of the predicate *open* in sentence (2a) above. Assume that the relevant expression of the lexical semantics for *letter* is as given in (4);

$$(4) \quad \begin{bmatrix} \textbf{letter} \\ \text{QUALIA} = \begin{bmatrix} \textbf{physobj·info-lcp} \\ \text{FORMAL} = \textbf{R(x,y)} \\ \text{TELIC} = \textbf{read(e,z,x.y)} \\ \cdots \end{bmatrix} \end{bmatrix}$$

In order to take advantage of the qualia-based information in the complement, the verbal semantics for *open* can be formulated so as to modally embed the relevant expression from the semantics of the complement phrase. A revised statement of the semantics of the verb *open* is presented in (5), where the modal statement making reference to the object's TELIC is explicitly given.

$$(5) \quad \begin{bmatrix} \textbf{open} \\ \text{EVENTSTR} = \begin{bmatrix} \text{E}_1 = \textbf{e}_1\textbf{:process} \\ \text{E}_2 = \textbf{e}_2\textbf{:state} \\ \text{RESTR} = <_\alpha \end{bmatrix} \\ \text{ARGSTR} = \begin{bmatrix} \text{ARG1} = \boxed{1} \\ \text{ARG2} = \boxed{2} \begin{bmatrix} \textbf{physobj} \\ \text{FORMAL} = \textbf{entity} \end{bmatrix} \end{bmatrix} \\ \text{QUALIA} = \begin{bmatrix} \textbf{dc-lcp} \\ \text{FORMAL} = \textbf{P}(\textbf{e}_2, \diamond[\text{TELIC}(\boxed{2})]) \\ \text{AGENTIVE} = \textbf{open\_act}(\textbf{e}_1, \boxed{1}, \boxed{2}) \end{bmatrix} \end{bmatrix}$$

Given these two expressions, the qualia structure resulting from co-composition within the VP can be expressed as in (6).

(6)

$$
\begin{bmatrix}
\textbf{open the\_letter} \\
\text{EVENTSTR} = \begin{bmatrix} \text{E}_1 = \textbf{e}_1\text{:process} \\ \text{E}_2 = \textbf{e}_2\text{:state} \\ \text{RESTR} = <_\propto \end{bmatrix} \\
\text{ARGSTR} = \begin{bmatrix} \text{ARG1} = \boxed{1} \\ \text{ARG2} = \boxed{2} \begin{bmatrix} \textbf{letter} \\ \text{QUALIA} = \begin{bmatrix} \textbf{physobj\cdot info-lcp} \\ \text{TELIC} = \boxed{3} = \textbf{read(e,z,x.y)} \end{bmatrix} \end{bmatrix} \end{bmatrix} \\
\text{QUALIA} = \begin{bmatrix} \textbf{dc-lcp} \\ \text{FORMAL} = \textbf{P}(\textbf{e}_2, \Diamond[\boxed{3}]) \\ \text{AGENTIVE} = \textbf{open\_act}(\textbf{e}_1, \boxed{1}, \boxed{2}) \end{bmatrix}
\end{bmatrix}
$$

What this expression says is the that the result of the open_act is a state asserting the possibility of the activity inherent in the TELIC role of the complement. This is another example of *co-composition*, where qualia unification results in a specific verbal sense in context, without the need to enumerate individual senses. The same verbal representation for *open* in (5) gives rise to the appropriate (but distinct) meaning of the verb in (2c) above, where the complement is the NP *the door* (cf. chapter 6 for discussion):

(7)
$$
\begin{bmatrix}
\textbf{door} \\
\text{QUALIA} = \begin{bmatrix} \textbf{physobj\cdot aperture-lcp} \\ \text{TELIC} = \textbf{walk\_through(e,z,y)} \\ \cdots \end{bmatrix}
\end{bmatrix}
$$

In this case, the denotation for the VP $[_{VP}$ open the door] makes reference to the ability to walk through the aperture as a result of the action of opening:

(8)

$$
\begin{bmatrix}
\textbf{open the\_door} \\
\text{EVENTSTR} = \begin{bmatrix} \text{E}_1 = \textbf{e}_1\text{:process} \\ \text{E}_2 = \textbf{e}_2\text{:state} \\ \text{RESTR} = <_\propto \end{bmatrix} \\
\text{ARGSTR} = \begin{bmatrix} \text{ARG1} = \boxed{1} \\ \text{ARG2} = \boxed{2} \begin{bmatrix} \textbf{door} \\ \text{QUALIA} = \begin{bmatrix} \textbf{physobj\cdot aperture-lcp} \\ \text{TELIC} = \boxed{3} = \textbf{walk\_through(e,z,y)} \end{bmatrix} \end{bmatrix} \end{bmatrix} \\
\text{QUALIA} = \begin{bmatrix} \textbf{dc-lcp} \\ \text{FORMAL} = \textbf{P}(\textbf{e}_2, \Diamond[\boxed{3}]) \\ \text{AGENTIVE} = \textbf{open\_act}(\textbf{e}_1, \boxed{1}, \boxed{2}) \end{bmatrix}
\end{bmatrix}
$$

In some sense, these functionally dependent verbs are modal causatives making reference to the qualia of their arguments. For this reason, we will call them *qualia modal causatives* (cf. Pustejovsky, forthcoming) to distinguish them from the class of modal causatives such as *risk*. Other examples of this type of underspecification with co-composition include the verbs *break* and *close*, which both make reference to the TELIC role of the complement as well, but in different ways. Briefly, the TELIC role for the complement of the verb *break* can be viewed as modally subordinated within the following context:

$$
(9) \quad
\begin{bmatrix}
\textbf{break NP} \\
\cdots \\
\text{ARGSTR} = \begin{bmatrix} \cdots \\ \text{ARG2} = \boxed{2}\, \begin{bmatrix} \textbf{NP} \\ \text{QUALIA} = \begin{bmatrix} \cdots \\ \text{TELIC} = \boxed{3} = \phi \end{bmatrix} \end{bmatrix} \end{bmatrix} \\
\text{QUALIA} = \begin{bmatrix} \textbf{dc-lcp} \\ \text{FORMAL} = \mathbf{P}(e_2, \neg\Diamond[\,\boxed{3}\,]) \\ \cdots \end{bmatrix}
\end{bmatrix}
$$

That is, the resulting state of a transitional event of breaking refers to the inability to use the object for that which it is intended; i.e., its TELIC role.[1]

The above discussion of functionally dependent verbs raises the issue of underspecified meanings more generally. Namely, when is it appropriate to "pack" many meanings into a single lexical representation, either with devices for semantic underspecification or by treating the item functionally, and when should one "unpack" several senses for a single lexical item, even when they are logically related? In the case of verbs such as *break* and *open*, co-compositional operations give rise to the contextualizing effects that the complements have on the phrase. Similarly, for cases of semantic type selection with multiple syntactic forms, such as *begin* and *believe*, the underspecification brought about by coercion seems generally correct and well-motivated by the data. Some cases of nominal polysemy, however, are not as straightforward, and complications arise when trying to account for all logical polysemies in terms of an underspecified representation. In particular, sense pairs related by "grinding" operations, as with the nouns *lamb* and *haddock*, are not homogeneously represented as single meta-entries, and may involve the application of lexical rules giving rise to sense extensions (cf. Copestake and Briscoe, 1992, 1995).[2] The nominal polysemy cases that do seem to involve "sense packing" are those analyzed above as dot objects, namely, nouns such as *lunch, sonata,* and *book.*

10.2   Stage-Level Predication

As mentioned in chapter 2 above, the stage-level/individual-level distinction in predicate types first made by Carlson (1977) is an important criterion for distinguishing the semantics of predication. Given the descriptive possibilities of qualia structure, one might view stage-level predicates as similar in some way to artifacts, and individual predicates as similar to natural kinds. Seen from this perspective, the distinction between states such as *be tall* and *be angry* is not a difference in event type, as argued in Pustejovsky (1991b), where stage-level predicates were analyzed as event transition functions, but rather is due to the presence or absence of reference to the mode of explanation which brings that state about, namely, the AGENTIVE quale.[3] Thus, rather than simply typing stage-level and individual level predicates distinctly, as Carlson proposed, the semantics should describe how a state is changeable. What distinguishes stage-levels from the general class of stative predicates is the inherent reference to that factor that brings this state about; as mentioned above, there is reference to the "coming into being" factor, the AGENTIVE role in the qualia. That is, a stage-level predicate is an *artifactual state.*

In order to make this proposal more explicit, let us develop the similarity to nominal artifacts more closely. Just as an artifact is defined by virtue of its AGENTIVE quale making reference to a specific event description of how it comes into being, let us assume that a changeable state also makes reference to such an event. As suggested in chapter 8, subevents, like arguments, may also have a *default* status in the event structure. For example, in (10) below, the predicate α is typed as a state, but reference to a default event, e_2, binds the argument in the stative predication to a relation preceding this state, in other words, the cause of the state.

$$(10) \quad \begin{bmatrix} \alpha \\ \text{ARGSTR} = \begin{bmatrix} \text{ARG1} = \mathbf{x{:}\tau_1} \\ \text{D-ARG1} = \mathbf{y{:}\tau_2} \end{bmatrix} \\ \text{EVSTR} = \begin{bmatrix} \text{E}_1 = \mathbf{e_1{:}state} \\ \text{D-E}_1 = \mathbf{e_2{:}\sigma} \\ \text{RESTR} = e_2 <_\alpha e_1 \\ \text{HEAD} = e_1 \end{bmatrix} \\ \text{QUALIA} = \begin{bmatrix} \text{FORMAL} = \mathbf{\alpha\_result(e_1,x)} \\ \text{AGENTIVE} = \mathbf{R(e_2,x,y)} \end{bmatrix} \end{bmatrix}$$

There are several reasons for thinking that a lexical item might make reference to default events, as opposed to the non-expression of an event due to lack of headedness. The function of heading an event, recall, is to both focus that event within a larger structure of events, as well as to filter the expressive output from the semantics to the syntax.

To illustrate the consequences of this proposal, consider the sentences in (11)–(13), involving the psych-stage-level predicates *angry, nervous,* and *upset.*

(11) a. John is <u>angry</u> at the newspaper.
      b. John is <u>angry</u> from reading the newspaper.

(12) a. ?There are musicians <u>nervous</u>.
      b. There are musicians <u>nervous</u> about tonight's competition.

(13) a. ?There are Americans <u>upset</u>.
      b. There are Americans <u>upset</u> with the way the President is handling foreign policy.

As Diesing (1992) points out, the *there*-insertion construction is a generally reliable test for pulling out the existential interpretation possible with stage-level predicates. Although (12a) and (13a) are marginal, notice how the PP-adjunct makes reference to the quale identifying the predicate as an artifactual state. The result in each case is a perfectly acceptable stage-level predication (cf. (12b) and (13b)). By specifying the AGENTIVE quale value in the qualia structure for *angry, nervous,* and *upset,* the predicate is appropriately identified for an existential interpretation. The lexical semantics for *angry* is given in (14) below, illustrating how causative adjuncts such as *from reading the newspaper* act to specify the AGENTIVE role for the predicate.

$$(14) \quad \begin{bmatrix} \textbf{angry} \\ \\ \text{EVENTSTR} = \begin{bmatrix} \text{E}_1 = \textbf{e}_1\textbf{:state} \\ \text{D-E}_1 = \textbf{e}_2\textbf{:process} \\ \text{RESTR} = e_2 <_\propto e_1 \\ \text{HEAD} = \textbf{e}_1 \end{bmatrix} \\ \\ \text{ARGSTR} = \begin{bmatrix} \text{ARG}1 = \boxed{1}\begin{bmatrix} \textbf{human} \\ \text{FORMAL} = \textbf{animate} \end{bmatrix} \\ \text{D-ARG}1 = \boxed{2}\begin{bmatrix} \top \end{bmatrix} \end{bmatrix} \\ \\ \text{QUALIA} = \begin{bmatrix} \text{FORMAL} = \textbf{angry}(\textbf{e}_1, \boxed{1}) \\ \text{AGENTIVE} = \textbf{exp\_act}(\textbf{e}_2, \boxed{1}, \boxed{2}) \end{bmatrix} \end{bmatrix}$$

The event of reading the newspaper is unified with the experiencer process identified as e_2 in the structure above. Notice that this is possible only because *read* is a subtype of experiencer predicates. Unlike its associated causative, *anger*, the predicate *angry* remains stative even when reference to the causing event is present through an adjunct expression, as in this case.

Assuming that this approach to stage-level predication is correct, let us now briefly revisit the problem of resultatives first mentioned in chapter 8, in the context of co-composition. As argued in Pustejovsky (1991a), the adjectival phrases entering into resultative constructions are just those stage-level predicates which "cohere" with the process predicate present in the phrase. For adjectives such as *clean* and *flat*, as used in (15b) and (16b) below,

(15) a. Mary waxed the car.
      b. Mary waxed the car <u>clean</u>.

(16) a. John hammered the metal.
      b. John hammered the metal <u>flat</u>.

composition with the VP can be accomplished by a modified version of qualia unification presented in chapter 8. To illustrate this derivation, consider the sentence in (15b). The lexical representation for the adjective *clean* is that given in (17).

(17)

$$
\begin{bmatrix}
\textbf{clean} \\
\text{EVENTSTR} =
\begin{bmatrix}
\text{E}_1 = \textbf{e}_1\textbf{:state} \\
\text{D-E}_1 = \textbf{e}_2\textbf{:process} \\
\text{RESTR} = e_2 <_\propto e_1 \\
\text{HEAD} = \textbf{e}_1
\end{bmatrix} \\
\text{ARGSTR} =
\begin{bmatrix}
\text{ARG1} = \boxed{1}\begin{bmatrix}\textbf{physobj} \\ \text{FORMAL} = \textbf{entity}\end{bmatrix} \\
\text{D-ARG1} = \boxed{2}\begin{bmatrix}\top\end{bmatrix}
\end{bmatrix} \\
\text{QUALIA} =
\begin{bmatrix}
\text{FORMAL} = \textbf{clean}(\textbf{e}_1, \boxed{1}) \\
\text{AGENTIVE} = \textbf{R}(\textbf{e}_2, \boxed{1}, \boxed{2})
\end{bmatrix}
\end{bmatrix}
$$

Here I am assuming that R is a predicate that is sortally structured to subsume *wax, wipe,* and related predicates. The stage-level predicate acts as a function over the VP *wax the car*, but under qualia unification, the FORMAL role of the adjective unifies with that of the VP, resulting in a derived causative and an aspectually telic interpretation (cf. Dowty, 1979).

(18)

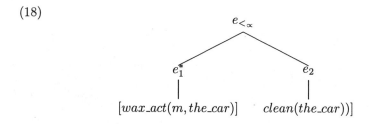

The structure in (18) is basically that of the default causative paradigm encountered in chapter 9; the difference, of course, is that it is a derived interpretation and is not lexicalized into one lexical item. In some sense, the stage-level predicative construction corresponding to (15b), namely, *The car is clean* can be thought of as a *potential* unaccusative. The proper unaccusative for (15b) would be (19):

(19) *The car <u>waxed</u> clean.

Obviously, the crucial difference here is an aspectual one, where the adjective can denote only a state and not a transition, as with unaccusatives. Stage-level predicates, therefore, facilitate or license reference to that which brings about that state, but only in specific constructions under co-compositional operations.

To close this section, it is interesting to see whether the distinction between stage-level and individual-level predicates as construed above might extend to the nominal domain as well. There is a difference between "role-defining" nominals such as *physicist, linguist,* and *violinist,* and "situationally-defined" nominals such as *pedestrian, student, passenger,* and *customer.* I will refer to these two classes as *individual-level nominals (ILNs)* and *stage-level nominals (SLNs),* respectively. Observe that, whereas ILNs successfully denote even when the defining characteristic is absent, SLNs denote only if there is existential force on the predicate defining the nominal.

(20) a. The <u>violinist</u> is eating lunch at the cafeteria.
      b. We met the <u>physicists</u> from the institute on the trail.

(21) a. The <u>passengers</u> are eating lunch on the plane.
      b. Bill is helping a <u>customer</u>.

The NPs in (20) still felicitously pick out the individual(s) denoted by the ILNs because of the generic nature of the interpretation. Hence, even though the TELIC quale for *violinist* refers to "playing the violin," it need not be an activity or state that holds at the time of reference. Similarly, "doing physics" in some official capacity would arguably define an individual as a physicist, but one need not be engaged in this activity in order to be individuated as one. Here again, the generic force of the occupational classification transcends any particular situation which that individual is part of.

Notice that the SLNs in (21), however, properly denote only if the activity defined by the noun is existentially closed; that is, in (21a) the passengers, defined in terms of the process of "travelling," must be engaged in this activity in order to be identified by this term. The same holds for *customer* in (21b), where it is a particular situation (i.e., "shopping") that determines the conditions for which this term will properly denote. There are cases, however, where a SLN may appropriately refer even after the situation identifying the individual has occurred, as in (22).

(22) Hey, you're the <u>passenger</u> from my flight yesterday!

What is important to point out about such examples, however, is that the situation referred to by the NP *the passenger* is still existentially quantified over, unlike the generic readings available for ILNs.

This distinction can be brought out in the semantics as a difference in qualia structure, where the situational reading of an SLN can be identified with the AGENTIVE quale of the noun (cf. (23)), while the generic readings available for ILNs are associated with the TELIC role of the noun, cf. (24).

$$(23) \quad \begin{bmatrix} \textbf{pedestrian} \\ \text{QUALIA} = \begin{bmatrix} \text{FORMAL} = \textbf{x} \\ \text{AGENTIVE} = \textbf{walk\_act(e,x)} \\ \dots \end{bmatrix} \end{bmatrix}$$

$$(24) \quad \begin{bmatrix} \textbf{violinist} \\ \text{QUALIA} = \begin{bmatrix} \text{FORMAL} = \textbf{x} \\ \text{TELIC} = \textbf{play(e,x,y:violin)} \\ \dots \end{bmatrix} \end{bmatrix}$$

Pustejovsky (1989,1991a) discusses how reference to the TELIC role of a nominal is a prototypical and defeasible inference, while Moravcsik (1990) makes the observation that the activity most typically associated with the use of an object is a generic statement. Applied to the interpretation of the two classes of nominals above, the genericity of the TELIC quale seems to provide an appropriate distinction in the way that they denote. Characterizing the SLN as involving an existential closure on the event in the AGENTIVE quale is explored in Busa (forthcoming), where this distinction is studied in greater detail.[4]

10.3 Further Applications of Coercion

In this section, I review briefly how type coercion might be usefully adopted in other parts of the grammar. The advantages of the approach described in this work are, I believe, seen in the application of the generative devices to widely diverse phenomena and constructions in language.[5]

Coercion in Temporal Connectives The standard interpretation of the temporal connectives *before*, *after*, *while*, and *during*, involves selection of an interval or event. Remaining neutral on this issue for now, it is clear that in order to account for the selectional behavior exhibited below, we must either posit two lexical entries for these items or reconstruct the interpretations in terms of type coercion. Consider, for example, the selectional distinctions available for the connectives *before* and *after* compared to that for the preposition *during*.

(25) a. I will call you <u>before</u> John gets here for his appointment.
      b. I will call you <u>before</u> my next appointment.
      c. My next appointment is John.
      d. *I will call you <u>before</u> my next appointment, who is John.
      e. *I will call you <u>before</u> John.
      f. Let's examine Mary <u>before</u> John. (ellipsis)

(26) a. Let's leave <u>after</u> we drink the coffee.
      b. Let's leave <u>after</u> dessert.
      c. Let's leave <u>after</u> the coffee.

(27) a. *I will call you <u>during</u> my next student.
      b. *I will read it <u>during</u> my coffee.

While *before* and *after* seem to generally license coercion, *during* does not. Many of these sentences point out that coercion can only facilitate type satisfaction, and pragmatic or contextual factors may be required to determine what the full meaning of a reconstructed interpretation is. The interaction between lexically-encoded linguistic knowledge and pragmatic effects on interpretation is studied in more detail in Asher and Lascarides (1995) and Nunberg (1995).

Functional Prepositions and the Role of Qualia   There is an interesting paradigm that has received little attention in the literature, concerning the use of English prepositions such as *at* and *in* to specify functional involvement. Consider the following sentences.

(28) a. John is <u>at</u> his desk.
      b. John is <u>by</u> his desk.

(29) a. The student is <u>at</u> the board.
      b. ??My 2-year old daughter is <u>at</u> the board.

(30) a. John is <u>at</u> the office.
      b. I left my computer <u>at</u> the office.

(31) a. Zac is <u>in</u> school from 9:00 am to 3:00 pm.

  b. The computers are finally <u>in</u> the school.

(32) a. Mary is <u>in</u> hospital with a broken leg.
  b. Mary is <u>in</u> the hospital visiting her brother.

There are two things to observe about these data and the broader paradigm. First, the preposition *at* seems to only select locations that have in their qualia structure a specific TELIC role. For example, blackboards are used for writing on, the desk is used for work, and so on. Secondly, when an individual is predicated of an *at*-PP, it suggests that the individual is participating in the TELIC role taken from the preposition's complement. That is, if I am at my desk, then I am situated in the specific orientation which would enable me to perform the activities typically associated with the desk. Similarly, if I am at the board, then I am in the process of or intending to or being forced to write something on the blackboard, i.e., the TELIC of the NP. Notice that if such an activity cannot reasonably be fulfilled, as with (29b) above, then the sentence is semantically odd, since my daughter doesn't have the ability to use the board for its proper function (cf. Li, 1994).[6]

   There is another parameter at play here involving definiteness and the *bare singular* predicative readings in (31a) and (32a). Namely, for many TELIC-specified nominals, most with dot object status, such as *hospital* and *school*, when they appear as bare singular expressions as complement to prepositions such as *in* (and *at*), they predicate not only the location of the individual but also the activity associated or events characterized as the function of that nominal. Thus, being "*in* hospital" is to be a patient, and being "*in* school" is to be a student, and so on. Although it is not completely clear what the constraints are on such interpretations, what is clear is that the qualia are contributing essential information to the interpretation of the expression in a way that is not a strict coercion.

10.4   Linguistic versus Commonsense Knowledge

From the discussion presented above, the boundary between what we formally take to be linguistic or lexical knowledge and that which is sometimes referred to as "commonsense knowledge" might appear fuzzier than ever.[7] Once we start enriching our lexicon with information that, to a linguist, appears better suited for a knowledge base, there may appear to be no systematic means to judge where to stop (cf. Herzog and Rollinger, 1991, and in particular, Lang, 1991). Yet, the fact that there appears to be a continuum between these two types of knowledge doesn't mean that there are not clear cases of paradigmatic linguistic behavior that are better treated as language specific knowledge, rather than in terms of general inferencing mechanisms. One of the goals of the present work has been not only to argue in favor of richer lexical representations and compositional mechanisms, but also to show that these structures and devices are still language specific in identifiable ways. What is different about the approach taken here is that there are clear and obvious means to interface lexical knowledge with commonsense and pragmatic inferences.

For example, recent work by Asher and Lascarides (1995) investigates how discourse structure can affect the selection of lexical senses, focusing in particular on the mechanisms whereby lexical semantics affects and contributes to discourse interpretation. To this aim, they integrate three components:

(A) a theory of discourse structure called SDRT (cf. Kamp and Reyle, 1993), which represents discourse in terms of rhetorical relations that connect together the propositions introduced by the text segments;

(B) an accompanying theory of discourse attachment called DICE (cf. Lascarides and Asher, 1993), which computes the rhetorical relations holding between constituents, on the basis of the reader's background information; and

(C) a formal language for specifying both the syntactic and semantic knowledg for a lexical item, called the LRL, lexical representation language (cf. Copestake and Briscoe, 1993), making use of a typed feature structure logic.

By integrating these separate components, they are able to model the information flow in both directions, from words to discourse, and from discourse to words. For the mapping from words to discourse, Asher and Lascarides show how the LRL permits the rules for computing rhetorical relations in DICE to be generalized and simplified, so that a single rule applies to several semantically related lexical items. From discourse to words, they encode two heuristics for lexical disambiguation:

- disambiguate words so that discourse incoherence is avoided; and
- disambiguate words so that rhetorical connections are reinforced.

With these heuristics, several cases of lexical disambiguation can be analyzed, that have until now been outside the scope of theories of lexical processing. Asher and Lascarides show how lexical processing can work in service to a theory of discourse attachment. The knowledge resources encoded in a theory of discourse attachment, however, are also useful to lexical processing. Consider the following examples and the ambiguities in them concerning the words *plant*, *bar* and *dock*.

(33) a. They ruined the view.
      b. They improved the view.
      c. They put a <u>plant</u> there.

(34) a. The judge demanded to know where the defendant Ross was.
      b. The barrister mumbled apologetically, and said that Ross had last been seen drinking heavily.
      c. The judge told the bailiff to escort Ross from the <u>bar</u> to the <u>dock</u>.

They argue that *bar* in the second example is disambiguated to its "drinking establishment" sense on the basis of constraints on coherent discourse. In contrast, *plant* in the first example is disambiguated on the basis of strengthening the rhetorical link between the sentences. The inference which leads to this disambiguation is driven by the lexical semantic information associated with the qualia structure for the words.

The examples above illustrate the disambiguation of contrastive senses with the help of contextual information. These are distinguished from the cases of logical polysemy studied in this work for reasons outlined in some detail in chapters 3 and 4. There are, however, some types of sense extension that I have not discussed in this work, and which do require some mention in this section. These are cases of *displaced reference*, studied in Nunberg (1979,1995), Fauconnier (1985), and Jackendoff (1992b). What distinguishes this from logical polysemy is the lexically idiosyncratic nature of the ambiguity, as well as the semi-productive status such extensions have in language. These involve sentences like those given in (35) below.

(35) a. I am parked out back.

b. Ringo squeezed himself into the parking space.

These sentences illustrate two types of referential transfer: a type-mismatch between subject and predicate in (35a), where it is the car that is parked, not the individual; and a mismatch between verb and object, together with a non-identity between antecedent and anaphor in the binding relation in (35b). Nunberg refers to such extensions of meaning as *predicate transfers*. In particular, he argues against a metonymic analysis, where the subject *I* in (35a) and the object *himself* in (35b) are interpreted as *my car* and *his car* respectively. Rather, his position is that there are pragmatically-licensed conditions which allow the predicate to extend its sense, where it is retyped to select for the subjects that are present in the syntax. The operation of predicate transfer allows a name of a property to be mapped into a new name denoting a property to which it functionally corresponds, as with the meaning of the predicate *parked out back* in (35a) above. Predicate transfer is responsible for the ability of this predicate to both refer to the car, but also to take syntactically as its subject, the driver of the car. According to Nunberg's (1995) formulation of the phenomena, predicate transfer is subject to two general conditions;

- the basic and derived property must stand in a functional correspondence to one another;
- the derived property should be a "noteworthy" feature of its bearer.

Nunberg argues that reference to predicate transfer allows us to maintain a very strict definition of syntactic identity, thereby ruling out all cases of "sortal crossing," where a term appears to refer to things of two sorts at the same time, as in examples like *Ringo squeezed himself into a tight space*; in such a case, the reflexive is strictly coreferential with its antecedent. Nunberg claims that these observations enhance the reliability of "zeugma" tests for ambiguity, while also highlighting a theoretical difficulty in distinguishing polysemy and generality. Furthermore, he claims that these results pose a difficulty for the view argued here that there is a legitimate distinction between logical polysemy and more general operations of sense transfer such as metaphor.[8]

Consider next the sentences first discussed in Jackendoff (1992b), for the effect of predicate transfer on reflexivization.

(36)   a. Ringo$_i$ squeezed himself$_i$ into a narrow space.
       b. Yeats$_i$ did not like to hear himself$_i$ read in an English accent.

Because of the restricted conditions on when such co-predications are
allowed, Nunberg suggests that these need not be cases of sortal crossing,
but rather instances of predicate transfer, where the individuals denoted
by the subject expressions are fixed, and it is the predicate which changes
its sense. The reliability of the zeugma as a test for determining the
polysemy of a word is preserved with this interpretation.

What emerges very clearly from the recent work on the interface between lexical and non-lexical semantic information is that polysemy is
not a single, monolithic phenomenon. Rather, it is the result of both
compositional operations in the semantics, such as coercion and co-
composition, and of contextual effects, such as the structure of rhetorical
relations in discourse and pragmatic constraints on co-reference. What
is necessary is for research to tackle the difficult question of how other
components in the natural language interpretation process interact with
the lexicon to disambiguate and fully determine the semantics of words
in context. This work, emerging from very different traditions, illustrates
how lexical semantics can be made sensitive to sentence level compositional processes as well as discourse level inference mechanisms, reacting
to the diverse and multiple causes of lexical ambiguity.

10.5   Lexical Inference and Rhetoric

If we look at the relation between inferential structures within compositional semantics and the larger structures of inference associated with
rhetoric, some interesting parallels emerge. These can perhaps best be
illustrated by examining the structure of *enthymemic inference* in the
structure of rhetoric; that is, the conditions which license *ellipsis* in
persuasive discourse. Within Aristotle's view of how logic and rhetoric
interact (cf. *Rhetoric*), rhetoric is viewed as the application of the general inferential mechanisms of the logic to a particular context, for a
specific goal. Inference is put to use for persuasive discourse, and that
which is persuasive is evaluated only in reference to some specific individual; because of this, the mode of ellipsis depends on the rhetorical
structure employed.

Consider the form of an *enthymeme*, which is a set of two propositions offered as an argument, such that the addition of a third results in a categorical syllogism. When the ellipsed proposition is the major premise, then we have what could be termed *enthymemic induction*. In this structure, propositions can be viewed as being coerced to a pattern of coherence to satisfy the inference. The following illustrates this pattern, where the bracketed expression is the ellipsed proposition.

A. James is a Texan.

B. Therefore, James is tall.

C. [All Texans are tall.]

$$A \wedge [_C A' \rightarrow B'] \implies B$$

The assumed belief is that the speaker and hearer share ellipsed propositions as common belief. The speaker, by using such a rhetorical form, is establishing coherence between (i.e., coercing) the propositions for the hearer.

If the ellipsed proposition is the minor premise, then an *enthymemic abduction* results. This is illustrated by the following argument.

A. Every American loves baseball.

B. Therefore, John loves baseball.

C. [John is American.]

$$[_A C' \rightarrow B'] \wedge B \implies C$$

The assumed belief here is that the speaker and hearer know that the ellipsed proposition is true. The speaker in this case is using a non-analytic proposition as the major premise. This is the coercive assumption from which, with the common belief of C, the syllogism has rhetorical force.

Finally, if the ellipsed proposition is the conclusion, then a simple *enthymemic deduction* results, shown below.

A. All politicians are corrupt.

B. Berlusconi is a politician.

C. [Berlusconi is corrupt.]

$$[_A B' \rightarrow C'] \wedge B \implies C$$

Common knowledge provides the valid rule of syllogistic reasoning. But the speaker does not complete the syllogism, leaving the inference as new and topical information *conveyed* or projected by the discourse.

The effect of coercion and co-composition, when projected to discourse-level interpretations, could be viewed as a type of lexical enthemymic inference. Consider the example below, where the qualia contribute information that can be used in the discourse in a method similar to the inferences discussed above.

A. Steven King began a new novel.

B. [Steven King is a writer.]

C. AGENTIVE(novel) $= \lambda z \lambda x.y \lambda e^T [write(e^T, z, x.y)]$

C'. Steven King began to write a new novel.

As argued in chapter 7, coercion requires that the verb *begin* selects an event function as its complement, but the interpretation is not fully determined by the lexical semantics alone. The knowledge of what the type of the NP *Steven King* is, and what qualia values may or may not contribute to further specifying this interpretation, can be seen as discourse inferences that are biased by the compositional semantics of the sentence. Similar remarks hold for data mentioned in chapter 4 above, where the full interpretation of the type required by the coercion on the complement is logically separate from the type coercion itself.

(37) a. Most commercial pilots <u>prefer</u> Kennedy to Logan.
      b. Most commercial pilots <u>prefer</u> New York to Boston.

These comments are merely suggestive, but establishing the contribution of lexical semantics to pragmatic and contextual inferences is an important area of research.

10.6 Summary

In this book, I have presented a framework for the semantic analysis of natural language, motivated by the following theoretical and computational concerns:

(1) Explaining the interpretation of words in context;

(2) Deriving a potentially infinite number of senses for words from finite resources;

(3) Accounting for the systematic relatedness between word senses in a formal and predictable way;

(4) Characterizing natural languages in terms of their polymorphic properties; more specifically, studying what types of polymorphisms exist and how productive they are in natural language;

(5) Providing a semantic representation that is applicable cross-categorially, and is not restricted to verb semantics alone.

By structuring the representation of words in a manner completely parallel to that of syntactic objects, we obviate the need to postulate lexical primitives, since the natural language vocabulary is itself the data set of primitives. Just as the generativity of syntactic structures is the major concern of syntactic theory, accounting for the generativity of senses in a language is the primary goal of lexical and compositional semantics. This, in my view, characterizes what a generative lexicon should be.

There are obviously many questions that have been left unanswered in the current work. For example, issues relating to parsing, details of interpretation concerning quantification, and connections to pragmatic and commonsense inferencing mechanisms have not been seriously dealt with here, although they have contributed to the design of the framework. I have attempted to present a model of semantics for natural language that provides the necessary lexical resources to perform these tasks, while simplifying and, I hope, clarifying the role of the lexicon in linguistic theory.

Notes

Chapter 1

1. Weinreich (1964), in making this distinction, was critiquing the somewhat arbitrary manner with which the Webster's Third Dictionary handled lexical items with multiple word senses. The observation shows an insight into the problem of distinguishing accidental sharing of lexical forms from linguistically motivated sense relations, that others did not generally recognize.

Chapter 2

1. Perhaps the most notable exception to this claim or movement would be Fillmore's recent move towards the encoding of larger units of phrasal structure, known as *constructions* (cf. Fillmore, 1985). Goldberg (1994) extends this perspective to a fairly broad range of phenomena, showing how constructions can adequately account for cases of polyvalency and polysemy. In some sense, this is not contradictory to my claim above, since larger structural units are essentially lexicalized rather than subject to general rules of composition (cf. chapter 8 below).

2. This is still a contentious point and is an issue that is not at all resolved in the community. Hobbs (1987) and Wilensky (1986,1991), for example, question the distinction between commonsense knowledge and lexical knowledge. Even more fundamentally, some previous research in NLP and computational linguistics, such as Wilks (1975) and Schank (1975) saw no utility in distinguishing knowledge of the world and knowledge of how we talk about the world. More recently, Wilks' work (cf. Wilks *et al.*, 1988,1993) has pointed to examining how faithfully lexical knowledge represents our knowledge of the world, as encoded in machine-readable formats such as dictionaries, e.g., LDOCE (cf. Procter, 1978). Schank has not recently addressed the issue of knowledge representation as it relates to language. Nevertheless, I will suggest below that there are good reasons, both methodological and empirical, for establishing just such a division. Pustejovsky and Bergler (1992) and Pustejovsky (1993) contain a good survey on how this issue is addressed by the community. Saint-Dizier and Viegas (1995) compare some recent approaches to addressing this distinction more formally. Cf. also Atkins and Zampolli (1994) for approaches to integration of lexicographic and computational methods.

3. The context within which an utterance is situated must reflect the state of the discourse, as many have recently argued, for example, Heim (1982), Kamp and Reyle (1993), Asher (1993), and recent trends within situation semantics. Just as important, however, is some notion of the purpose of the utterance. Grosz and Sidner (1986), Pollack (1986), Cohen, Morgan, and Pollack (1990), and others have rightly stressed the importance of goals in laying the contextual groundwork for the communicative act. Thus, in some sense, the rhetorical structure of the discourse defines what the speaker wants to accomplish (cf. Hovy, 1993). I will return to this point in chapter 10.

4. See Dixon (1991) and Levin (1993) for discussion.

5. The generalization, as Levin (1993) sees it, bears on verbs denoting both contact and motion (or perhaps more correctly, motion towards contact). Notice, however, that (9b) above becomes much better if we contextualize the sense with adjunct modification:

(i) ?Under the table, the cat kept <u>touching</u> at my leg with its front paw.

The issue of sense contextualization will figure more prominently later in our discussion of co-composition in chapter 7.

6. As we will see below, however, even this distinction requires modification, since all three of the lexically marked activity verbs can phrasally or sententially appear in transitional (i.e., telic) contexts. See chapter 9 below for further discussion.

7. I argue in Pustejovsky (1995c) that the aspectual distinction in the indefinite NP deletion cases is in fact sufficient to explain which verbs license the alternation. For the broader class of complement-drop phenomena, however, including the infinitival complement cases in (17) and (18) above, more is involved than simple aspect.

8. On details of this, see Dowty (1979).

9. It is useful here to point out the distinction between *temporal culmination*, where an event of whatever sort simply stops, and *logical culmination*, whereby something is fulfilled or finished as a result of the activity (cf. also Parsons, 1990 and Tenny, 1992).

10. The issue of variable aspectuality is discussed in some detail in chapter 9 in terms of polysemy and event coercion.

11. Although there are several diagnostics for indicating membership in one or the other class, many of them are simply inadequate to accord with speaker intuitions. For example, both *there*-insertion and progressive tests seem to favor stage-level predicates over individual-level ones, but there are many counterexamples to the generalization. I discuss the general issue of stage-level predication below in chapter 10.

12. For crystallographers, of course, there is a very different experience with sand as a material. They might very well refer to individual grains of sand as "sand." The classification of a material or thing in the world is obviously driven by how we perceive it and construct the reality for that object, given a certain mode of measurement. See Modrak (1987) and Hacking (1983).

13. I return to a discussion of this issue later in chapter 7.

14. Chomsky (1957) sees this as a clear mismatch between the structure that Markov models assign to such sentences and the underlying representations necessary to understand them.

15. Any property is of course possible as the complement of *easy* or *difficult* when overt complementation is used, as illustrated in (i) and (ii):

    (i) a. That exam was <u>difficult</u> to grade.
       b. The exam has been <u>easy</u> to write, but it's going to be very <u>difficult</u> for the students to take.

    (ii) This highway will be <u>easy</u> for the work crew to pave in the summer.

Default interpretations of ellipsed expressions will always give way to overt linguistic expressions.

16. This definition ignores the issue of opacity and non-substitutability in opaque contexts. Katz (1972) has a useful discussion on the general nature of semantic relations, while Bierwisch and Schreuder (1992) discuss the issues of representation and access for the different semantic relations between lexical items. Apresjan (1973a) examines the linguistic contexts for synonymy in particular, and how it is structurally identified. Sparck Jones (1986) presents a helpful study of criteria for semantic classification and the identification of terms as synonyms.

17. The issue of presupposition and how lexical meaning relates to projection cannot be given a full discussion in this work. I will return, however, to these issues briefly in the context of factivity in chapter 7. Soames (1989) presents a helpful guide to most of the recent approaches to the treatment of presupposition in natural language.

Chapter 3

1. Hirst treats *taxied* as ambiguous in this sentence as well. Although the uninflected form *taxi* is certainly ambiguous, the past tense marker here acts to disambiguate the form, therefore we need not consider it for disambiguation purposes.

2. See original articles by Katz (1965), Vendler (1963), on the use of "good." But we return to this in the next chapter.

3. In some sense, things haven't changed that much since Katz and Fodor (1963) proposed essentially the same system for representing ambiguous forms. It is interesting that early connectionist attempts at word sense disambiguation constructed a feature structure model of lexical senses almost identical to that of the early Katz-Fodor theory (cf. Rumelhart and McClellan (1986)). Not surprisingly, the critics of this work (cf. the papers in Pinker and Mehler, 1988) raise the same issues that the strongest Katz-Fodor critic had raised, namely, Weinreich, in his essay "Explorations in Semantic Theory."

4. It is clear that for some contrastive ambiguities, the sense enumerative approach will have to employ a fairly rich system of selectional features to properly disambiguate senses. Some researchers have suggested using sets of synonyms to aid in disambiguating senses of a lexical item (cf. Miller *et al.*, 1990a). On this view, a lexical item would, in addition to CAT and GENUS information, also store a SYNSET, the set of synonyms associated with the word; i.e., those words that it extensionally appears in complementary distribution with. This would help in distinguishing the sense of *line* given above in (2), for example:

(i) $\begin{bmatrix} \textbf{line}_1 \\ \text{CAT} = \textbf{count-noun} \\ \text{SYNSET} = \textbf{message} \end{bmatrix}$

(ii) $\begin{bmatrix} \textbf{line}_2 \\ \text{CAT} = \textbf{count-noun} \\ \text{SYNSET} = \textbf{border} \end{bmatrix}$

5. This approach starts with *Aspects*-like lexical representations and is recently codified in the HPSG work of Pollard and Sag (1994).

6. Although the exact mechanisms for such selection are not trivial, and the details of how such word sense search and selection is performed varies from system to system, most researchers will acknowledge the same basic strategy for disambiguation of contrastive senses. Strategies do vary quite a bit, of course, from Marker Passing techniques, reported on in several implementations (cf. Hendler 1980, 1987, Hirst, 1988), to Memory-Based Retrieval techniques such as Waltz and Pollack (1987) and Bookman (1994).

Chapter 4

1. The context-dependence of the predicates mentioned above was noticed by Aristotle in the *Categories* and the *Nicomachean Ethics*, where he speaks of the *particular aspect* of an individual to which is attributed a quality such as *goodness*; for example a *good lyre-player* or a *good sculptor* speaks to the function of

particular aspect of an individual to which is attributed a quality such as *good-ness*; for example a *good lyre-player* or a *good sculptor* speaks to the function of that individual in that capacity, i.e., at playing the lyre or sculpting. Vendler (1963,1967) discusses the role of function and how it interacts with adjectival modification. Moravcsik (1975) expands on the general strategy in Aristotle's theory of understanding by looking at *modes of meaning*. I return to this in chapter 6.

2. Examples here, and in the remainder of the book, are taken from various corpus sources. These are: *the Birmingham Collection of English Text* (BCET), *Wall Street Journal, 1989* (WSJ), *Readers Digest* (RD), *Longman Dictionary of Contemporary English* (LDOCE).

3. Others who have addressed the general issue of related word senses and how to represent them semantically are Bierwisch (1983), Apresjan (1973b,1981), and to a lesser extent, Katz (1964), Nunberg (1979) is a rich study of the pragmatics of polysemy and sense extensions, and we return to Nunberg's recent proposals in chapter 10.

4. The subselectional properties of adjectives in general are explored in Pustejovsky (1993) and (1994). For further details on this and related classes of adjectives, see Pustejovsky (1995a). Also, for a cross-linguistic perspective on the polysemy demonstrated by these adjectives, see Bouillon and Viegas (1994) and Bouillon (1995), where psychological adjectives are examined.

5. Elliott (1974) distinguishes "exclamations" from "questions" on the basis of tests involving negation, polarity, and sensitivity to *whether* wh-complementation. Observe that the ambiguity in (i) between exlamations and questions disappears with matrix negation in (ii).

(i) I know how tall he is.

(ii) I don't know how tall he is. (only indirect question)

The matrix negation in (ii) blocks the exclamation complement interpretation just as it blocks the factive in (iii):

(iii) *I don't know that he is tall.

Whatever filters the exclamation reading also appears to filter the factive in (iii).

6. Van Valin and Wilkins (1993) provide an interesting analysis of the verb *re-member*, and the relation between its possible complementation patterns and the underlying semantics of the verb. In a related manner, Jackendoff (1993) examines the underlying conceptual structure of the verb *intend* and the syntactic realizations associated with it, while Wheeler (1990), in a somewhat related manner, discusses the selectional properties of the verb *understand*. I return to this question in chapter 7 below.

7. See Verma and Mohanan (1991) for an extensive survey of experiencer subject constructions in different languages.

8. Morrill and Carpenter (1990) make a distinction between weak and strong compositionality as it relates to the degree of how strongly the composition respects the constituent structure of the sentence. Although this is an important distinction, we do not address this dimension here, but see rather Pustejovsky (1994).

9. See Pustejovsky (1994b) for further discussion.

Chapter 5

1. As an operation on types within a λ-calculus, type coercion can be seen as transforming a monomorphic language into one with polymorphic types (cf. Cardelli and Wegner, 1985, Klein and van Benthem, 1987).

2. Both Levin and Rappaport (1988, 1995) and Marantz (1984) make further refinements involving *direct* versus *indirect* internal arguments. This distinction separates arguments receiving θ-assignment directly from the verb, from those arguments assigned a θ-role from a preposition.

3. The operations involved with the expression of shadow arguments appear to obey the type of behavior described in Wunderlich (1987), who discusses incorporation within derivational processes in German. Wunderlich's proposal is closer to the analysis presented here than is Baker's (1988) theory, athough many of Baker's syntactic operations translate fairly directly into the type of semantic operations available in a generative lexicon (cf. Pustejovsky, 1995b).

4. Viewed from the perspective of default and shadow arguments, one might be tempted to rethink the classification of certain constructions. For example, the resultative construction, discussed briefly in chapter 2, is not a semantically homogeneous class, in terms of the verbs entering into the construction. For although it would appear that all verbs in the construction are process-like (although see Levin and Rappaport (1995) and chapter 7 for discussion), the nature of the arguments can differ from verb to verb. For verbs such as *hammer* and *wipe*, the semantics of the resulting state is contributed by the adjunct adjectival predicate. Restrictions on this predicate type come from both the complement itself as well as the verb. But notice that some verbs restrict the resultative phrase type in an even tighter fashion, where the predicate is logically restricted by a subtyping relation to a shadow argument of the verb:

> (i) a. Mary <u>painted</u> the house white.
>   b. John <u>dyed his</u> jeans purple.
>   c. Zac <u>colored</u> the dragon green.

For the verbs *paint*, *dye*, and *color*, there is a shadow argument associated with the incorporated semantics of paints, dyes, and colors, respectively. ¿From a selectional point of view, we have the following relations: $white \leq paint\_color$, $purple \leq dye\_color$, and $green \leq color$. These seem to be positioned between the pure resultatives and the emphatic resultatives discussed in Pustejovsky (1991b).

5. More specifically, within a purely Davidsonian representation, the verb *build* would denote the following expression, where the event is added as an argument to the relation directly:

> (i) $\lambda y \lambda x \lambda e[build(e, x, y)]$

Parsons (1990) captures the relational structure of the verb through a set of functions, $\theta_1(e, x)$, $\theta_2(e, y)$, corresponding roughly to θ-roles as used by Chomsky (1981) and formal interpretations of these roles as in Dowty (1989, 1991).

> (i)$\lambda y \lambda x \lambda e[building(e) \wedge \theta_1(e, x) \wedge \theta_2(e, y)]$

On this view, the event is essentially identified by predication, as with any other individual in the logic.

6. This is the view taken by Dahl (1973), Comrie (1976), Mourelatos (1978), Desclés (1989), and Guentcheva (1990). The view of structural decomposition of events espoused here, however, would not necessarily be shared by these authors.

7. Landman (1991) provides a useful discussion of how Kamp's (1979) system differs from van Benthem's (1983) logic for events. In Kamp's event structure, both precedence and overlap are primitive relations, while van Benthem's structures contain only precedence. We follow Landman's suggestion to define overlap in terms of temporal inclusion. This, furthermore, allows us to define "exhaustive overlap part of" as well.

8. Allen (1983,1984) illustrates what the possible orderings are given a set of events. Crouch and Pulman (1993) explore the restrictions on the planning of events for discourse in a natural language interface.

9. Discussion of the richness of this new event typology.

10. As pointed out in Higginbotham (1985) and McConnell-Ginet (1982), some adverbs allow a wide-scope interpretation on the adverb, such as in (i):

   (i) Mary rudely departed.

   (ii) Mary departed rudely.

   Higginbotham (1985) observes that reference to part of the event in (ii) above gives the manner reading while wide-scope gives the subject-oriented interpretation (cf. Jackendoff, 1972).

11. These lexical or collocational differences are of course only a reflection of how they differ semantically. Nevertheless, these are informative distinctions and contribute to the sortal classification of objects in our ontology of the world. It might be argued that these distinctions are difficult to maintain, however. For example, it is certainly possible to read a dictionary (the case of Malcolm X mentioned above), and refer to a novel (e.g., for a particular passage or quote). It might also be argued that dictionaries are also written in some particular way, and therefore the AGENTIVE must also make reference to the activity which characterizes novels. I argue in chapter 8, however, that our use of the term *dictionary* refers more to the structure of a listing along with the general strategy for constructing lists, i.e., compilation. Hence, we have many kinds of dictionaries, e.g., term dictionaries, visual dictionaries, music dictionaries, etc. The German word *Lexikon* is even more broadly construed as a structured listing of information of some sort.

12. For the purpose of exposition, I adopt a feature notation and style of HPSG (cf. Pollard and Sag, 1987, 1994). Furthermore, I am ignoring certain aspects of syntactic variation as discussed in Sanfilippo (1993). These are addressed more fully in Pustejovsky and Johnston (forthcoming). The treatment of verbal alternation given in Sanfilippo (1993) is closest to that presented here, and we discuss this more fully in chapter 10 below.

Chapter 6

1. Much of the perspective taken here has been influenced directly or indirectly by readings of Aristotle's *Organon* and subsequent commentaries on it.

2. Hobbs' (1987) "systems," within the model of commonsense reasoning he assumes, are good approximations for the type of understanding needed to categorize and name things in the world. Nirenburg's (1989a,1989b) notion of "microtheory" is a rich model of what language maps into after superficial linguistic interpretation has occurred. Miller's ideas regarding the structure of the mental lexicon are also interesting in this respect, since the qualia can be viewed as "distinguished" links between lexical concepts in the lexicon.

3. As in Moravcsik's (1990) treatment of Aristotle's *aitiae*—the modes of explanation mentioned above—the goal is to explore a sound cognitive view on semantics, largely based on the constructivist assumptions in Aristotle's metaphysics.

   Qualia structure, as interpreted in a generative lexicon, is an integrated part of a larger methodological shift from conventional approaches to lexical semantics. The qualia provide the foundation for an inherently polymorphic approach to semantics. But they are only one tool for the characterization of natural language as appropriately polymorphic. What gives the qualia their true generative power is an explicit statement of how they are typed, i.e., what the expression in the quale role actually refers, as well as reference to explicit mechanisms of enriched composition, such as coercion, selective binding, and co-composition. to be discussed in chapter 7. Hence, as presented in the literature, there is some divergence between our use of qualia structure and Moravcsik's use of aitiae. GL makes explicit just what the generative devices are that allow qualia to provide different ways of explaining what an object is. What these approaches share is the goal of looking beyond conventional truth-theoretic models of semantics to a model of meaning which admits of a multiplicity of reference in linguistics expressions. For further exposition of this position, see Pustejovsky (forthcoming).

   There is possibly some similarity between aspects of qualia theory and the ontological theory of *moments* put forth by Smith and Mulligan (1983). They argue for an ontology consisting of "dependent parts" of objects, which are not properly characterizable in standard mereological terms. Many of these "parts" are characteristic properties of an object which might be viewed as qualia associated with it.

   Another theoretical similarity exists between GL's use of qualia structure and the notion of "lexical function" as employed by Mel'čuk and his colleagues (cf. Mel'čuk (1973a,1988a), within the Meaning-Text Model. Heylen (1995), in fact, compares qualia structure and lexical functions as descriptive mechanisms for accounting for semantic relatedness in potential, as well as actual, collocational usage. Finally, some of the proposals given in Bés and Lecomte (1995) are much in line with the methodology here, concerning what level of lexical knowledge is both appropriate and necessary for linguistic theory.

4. It might be argued that the subject always stands in a containment relation to the substance denoted by the complement NP. That is, yeast is contained in beer, tomatoes are contained in the pasta sauce, and so on. There are some interesting counter-examples, however, to this generalization, as (i) illustrates.

   (i) Methylene Chloride is used in decaffeinated coffee.

   This example suggests that the construction is actually making reference to some process involved in bringing about the substance, as opposed to the substance itself, since the chemical in subject position is not present in the resulting liquid.

5. The notion of defeasibility here is that as used in Lascarides *et al.* (1994). Another way of viewing the distinction between these sentences is that the space of interpretations available to the NPs *New York* and *Boston* is larger than that available to the more sortally restricted airport proper names in (4a).

6. In Pustejovsky and Anick (1988), the senses are "split" according to separate qualia assignments. Under this analysis, the FORMAL role takes as its value the *Figure* of a physical object, while the CONST role assumes the *Invert-Figure* value of an aperture. The polysemy was seen as resulting from the foregrounding or backgrounding of a nominal's qualia. That is, in (9a) *paint* applies to the FORMAL role of *the door*, while in (9b), *through* will apply to the CONST interpretation of the same NP. The problem, however, with sense splitting inside the qualia structure for a lexical item is that it fails to capture the selectional behavior of the item for all contexts. The interpretation of complex types such as these first given in Pustejovsky (1994) overcomes these difficulties, as we see below in chapter 8.

7. Pustejovsky and Boguraev (1994) show how these logical polysemies are in fact regularly encoded in dictionary definitions for these words.

8. See Leiß (1991) and Gunter (1992) for an explanation of formal mechanisms of type inference within the λ-calculus, and Copestake (1993), Morrill (1994), Buitelaar and Mineur (1994) for its application to lexical representation. Shieber (1992) discusses general issues of type inference for natural language processing. It should be pointed out that the details of the typing assumptions discussed in those works differ in ways that are beyond the scope of the present discussion. For further details of the typing rules and the use of typed feature structures within generative lexicons, see Pustejovsky and Johnston (forthcoming) .

9. Following a suggestion by Manfred Krifka and Nicholas Asher (personal communication), the specific relation that structures the types can be built into the type structure itself. This is essentially the analysis pursued below in 8.3.

10. For expository purposes, I ignore the other qualia roles until the discussion below.

11. In previous treatments of the semantics for dotted types, I associated a unique AGENTIVE and TELIC role value for each argument in the argument structure (cf. Pustejovsky (1994), Viegas and Bouillon (1994)). This seemed appropriate since the information for both modes of presentation for an object must be accounted for. For example, on this view, for a two-argument dotted type nominal such as *book*, there is a mode of explanation for both the coming about of the information and the coming about of the physical object as well. That is, the qualia structure was given as follows:

$$
\begin{bmatrix}
\textbf{book} & & \\
\text{ARGSTR} = & \begin{bmatrix} \text{ARG1} = \text{x:information} \\ \text{ARG2} = \text{y:phys\_obj} \end{bmatrix} & \\
\text{QUALIA} = & \begin{bmatrix} \textbf{information-phys\_obj- container-lcp} \\ \text{FORM} = \text{hold(y,x)} \\ \text{TELIC} = \text{read(P,w,x)} \\ \text{AGENT} = \text{write(T,v,x), publish(T,z:printer,y)} \end{bmatrix}
\end{bmatrix}
$$

The problem with this interpretation is that the predicates that are sui generis to entities that are both physical objects and information bearing objects are actually mistyped here; that is, both *read* and *write* are only understandable in terms of a complex typing system, such as that outlined in the previous chapter. The objects selected for by a predicate such as *read* and the predicates made reference to by objects such as *books* are the characteristic functions for those entities.

12. Aristotle *Metaphysics, Physics II*, and Moravcsik (1975).

13. These strategies replace the mapping rules discussed in Pustejovsky (1991b), where it was less clear what type of semantic representation the mapping to syntax actually allows. These were given as follows:

> (A) The semantic participant involved in a predicate opposition is mapped onto the "internal" argument position of the lexical structure.

All transitions involve a predicate opposition of some sort. Independent of this principle, Pustejovsky (1988) and Grimshaw (1990) argue that the notions of causer and agent are associated with the initial subevent of an event structure.

> (B) The agentive participant in the initial subevent or event structure is mapped onto the external argument position of the lexical structure.

The result of both principles A and B applying in the structures above is not general enough, however, to account for the mapping to passive constructions as well as to experiencer constructions (cf. chapter 9 for discussion).

14. This proposal should be compared to the lexical mapping theory, as outlined in Bresnan and Kanerva (1989) and Bresnan and Moshi (1990), where semantc arguments are related to their morphosyntactic expressions by means of specific syntactic functions. Along with these principles, they assume a universal hierarchy of thematic roles, as given below:

> (i) ag > ben > goal > inst > patient > locative

Cf. also Alsina and Mchombo (1990) for further discussion.

Chapter 7

1. Briefly, we can summarize some of the type shifting operations that have been suggested in the literature (cf. Partee (1985), Chierchia (1984), Hendriks (1987), Dowty (1988).

> (i) Type Shifting functions:
> a. lift: $j \Rightarrow \lambda P[P(j)]$
> b. lower: $lower(lift(j)) = j$
> c. ident: $j \Rightarrow \lambda x[x = j]$
> d. iota: $P \Rightarrow \iota P[P(x)]$
> e. nom: $P \Rightarrow^{\cap} P$
> f. pred: $x \Rightarrow^{\cup} x$
> g. general lifting: $\alpha \Rightarrow \lambda X_{<a,t>}[X(\alpha)]$

2. There is a long controversy over how to best analyze the infinitival in such constructions; namely, as either a VP of some sort or as a full sentence with a PRO-subject. In order to focus on issue of the coercion phenomena themselves, I will not discuss this issue here. Cf. Chomsky, 1981 and Pollard and Sag, 1994.

3. As we see in 7.4 below, this is in agreement with the general strategy outlined in Chomsky (1986) moving towards constraints making reference to semantic selection rather than syntactic configurations directly. See below for discussion.

4. For details see Klein and Sag (1985) and Gazdar *et al.* (1985).

5. One recent proposal which would disagree with this conclusion is Chierchia and Turner (1989), where properties are allowed as arguments.

6. If we return to the type selection of *consider* in (3) above, we can see another way of solving this type clash; namely, to allow the NP to shift in denotation according to the reference type ladder. Following the proposals just discussed, however, there is another possibility; to shift the type of the verb itself, so that it would accept an NP as type $<<e,t>,t>$, without the NP shifting at all. Assume that this could be accomplished by a type-shifting operator, f_{sc}, (for *small clause*), which would act to relate the two structures in (ia) and (ib).

> (i) a. John considers Mary to be an honest person.
>   b. John considers Mary an honest person.

Thus, f_{sc} exhibits the shifting shown in (ii) below.

> (ii) a. *consider* $\in$: `<VP,<NP,<NP,S>>>`
>   b. $f_{sc}(\textit{consider}) \in$ `<NP,<NP,<NP,S>>>`

We then associate with this operation the meaning postulate in (iii), guaranteeing the correct predicative interpretation of the second phrase.

> (iii) $\forall \mathcal{P}_1 \forall \mathcal{P}_2 \forall \mathcal{P}_3 \Box [f_{sc}(\zeta)(\mathcal{P}_1)(\mathcal{P}_2)(\mathcal{P}_3) \leftrightarrow \zeta(\lambda \mathcal{P}_1 \lambda x \mathcal{P}_1\{\lambda y[x=y]\})(\mathcal{P}_2)(\mathcal{P}_3)]$

The derivation of sentence (ib) is shown in (iv) below, along with the corresponding semantic translation (assuming a right-wrap operation of some sort, cf. Bach (1977)).

> (iv) a. John considers John an honest person.
>   b. $f_{sc}(\textbf{consider'})(\textbf{an-honest-person})(\textbf{m})(\textbf{j})$
>   c. $\textbf{consider'}(\lambda \mathcal{P} \lambda x \mathcal{P}\{\lambda y[x=y]\}(\lambda Q \exists x[honest.person'(x) \wedge Q(x)])(\textbf{m})(\textbf{j})$
>   d. $\textbf{consider'}(\lambda x \exists z[honest.person'(z) \wedge \lambda y[x=y](z)])(\textbf{m})(\textbf{j})$
>   e. $\textbf{consider'}(\exists z[honest.person'(z) \wedge [\textbf{m}=z]])(\textbf{j})$
>   f. $\textbf{consider'}(honest.person'(\textbf{m}))(\textbf{j})$

As the structure above makes clear, this rule allows the second internal argument to be treated predicatively of the first. This solution is more in keeping with the proposal in Klein and Sag (1985), since the verb is the element shifting its type.

7. As discussed in Pustejovsky (1993), more in line with the proposals above, we can imagine two alternative ways of capturing the relatedness between the above sentences involving *want*: either the verb shifts its type due to a lexical specification, or the NP shifts with reference to a type ladder. Adopting a Klein and Sag-style analysis, we can propose an operator f_{hd} (for *have*-deletion) that would relate the two uses of *want* in (1).

> (i) a. Mary wants to have John.
>   b. Mary wants John.

It operates in the following way. Given that the usage in (1a) is already derived from applying f_E to the underlying type for *want*, i.e., $<S,<NP,S>>$, we apply f_{hd} to $f_E(\textit{want})$:

> (ii) a. $f_E(\textit{want}) \in$ `<VP,<NP,S>>`
>   b. $f_{hd}(f_E(\textit{want})) \in$ `<NP,<NP,S>>`

We would need to propose a meaning postulate to generate these equivalences:

(iii) $\forall \mathcal{P}_1 \ldots \mathcal{P}_n \Box[f_{hd}(\zeta)(\mathcal{P}_1) \ldots (\mathcal{P}_n) \leftrightarrow \zeta(have'(\mathcal{P}_1)) \ldots (\mathcal{P}_n)]$

This would allow for the derivation in (iv).

(iv) a. Mary wants <u>John</u>.
   b. $f_{hd}(f_E(\textbf{want'}))(\hat{}\textbf{j})(\textbf{m}) \Rightarrow$
   c. $f_E(\textbf{want'})(\hat{}have'(\textbf{j}))(\textbf{m}) \Rightarrow$
   d. $\textbf{m}\{\lambda x[\textbf{want'}(\hat{}have'(\textbf{j})(x^*))(x^*)]\}$

This solution accounts for one interpretation of *want*, but as Dowty (1979) and (1985) point out, there might be many possible such operators, depending on the denotation of the complement, as we see later in this chapter.

8. I assume that the basic rule of function application is given simply as:

(i) If α is of type **a**, and β is of type **<a,b>**, then $\beta(\alpha)$ is of type **b**.

It should be pointed out that the revised rule of application, FAC, is equivalent to the standard formulation in (i) just in case Σ_α is null; that is, when the grammar provides no type shifting operators that can apply to the argument.

9. One might consider a mixed solution, making use of type shifting over the verb and type coercion on the complement as well. Briefly, this involves shifting the type, essentially embedding the NP denotation within an empty predicate (cf. Dowty, (1979). Let us simply call this operation ρ and characterize it in (i).

(i) ρ: **<<e,t>,t>** $\Rightarrow$ **<e,t>**

The meaning postulate associated with this type shifting rule is given below in (ii):

(ii) $\forall \mathcal{P} \Box[\rho(\mathcal{P}) \leftrightarrow \lambda x \exists P[P(\mathcal{P})(x)]]$

The result of applying this operator to an NP is effectively to create a *metonymic extension* of the NP meaning. In the case of the NP *John*, for example, the operator produces the following:

(iii) $\rho(\lambda P[P(j)]) \Rightarrow \lambda x \exists Q[Q(\lambda P[P(j)])(x)]$

This operator, together with the independently motivated *Equi* operator, f_E, is able to generate an "underspecified" translation of (iv), as shown in (v) below.

(iv) Mary wants John.

(v) a. $f_E(\textbf{want'})(\hat{}\rho(\textbf{j}))(\textbf{m}) \Rightarrow$
   b. $f_E(\textbf{want'})(\hat{}\lambda x \exists P[P(\textbf{j})(x)])(\textbf{m}) \Rightarrow$
   c. $\textbf{m}\{\lambda x[\textbf{want'}(\hat{}\lambda x \exists P[P(\textbf{j})(x)](x^*))(x^*)]\} \Rightarrow$
   d. $\textbf{m}\{\lambda x[\textbf{want'}(\hat{}\exists P[P(\textbf{j})(x^*)])(x^*)]\} \Rightarrow$
   e. $\textbf{want'}(\hat{}\exists P[P(\textbf{j})(\textbf{m})])(\textbf{m})$

The expression in (ve) leaves the relation between Mary and John underspecified. This actually happens to be an advantage rather than a problem, since lexical information from the particular elements in composition with the verb may act to specify this relation in unique ways.

10. Pollard and Sag (1994) discuss a type of complement coercion that can properly be considered a subset of the more general phenomenon being examined here. In particular, they discuss the "coercion" involved in the controller shift in (ii) below, from subject-control to object-control.

  (i) a. Sandy was promised to be allowed to attend the party.
     b. John promised Sandy to be allowed to attend the party.

  Pollard and Sag show how *to be allowed to attend* in (ii) is coerced into "to cause x to be allowed to attend." They employ a lexical rule to shift the controller in order to arrive at the correct interpretation. These data have not been studied in GL, but the general methodology would be to have the complement sense systematically coerced by virtue of one underlying semantic type for *promise*.

11. In an interesting and relevant article, Harris (1965) treats many cases of what we have considered type coercions in terms of specific transformations on surface syntactic forms. In particular, Harris introduces a "zeroing transformation" that eliminates secondary members of a sequence, as long as the meaning can be preserved. This transformation, for example, is responsible for the zeroing of the subject of the complement NP in (ib) below:

  (i) a. He denied his having slept.
     b. He denied having slept.

  In a similar manner, but under different conditions for "appropriateness," Harris suggests that (iib) can be derived from (iia) .

  (ii) a. I began to read the book.
      b. I began the book.

  Harris calls the appropriatedness context variable X_{ap}, and admits that the conditions under which it licenses the zeroing transformation are unclear and in need of further study, in order to prevent X_{ap} from applying in (iiia), for example.

  (iii) a. I began to buy the book.
       b. *I began the book.

  Unfortunately, Harris' later work never revisits this problem. Notice that, from the point of view of a generative lexicon, the question of appropriateness is answered directly by the qualia values associated with the complement NP and the operation of coercion over this representation. Hence, Harris' basic insights can be preserved, but within a richer lexical framework for the language.

12. In chapter 8 I discuss some issues related to inheritance through the type lattice. In particular, I examine how *book* differs from *novel* and *newspaper* formally in the type hierarchy and their qualia structures.

13. For purposes of exposition, I have been ignoring the issue of quantification in complement position. Krifka (1989) and Verkuyl (1993) discuss at some length the aspectual consequences of verbal complement types.

14. For this and all subsequent examples in this section, we will not concern ourselves with further aspects of the verbal lexical semantics, since we are here interested primarily in semantic type behavior alone.

15. The rule should apply to generalized quantifiers as well. The type derivation can now be given as follows, where S' abbreviates the type t, and NP' the type <<e,t>,t>.

$$\text{(i)} \quad \frac{believe : \text{S}' \to (\text{NP}' \to \text{S}') \quad \oplus \quad \dfrac{John\text{:NP}' \quad \oplus \quad \rho_2[\text{NP}',\text{S}']\text{:NP}' \to \text{S}'}{\rho_2[\text{NP}',\text{S}'](John)\text{:S}'}}{believe(\rho_2[\text{NP}',\text{S}'](John)) : \text{NP}' \to \text{S}'}$$

16. In some sense, this can be seen as similar to the goals of the lexical subordination operation in Levin and Rapoport (1988). In fact, co-composition provides an elegant solution to the polysemy involving resultative verbs such as *hammer* and *wipe*, as well as with verbs such as *rattle* in *rattle down the hill* (cf. Jackendoff, 1990 and Levin, 1993). See chapter 10 for discussion.

17. As we shall see in chapter 10, *light verb specification* characterizes the way in which a specific "sense in context" of certain verbs is determined by the complement. In many of these cases, the verb acts only as a general function over qualia-based information from the complement; e.g., the verbs *open, close, break,* and *fix.* This is formally distinct from the types of constructions discussed in Di Sciullo and Rosen (1990) and related work, however.

Two other cases discussed in Pustejovsky (forthcoming) include *manner co-composition* and *feature transcription.* The former determines how an argument to the verb may itself specify the manner in which that object is acted upon. There are two basic subtypes considered: (a) where the complement specifies manner, e.g., the verbs *try* and *sample;* and (b) where the subject specifies manner, e.g., the verbs *break* and other causatives, as well as psych verbs.

Feature transcription involves those constructions where a modifier to an expression contributes information to further specify a semantic feature of that expression that was left unspecified. For example, adjectives such as *pregnant,* when applied to terms not sensitive to gender, such as *professor,* will specify the expression for that feature. Weinreich (1972), in his critique of the Katz and Fodor model of semantic description, called such constructions "feature transfers."

What is interesting about these operations is that, although they are similar to coercions in some respect, they are not type changing operations; rather, they make use of qualia-based information to further specify the verb's "sense in context."

18. This type of modification might at first seem similar to the "anaphoric island" effects discussed in Postal (1971), illustrated in (i) below.

(i) *John is an <u>orphan</u> and he misses them$_i$ very much.

Obviously, in (i) the indexed pronoun is unable to refer to the putative implicit reference to (John's) parents, and the sentence is ungrammatical under this interpretation. The anaphoric binding in (i) is qualitatively different from the selective binding operations above, however. Notice that an adjective such as *fast* or *good* is able to identify part of the qualia structure of the expression it is in composition with. Making an expression available for modification is not the same as elevating it to a position of antecedenthood for subsequent anaphora, as in (i) above. We can think of the qualia with their values as a more explicit statement of the type of the noun itself. In this sense, selective binding allows an adjective to modify a type fragment of the expression. Such an interpretation would prevent the projection of implicit features expressing aspects of the FORMAL role for the noun *orphan.* Notice that, although anaphoric island effects are preserved, event predicate selection is in fact possible with *orphan,* as illustrated in (ii):

(ii) a recent <u>orphan</u>

This supports the view that these are very different phenomena.

19. It might be argued that the modification by adjectives such as *good* as illustrated in (67) above is not licensed by the type within the qualia, but rather by the qualia themselves. That is, the rule might better be stated in terms of qualia selection:

   (i) SELECTIVE BINDING (by quale):

   If α is of type $< q, q >$, β is of type b, and the qualia structure of β, QS_β, has quale, q, then $\alpha\beta$ is of type b, where

   $$[\![\alpha\beta]\!] = \beta \cap \alpha(q_\beta).$$

   Although it may appear that specific qualia are selected for, in general, such statements can be recast in terms of types. If the formulation of selective binding in (66) is correct, then we would predict that any quale satisfying the type required by the adjective would be available for selective interpretation. This does seem to be the case, as illustrated in (ii) below.

   (ii) a <u>good</u> knife: a knife that is well-made;

   (ii) That's a good knife, but it doesn't cut very well.

   If such distinctions are grammatical, which they appear to be, then the adjective is able to select the AGENTIVE quale of the noun, supporting the view that a *type* rather than a *quale* is selected.

20. As stated above, strictly speaking the modification is in terms of type satisfaction and not a particular quale role. Hence, either TELIC or AGENTIVE would be a possible target of the modification.

21. One can imagine some use of *house* in a sublanguage where things are different, for example, Victorian or Edwardian England, where a family might have any number of houses. *Blandings Castle*, for example might be *an old house of mine*, still in my possession, while I might typically live in a newer house. The word *house* wouldn't have changed significantly in this subculture, but enough to reconceptualize it as an object with a different intension. The issue of how much of this semantic shift is cultural and what is lexical is beyond the scope of the present investigation. My methodological assumption throughout has been to attribute specific grammatical effects to predominantly linguistic distinctions, which by their very nature, reveal the particular conceptualizations of the world constructed by a word or phrase.

22. For some states, being modified by an adjective such as *old* will refer to relations that are possibly extensionally equivalent in duration to the interpretation of the object itself. For example, *an old brother* sounds particularly odd under this interpretation for this reason (i.e., there is no "He is old as my brother" reading). The relationship of brotherhood or sisterhood does not allow this.

23. Kiparsky and Kiparsky (1971) attempt to relate the syntactic behavior of complements to the semantics of the predicate, the complement, and the relation between them. Grimshaw (1979) distinguishes the behavior of syntactic complementation in English in terms of semantic selection over three complement types, propositions, interrogatives, and exclamations (cf. Bresnan, 1972). As Van Valin and Wilkins (1993) point out, the tradition of semantic selection has been pursued by functionalists, and is central to the goals of Role and Reference Grammar (RRG) theorists (cf. Van Valin, 1993 and the papers therein).

Wierzbicka (1980,1982,1988) develops an increasingly rich system of semantic selection, with many interesting insights regarding the role of semantic categories
for syntactic form. Yet the goal of semantic theory in this respect should be
to capture the most elegant generalizations concerning syntactic expressiveness
from semantic selection, and not to completely recreate the richness of the syntactic descriptive system within semantics. The observations by Grimshaw (1982)
and Jacobson (1992) concerning the limitations of semantic selection are worth
noting, and there is no reason to think that syntax is completely parasitic on
semantic types.

24. That something besides case assignment is involved can be seen from sentences
    such as the following:

    (i) John asked me about my name.

    (ii) John asked me my name.

    In sentence (i), the preposition is not just case marking the complement but
    shifting the interpretation of the predicate as well.

25. Groenendijk and Stokhof (1989) discuss the scope distinctions allowed by these
    verbs in sentences like (i) and (ii) below.

    (i) Peter <u>knows</u> who John loves or who Mary loves.

    (ii) Peter <u>wonders</u> who John loves or who Mary loves.

    The sentence in (ii) is ambiguous where the disjunction may take wide or narrow
    scope relative to *wonder*.

Chapter 8

1. In Pustejovsky (1991) and Pustejovsky and Boguraev (1993), a distinction is
   made between *fixed* and *projective* inheritance. Following Touretzky (1986), the
   fixed inheritance structure of a lexical item is defined as follows, where Q and P
   are concepts in our model of lexical network. Then:

   (i) DEFINITION: A sequence $< Q_1, P_1, \ldots, P_n >$ is an *inheritance path*, which
   can be read as the conjunction of ordered pairs $\{< x_1, y_i > | 1 \leq i \leq n\}$.

   Furthermore, from this the set of concepts that lie on an inheritance path is
   defined, as distinguished by a particular quale role (e.g., TELIC vs. FORMAL).
   This is called the *conclusion space* for a given quale, Φ_q.

   (ii) DEFINITION: The *conclusion space* of a set of sequences, Φ_q, is the set of
   all pairs $< Q, P >$ such that a sequence $< Q, \ldots, P >$ appears in Φ_q,
   where q is one of the qualia for the concept Q.

   (iii) DEFINITION: The *complete conclusion space* Φ is the set of all conclusion
   spaces defined for each quale for a concept: $\Phi = \Phi_{q_i}$.

   Finally, by adopting Touretzky's operator Inh—where, for every set of sequences
   S, $Inh(S)$ denotes the set of values inheritable from S—the lattice structures
   shown above for *book* can be differentiated as follows:

Let $[\![\alpha]\!]^{\Phi}$ stand for the denotation of α with respect to a model of inheritance over the set of sequences, Φ. Then,

$[\![book]\!]^{\Phi} =$
$\quad \lambda x\, [\, book(x) \quad \wedge\, Formal(x) = Inh(physobj')$
$\qquad\qquad\qquad \wedge\, Telic(x) = Inh(literature')$
$\qquad\qquad\qquad \wedge\, Agentive(x) = Inh(literature')\,]$

By viewing the different facets of meaning of a lexical item (i.e. its qualia) as inheriting from orthogonally typed lattice structures, this approach hoped to avoid the problems associated with multiple inheritance, although this has not been fully explored within this system. Briscoe *et al.* (1993) address the issues relating to multiple inheritance in a more comprehensive manner; cf. also Klein and van Benthem, 1987, Evans and Gazdar, 1990, and Russell *et al.*, 1993.

2. Details on how nouns with "horizontal relations" such as *brother, neighbor,* and *sister* differ formally from those denoting "hierarchical relations," such as *father, daughter,* and *son,* are discussed in Pustejovsky (1995b).

3. Besides the two types of dot objects discussed above, *book* and *newspaper,* there is at least one other type we will consider, that involved in defining nouns such as *sonata,* discussed in 8.5. What distinguishes these nominals is the way in which the qualia structure relate the dot elements. For a noun such as *book,* the FORMAL role refers only to the two elements, $hold(x, y)$, and both AGENTIVE and TELIC qualia are defined in terms of the dot object, $x.y$, itself. For *newspaper,* the dot elements are "split" between qualia values, where the producer sense functions separately from the product sense in the qualia. No quale role makes reference to the dot object, however, which presumably restricts the noun's denotational possibilities; that is, *newspaper* can never refer simultaneously to the organization and the product on the same predicative level. Finally, the dot object for a noun such as *sonata* is constructed with the specific relation of "performing," as is discussed below. In this case, the relation is not saturated by the dot elements as arguments, but makes reference to other arguments as well. Cf. Pustejovsky and Johnston (forthcoming) for discussion of the formal difference in dot object qualia structures.

4. The case of (59c) above is similar to the issue of anaphoric islandhood mentioned in Postal (1971), where an adjective seems to be filling the role of a true argument to the noun. Cf. footnote 17 for chapter 7.

5. There are some interesting complications, however, suggesting that simple control between the subject and the infinitival phrase is not mediated by constraints on agentive controllability.

   (i) Our house <u>needs</u> a new roof.

   (ii) The soup <u>needs</u> more salt.

   (iii) The carpet <u>needs</u> vacuuming.

The interesting thing about such examples, however, is that we predicate *need* of only those things that we can or want to affect or act on in some way. Thus, I might say of a lawn, that it needs mowing, but I would not say of a tree, that it needs cutting down, unless there is some reason (i.e., TELIC state) that precipitates this comment, e.g., it is rotting, it is blocking the view to the city, and so on. Similarly, a house needs a new roof only because of how it impacts the integrity of the house, while the carpet needs to be vacuumed because it is dirty, and someone (the speaker) wants it clean, and so on.

This is not to say that *need* entails a decomposition or reconstruction into the appropriately modal statement capturing the above intuitions. It does mean, however, that when we predicate something of *need*, the conditions on licensing this predication must include the ability for an agent to act to bring about the change of state implicitly referred to by the complement NP or gerundive.

6. The verb *burn* has both causative and unaccusative forms, according to the analysis in chapter 9. The representation will change slightly to reflect this polysemy, but not in any significant way for our discussion here. The expression of the underlying agentive argument in the causative readings of such *ing*-nominals is optionally defaulted, while the object is not, as the example in (ia) suggests.

    (i) a. The Allied Forces' burning *(of Dresden) was viewed with horror.
       b. We witnessed the arson's burning *(of the house).

7. Grimshaw (1990) discusses many of these same issues from the point of view of syntactic expressibility. Grimshaw's goal is to account for the classic problem of complement optionality in NPs in a systematic way. For example, it is well known that verbal argument patterns appear quite systematic compared to the apparent optionality of arguments within the nominal system (cf. (i) and (ii)):

    (i) a. *The doctor examined.
       b. The doctor's examination (of the patient) was successful.
    (ii) a. *They attempted.
       b. Their attempt (to reach the top) was successful.

As Grimshaw points out, however, complements in the NP system are not completely optional. She proposes that the argument structure of a lexical item is derived from two independent components of predicate meaning; the *aspectual structure* and *thematic structure*. Any item lacking an aspectual structure (e.g., the event structure of Pustejovsky (1991b)) will have no argument structure and will take only optional arguments. This is Grimshaw's distinction between nouns such as *exam* and *examination*. Although I generally agree with Grimshaw's analysis of aspectual structure, the semantics of these nominals is much more complex and subtle.

To begin with, the distinction Grimshaw makes in grammatical behavior between *exam* and *examination* does not completely accord with the data. For example, although it is true that sentence (iiia) and (iiib) are both grammatical, both (iva) and (ivb) are ungrammatical.

    (iii) a. The examination was long.
        b. The exam was long.
    (iv) a. *The examination of the patients was on the table.
       b. *The examination was on the table.

As Grimshaw correctly points out, the noun *examination* is ambiguous between a process reading and a result reading. Namely, it can refer to the act of the examining, or to the specific results of the examination.

Furthermore, observe that, contrary to Grimshaw's proposal, *examination* does not require its full argument structure to be satisfied when the genitive agentive NP is present:

(v) a. An unskilled instructor's examination (in this area) will always take a
      long time.
    b. Any examination by an unskilled instructor (in this area) will always take
      a long time.

There is no room to discuss the consequences of syntactic projection from event
nominalizations as dot objects presented here. Busa (forthcoming) provides substantial evidence suggesting that the analysis of nominalizations outlined in this
chapter extends nicely to cover cross-linguistic data in Italian and English. Busa
furthermore shows that the problem of argument expression in NPs follows from
the systematic projection of semantic types within a generative lexical approach
to grammar.

8. Nunes (1993) presents a discussion of how the semantics of the verb affects the
   range of interpretations possible in the nominalizations they form. Lebeaux
   (1986) also presents some interesting constraints on the formation of derived
   nominals.

9. As pointed out by psychologists such as Miller (1991), social artifacts are very
   different from simple physical artifacts, in that their function is defined in a more
   complex manner. For example, in defining the TELIC role for an event object
   such as *symphony*, one cannot ignore the role of the listener (the experiencer).
   That is, music is performed *for* an audience. In Pustejovsky and Bouillon (1995),
   this is reflected in the qualia structure as a conjunction of relational values in
   the TELIC role, i.e., *perform* and *listen*. Recovering the event *listen* in the
   metonymic reconstruction due to coercion without also recovering *perform* is
   similar to binding a variable with a partial value; that is, *listen* is a dependent
   event while *perform* is independent, being projectable through coercion by itself.
   This will be important for our discussion of coercion in aspectual and experiencer
   predicates in chapter 9.

10. One issue that we cannot adequately address here is the finer sortal structure of
    the propositional domain. Following the discussion begun in chapter 7, where
    semantic types were associated with canonical syntactic forms (csfs), it is curious
    that traditional propositional attitude verbs and their nominals behave heteroge-
    neously with respect to complement selection. Even the verbs *believe* and *think*
    along with their nominalizations *belief* and *thought* differ in this respect. For
    example, while *believe* is a stative predicate, *think* has a prominent use as a pro-
    cess predicate, in (ii) below (cf. Desclés, 1989 and Guentcheva, 1990 for related
    observations):

    (i) *John is believing that he should go not go to the conference.

    (ii) John is thinking that he should not go to the conference.

    Furthermore, the verb *think* and its nominalized forms enter into complex predi-
    cate constructions such as *do some thinking* and *give it some thought*, which are
    unavailable to *believe* and *belief* (cf. Cattell, 1984).

    I believe that we can sortally structure our space of propositions into subtypes
    of attitudes, including at least the following: propositions, beliefs, suppositions,
    superstitions, proposals, debates, issues, and so on. The justification for such a
    move would be to account for systematic syntactic differences in how these types
    are expressed phrasally, as well as motivated semantic distinctions between them.

11. This raises an obvious question concerning the interdependencies possible be-
    tween qualia structures. The relation, for example, between *bake* and *baker* is

typically construed as that between an activity and the agentive nominal associated with that activity. Thus, the suffix *-er* is treated as a function over the relation and returns the individual associated with the agentive aspect of the relation (cf. Williams, 1981, Travis and Williams, 1983 and Moortgat, 1988). The qualia structure for an agentive nominal would have roughly the following form, here illustrated with *baker*:

$$
\text{(i)} \quad
\begin{bmatrix}
\textbf{baker} \\
\text{FORMAL} = \textbf{human(x)} \\
\text{TELIC} = \textbf{bake(e,x,y:bread)}
\end{bmatrix}
$$

While English *-er* functions both as the agentive nominalizer and the instrumental nominalizer, many languages use distinct suffixation for these roles. For example, Comrie and Thompson (1985) point out that in the Californian Indian language Wappo, the suffix *-(e)ma* designates purpose as applied to a verb root, such that from the verb kač (*plow*), the instrument/tool kačema (*plow*) is derived.

Returning to the example in English above, the instrumental nominal for *baking* is, of course, the noun *oven*. What *oven* and *baker* share is a more or less common TELIC quale specification, where *baker* is as represented in (i) and *oven* has the qualia structure in (ii).

$$
\text{(ii)} \quad
\begin{bmatrix}
\textbf{oven} \\
\text{FORMAL} = \textbf{container(x)} \\
\text{TELIC} = \textbf{bake(e,w,y:bread)} \wedge \textbf{loc(e,x)} \\
\ldots
\end{bmatrix}
$$

This is quite unlike the TELIC values for tools such as *knife* and *umbrella*, encountered above. The locative relation in (ii), however, is a necessary feature for distinguishing the semantics of locative nominalizations from instrumental nominalizations (cf. Comrie and Thompson, 1985 for discussion).

Chapter 9

1. Support for the distinction made above with respect to argument coherence and causation comes from Abusch (1985), who argues, independently, that accomplishments and causatives are not co-extensive, on the basis of data such as that in (i), which show that causatives may involve processes a well.

    (i) John galloped the horse for three hours.

    This view is assumed in the statement of causation above.

2. Matters may not be as straightforward as this, however. Alsina (1992) argues that, in some languages, the causative morpheme is a three place predicate, involving the semantic role of PATIENT as well as CAUSER and CAUSEE. On this account, morphological causatives cannot be reduced to a syntactic derivation, such as that proposed by Incorporation Theory (cf. Baker, 1988). Ackerman (1993) proposes a proto-role account of related data, and argues that the argument-linking account in Alsina (1992) is unable to explain certain causative marking cases in Hungarian. Cf. also Saksena (1980) and Dowty (1991).

3. A similar proposal is made in Pustejovsky (1988, 1991b), but a slightly different phenomenon is being examined, namely, how the "deep object" of an unaccusative surfaces as a subject in English.

4. The verb *arrive*, of course, is not a default causative in the sense of *break*. The initial event, e_1, involves a motion predicate, and carries a causal interpretation only co-compositionally with an agentive subject; compare (i) with (ii) below:

   (i) *The package intentionally arrived late.

   (ii) The guests intentionally arrived late.

   Clearly, the verb itself is not changing, but rather, a derived sense exists in (ii) incorporating the elements of agency, inherited from the agentive subject NP. Cf. Pustejovsky (1995b) and Pustejovsky and Johnston (forthcoming) for further discussion.

5. This is needed to constrain the output on forms, just as the Projection Principle and θ-Criterion provide principled limitations on argument structure-to-phrase structure mappings; cf. Chomsky (1981, 1986).

6. Essentially, the ability to reconstruct a coherent link between the causing event and the resulting state is dependent on the referential transparency of the NP in the adjunct phrase, and typing restrictions on the event description in the AGENTIVE quale. These two factors will determine the range of semantic well-formedness judgments for such sentences.

7. There are at least two other major properties of raising predicates that should be mentioned, but that are not as important to our discussion. These are: (a) the inheritance property, which ensures that any syntactic restrictions imposed by the embedded VP on the subject are inherited or reflected in the "raised" position; and (b) the narrow scope interpretation of the raised NP relative to the raising verb. See Jacobson (1990) and Di Sciullo and Williams (1987) for discussion.

8. Further discussion of the syntactic patterning associated with aspectual predicates in English can be found in Freed (1979) and Rudanko (1989).

9. There do appear to be some counterexamples to this basic distinction. Sentences such as (27a) and (27b) appear to have a control component to their interpretation, even though the complement event-type in each case is atelic.

   (i) a. John is beginning to look for a job.
       b. James began to work at Brandeis in 1986.

   Notice, however, that although verbs such as *look for* in (27) and *work on* in (28) are indeed atelic,

   (i) a. Mary is working on a book.
       b. Mary is beginning to work on a book.

   their semantics incorporates an obvious "telicity" in the qualia sense. That is, the intensional context involves mention of the goal state, or TELIC role of the activity. For example, the relation *look-for(x,y)* modally incorporates the relation *have(x,y)*; similarly, in (28), *work-on(x,y)* modally incorporates the goal state of *exist(y)*. Hence, in some sense, the aspectual classification of these predicates as simple processes does not reflect this goal-oriented property. In order to explain the behavior of these verbs with respect to controllability in the sentences in (27a) and (28a), Pustejovsky and Bouillon (1995) refer to this class of predicates as *intensionally telic*, and suggest that this is why control readings are acceptable. That is, it is due to this implicit goal state that these verbs pass the tests for controllability. Other verbs in this natural class include *grope for*, *reach for*, and other conative verbs as well.

10. See Pustejovsky (1993) for details on the control relation. We follow generally Klein and Sag (1985) for how binding is achieved in Equi-constructions such as *begin*.

11. In Pustejovsky and Bouillon (1995), Dowty's (1979) analysis of *finish* is placed within a generative lexical framework, where this verb is analyzed as making ireference to two events: (1) that subevent which brings about, *sine qua non*, the culmination of the event as a whole; and (2) an assertion that the entire event has occurred. As Dowty makes clear, this presupposes that the event has a natural division into two subparts. This would seem to indicate that *finish* is an aspectualizer which type-shifts the complement event into an achievement (i.e., a right-headed transition). It does this, however, by preserving the integrity of the complement event, for notice how *finish*-sentences behave in many respects as both accomplishments and achievements:

   (i) a. Mary finished building the house in 3 months.
       b. Mary finished building the house at 3:00 pm today.

   Hence, even lexical accomplishments (left-headed transitions) can be interpreted as achievements (right-headed transitions) when complements of *finish*. In order to capture this intuition while still satisfying Dowty's fundamental interpretation of *finish*, we define a general relation of logical culmination, *cul*, between an event and one of its subevent:

   (i) $\forall e_1 \forall e_2 [cul(e_1) = e_2 \leftrightarrow \neg \exists e [e_2 \preceq e_1 \land e_2 < e \land e \preceq e_1]]$

   we can build this relation directly into the event structure itself, in which case it would be a relation on event trees. This would essentially be a logical culmination relation between events; $cul_\propto(e_1, e_2)$. Now we can express the semantics of *finish* as a right-headed transition, where the subevent standing in the culminating relation with the larger event is seen as the AGENTIVE of the overall aspectual event. Furthermore, the FORMAL or result of the aspectual event is the assertability of the entire transition, of which the AGENTIVE is a part.

   (i) $\lambda x \lambda e_2^T \exists e_1 \exists R \exists P$ [finish: ES= $e_1 cul_\propto e_2 \land$ FORMAL= $[P(x)(e_2^{*T})]]$
       $\land$ AGENTIVE = $[R(e_1, x)]]$

12. An interesting paradigm showing how control and raising interpretations differ for verbal and nominal forms is illustrated below in (i) and (ii).

    (i) a. When you go underwater, you stop breathing. (Control)
        b. When you die, you stop breathing. (raising)
    (ii) a. *When you go underwater, your breathing stops. (no control)
         b. When you die, your breathing stops. (only raising)

    The nominalization in (ii) does not allow the intransitive control reading, thereby ruling out (iia). The only reading available in the intransitive form is the conventional raising interpretation.

13. These examples are related to the discussion of "Super Equi-NP Deletion," begun by Grinder (1970), where sentences such as (i) and (ii) are discussed:

    (i) Roger$_i$ thinks it is easy PRO$_i$ to protect himself$_i$.
    (ii) That washing herself$_i$ in public was enjoyable surprised Louise$_i$.

Within the approach taken here, the sentence in (ii) would be treated along a similar analysis to that presented above.

14. Such observations are not new, of course. One early analysis making a related observation is Gruber (1967), who attributes the difference between *look* and *see* in terms of agentivity. Notice the following sentence pairs:

> (i) a. John looked through the glass carefully.
> b. *John saw through the glass carefully.

> (ii) a. What John did was to look at Bill.
> b. *What John did was to see Bill.

The reconstructions possible with *startle* versus *anger* seem to pattern along similar lines to the difference shown above.

15. There are of course two readings for 'frighten' type verbs: one which is purely causative (x occasions fear in y), and the other which is being considered here. As Pesetsky (1987) notes, the backwards binding effects introduced below obtains only in the second interpretation.

16. Williams' (1987) proposal is somewhat different from Grimshaw's, but we will not review the differences here.

17. This topic is addressed in more detail in Pustejovsky (forthcoming) where I address the general nature of argumenthood and what logical distinction is possible between argument types. In particular, I examine the general conditions allowing *lexical shadowing*. Shadowing, discussed briefly in chapter 5, can be defined as the relation between an argument and the underlying semantic expression which blocks its syntactic projection in the syntax. As discussed in chapter 5, shadowing is responsible for the grammaticality of (ib) and (iib), and the unacceptability of (ic) and (iic).

> (i) a. Mary buttered her bread.
> b. Mary buttered her bread with an expensive butter from Wisconsin.
> c. *Mary buttered her bread with butter.

> (ii) a. John and Mary danced.
> b. John and Mary danced a fast waltz.
> c. *John and Mary danced a dance.

These alternations are related by the fact that the grammatical expression of a particular argument NP (in (ib) and (iib)) is licensed only when the NP stands in a subtype relation with certain "implicit semantic content" of the verb, as mentioned in chapter 5. That is, the underlying semantics of the verb *butter*, for example, shadows the expression of the material which is spread and obviates its expression as an argument. However, when a specialization of this shadow argument is made, the shadow is "lifted" and grammatical expression of this information as an argument is possible. Similarly, with *dance*, the expression of an object is shadowed by the underlying semantics of the verb.

There is another type of shadowing which is not purely lexical, but is the result of compositional operations in the syntax; namely, that discussed in chapter 2 with ditransitive verbs such as *give* and *mail*.

> (iii) a. John gave a talk to the academy today.
> b. John gave a talk today.
> c. *John gave a book today.

(iv) a. Mary mailed a letter to me.
    b. Mary mailed a letter.
    c. *Mary mailed a book.

Here it is the specific semantics of the complements *talk* and *letter*, respectively, which are obviating the obligatory expression of the indirect object.

It is possible, therefore, to identify the following three types of lexical shadowing:

(A) *Argument Shadowing*: Expression of an argument is shadowed by the verbal semantics (as in the cognate constructions) or by the semantics of the phrase (as with the *build*-examples.

(B) *Complementary Shadowing*: Expression of one argument shadows the expression of another in a complementary fashion (as in the *risk*-examples).

(C) *Co-compositional Shadowing*: Expression of an argument is made optional by virtue of how the verb "co-composes" with its complement (as with the *give a lecture* cases).

For further discussion of these issues, cf. Pustejovsky (forthcoming).

18. Privation is but one part of Aristotle's original theory of oppositions. As presented in the *Categories* 11b18, there are four basic classes of opposition:

(i) Correlatives (between two relatives): <u>double</u> vs. <u>half</u>.

(ii) Contrariety: <u>good</u> vs. <u>bad</u>.

(iii) Privation (Privatives to positives): <u>blindness</u> vs. <u>sight</u>.

(iv) Contradiction (Affirmatives to negatives): "He is sitting." vs. "He is not sitting."

For the concept of privation, there is an inherent modality related to Aristotle's notion of potentiality of a subject. That is, it is not sufficient to merely translate a privative predicate such as *sick* or *blind* as *not healthy* or *unable to see*, since the individual to which a privative applies must have the *ability* to be predicated of that term. Privation, therefore, correctly applies to a subject of which the positive should, by its nature, be able to apply. Thus, a dog cannot properly said to be *illiterate*, because it is not possibly literate, by its very nature (cf. Horn, 1989 for discussion).

19. We ignore, for now, quantification over the individual variables in the expressions below.

20. In Pustejovsky (forthcoming), this is explained in terms of a more general process of lexical shadowing operating in the grammar.

21. Saksena (1980) discusses this issue at some length. She makes the claim that an "affected"/"non-affected" distinction is more primary than that of AGENT and PATIENT in causative constructions. Saksena argues that the concept of AGENT is not a single category, but itself has a dimension of affectedness (cf. Anderson, 1979, 1984). This view emerges from observations in Hindi, where there are two ways of realizing a causatives, corresponding to affected and non-affected readings, as in(?? and (91) above (cf. also Saksena, 1982). As with the analysis above for Italian, it should be possible to distinguish these two readings in terms of the event structures associated with the sentences, where distance in a tree structure is correlated with non-affectedness on the arguments. A related statement of this proposal can be found in Pustejovsky (1988).

Chapter 10

1. There are many issues raised by a semantics with co-composition and under-specified representations. The interesting thing about an operation such as co-composition is that specific values for the qualia roles may emerge in composition through qualia unification (cf. chapter 8), where otherwise they were not lex-ically specified for a verb or noun. For example, in the compound *book shelf*, the TELIC role of the noun *shelf* is specialized by virtue of the typing restriction imposed by the noun *book*; that is, the TELIC for the compound is specialized from "holding" to "holding books" (cf. Levi, 1989). Similarly, within the verbal system, complements can contribute information specifying TELIC values associated with the entire VP, although not necessarily associated with the head verb. Adjectives, too, can compound to further specify qualia-related information, such as the AGENTIVE role in the compound adjective *American made*. Johnston, Boguraev, and Pustejovsky (1995) discuss the semantics of compounds, while Pustejovsky (1995d,forthcoming) and Johnston (1995) discusses the semantics of underspecification more generally. A related issue concerning semantic specificity and markedness in morphological operations is discussed in Kiefer (1992).

2. Although I have not discussed it at any length in this work, another well-studied type of logical polysemy involves the pair of *package* and *grind* operations, which can themselves be categorized as coercion operations. Each of the sentences in (i) below involves a mass noun which has been packaged by a determiner or a combination of the predicate type and Aktionsarten of the sentence (cf. Verkuyl, 1993, Dölling, 1992, and Hendriks, 1987).

   (i) a. Mary loves the <u>wine</u> John brought.
       b. Mary ate the <u>cheese</u>.
       c. John drank the <u>beer</u>.
       d. <u>Sand</u> drifted into the tent for hours.

Examples involving count nouns which have been ground by a term explicitly typed as applying to mass nouns (i.e., *more*) are given in (ii). These sentences involve a particular kind of "fruit-grinding " which can be seen as a subtype of a more general grinding mechanism (cf. Link, 1983 and Bach, 1986). In these cases, an countable "food individual" is typed shifted to "food substance:"

   (ii) a. Mary put <u>apple</u> in the yogurt.
        b. We should add some more <u>wall</u> to this side of the room.
        c. Adding <u>banana</u> to your diet will lower heart attack risks.

As Copestake and Briscoe (1992) point out, however, the problem of "animal grinding" is more involved, since the basic type of the noun is being shifted, as well as its countability. Consider the pairs in (iii) and (iv) below.

   (iii) a. Bill caught a <u>haddock</u> this morning.
         b. We're having <u>haddock</u> for dinner today.

   (iv) a. Zac wants a pet <u>lamb</u> for his birthday.
        b. Sophia loves <u>lamb</u> with gravy.

Within an approach such as theirs, the semantics for an individual count noun such as *haddock* is typed underlyingly as a countable animal, as illustrated below:

$$
\begin{bmatrix}
\textbf{count-noun} \\
\text{ORTH} = \text{``haddock''} \\
\text{SYNTAX} = \begin{bmatrix} \text{COUNT} = + \end{bmatrix} \\
\text{RQS} = \begin{bmatrix}
\textbf{animal} \\
\text{SEX} = \textbf{gender} \\
\text{AGE} = \textbf{scalar} \\
\text{EDIBLE} = \textbf{boolean} \\
\text{PHYSICAL-STATE} = \textbf{solid} \\
\text{FORM} = \begin{bmatrix} \textbf{physform} \\ \text{SHAPE} = \textbf{individuated} \end{bmatrix}
\end{bmatrix}
\end{bmatrix}
$$

Copestake and Briscoe (1992) argue for generative principles of sense derivation, and propose that a lexical rule such as the grinding operation below accounts for the "edible mass" sense of individual animals.

$$
\text{animal\_grinding} \quad
\begin{bmatrix}
\textbf{grinding} \\
1 = \begin{bmatrix} \text{RQS} = \begin{bmatrix} \textbf{animal} \\ \text{EDIBLE} = + \end{bmatrix} \end{bmatrix} \\
0 = \begin{bmatrix} \text{RQS} = \textbf{food\_substance} \end{bmatrix}
\end{bmatrix}
$$

This derives the sense of "haddock meat" from the individual fish. Seen in a larger context, this lexical rule is a type coercion operation applying with very specific constraints. Copestake and Briscoe's arguments for generating the mass sense through the application of lexical rules are generally convincing, since the rule is necessary for creative grindings over other lexical items.

Within the framework of a generative lexicon, however, another approach is also possible, one involving coercion and selection compositionally, without the application of lexical rules. Polysemous nouns such as *haddock* could be represented as complex types, where the relation between the dot elements expresses what the lexical rule does for Copestake and Briscoe: $\lambda x.y \exists R[haddock(x.y) \land R(x,y)]$. Not surprisingly, the TELIC for a complex type such as *haddock* or *lamb* will make reference only to the type which itself has a TELIC value, in this case the type food, whose TELIC is specified as "eating:"

$$
(38) \quad
\begin{bmatrix}
\textbf{haddock} \\
\text{ARGSTR} = \begin{bmatrix} \text{ARG1} = \text{x:ind\_animal} \\ \text{ARG2} = \text{y:food\_stuff} \end{bmatrix} \\
\text{QUALIA} = \begin{bmatrix} \textbf{ind\_animal·food\_lcp} \\ \text{FORMAL} = \textbf{R(x,y)} \\ \text{TELIC} = \textbf{eat(e,w,y)} \\ \dots \end{bmatrix}
\end{bmatrix}
$$

It is very possible that the language makes use of both devices, namely complex types such as dot objects as well as the application of lexical rules. Regardless, both types of devices must be seriously constrained by the grammar in order not to overgenerate unwanted forms (cf. Johnston, 1995 for evidence in favor of dot object representations).

3. As with the interpretation of qualia structures above, if an event or argument is not mentioned explicitly in the parameter list, then it is assumed that existential closure applies to the variables mentioned in the qualia. The feature structure given in (1) above will correspond to the λ-expression given in (1):

(i) $\lambda x \lambda e_2 \exists e_1 \exists y \exists P \exists R$ [α: FORMAL=$[P(e_2, x)]$ $\wedge$ AGENTIVE=$[R(e_1, y, x)]$]]

4. The semantic distinction between ILNs and SLNs made above is explored in Busa (forthcoming). Her analysis is embedded within a larger study of the semantics of nominalizations in English and Italian, and approaches these phenomena within the generative lexicon framework.

5. In Pustejovsky (1995a), type coercion is invoked as an explanation for the interpretation of concealed questions, mentioned in chapter 4. It is useful to think of this alternation in terms of coercion, as it explains which noun classes participate in this particular "metonymic extension." Under a generative lexical analysis, coercion would account for the multiple subcategorizations available in these examples. That is, these verbs would be typed as taking an argument of an interrogative type, while also allowing a simple propositional interpretation. Following Groenendijk and Stokhof (1989), we can assume that embedded interrogatives can be typed as <s,t>. Then the type for *understand* and *reveal* as used above would be <<s,t>,<e,t>>. The verb *know* would presumably also be so typed, but without some further remarks on syntactic constraints on coercion, we might expect all of the sentences below to be well-formed, which of course they are not.

> (i) a. John knows that Mary bought a car.
>   b. John knows what Mary bought.
>   c. *John knows Mary's buying the car.
>   d. *John knows the purchase of the car.
>   e. John knows the answer.

Thus, for coercion to apply in a completely unconstrained fashion in these cases overgenerates and leaves unexplained why (ic) and (id) are ungrammatical. This problem awaits further research, and a solution should prove helpful in determining how syntactic effects can contribute to limiting the application of semantic coercion.

It is perhaps worth mentioning another interesting case of coercion, involving *sort shifting*, pointed out by Hobbs *et al.* (1987a,1987b). Notice how the complement in each sentence is embedded within an interpretation predicted by the typing of the verb.

> (ii) a. Thatcher <u>vetoed</u> the channel tunnel. (*the proposal*)
>   b. The board <u>vetoed</u> an increase in pay for the teachers. (*the proposal*)
>
> (iii) The organizers have <u>booked</u> Ella into Symphony Hall. (*the concert*)
>
> (iv) Her secretary has <u>scheduled</u> John for next week. (*the appointment*)

That is, in (ii) the complements are modally subordinated within the type of proposal, which is the type selected by the verb *veto*. This produces a weak intensional context for the complement, since it is intensionally "wrapped" by the denotation of another sort. A similar explanation accounts for the apparent metonymies in (iii) and (iv), where, in fact, strict typing is being obeyed, and sort coercion is providing for the correct interpretation (cf. Pustejovsky (1995c) for further discussion).

6. Li (1994) discusses spatial prepositions and their interpretation in German, within Lang's (1989) theory of spatial relations and Bierwisch's model of conceptual structures (cf. also Bierwisch and Lang, 1989).

7. One lexical knowledge base that is designed according to psychological considerations is (WordNet, Miller, 1990a,1990b), where the fundamental lexical relation
is that of *synonymy*. WordNet currently contains over 64,000 different lexical
entries which are organized into about 39,000 sets of synonyms. In WordNet,
the lexicon is divided into four categories: nouns, verbs, modifiers, and function
words. The function words are actually not represented explicitly, leaving three
classes of words: nouns, verbs, and adjectives.

From the view of lexical organization principles, WordNet is interesting in the
way that it structures these three categories. Nouns are organized into topical
hierarchies, while verbs are organized by means of various entailment relations.
Adjectives, on the other hand, are structured as n-dimensional hyperspaces.

The relation between nouns is the conventional hyponymy relation, which is
equivalent to the is-a relation of knowledge representation languages. Rather
than assuming a single hierarchical structure with *entity* as the topmost element,
for example, WordNet partitions the nouns into a set of semantic primes, each a
generic concept which forms a separate hierarchy. These actually correspond to
distinct semantic fields. For example, some of these fields are listed below:

{act, action, activity}	{natural object}
{animal, fauna}	{natural phenomenon}
{artifact}	{person}
{attribute}	{plant, flora}
{cognition, knowledge}	{process}
{food}	{state, condition}

Nouns are further distinguished by features which characterize them uniquely,
for example a noun concept's function or attributes.

The organization of adjectives in WordNet follows a different set of principles.
Adjectives divide into two classes: *ascriptive* and *nonascriptive*. The former
involves a typically bipolar attribute predicates of the noun it modifies. For
example, the adjective *heavy* in *the package is heavy* ascribes a value of the
attribute of weight to the noun *package*. The antonym of this adjective, *light*,
refers to the same attribute, i.e. weight. Thus, the class of ascriptive adjectives
is organized along very different principles.

Nonascriptive adjectives include those words which do not directly predicate
the noun, but "pertain to it" in some unspecified way. For example, a *musical
instrument* is an instrument *used for* music, not one that is musical.

Finally, verbs in WordNet are structured according to a set of lexical entailment
relations. For example, the verb *snore* lexically entails *sleep* since *He is snoring*
entails *He is sleeping*. This organization is similar to theories in formal semantics
which adopt meaning postulates as the formal device relating lexical items. For
more details and information on WordNet, see Miller (1990a) and Miller and
Fellbaum (1991).

8. The issue of metaphor has largely been ignored in this work, and I have instead
focused my attention on more systematic patterns of polysemy and metonymy.
The phenomena are not always so easy to delineate, of course, and much of the
literature assumes that most forms of metonymy, as discussed in the context
of coercion (cf. chapter 7), are no different from certain types of metaphorical
inferencing (cf. Fass, 1988,1993, and Martin, 1990,1992). Brugman and Lakoff
(1988), Lakoff (1987), and Sowa (1984,1993) also argue that it is difficult to

maintain any clear separation between lexical and linguistic knowledge, on the one hand, and general conceptual knowledge on the other, based on the modes of sense extension associated with the metaphorical usage of lexical items. This is similar to the position held by Nunberg (1995) as discussed above, but Nunberg would presumably still distinguish between lexically and non-lexically based inferences.

Bibliography

Abraham, W. 1986. "Unaccusatives in German," *Groningen Arbeiten zur Germanistischen* 28:1-72.

Abusch, D. 1985. *On Verbs and Time*, Doctoral dissertation, University of Massachusetts, Amherst, MA.

Ackerman, F. 1992. "Complex Predicates and Morphological Relatedness: Locative Alternation in Hungarian," in I. Sag and A. Szabolcsi (eds.), *Lexical Matters*, CSLI Lecture Notes, Stanford, distributed by U. of Chicago Press.

Ackerman, F. 1993. "Entailments of Predicates and the Encoding of Causees," *Linguistic Inquiry* 24:535-546.

Allen, J. 1983. " Maintaining Knowledge About Temporal Intervals," *Communications of the ACM* 26:832-843.

Allen, J. 1984. "Towards a General Theory of Action and Time," *Artificial Intelligence* 23:123-154.

Alsina, A. 1992. "On the Argument Structure of Causatives," *Linguistic Inquiry* 23:517-555.

Alsina, A. and S. Mchombo. 1990. "The Syntax of Applicatives in Chicheŵa," *Natural Language and Linguistic Theory* 8:493-506.

Amsler, R. A. 1980. *The Structure of the Merriam-Webster Pocket Dictionary*, Doctoral dissertation, University of Texas, Austin, TX.

Anderson, M. 1979. *Noun Phrase Structure*, Doctoral dissertation, University of Connecticut, Storrs.

Anderson, M. 1984. "Prenominal Genitive NPs," *The Linguistic Review* 3:1-24.

Anick, P. and S. Bergler. 1992. "Lexical Structures for Linguistic Inference," in J. Pustejovsky and S. Bergler (eds.), *Lexical Semantics and Knowledge Reperesentation*, Springer Verlag, Berlin.

Anick, P. and J. Pustejovsky. 1990. "An Application of Lexical Semantics to Knowledge Acquisition from Corpora," in *Proceedings of 13th International Conference on Computational Linguistics*, Helsinki, Finland, 1990, pp.7–12.

Apresjan, J. D. 1973a. "Synonymy and Synonyms," in F. Kiefer (ed.), 173-199.

Apresjan, J. D. 1973b. "Regular Polysemy," *Linguistics* 142:5-32.

Apresjan, J. D. 1981. "Semantic Amalgamation Rules for Russian Verbs," in P. Jacobson and H. L. Krag (eds.), *The Slavic Verb*, Rosenkilde and Bagger, Copenhagen, 7-13.

Asher, N. and M. Morreau. 1991. "Common Sense Entailment: A Modal Theory of Nonmonotonic Reasoning," in *Proceedings to the 12th International Joint Conference on Artificial Intelligence*, Sydney, Australia.

Atkins, B. T. 1987. "Semantic ID Tags: Corpus Evidence for Dictionary Senses," in *Proceedings of 3rd Annual Conference at University of Waterloo*, Center for the New OED, pgs. 17-36.

Atkins, B. T. 1991. "Building a Lexicon: Reconciling Anisomorphic Sense Differentiations in Machine-Readable Dictionaries," *International Journal of Lexicography*.

Atkins, B. T and B. Levin. 1991. "Admitting Impediments," in Zernik (ed.), *Lexical Acquisition: Using On-Line Resources to Build a Lexicon*, LEA, Hillsdale, NJ.

Atkins, B. T., J. Kegl and B. Levin. 1986 "Explicit and Implicit Information in Dictionaries," *Advances in Lexicology*, Proceedings of the Second Conference of the Centre for the New OED, University of Waterloo, Waterloo, Ontario.

Atkins, B. T., J. Kegl and B. Levin. 1988. "Anatomy of a Verb Entry: From Linguistic Theory to Lexicographic Practice," *International Journal of Lexicography* 1:84-126.

Austin, J. L. 1962. *How to Do Things with Words*, Harvard University Press, Cambridge, MA.

Bach, E. 1981. "On Time, Tense, and Aspect: an Essay in English Metaphysics," in P. Cole (ed.), *Radical Pragmatics*, Academic Press, New York, 63-81.

Bach, E. 1986. "The Algebra of Events," in *Linguistics and Philosophy* 9:5-16.

Baker, C.L. 1969. "Concealed Questions," paper delivered at LSA.

Baker, M. 1988. *Incorporation: A Theory of Grammatical Function Changing*, University of Chicago Press, Chicago.

Bar-Hillel, Y. 1953. "A Quasi-arithmetical Notation for Syntactic Description," *Language* 29:47-58.

Bartsch, R. 1985. "The Structure of Word Meanings: Polysemy, Metaphor, Metonymy" in F. Landman and F. Veltman (eds.) *Varieties of Formal Semantics*, Foris, Dordrecht.

Beard, R. 1991. "Decompositional Composition: The Semantics of Scope Ambiguities and 'Bracketing Paradoxes'," in *Natural Language and Linguistic Theory* 9:195- 229.

Beckwith, R., C. Fellbaum, D. Gross, and G. Miller. 1989. "WordNet: A Lexical Database Organized on Psycholinguistic Principles," in U. Zernik (ed.), *Proceedings of the First International Workshop on Lexical Acquisition*, at IJCAI, Detroit.

Beckwith, R. and G. A. Miller. 1990. "Implementing a Lexical Network," *International Journal of Lexicography* 3:302-312.

Beierle, C., U. Hedtstück, U. Pletat, P. H. Schmitt, and J. Siekmann. 1992. "An Order-Sorted Logic for knowledge Representation Systems," *Artificial Intelligence*, 55:149-191.

Belletti, A. and L. Rizzi. 1988. "Psych-verbs and Theta-Theory," *Natural Language and Linguistic Theory* 6:291-352.

Benthem, J. van. 1983. *The Logic of Time*, Kluwer Academic Publishers, Dordrecht.

Benthem, J. van. 1991. *Language in Action: Categories ,Lambda, and Dynamic Logic*, Studies in Logic and the Foundations of Mathematics, Volume 130, Noth-Holland, Amsterdam, also published in 1994, by MIT Press, Cambridge.

Bergler, S. 1991. "The semantics of collocational patterns for reporting verbs," in *Proceedings of the Fifth Conference of the European Chapter of the Association for Computational Linguistics*, Berlin, April 9-11.

Bergler, S. 1992. *Evidential Analysis of Reported Speech*. PhD dissertation, Brandeis University.

Bés, G. and A. Lecomte. 1995. "Semantic Features in a Generic Lexicon," in P. Saint-Dizier and E. Viegas (eds)., *Computational Lexical Semantics*, Cambridge University Press.

Bierwisch, M. 1983. "Semantische und konzeptuelle Repräsentationen lexikalischer Einheiten," in R. Ruzicka and W. Motsch (eds)., *Untersuchungen zur Semantik*, Berlin, Akademische-Verlag.

Bierwisch, M. and E. Lang. 1989. *Dimensional Adjectives. Grammatical Structure and Conceptual Interpretation*, Springer Verlag, Berlin.

Bierwisch, M. and R. Schreuder. 1992. "From Concepts to lexical Items," *Cognition* 42:23-60.

Bobrow, D. G. and T. Winograd. 1977. "An Overview of KRL, a Knowledge Representation Language," *Cognitive Science*, 1:3-46.

Boguraev, B. 1991. "Building a Lexicon: The Contribution of Computers," in B. Boguraev (ed.), Special issue on computational lexicons, *International Journal of Lexicography* 4(3).

Boguraev, B. and T. Briscoe, eds. 1988. *Computational Lexicography for Natural Language Processing* , Harlow, Essex, Longman.

Boguraev, B. and J. Pustejovsky. 1990. "Lexical Ambiguity and The Role of Knowledge Representation in Lexicon Design," *Proceedings of COLING-1990*,

Helsinki.

Boguraev, B. and J. Pustejovsky. 1994. "A Richer Characterization of Dictionary Entries" in B. Atkins and A. Zampolli (eds.), *Automating the Lexicon*, Oxford University Press.

Boguraev, B. and J. Pustejovsky, eds. 1996. *Corpus Processing for Lexical Acquisition*, MIT Press, Cambridge, MA.

Bolinger, D. 1967. "Adjective Comparison: A Semantic Scale," *Journal of English Linguistics* 1:2-10.

Bolinger, D. 1968. "Entailment and the Meaning of Structures," *Glossa* 2:119-127.

Bolinger, D. 1971a. "A Further Note on the Nominal in the Progressive," *Linguistic Inquiry* 2:584-586.

Bolinger, D. 1971b. "Semantic Overloading: a study of the Verb 'Remind'," *Language* 47:522-547.

Bookman, L. 1994. *Trajectories through Knowledge Space: a Dynamic Framework for Machine Comprehension*, Kluwer Academic Publishers, Boston.

Bouillon, P. and E. Viegas. 1994. "A Semi-Polymorphic Approach to the Interpretation of Adjectival Constructions: A Cross-linguistic Perspective," *Proceedings of Euralex 94*, Amsterdam.

Bouillon, P. 1995. "The Semantics of Adjectival Modification," ms. ISSCO, Geneva.

Brachman, R. J. 1979. "On the Epistemelogical Status of Semantic Networks," in N. Findler, ed., *Associative Networks: Representation and Use of Knowledge by Computers*, Academic Press, New York.

Brachman, R. J. and J. Schmolze. 1985. "An Overview of the KL-ONE Knowledge Representation System," *Cognitive Science* 9.2.

Bresnan, J., ed. 1972. *Theory of Complementation in English Syntax*, Ph.D. Dissertation, MIT.

Bresnan, J., ed. 1982. *The Mental Representation of Grammatical Relations*, MIT Press, Cambridge, MA.

Bresnan, J. and J. Kanerva. 1989. "Locative Inversion in Chicheŵa," *Linguistic Inquiry* 20:1-50.

Bresnan, J. and L. Moshi. 1990. "Object Asymmetries in Comparative Bantu Syntax," *Linguistic Inquiry* 21:147-185.

Bresnan, J. and A. Zaenen. 1990. "Deep Unaccusativity in LFG," in K. Dziwirek et al., eds., *Grammatical Relations: A Cross-Theoretical Perspective*, CSLI, Stanford and U. of Chicago, Chicago.

Briscoe, E., A. Copestake, and B. Boguraev. 1990. "Enjoy the Paper: Lexical Semantics via Lexicology," *Proceedings of 13th International Conference on Computational Linguistics*, Helsinki, Finland, pp. 42–47.

Briscoe,T., V. de Paiva, and A. Copestake (eds.). 1993. *Inheritance, Defaults, and the Lexicon*, Cambridge University Press, Cambridge.

Brugman, C. 1981. *The Story of 'Over': Polysemy, Semantics, and the Structure of the Lexicon*, Master's Thesis, University of California, Berkeley.

Brugman, C. and G. Lakoff. 1988. "Cognitive Topology and Lexical Networks," in S. I. Small, G. W. Cottrell, and M. K. Tanenhaus, eds., *Lexical Ambiguity Resolution*, Morgan Kaufmann, San Mateo, CA., p. 477-508.

Buitelaar, P., and A.-M. Mineur. 1994. "Compositionality and Coercion in Categorial Grammar," in *Proceedings of Ninth Amsterdam Colloquium*, December 14-17, 1993, Amsterdam.

Burge, T. 1972. "Truth and Mass Terms," *Journal of Philosophy* 69, 263-282.

Burzio, L. 1986. *Italian Syntax: A Government and Binding Approach*, Reidel, Dordrecht.

Cardelli, L. 1988. "A Semantics of Multiple Inheritance," *Information and Computation* 76:138-164.

Cardelli, L. and P. Wegner. 1985. "On Understanding Types, Data Abstraction, and Polymorphism," *ACM Computing Surveys*, 17:471-522.

Carlson, G. 1977. *Reference to Kinds in English*, PhD. dissertation, University of Massachusetts, Amherst.

Carlson, G. 1984. "Thematic Roles and Their Role in Semantic Interpretation," *Linguistics* 22:259-279.

Carlson, G. 1989. "On the Semantic Composition of English Generic Sentences," in G. Chierchia, B. Partee and R. Turner (eds.), *Properties, Types and Meaning, II* , Kluwer, Dordrecht, 167-192.

Carnap, R. 1956. *Meaning and Necessity*, University of Chicago Press, Chicago.

Carpenter, B. 1992. "Typed Feature Structures," *Computational Linguistics*, 18:2.

Carrier, J. and J. H. Randall. 1992. "The Argument Structure and Syntactic Structure of Resultatives," *Linguistic Inquiry* 23:173-234.

Carter, R. 1988a. *On Linking: Papers by Richard Carter*, B. Levin and C. Tenny., eds., MIT Lexicon Project Working Papers 25, Center for Cognitive Science, MIT, Cambridge, MA.

Carter, R. 1988. "Compositionality and Polysemy," in B. Levin and C. Tenny, (eds.), *On Linking: Papers by Richard Carter*, MIT Lexicon Project Working Papers no. 25, Dept. of Linguistics and Philosophy, MIT, Cambridge.

Cattell, R. 1984. *Composite Predicates in English*, Syntax and Semantics 17, Academic Press, New York, NY.

Centineo, G. 1986. "A Lexical Theory of Auxiliary Selection in Italian," *Davis Working Papers in Linguistics*, 1:1-35.

Charniak, E. and R. Goldman. 1988. "A Logic for Semantic Interpretation," in *Proceedings of the 26th Annual Meeting of the Association for Computational Linguistics*, Buffalo.

Chierchia, G. 1982. "Bare Plurals, Mass Nouns, and Nominalization," *WCCFL 1*, 243-255.

Chierchia, G. 1984. *Topics in the Syntax and Semantics of Infinitives and Gerunds*, Doctoral dissertation, University of Massachusetts, Amherst, MA.

Chierchia, G. 1989. "A Semantics for Unaccusatives and its Syntactic Consequences," unpublished ms., Cornell University, Ithaca, NY.

Chierchia, G. 1989. "Structured Meanings, Thematic Roles, and Control," in G. Chierchia, B. Partee, and R. Turner, eds., *Properties, Types, and Meaning, vol. 2*, Kluwer Academic Publishers, Dordrecht, The Netherlands, 131-166.

Chierchia, G. and S. McConnell-Ginet. 1990. *Meaning and Grammar: An Introduction to Semantics*, MIT Press, Cambridge.

Chomsky, N. 1955. *The Logical Structure of Linguistic Theory*, University of Chicago Press, first published 1975.

Chomsky, N. 1957. *Syntactic Structures*, Mouton, The Hague.

Chomsky, N. 1965. *Aspects of the Theory of Syntax*, MIT Press, Cambridge.

Chomsky, N. 1970. "Remarks on Nominalization," in R. Jacobs and P.S. Rosenbaum (eds.), *English Tranformational Grammar*, Ginn, Waltham, MA.

Chomsky, N. 1972. *Studies on Semantics in Generative Grammar*, Mouton, The Hague.

Chomsky, N. 1973. "Conditions on Transformations," in S. Anderson and P. Kiparsky, (eds.), *A Festschrift for Morris Halle*, Holt, Rinehart, and Winston, New York.

Chomsky, N. 1975. *Reflections on Language*, Pantheon, New York.

Chomsky, N. 1981. *Lectures on Government and Binding*, Foris Publications, Dordrecht.

Chomsky, N. 1986. *Knowledge of Language, its Nature, Origin, and Use*, Praeger, New York.

Chomsky, N. 1994a. *Language and Thought*, Moyer Bell, Wakefield, R.I.

Chomsky, N. 1994b. "Language as a Natural Object," Jacobsen Lecture, University College, London, May 23, 1994.

Cohen, P.R., J. Morgan, and M. Pollack, eds. 1990. *Intentions in Communication*, MIT Press, Cambridge, MA.

Collins, A. and M. Quillian. 1969. "Retrieval Time from Semantic Memory," *Journal of Verbal Learning and Verbal Behavior*, 9:240-247.

Comrie, B. 1976. *Aspect*, Cambridge University Press, Cambridge.

Comrie, B. 1980. *Tense*, Cambridge University Press, Cambridge.

Comrie, B. and S. Thompson. 1985. "Causative Verb Formation and Other Verb-deriving Morphology," in T. Shopen (ed.), *Language typology and syntactic description: Grammatical categories and the lexicon*, Cambridge University Press, Cambridge.

Copestake, A. 1991. "Defaults in the LRL," in T. Briscoe, A. Copestake, and V. de Paiva, eds., *Proceedings of the Acquilex Workshop on Default Inheritance in the Lexicon*, University of Cambridge Computer Laboratory Technical Report No. 238, 1991.

Copestake, A. 1992. *The Representation of Lexical Semantic Information*, CSRP 280, University of Sussex.

Copestake, A. 1995. "The Representation of group denoting nouns in a lexical knowledge base," in P. Saint-Dizier and E. Viegas, eds., *Computational Lexical Semantics*, Cambridge University Press.

Copestake, A. and T. Briscoe 1992. "Lexical Operations in a Unification-based Framework," in J. Pustejovsky and S. Bergler, eds., *Lexical Semantics and Knowledge Reperesentation*, Springer Verlag, Berlin.

Copestake, A. and T. Briscoe 1995. "Semi-Productive Polysemy and Sense Extension," *Journal of Semantics* 12.

Copestake, A., A. Sanfilippo, T. Briscoe, and V. de Paiva. 1993. "TheACQUILEX LKB: An Introduction," in T. Briscoe, V. de Paiva, and A. Copestake (eds.), *Inheritance, Defaults, and the Lexicon*, Cambridge University Press, Cambridge.

Croft, W.A. 1990. "A Conceptual Framework for Grammatical Categories: A Taxonomy of Propositional Acts.," *Journal of Semantics* 7:245-79.

Croft, W. 1991. *Typology and Universals*, Cambridge University Press.

Croft, W. 1991b. *Categories and Relations in Syntax: The Clause-Level Organization of Information*, University of Chicago Press.

Crouch, R. and S. Pulman. 1993. "Time and Modality in a Natural Language Interface to a Planning System," *Artificial Intelligence* 63:265-304.

Cruse, D. A. 1986. *Lexical Semantics*, Cambridge University Press.

Cruse, D. A. 1995. "Polysemy and related phenomena from a cognitive linguistic viewpoint," in P. Saint-Dizier and E. Viegas (eds.), *Computational Lexical Semantics*, Cambridge University Press.

Dahl, Ö. 1981. "On the Definition of the Telic-Atelic (Bounded-Nonbounded. Distinction," *Syntax and Semantics: Tense and Aspect* 14, p. 79-90.

Davidson, D. 1967. "The Logical Form of Action Sentences," in N. Rescher, ed., *The Logic of Decision and Action*, Pittsburgh University Press, Pittsburgh.

Davidson, D. and G. Harman, eds., 1972. *Semantics of Natural Language*, Reidel, Dordrecht.

Déclés, J.-P. 1989. "State, Event, Process, and Topology," *General Linguistics* 29:159-200.

de Paiva, V. 1993. "Types and Constraints in the LKB," in T. Briscoe, V. de Paiva, and A. Copestake (eds.), *Inheritance, Defaults, and the Lexicon*, Cambridge University Press, Cambridge.

Diesing, M. 1992. *Indefinites*, MIT Press, Cambridge.

Dini L. and F. Busa. 1994. "Generative Operations in a Constraint-based Grammar," in *Proceedings of KONVENS-94*, Vienna, Austria, September 28-30.

Di Sciullo, A. M. and S. T. Rosen 1990. "Light and Semi-Light Verb Constructions," in K. Dziwirek, P. Farrell and E. Mejías-Bikandi, eds., *Grammatical Relations: A Cross-Theoretical Perspective*, Center for the Study of Language and Information, Stanford University, Stanford, CA, 109-125.

DiScuillo, A. M. and E. Williams 1987. *On the Definition of Word*, MIT Press, Cambridge.

Dixon, R. M. W. 1984. "The Semantic Basis of Syntactic Properties," *BLS* 10, 583-595.

Dixon, R. M. W. 1991. *A New Approach to English Grammar, on Semantic Principles*, Oxford University Press.

Dölling, J. 1992. "Flexible Interpretationen durch Sortenverschiebung," in I. Zimmermann and A. Strigen (eds.), *Fügungspotenzen*, Berlin, Akademie Verlag.

Dor, D. 1992. "Towards a Semantic Account of Concealed Questions," ms. Stanford University.

Dowty, D.R. 1976. "Montague Grammar and the Lexical Decomposition of Causative Verbs," in B. Partee, ed., *Montague Grammar*, Academic Press, New York, NY, 201-246.

Dowty, D. R. 1979. *Word Meaning and Montague Grammar*, D. Reidel, Dordrecht, Holland.

Dowty, D.R. 1982. "Grammatical Relations in Montague Grammar," in P. Jacobson and G.K. Pullum, eds., *The Nature of Syntactic Representation*, Reidel, Dordrecht, 79-130.

Dowty, D. R. 1985. "On Some Recent Analyses of Control," *Linguistics and Philosophy* 8:1-41.

Dowty, D. R. 1989. "On the Semantic Content of the Notion 'Thematic Role'," in G. Chierchia, B. Partee, and R. Turner, eds. *Properties, Types, and Meaning, Vol. 2, Semantic Issues*, Dordrecht.

Dowty, D. R. 1991. "Thematic Proto-Roles and Argument Selection," *Language* 67:547-619.

Eberle, K. 1988. "Partial Orderings and Aktionsarten in Discourse Representation Theory," in *Proceedings of COLING-88*, Budapest, 1988, pg. 160-165.

Elliott, D. E. 1974. "Towards a Grammar of Exclamations," *Foundations of Language* 11.

Enç, M. 1981. *Tense without Scope*, Ph.D. Dissertation, University of Wisconsin, Madison.

Enç, M. 1987. "Anchoring Conditions for Tense," *Linguistic Inquiry* 18:633-658.

Eschenbach, C. 1993. "Semantics of Number," *Journal of Semantics*, 10:1-23.

Evans, R. and G. Gerald. 1989. "Inference in DATR," in the *Proceedings of the Fourth European ACL Conference*, April 10-12, 1989, Manchester, England.

Evans, R. and G. Gerald. 1990. "The DATR papers: February 1990." Cognitive Science Research Paper CSRP 139, School of Cognitive and Computing Science, University of Sussex, Brighton, England.

Evens, M. 1987. *Relational Models of the Lexicon*, Cambridge University Press, Cambridge.

Farkas, D. F. 1988. "On obligatory Control," in *Linguistics and Philosophy*, 11:27-58.

Fass, D. 1988a. "An Account of Coherence, Semantic Relations, Metonymy, and Lexical Ambiguity Resolution," in S.I. Small, G.W. Cottrell, and M.K. Tanenhaus, eds. *Lexical Ambiguity Resolution*, Morgan Kaufmann, San Mateo, CA.

Fass, D. 1993. "Lexical Semantic Constraints," in J. Pustejovsky (ed.) *Semantics and the Lexicon*, Kluwer Academic Publishers, Dordrecht.

Fauconnier, G. 1985. *Mental Spaces*, MIT Press, Cambridge.

Fellbaum, C. 1990. "English Verbs as a Semantic Net," *International Journal of Lexicography*, 3:278-301.

Fillmore, C. 1968. "The Case for Case," in *Universals in Linguistic Theory*, E. Bach and R. Harms, eds.,. New York, Holt, Rinehart, and Winston.

Fillmore, C. 1971. "Types of Lexical Information," in D. Steinberg and L. Jakobovits, eds., 370-392.

Fillmore, C. 1977a. "Topics in Lexical Semantics," in R. W. Cole, ed., *Current Issues in Linguistic Theory*, Indiana University Press, Bloomington.

Fillmore, C. 1977b. "The Case for Case Re-opened," in P. Cole, ed., *Syntax and Semantics, Vol. 8*, Academic Press, New York.

Fillmore, C. 1986. "Pragmatically Controlled Zero Anaphora," *BLS* 12, 95-107.

Fillmore, C. 1988. "The Mechanisms of Construction Grammar,"*BLS* 14, 35-55.

Fillmore, C. and B. T. Atkins. 1991. "Toward a Frame-Based Lexicon: The Semantics of Risk," paper delivered at ACL, Berkeley, CA.

Fillmore, C. and B. T. Atkins. 1994. "Starting where the dictionaries stop: the Challend of corpus lexicography," in B. T. Atkins and A. Zampolli, eds. *Computational Approaches to the Lexicon*, Oxford University Press, Oxford.

Fillmore, C. and D. T. Langendoen, eds., 1971. *Studies in Linguistic Semantics*, Holt, Rinehart and Winston, New York, NY.

Fisher, C., H. Gleitman, and L. R. Gleitman 1991. "On the Semantic Content of Subcategorization Frames," *Cognitive Psychology* 23.

Flickinger, D. C. Pollard, and T. Wasow 1985. "Structure-Sharing in Lexical Representation," *Proceedings of 23rd Annual Meeting of the ACL*, Chicago, IL, pp.262–267.

Fodor, J. 1975. *The Language of Thought*, Harvard University Press, Cambridge.

Foley, W.. and R. Van Valin 1984. *Functional Syntax and Universal Grammar*, Camrbidge University Press, Cambridge.

Freed, A. F. 1979. *The Semantics of English Aspectual Complementation*, Dordrecht: Reidel.

Gawron, M. 1983. *Lexical Semantics and the Semantics of Complementation*, Ph.D. dissertation, University of California at Berkeley.

Gazdar, G. , E. Klein, G. Pullum, and I. Sag. 1985. *Generalized Phrase Structure Grammar*, Harvard University Press.

Gentner, D. and I. M. France 1988. "The Verb Mutability Effect: Studies of the Combinatorial Semantics," in S. I. Small, G. W. Cottrell, and M. K. Tanenhaus, eds., *Lexical Ambiguity Resolution*, Morgan Kaufmann, San Mateo, CA.

Gleitman, L. 1990. "The Structural Sources of Verb Meaning," *Language Acquisition, 1*, 3-55.

Godard, D. and J. Jayez. 1993. "Towards a proper treatment of Coercion Phenomena," in *Proceeding of the 1993 European ACL*.

Goldberg, A. 1992. *Argument Structure Constructions*. Ph.D. Dissertation, University of California, Berkeley.

Goldberg, A. 1995. *Constructions: A Construction Grammar Approach to Argument Structure*, University of Chicago Press, Chicago.

Goodman, N. 1951. *The Structure of Appearance* , Reidel Publishing, Dordrecht, The Netherlands.

Green, G. 1974. *Semantics and Syntactic Regularity*, Indiana University Press, Bloomington.

Grice, H. P. 1971. "Meaning," in D. Steinberg and L. Jacobovits, eds., *Semantics: An Interdisciplinary Reader in Philosophy, Linguistics, and Psychology*, Cambridge, Cambridge University Press.

Grimshaw, J. 1979. "Complement Selection and the Lexicon" *Linguistic Inquiry* 10:279-326.

Grimshaw, J. 1982. "Subcategorization and Grammatical Relations," in A. Zaenen (ed.), *Subjects and other Subjects: Proceedings of the Harvard Conference on Grammatical Relations*, Bloomington, Indiana Linguistics Club, p. 35-55.

Grimshaw, J. 1990. *Argument Structure*, MIT Press, Cambridge, MA.

Grimshaw, J. and S. Vikner 1993. "Obligatory Adjuncts and the Structure of Events,"in E. Reuland and W. Abraham (eds.), *Knowledge and Language*, Vol. II, Kluwer Academic Publishers, Dordrecht, p. 143-155.

Grinder, J. 1970. "Super Equi-NP Deletion," *CLS 6*.

Groenendijk, J., and M. Stokhof. 1989. "Type-Shifting Rules and the Semantics of Interrogatives", in G. Chierchia, B. Partee, and R. Turner (eds.), *Properties, Tpyes, and Meaning*, Dordrecht, Reidel.

Gropen, J., S. Pinker, M. Hollander, and R. Goldberg 1991. "Affectedness and Direct Objects: the Role of Lexical Semantics in the Acquisition of Verb Argument Structure," *Cognition* 41:153-195.

Gross, D. and K. Miller 1990. "Adjectives in WordNet," *International Journal of Lexicography*, 3, pp. 265-277.

Grosz, B. and C. Sidner. 1986. "Attention, Intentions, and the Structure of Discourse," *Computational Linguistics* 12:175-204.

Gruber, J. S. 1967. *"Look* and *See," Language* 43, 937-947.

Gruber, J. S. 1976. *Lexical Structures in Syntax and Semantics*, North-Holland, Amsterdam.

Guentcheva, Z. 1990. "L'oppostion perfectif/imperfectif et la notion d'achèvement," in J. Fontanille (ed.), *Le discours aspectualisé*, Collection Nouveaux Actes Sémiotiques, Benjamins, Paris.

Gunter, C. 1992. *Semantics of Programming Languages*, MIT Press, Cambridge.

Hacking, I. 1983. *Representing and intervening: introductory topics in the philosophy of natural science*, Cambridge University Press, New York.

Hale, K. and S. J. Keyser. 1986. "Some Transitivity Alternations in English," Lexicon Project Working Papers 7, Center for Cognitive Science, MIT, Cambridge, MA.

Hale, K. and S. J. Keyser. 1987. "A View from the Middle," Lexicon Project Working Papers 10, Center for Cognitive Science, MIT, Cambridge, MA.

Hale, K.L. and S. J. Keyser 1992. "The Syntactic Character of Thematic Structure," in I. M. Roca, ed., *Thematic Structure: Its Role in Grammar*, Foris, Berlin, 107-143.

Harris, Z. 1951. *Methods in Structural Linguistics*, University of Chicago Press, Chicago.

Harris, Z. 1952. "Discourse Analysis" *Language* 28:130.

Harris, Z. 1957. "Co-Occurrence and Transformation in Linguistic Structure" *Language* 33:283-340.

Harris, Z. 1965. "Transformational Theory," *Language* 41:363-401.

Hayes, P. 1979. "Naive Physics Manifesto," in D. Mitchie (ed.), *Expert Systems in the Micro-electronic Age*, Edinburgh University Press, Edinburgh, Scotland.

Heim, I. 1979. "Concealed Questions", in R. Bäuerle, U. Egli, and A. von Stechow (eds.), *Semantics from Different Points of View*, Springer, Berlin.

Hendriks, H. 1987. "Type Change in Semantics: The Scope of Quantification and Coordination," in E. Klein and J. van Benthem (eds.), *Categories, Polymorphism, and Unification*, Centre for Cognitive Science, University of Edinburgh, and Institute for Language, Logic and Information, University of Amsterdam.

Heylen, D. 1995. "Lexical Functions and Knowledge Representation," in P. Saint-Dizier and E. Viegas (eds.), *Computational Lexical Semantics*, Cambridge University Press.

Herskovits, A. 1987. *Language and Spatial Cognition*, Cambridge University Press, Cambridge, UK.

Herskovits, A. 1988. "Spatial Expressions and the Plasticity of Meaning," in B. Rudzka-Ostyn (ed.), *Topics in Cognitive Grammar*, John Benjamins, Amsterdam, 271-297.

Herzog, O. and C.-R. Rollinger, eds. 1991. *Text Understanding in LILOG: Integrating CL and AI*, Springer-Verlag, Berlin.

Higginbotham, J. 1983. "The Logic of Perceptual Reports: An Extensional Alternative to Situation Semantics," *The Journal of Philosophy* 80, 100-127.

Higginbotham, J. 1983. "Logical Form, Binding, and Nominals," *Linguistic Inquiry* 14:395-420.

Higginbotham, J. 1985. "On Semantics," *Linguistic Inquiry* 16:547-593.

Higginbotham, J. 1989. "Elucidations of Meaning," *Linguistics and Philosophy* 12:465-517.

Hinrichs, E. 1985. *A Compositional Semantics for Aktionarten and NP Reference in English*. PhD Dissertation, Ohio State University.

Hirst, G. 1987. *Semantic Interpretation and the Resolution of Ambiguity*, Cambridge University Press, Cambridge.

Hirst, G. 1988. "Resolving Lexical Ambiguity Computationally with Spreading Activation and Polaroid Words," in S.I. Small, G.W. Cottrell, and M.K. Tanenhaus (eds.), *Lexical Ambiguity Resolution*, Morgan Kaufmann, San Mateo, CA.

Hobbs, J. 1982. "Towards an Understanding of Coherence in Discourse," in *Strategies for Natural Language Processing*, W. Lehnert and M. Ringle, eds., Hillsdale, NJ, Lawrence Erlbaum Associates.

Hobbs, J. 1987. "World Knowledge and Word Meaning," in *Proceedings of TINLAP-3*, Las Cruces, New Mexico.

Hobbs, J., W. Croft, T. Davies, D. Edwards, and K. Laws. 1987a. "Commonsense Metaphysics and Lexical Semantics," *Computational Linguistics* 13.

Hobbs, J., W. Croft, T. Davies, D. Edwards, and K. Laws. 1987b. "The TACITUS Commonsense Knowledge Base," Artificial Intelligence Center, SRI International.

Hobbs, J., M. Stickel, P. Martin, D. Edwards. 1993. "Interpretation as Abduction," *Artificial Intelligence* 63:69-142.

Hoekstra, T. 1992. "Aspect and Theta Theory," in I. M. Roca (ed.), *Thematic Structure: Its Role in Grammar*, Foris, Berlin, 145-174.

Horn, L. R. 1980. "Affixation and the Unaccusative Hypothesis," *CLS* 16, 134-146.

Horn, L. R. 1989. *A Natural History of Negation*, University of Chicago Press, Chicago.

Hout, A. van. 1995. "Projection based on Event Structure," in P. Coopmans, M. Everaert, and J. Grimshaw (eds.), *Lexical Specification and Lexical Insertion*, Lawrence Erlbaum Associates, Hillsdale, N.J.

Hovy, E. 1993. "Automated Discourse Generation using Discourse Structure Relations," *Artificial Intelligence* 63:341-385.

Ilson, R. and I. Mel'čuk 1989. "English *Bake* Revisited," *International Journal of Lexicography* 2:325-346.

Ingria, R. and J. Pustejovsky. 1990. "Active Objects in Syntax, Semantics, and Parsing," in C. Tenny, ed., *The MIT Parsing Volume, 1988-1989*, Parsing Project Working Papers 2, Center for Cognitive Science, MIT, Cambridge, MA, 147-169.

Jackendoff, R. 1972. *Semanic Interpretation in Generative Grammar*, MIT Press, Cambridge, MA.

Jackendoff, R. 1983. *Semantics and Cognition*, MIT Press, Cambridge, MA.

Jackendoff, R. 1985a. "Multiple Subcategorization and the θ-Criterion," *Natural Language and Linguistic Theory* 3:271-295.

Jackendoff, R. 1985b. "Believing and Intending: Two Sides of the Same Coin," *Linguistic Inquiry* 16:445-460.

Jackendoff, R. 1985c. "Multiple Subcategorization and the Theta-Criterion: The Case of *Climb*," *Natural Language and Linguistic Theory* 3:271-295.

Jackendoff, R. 1987. "The Status of Thematic Relations in Linguistic Theory," *Linguistic Inquiry* 18:369-411.

Jackendoff, R. 1990. *Semantic Structures*, MIT Press, Cambridge, MA.

Jackendoff, R.S. 1992a. "Babe Ruth Homered His Way into the Hearts of America," in T. Stowell and E. Wehrli (eds.), *Syntax and the lexicon*, Academic Press, San Diego, 155-178.

Jackendoff, R. 1992b. "Mme. Tussaud Meets the Binding Theory," *Natural Language and Linguistic Theory* 21:427-455.

Jackendoff, R. 1993. "The Conceptual Structure of Intendingand Volitional Action," in H. Campos and P. Kempchinsky (eds.), *Festschrift for Carlos Otero*, Georgetown University Press, Georgetown.

Jacobs, R. and P. Rosenbaum, eds. 1967. *Readings in English Transformational Grammar*, Ginn, Waltham, MA.

Jakobson, R. 1970. *Recent Developments in Linguistic Science*, Perenial Press.

Jacobson, P. 1990. "Raising as Function Composition," in *Linguistics and Philosophy* 13:423-476.

Jacobson, P. 1992. "The Lexical Entailment Theory of Control and the *Tough*-Construction," in I.A. Sag and A. Szabolcsi, (eds.), *Lexical Matters*, CSLI, Stanford, 269-299.

Jespersen, O. 1924. *The Philosophy of Grammar*, Norton, New York.

Johnston, M. 1995. "Semantic Underspecification and Lexical Types: Capturing Polysemy without Lexical Rules," in *Proceedings of ACQUILEX Workshop on Lexical Rules*, August 9-11, 1995, Cambridgeshire.

Johnston, M., B. Boguraev, and J. Pustejovsky. 1995. "The Acquisition and Interpretation of Technical Complex Nominals," in *Proceedings of AAAI Symposium on Lexical Acquisition*, March 29-31, Stanford.

Kamp, H. 1979. "Some Remarks on the Logic of Change: Part 1" in C. Rohrer, (ed.), *Time, Tense, and Quantifiers*, Tübingen, Niemeyer.

Kamp, H. and U. Reyle. 1993. *From Discourse to Logic*, Kluwer Academic Publishers, Dordrecht.

Kamp, H. and A. Roßdeutscher. 1992. "Remarks on Lexical Structure, DRS Construction, and Lexically Driven Inferences," Arbeitspapiere des Sonderforschungsbereichs 340 *Sprachtheoretische Grundlagen für die Computerlinguistik*, Nr. 21, Stuttgart.

Karttunen, L. 1971. "Implicative Verbs". *Language* 47:340-58.

Karttunen, L. 1974. "Presupposition and Linguistic Context". *Theoretical Linguistics* 1:181-93.

Katz, J. 1964. "Semantic Theory and the Meaning of 'Good'," *Journal of Philosophy* 61:739-766.

Katz, J. 1972. *Semantic Theory*, Harper and Row, New York.

Katz, J. and J. Fodor. 1963. "The Structure of a Semantic Theory," *Language* 39:170-210.

Kautz, H. 1987. *A Formal Theory of Plan Recognition*, Ph.D. Dissertation, University of Rochester.

Keenan, E. and L. Faltz. 1985. *Boolean Semantics for Natural Language*, Reidel Publishing, Dordrecht.

Kenny, A. 1963. *Action, Emotion, and Will*, Routledge and Kegan Paul, London.

Keyser, S. J. and T. Roeper. 1984. "On the Middle and Ergative Constructions in English," *Linguistic Inquiry* 15:381-416.

Keyser, S. J. and T. Roeper. 1992. "Re: The Abstract Clitic Hypothesis," *Linguistic Inquiry* 23:89-125.

Kiefer, F. 1992. "Hungarian Derivational Morphology, Semantic Complexity, and Semantic Markedness," in I.A. Sag and A. Szabolcsi, (eds.), *Lexical Matters*, CSLI, Stanford, 183-208.

Kilgarriff, A. 1995. "Inheriting Polysemy," in P. Saint-Dizier and E. Viegas (eds.), *Computational Lexical Semantics*, Cambridge University Press, Cambridge.

Kiparsky, P. and C. Kiparsky. 1971. "Fact," in D. Steinberg and L. Jakobovitz, (eds.), *Semantics*, Cambridge University Press, Cambridge, 345-369.

Klavans, J., M. Chodorow, N. Wacholder. 1990. "From Dictionary to Knowledge Base via Taxonomy," *Proceedings of the 6th Conf. UW Centre for the New OED*, Waterloo, 110-132.

Klein, E. and I. Sag. 1985. "Type-Driven Translation," *Linguistics and Philosophy* 8:163-202.

Klein, E. and J. van Benthem. 1987. *Categories, Polymorphism, and Unification*, Centre for Cognitive Science, University of Edinburgh, and Institute for Language, Logic and Information, University of Amsterdam.

Kowalski, R. and M. Sergot. 1986. "A Logic-based Calculus of Events," *New Generation Computing* 4:67-95.

Kratzer, A. 1988. "Stage-level vs. Individual-level Predicates," ms. UMASS, Amherst.

Kratzer, A. 1989. "An Investigation into the Lumps of Thought," *Linguistics and Philosophy*, 12:607-653.

Krifka, M. 1989. "Nominal Reference, Temporal Constitution, and Quantification in Event Semantics," in R. Bartsch, J. van Ebthe, and P. van Emde Boas (eds.), *Semantics and Contextual Expressions*, Foris, Dordrecht, pg. 75-115.

Krifka, M. 1992. "Thematic Relations as Links between Nominal Reference and Temporal Constitution," in I. Sag and A. Szabolcsi, (eds.), *Lexical Matters*, CSLI Lecture Notes, University of Chicago Press, Chicago, Ill.

Kunze, J. 1991. *Kasusrelationen und semantische Emphase*, Akademie Verlag, Berlin.

Ladusaw, W. and D. Dowty 1988. "Toward a Nongrammatical Account of Thematic Roles," in W. Wilkins, (ed.), 62-73.

Lakoff, G. 1968. "Instrumental Adverbs and the Concept of Deep Structure," *Foundations of Language*, 4:4-29.

Lakoff G. 1970. *Irregularity in Syntax*. Holt, Rinehart, and Winston.

Lakoff G. 1971. "On Generative Semantics," in *Semantics: An Interdisciplinary Reader*, D. Steinberg and L. Jakobovits, eds., Cambridge University Press.

Lakoff, G. 1972. "Linguistics and Natural Logic," in D. Davidson and G. H. Harmon, eds., *The Semantics of Natural Language*, Reidel, Dordrecht, 545-665.

Lakoff G. 1987. *Women, Fire, and Dangerous Objects*, University of Chicago Press, Chicago, 1987.

Lambek, J. 1958. "The Mathematics of Sentence Structure," *American Mathematical Monthly* 65, 154-170, also in W. Buskowski, W. Marciszewski, and J. van Benthem (eds.), 1988, *Categorial Grammar*, John Benjamins, Amsterdam, 153-172.

Lambek, J. 1961. "The the Calculus of Syntactic Types," in R. Jakobson (ed.), *Structure of Language and its Mathematical Aspects*, Proceedings of the Symposia in Applied Mathematics XII, American Mathematical Society, 166-178

Lamiroy, B. 1987. "Les Verbes de Mouvement Emplois Figurés et Extensions Métaphoriques," *Langue Française* 26:41-58.

Lamiroy, B. 1987. "The complementation of aspectual verbs in French," in *Language*, 63.

Landman, F. 1991. *Structures for Semantics*, Kluwer Academic Publishers, Dordrecht.

Lang, E. 1989. "The Semantics of Dimensional Designation of Spatial Objects," in M. Bierwisch and E. Lang (eds.), *Dimensional Adjectives: Grammatical Structures and Conceptual Interpretation*, Springer Verlag, Berlin.

Lang, E. 1991. "The LILOG Ontology from a Linguistic Point of View," in O. Herzog and C.-R. Rollinger (eds.), *Text Understanding in LILOG: Integrating CL and AI*, Springer-Verlag, Berlin.

Langacker, R.W. 1991. *Foundations of Cognitive Grammar: Descriptive Application*, Vol. 2, Stanford University Press, Stanford, CA.

Lascarides A. and N. Asher. 1993. "Temporal Interpretation, Discourse Relations and Commonsense Entailment," in *Linguistics and Philosophy* 16:437-494.

Lascarides, A., E.J. Briscoe, N. Asher and A. Copestake. 1994. "Persistent associative default unification," *Linguistics and Philosophy* 17.

Lasnik, H. and R, Fiengo. 1974. "Complement Object Deletion," *Linguistic Inquiry* 5:535-571.

Lebeaux, D. 1986. "The Interpretation of Derived Nominals," *CLS 22, Part 1, Papers from the General Session*, 231-247.

Lees, R. B. 1966. *The Grammar of English Nominalizations*, Mouton, The Hague.

Leiß, H. 1991. "Polymorphic Constructs in Natural and Programming Languages," *Semantics of Programming Languages*, Springer, Berlin.

Lenders, W. 1989. "Computergestützte Verfahren zur semantischen Beschreibung von Spracher," in *Handbuch Computerlinguistik*, Berlin, De Gruyter, pg. 231-244.

Levi, J. N. 1978. *The Syntax and Semantics of Complex Nominals*, Academic Press, New York.

Levin, B., ed. 1985. *Lexical Semantics in Review*, Lexicon Project Working Papers 1, MIT.

Levin, B. 1985. "Introduction," in B. Levin, (ed.), *Lexical Semantics in Review*, Lexicon Project Working Papers 1, Center for Cognitive Science, MIT, 1-62.

Levin, B. 1993. *Towards a Lexical Organization of English Verbs*, University of Chicago Press, Chicago.

Levin, B. and T. R. Rapoport 1988. "Lexical Subordination," *Proceedings of CLS 24*, 275-289, 1988.

Levin, B. and M. Rappaport. 1986. "The Formation of Adjectival Passives," *Linguistic Inquiry*, 17.4.

Levin, B. and M. Rappaport. 1988. "On the Nature of Unaccusativity," in *Proceedings of NELS 1988*.

Levin, B. and M. Rappaport Hovav. 1991. "Wiping the Slate Clean: A Lexical Semantic Exploration," *Cognition* 41:123-151.

Levin, B. and M. Rappaport Hovav. 1995. *Unaccusatives: At the Syntax-Lexical Semantics Interface*, MIT Press, Cambridge, MA.

Levin, L. 1986. *Operations on Lexical Forms*. Ph.D. dissertation, MIT, Cambridge.

Li, J. 1994. *Räumliche Relationen und Objektwissen: am Beispiel 'an' und 'bei'*, Gunter Narr, Tübingen.

Link, G. 1983. "The Logical Analysis of Plurals and Mass Terms: A Lattice-Theoretic Approach," in r. Bäuerle, C. Schwarze, and A. von Stechow, (eds.), *Meaning, Use, and Interpretation of Language*, Mouton, Berlin.

Lloyd, G. E. R. 1968. *Aristotle: The Growth and Structure of his Thought*, Cambridge University Press.

LoCascio, V. and C. Vet, eds. 1986. *Temporal Structure in Sentence and Discourse*, Foris, Dordrecht.

Lytinen, S. L. 1988. "Are Vague Words Ambiguous?" in S. I. Small, G. W. Cottrell, and M. K. Tanenhaus, eds., *Lexical Ambiguity Resolution*, Morgan Kaufmann, San Mateo, CA.

McArthur, T. 1981. *Longman Lexicon of Contemporary English*, Longman, Harlow, Essex.

McCawley, J. D. 1968b. "The Role of Semantics in a Grammar," in E. Bach and R. T. Harms (eds.), *Universals in Linguistic Theory*, Holt, Rinehart, and Winston, New York, NY.

McCawley, J. D. 1975. "Lexicography and the Count-Mass Distinction," *BLS* 1, 314-321. Reprinted in J.D. McCawley (1979), p. 165-173.

McCawley, N. 1976. "On Experiencer Causatives," in M. Shibatani (ed.), 181-203.

McCawley, J. 1979. *Adverbs, Vowels, and other Objects of Wonder*, University of Chicago Press, Chicago.

McClure, W. 1990. "A Lexical Semantic Explanation for Unaccusative Mismatches," in K. Dziwirek, P. Farrel, and E. Mejías-Bikandi (eds.), *Grammatical Relations: A Cross-Theoretical Perspective*, CSLI, Stanford.

McConnell-Ginet, S. 1982. "Adverbs and Logical Form: A Linguistically Realistic Theory," *Language* 58:144-184.

McKeon, R., ed. 1968. *The Basic Works of Aristotle*, Random House, New York.

Marantz, A.P. 1984. *On the Nature of Grammatical Relations*, MIT Press, Cambridge, MA.

Martin, J. 1990. *A Computational Model of Metaphor Interpretation*, Academic Press, Cambridge, MA.

Martin, J. 1992. "Conventional Metaphor and the Lexicon," in J. Pustejovsky and S. Bergler (eds.), *Lexical Semantics and Knowledge Reperesentation*, Springer Verlag, Berlin.

Mel'čuk, I. A. 1973a. "Lexical Functions in Lexicographic Description," *BLS* 8, 427-444.

Mel'čuk, I. A. 1988a. "Semantic Description of Lexical Units in an Explanatory Combinatorial Dictionary: Basic Principles and Heuristic Criteria," *International Journal of Lexicography* 1:165-188.

Mel'čuk, I. A. 1988b. *Dependency Syntax*, SUNY Press. Albany, New York.

Miller, G. 1985. "Dictionaries of the Mind" in *Proceedings of the 23rd Annual Meeting of the Association for Computational Linguistics*, Chicago.

Miller, G. 1989. "Contexts of Antonymous Adjectives," *Applied Psycholinguistics* 10:357-375.

Miller, G. 1990a. "Nouns in WordNet: A Lexical Inheritance System," *International Journal of Lexicography* 3:245-264.

Miller, G., ed. 1990b. "WordNet: An On-Line Lexical Database," *International Journal of Lexicography* 3:4.

Miller, G. 1991. *The Science of Words*, Scientific American Press, New York.

Miller, G., R. Beckwith, C, Fellbaum, D. Gross and K. J. Miller. 1990. "Introduction to WordNet: An On-line Lexical Database," *International Journal of Lexicography* 3:235-244.

Miller, G. and C. Fellbaum 1991. "Semantic Networks of English," *Cognition* 41:197-229.

Miller, G. and P. Johnson-Laird. 1976. *Language and Perception*, Belknap, Harvard University Press, Cambridge, MA.

Mineur, A.-M. and P. Buitelaar. 1995. "A Compositional Treatment of Polysemous Arguments in Categorial Grammar," in S. Peters and K. van Deemter (eds.), Ambiguity and Underspecification, CSLI, Stanford University.

Minsky, M. 1975. "A Framework for Representing Knowledge" in P. Winston, ed., *The Psychology of Computer Vision*, McGraw-Hill, New York.

Mitchell, J. C. 1988. "Polymorphic Type Inference and Containment," *Information and Computation* 76.

Mitchell, J. C. 1991. "Type Inference with Simple Subtypes," *Journal of Functional Programming* 1:245-285.

Modrak, D. 1987. *Aristotle: the Power of Perception*, University of Chicago Press, Chicago.

Moens, M. 1987. *Tense, Aspect and Temporal Reference*. Ph.D. Dissertation, Edinburgh.

Moens, M. and M. Steedman. 1988. "Temporal Ontology and Temporal Reference," *Computational Linguistics* 14:15-28.

Montague, R. 1970. "Universal Grammar," *Theoria* 36:373-398. Reprinted in Thomason 1974, pp. 222-246.

Montague, R. 1973. "The Proper Treatment of Quantification in Ordinary English," in K. Hintikka, J. Moravcsik and P. Suppes (eds.), *Approaches to Natural Language*, Dordrecht, Kluwer, pp. 221-242. Reprinted in Thomason 1974, pp. 247-270.

Moortgat, M. 1988. *Categorial Investigations: Logical and Linguistic Aspects of the Lambek Calculus*, Foris, Dordrecht.

Moravcsik, J. M. 1975. "Aitia as Generative Factor in Aristotle's Philosophy," *Dialogue* 14:622-36.

Moravcsik, J. M. 1981. "How do Words get their Meanings?," *Journal of Philosophy* 78:5-24.

Moravcsik, J. M. 1990. *Thought and Language*, Routledge, London.

Morrill, G. 1992. *Type-Logical Grammar*, Onderzoeksinstituut voor Taal en Spraak, Utrecht.

Morrill, G. 1994 *Type-Logical Grammar*, Kluwer Academmic Publishers, Dordrecht.

Morrill, G., and B. Carpenter. 1990. "Compositionality, Implicational Logics, and Theories of Grammar," *Linguistics and Philosophy* 13:4.

Mourelatos, A. P. D. 1978. "Events, Processes and States," *Linguistics and Philosophy* 2:415-434. Also published in P. Tedeschi and A. Zaenen (eds.), 1981. *Syntax and Semantics 14: Tense and Aspect*, Academic Press, New York, NY, 191-212.

Nebel, B. 1990. *Reasoning and Revision in Hybrid Representation Systems*, Springer Verlag, Berlin.

Nirenburg, S. 1989a. "Lexicons for Computer Programs and Lexicons for People," in *Proceedings of the 5th Annual Conference of the UW Centre for the New Oxford English Dictionary*, pp. 43-66. St. Catherine's College, Oxford, England.

Nirenburg, S. 1989b. "Knowledge-Based Machine Translation," *Machine Translation* (special issue on knowledge-based MT), 4:1.

Nirenburg, S. and L. Levin. 1989. "Knowledge Representation and Support," *Machine Translation* (special issue on knowledge-based MT), 4:1.

Nirenburg, S. and V. Raskin. 1987. "The Subworld Concept Lexicon and the Lexicon Management System," *Computational Linguistics* 13:3.

Nunberg, G. 1978. *The pragmatics of Reference*. Indiana University Linguistics Club: Bloomington, Indiana.

Nunberg, G. 1979. "The Non-uniqueness of Semantic Solutions: Polysemy," *Linguistics and Philosophy* 3:143-184.

Nunberg, G. 1995. "Transfers of Meaning," *Journal of Semantics* 12.

Nunberg, G. and A. Zaenen. 1992. "Systematic Polysemy in Lexicology and Lexicography," in H. Tommola, K. Varantola, T. Tolonen, and J. Schopp (eds.), *Proceedings of Euralex II*, Tampere, Finland, University of Tampere.

Nunes, M. 1993. "Argument Linking in English Derived Nominals," in R. van Valin, Jr. (ed.), *Advances in Role and Reference Grammar*, John Benjamins Publishing, Philadelphia.

Quillian, M. R. 1968. "Semantic Memory," in M. Minsky (ed.), *Semantic Information Processing*, MIT Press, Cambridge, MA.

Ostler, N. and B. T. Atkins. 1991. "Predictable Meaning Shift: Some Linguistic Properties of Lexical Implication Rules," in J. Pustejovsky and S. Bergler (eds.), *Lexical Semantics and Knowledge Representation*, ACL SIG Workshop Proceedings, 76-87.

Ostler, N. and B. T. Atkins. 1992. "Predictable Meaning Shift: Some Linguistic Properties of Lexical Implication Rules," in J. Pustejovsky and S. Bergler (eds.), *Lexical Semantics and Knowledge Reperesentation*, Springer Verlag, Berlin.

Parsons, T. 1985. "Underlying Events in the Logical Analysis of English," in E. LePore and B.P. McLaughlin (eds.), *Actions and Events*, Basil Blackwell, Oxford, 235-267.

Parsons, T. 1989. "The Progressive in English: Events, States, and Processes," *Linguistics and Philosophy* 12:213-241.

Parsons, T. 1990. *Events in the Semantics of English*, MIT Press, Cambridge, MA.

Partee, B. 1992. "Syntactic Categories and Semantic Type," in M. Rosner and R. Johnson (eds.), *Computational Linguistics and Formal Semantics*, Cambridge University Press

Partee, B. and M. Rooth. 1983. "Generalized Conjunction and Type Ambiguity," in *Meaning, Use, and Interpretation of Language*, Bäuerle, Schwarze, and von Stechow eds., Walter de Gruyter.

Passonneau, R. 1988. "A Computational Model of the Semantics of Tense and Aspect," *Computational Linguistics*, 14.2.

Paul, H. 1880. *Prinzipien der Sprachgeschichte*, 9th Edition, 1975, Niemeyer, Tübingen.

Pelletier, F. J. and L. K. Schubert. 1988. "Problems in the Representation of the Logical Form of Generics, Plurals, and Mass Nouns," in B. LePore (ed.), *New Directions in Semantics*, Academic Press, London.

Pelletier, F. J. and L. K. Schubert. 1989. "Mass Expressions," in D. Gabbay and F. Guenthner (eds.), *Handbook of Philosophical Logic*, Vol. IV, Reidel, Dordrecht.

Perlmutter, D. M. 1970. "On the Two Verbs *Begin*," in R. Jacobs and P. Rosenbaum (eds.), 107-119.

Perlmutter, D. M. 1978. "Impersonal Passives and the Unaccusative Hypothesis," *BLS* 4, 157-189.

Pinker, S. 1984. *Language Learnability and Language Development*, Harvard University Press, Cambridge, MA.

Pinker, S. 1989. *Learnability and Cognition: The Acquisition of Argument Structure*, MIT Press, Cambridge, MA.

Pinker, S. and J. Mehler. 1988. *Connections and Symbols*, MIT Press, Cambridge, MA.

Pollack, M. 1986. "A Model of Plan Inference that distinguishes between the Beliefs of Actors and Observers," in *Proceedings 24th Annual Conference of the Association of Computational Linguistics*, New York, 207-214.

Pollard, C. and I. Sag. 1987. *Information-Based Syntax and Semantics*, CSLI Lecture Notes Number 13, Stanford, CA.

Pollard, C. and I. Sag. 1994. *Head-Driven Phrase Structure Grammar*, University of Chicago Press and Stanford CSLI, Chicago.

Postal, P. 1970. "On the Surface Verb 'Remind'," *Linguistic Inquiry* 1:37-120.

Postal, P. 1971. *Cross-over Phenomena*, Holt, Rinehart, and Winston, New York.

Prince, A. and P. Smolensky 1994. *Optimality Theory*, ms. Johns Hopkins University and Rutgers University.

Pustejovsky, J. 1988. "The Geometry of Events," in *Studies in Generative Approaches to Aspect*, C. Tenny, ed., Lexicon Project Working Papers 24, MIT, Cambridge, MA.

Pustejovsky, J. 1989. "Issues in Computational Lexical Semantics," in the *Proceedings of the Fourth European ACL Conference*, April 10-12, Manchester, England.

Pustejovsky, J. 1991a. "The Generative Lexicon," *Computational Linguistics*, 17:409-441.

Pustejovsky, J. 1991b. "The Syntax of Event Structure," *Cognition* 41:47-81.

Pustejovsky, J. 1992. "Principles versus Criteria: On Randall's Catapult Hypothesis," in J. Weissenborn, H. Goodluck, and T. Roeper (eds.), *Theoretical Issues in Language Acquisition*, Kluwer Academic Publishers, Dordrecht.

Pustejovsky, J. 1993. "Type Coercion and Lexical Selection," in J. Pustejovsky (ed.), *Semantics and the Lexicon*, Kluwer Academic Publishers, Dordrecht, The Netherlands.

Pustejovsky, J. 1994. "Semantic Typing and Degrees of Polymorphism," in C. Martin-Vide (ed.), *Current Issues in Mathematical Linguistics*, Elsevier, Holland.

Pustejovsky, J. 1995a. "Linguistic Constraints on Type Coercion," in P. Saint-Dizier and E. Viegas (eds.), *Computational Lexical Semantics*, Cambridge University Press.

Pustejovsky, J. 1995b. "Extensions to Qualia Structure," ms., Computer Science Department, Brandeis University.

Pustejovsky, J. 1995c. *Language and The Multiplicity of Meaning*. ms. Dept. of Computer Science, Brandeis University.

Pustejovsky, J. 1996. "Lexical Underspecification for Semantic Forms," *Folia Lingua*.

Pustejovsky, J. Forthcoming. *The Semantics of Underspecification*. unpublished ms. Dept. of Computer Science, Brandeis University.

Pustejovsky, J. and P. Anick. 1988. "On The Semantic Interpretation of Nominals," in *Proceedings of COLING-1988*, Budapest, 1988.

Pustejovsky, J. and B. Boguraev. 1993. "Lexical Knowledge Representation and Natural Language Processing," *Artificial Intelligence* 63:193-223.

Pustejovsky, J. and B. Boguraev 1995. "Lexical Semantics in Context," *Journal of Semantics* 12:1-14.

Pustejovsky, J. and P. Bouillon 1995. "Logical Polysemy and Aspectual Coercion," *Journal of Semantics* 12:133-162.

Pustejovsky, J. and F. Busa. 1995. "Unaccusativity and Event Composition," in P. M. Bertinetto, V. Binachi, J. Higginbotham, and M. Squartini (eds.), *Temporal Reference: Aspect and Actionality*, Rosenberg and Sellier, Turin.

Pustejovsky, J. and F. Busa. Forthcoming. *Semantic Parameters and Lexical Universals*, MIT Press, Cambridge.

Pustejovsky, J. and M. Johnston. Forthcoming. *Generative Lexical Grammar*, ms. Department of Computer Science, Brandeis University.

Rapoport, T. R. 1990. "Secondary Predication and the Lexical Representation of Verbs," *Machine Translation* 4:31-55.

Rapoport, T. R. 1993. "Verbs in Depictives and Resultatives," in J. Pustejovsky (ed.), *Semantics and the Lexicon*, Kluwer Academic Publishers, Dordrecht.

Rappaport, M., B. Levin, and M. Laughren. 1993. "Levels of Lexical Representation," in J. Pustejovsky (ed.), *Semantics and the Lexicon*, Kluwer Academic Publishers, Dordrecht.

Ravin, Y. 1990. *Lexical Semantics Without Thematic Roles*, Oxford University Press, Oxford.

Reichenbach, H. 1978. *Selected writings, 1909-1953*, Reidel, Dordrecht.

Roberts, R. B. and Goldstein. 1977. "The FRL Manual," Technical Report AI Memo 409, MIT Artificial Intelligence Laboratory.

Roeper, T. 1987. "Implicit Arguments and the Head Complement Relation," *Linguistic Inquiry* 18.

Roeper, T. 1993. "Explicit Syntax in the Lexicon: the Representation of Nominalizations," in J. Pustejovsky (ed.), *Semantics and the Lexicon*, Kluwer Academic Publishers, Dordrecht.

Rooth, M. 1985. *Association with Focus*, Ph.D. Dissertation, University of Massachusetts, Amherst.

Rudanko, J. 1989. *Complementation and Case Grammar: A Syntactic and Semantic Study of Selected Patterns of Complementation in Present-Day English*, SUNY Press, Albany, NY.

Ruhl, C. 1989. *On Monosemy: A Study in Linguistic Semantics*, State University of New York Press, Albany, NY.

Rumelhart, D.E. and J.L. McClellan. 1986. *Parallel distributed processing : explorations in the microstructure of cognition*, MIT Press, Cambridge, MA.

Russell, G., J. Carroll, and S. Warwick. 1990. "Multiple Default Inheritance in a Unification-Based Lexicon," in *Proceedings of Workshop on Inheritance in Natural Language*, Tilburg, August.

Russell, G., A. Ballim, J. Carroll, and S. Warwick-Armstrong. 1993. "A Practical Approach to Multiple Default Inheritance for Unification-Based Lexicons," in T. Briscoe, V. de Paiva, and A. Copestake (eds.), *Inheritance, Defaults, and the Lexicon*, Cambridge University Press, Cambridge.

Ryle, G. 1966. *The Concept of the Mind*, Hutchinson, London.

Sag, I. A. and C. Pollard. 1991. "An Integrated Theory of Complement Control," *Language* 67:63-113.

Sag, I. A. and A. Szabolcsi, eds. 1992. *Lexical Matters*, CSLI Lecture Notes 24, Center for the Study of Language and Information, Stanford University, Stanford, CA.

Saint-Dizier, P. 1995. "Constraint Propagation Techniques for Lexical Semantic Descriptions," in P. Saint-Dizier and E. Viegas, eds., *Computational Lexical Semantics*, Cambridge University Press.

Saint-Dizier, P. and E. Viegas, eds. 1995. *Computational Lexical Semantics*, Cambridge University Press, Cambridge.

Saksena, A. 1980. "The Affected Agent," *Language* 56:812-826.

Saksena, A. 1982. "Contact in Causation," *Language* 58:820-831.

Sanfilippo, A. 1990. *Grammatical Relations, Thematic Roles, and Verb Semantics*. Ph.D. Dissertation, Centre for Cognitive Science, University of Edinburgh.

Sanfilippo, A. 1991a. "Thematic and Aspectual Information in Verb Semantics," unpublished ms., University of Cambridge, Cambridge, UK.

Sanfilippo, A. 1991b. "Argument Selection and Selection Change: An Integrated Approach," *CLS* 27.

Sanfilippo, A. 1993. "LKB Encoding of Lexical Knowledge," in T. Briscoe, V. de Paiva, and A. Copestake (eds.), *Inheritance, Defaults, and the Lexicon*, Cambridge University Press, Cambridge.

Sanfilippo, A. K. Benkerimi, and D. Dwehus. 1994. "Virtual Polysemy," in *Proceedings of COLING-1994*, Nantes, France.

Scha, R. 1983. "Logical Foundations for Question Answering," MS 12.331 Philips Research Laboratories, Eindhoven, The Netherlands.

Schank, R. C. 1972. "Conceptual Dependency: A Theory of Natural Language Understanding," *Cognitive Psychology* 3:552-631.

Schank, R.C. 1973. "Identification of Conceptualizations Underlying Natural Language" in R.C. Schank and K.M. Colby (eds.), *Computer Models of Thought and Language*, W.H. Freeman, San Francisco, CA, 187-247.

Schank, R. 1975. *Conceptual Information Processing*, Amsterdam, North-Holland.

Searle, J. 1979. *Expression and Meaning*, Cambridge, Cambridge University Press.

Seuren , P. 1985. *Discourse Semantics*, Blackwell Publishers, Oxford.

Shibatani, M., ed. 1976. *Japanese Generative Grammar*, Academic Press, New York.

Shieber, S. 1992. *Constraint-based grammar formalisms: parsing and type inference for natural and computer languages*, MIT Press, Cambridge, MA.

Small, S. I., G. W. Cottrell, and M. K. Tanenhaus, eds. 1988. *Lexical Ambiguity Resolution*, Morgan Kaufmann, San Mateo, CA.

Sparck Jones, K. 1986. *Synonymy and Semantic Classification.*. Ph.D. Dissertation with new Foreword. Edinburgh Information Technology Series (EDITS). Edinburgh: Edinburgh University Press.

Smith, B. and K. Mulligan. 1983. "Framework for Formal Ontology," *Topoi* 2:73-85.

Smolka, G. 1988. "A Feature Logic with Subsorts," Wissenschaftliches Zentrum der IBM Deutschland, LILOG-Report 33.

Soames, S. 1989. "Presupposition," in D. Gabbay ad F. Guenthner (eds.), *Handbook of Philosophical Logic* Vol. IV, 553-616.

Sowa, J. 1984. *Conceptual Structures*, Addison-Wesley, Boston.

Sowa, J. 1993. "Lexical Structures and Conceptual Structures," in J. Pustejovsky (ed.), *Semantics and the Lexicon*, Kluwer, Dordrecht.

Steinberg, D. and L. Jakobovits, eds. 1971. *Semantics*, Cambridge University Press, Cambridge.

Strachey, C. 1967. "Fundamental Concepts in Programming Languages," *Lecture Notes for International Summer School in Computer Programming*, Copenhagen.

Talmy, L. 1975. "Semantics and Syntax of Motion," in J. P. Kimball (ed.), *Syntax and Semantics 4*, Academic Press, New York, 181-238.

Talmy, L. 1976. "Semantic Causative Types," in M. Shibatani (ed.), 43-116.

Talmy, L. 1985. "Lexicalization Patterns: Semantic Structure in Lexical Forms," in T. Shopen (ed.), *Language Typology and Syntactic Description* 3, Grammatical Categories and the Lexicon, Cambridge University Press, Cambridge, UK, 57-149.

Tedeschi, P. and A. Zaenen, eds. 1981. *Tense and Aspect*, Syntax and Semantics 14, Academic Press, New York, NY.

Tenny, C., ed. 1988. *Studies in Generative Approaches to Aspect*, Lexicon Project Working Papers 24, Center for Cognitive Science, MIT, Cambridge, MA.

Tenny, C. 1992. "The Aspectual Interface Hypothesis," in I. A. Sag and A. Szabolcsi (eds.), 1-27.

Thomason, R., ed. 1974. *Formal Philosophy: The Collected Papers of Richard Montague*, New Haven, Yale University Press.

Touretzky, D. 1986. *The Mathematics of Inheritance Systems*, Morgan Kaufmann, Los Altos, CA.

Travis, L. and E. Williams 1983. "Externalization of Arguments in Malayo-Polynesian Languages" *The Linguistic Review* 2.

Trier, J. 1931. *Der deutsche Wortschatz im Sinnbezirk des Verstandes: Die Geschichte eines sprachlichen Feldes. Band I*. Heidelberg.

Van Valin, R. D. Jr. 1987. "The Unaccusative Hypothesis vs. Lexical Semantics: Syntactic vs. Semantic Approaches to Verb Classification," *NELS* 17, 641-661.

Van Valin, R. D. Jr. 1990. "Semantic Parameters of Split Intransitivity," *Language* 66:221-260.

Van Valin, R.D. Jr. 1993. "A Synopsis of Role and Reference Grammar," in R. van Valin, Jr. (ed) *Advances in Role and Reference Grammar*, John Benjamins Publishing, Philadelphia.

Van Valin, R.D. Jr. and D. Wilkins. 1993. "Predicting Syntax from Semantics," in R. van Valin, Jr. (ed.) *Advances in Role and Reference Grammar*, John

Benjamins Publishing, Philadelphia.

Van Voorst, J. 1986. *Event Structure.* Ph.D. Dissertation, University of Ottawa, Ottawa, Ontario.

Van Voorst, J. 1992. "The Aspectual Semantics of Psychological Verbs," *Linguistics and Philosophy* 15:65-92.

Vendler, Z. 1967. *Linguistics in Philosophy,* Cornell University Press, Ithaca.

Vendler, Z. 1984. "Agency and Causation," *Midwest Studies in Philosophy* 9:371-384.

Verkuyl, H. 1972. *On the Compositional Nature of the Aspects,* Reidel, Dordrecht.

Verkuyl, H. . 1973. "Temporal Prepositions as Quantifiers," in F. Kiefer and N. Ruwet (eds.), 582-615.

Verkuyl, H. 1989. "Aspectual Classes and Aspectual Composition," *Linguistics and Philosophy* 12:39-94.

Verkuyl, H. 1993. *A Theory of Aspectuality,* Cambridge University Press, Camrbridge.

Verkuyl, H. and J. Zwarts. 1988. "Time and Space in Conceptual and Logical Semantics: the notion of Path," *Linguistics* 30:483-511.

Verma, M. and K. P. Mohanan 1991. *Experiencer Subjects in South Asian Languages,* CSLI, University of Chicago Press.

Viegas, E. 1995. "The Semantics-Pragmatics of Lexicalization," in P. Saint- Dizier and E. Viegas (eds.), *Computational Lexical Semantics,* Cambridge University Press.

Vikner, C. and P. Hansen. 1994. "Knowledge Bases and Generative Lexicons," paper presented at *Workshop on Lexical Semantics,* November 11, University of Copenhagen.

Vlach, R. 1981. "The Semantics of the Progressive," *Syntax and Semantics: Tense and Aspect* 14, 271-92.

Vossen P. 1991. "The End of the Chain: Where Does Decomposition of Lexical Knowledge Lead Us Eventually?," unpublished ms., University of Amsterdam, Amsterdam.

Walker, D. E., and R. A. Amsler. 1986. "The Use of Machine-Readable Dictionaries in Sublanguage Analysis," in R. Grishman and R. Kittredge, eds., *Analyzing Language in Restricted Domains,* Lawrence Erlbaum: Hillsdale, NJ.

Walker, D., A. Zampolli, and N. Calzolari, eds. 1994. *Automating the Lexicon,* Oxford University Press.

Weinreich, U. 1959. "Travels through Semantic Space," *Word* 14:346-366.

Weinreich, U. 1963. "On the Semantic Structure of Language," in J. Greenberg (ed.), *Universal of Language,* MIT Press, Cambridge, MA.

Weinreich, U. 1964. "*Webster's Third*: A Critique of its Semantics," *International Journal of American Linguistics* 30:405-409.

Weinreich, U. 1972. *Explorations in Semantic Theory,* Mouton, The Hague.

Wheeler, R. S. 1990. "Sense and Subsense: The Meanings of the English Verb *Understand,*" ms., Utah State University.

Whorf, B. L. 1956. *Language, Thought, and Reality,* MIT Press, Cambridge, MA.

Wierzbicka, A. 1972. *Semantic Primitives,* Athenaum, Frankfurt.

Wierzbicka, A. 1980. *Lingua Mentalis: The Semantics of Natural Language,* Academic Press, New York, NY.

Wierzbicka, A. 1982. "Why Can You *Have a Drink* When You Can't *Have an Eat?,*" *Language* 58:753-799.

Wierzbicka, A. 1988. *The Semantics of Grammar,* Amsterdam, John Benjamins.

Wilensky, R. 1986. "Some Problems and Proposals for Knowledge Representation," Cognitive Science Report 40, University of California, Berkeley.

Wilensky, R. 1991. "Extending the Lexicon by Exploiting Subregularities," Report UCB/CSD 91/618, Computer Science Department, University of California,

Berkeley.

Wilks, Y. 1975a. "A Preferential Pattern Seeking Semantics for Natural Language Inference," *Artificial Intelligence*, 6:53-74.

Wilks, Y. 1975b. "An Intelligent Analyser and Understander for English," *Communications of the ACM*, 18:264-274.

Wilks, Y. 1978. "Making Preferences More Active," *Artificial Intelligence* 10:75-97.

Wilks, Y., D. Fass, C. M. Guo, J. McDonald, T. Plate, and B. Slator. 1988. "A Tractable Machine Dictionary as a Resource for Computational Semantics," in B. Boguraev and T. Briscoe (eds.), *Computational Lexicography for Natural Language Processing* , Harlow, Essex, Longman.

Wilks, Y., D. Fas, C. M. Guo, J. McDonald, T. Plate, and B. Slator. 1993. "Providing Machine Tractable Dictionary Tools," in J. Pustejovsky (ed.), *Semantics and the Lexicon*, Kluwer Academic Publishers, Dordrecht.

Williams, E. 1980. "Predication," *Linguistic Inquiry* 11:203-238.

Williams, E. 1981. "Argument Structure and Morphology," *The Linguistic Review* 1:81-114.

Williams, E. 1982. "Another Argument that Passive is Transformational," *Linguistic Inquiry* 13:160-163.

Williams, E. 1983. "Against Small Clauses," *Linguistic Inquiry* 14:287-308.

Williams, E. 1983. "Semantic vs. Syntactic Categories," *Linguistics and Philosophy* 6:423-446.

Williams, E. 1987. "Implicit Arguments, the Binding Theory, and Control," *Natural Language and Linguistic Theory* 5:151-180.

Williams, E. 1994. *Thematic Structure in Syntax*, MIT Press, Cambridge.

Woods, W. 1975. "What's in a link: foundations of semantic networks," in D. G. Bobrow and A. Collins (eds.), *Representation and Understanding: Studies in Cognitive Science*, Academic Press, New York.

von Wright, G. 1963. *Norm and Action: A Logical Inquiry*, Routledge and Kegan Paul, London.

Wunderlich, D. 1987. "An Investigation of Lexical Composition: The Case of German *be*-Verbs," *Linguistics* 25, 283-331.

Wunderlich, D. 1991. "How Do Prepositional Phrases Fit into Compositional Syntax and Semantics," *Linguistics* 29:591-621.

Wunderlich, D. 1994. "Models of Lexical Decomposition," in E. Weigand and F. Hundsnurscher (eds.), *Proceedings of the International Conference on 'Lexicology and Lexical Semantics'*, Münster, Tübingen, Niemeyer.

Zaenen, A. 1993. "Unaccusativity in Dutch: The Interface of Syntax and Lexical Semantics," in J. Pustejovsky (ed.), *Semantics and the Lexicon*, Kluwer, Dordrecht.

Zubizarreta, M. L. 1987. *Levels of Representation in the Lexicon and in the Syntax*, Foris, Dordrecht.

Zucchi, A. 1993. *The Language of Propositions and Events*, Kluwer Academic Publishers, Dordrecht.

Author Index

Subject Index